9/11 AND THE WAR ON TERROR

A Documentary and Reference Guide

Paul J. Springer

Documentary and Reference Guides

GREENWOOD™

An Imprint of ABC-CLIO, LLC
Santa Barbara, California • Denver, Colorado

Library of Congress Cataloging-in-Publication Data

Names: Springer, Paul J., author.
Title: 9/11 and the War on Terror : a documentary and reference guide / Paul J. Springer.
Description: Santa Barbara, California : Greenwood, [2016] | Series: Documentary and
    reference guides | Includes bibliographical references and index.
Identifiers: LCCN 2016013870 (print) | LCCN 2016022726 (ebook) | ISBN
    9781440843334 (hardcopy : alk. paper) | ISBN 9781440843341 (ebook)
Subjects: LCSH: September 11 Terrorist Attacks, 2001—Sources. | War on Terrorism,
    2001–2009—Sources. | Terrorism—United States—Prevention—Sources.
Classification: LCC HV6432.7 .S6875 2016 (print) | LCC HV6432.7 (ebook) |
    DDC 973.931—dc23
LC record available at https://lccn.loc.gov/2016013870

ISBN: 978–1–4408–4333–4
EISBN: 978–1–4408–4334–1

20 19 18 17 16   1 2 3 4 5

This book is also available as an eBook.

Greenwood
An Imprint of ABC-CLIO, LLC

ABC-CLIO, LLC
130 Cremona Drive, P.O. Box 1911
Santa Barbara, California 93116-1911
www.abc-clio.com

This book is printed on acid-free paper ∞

Manufactured in the United States of America

CONTENTS

Contents

READER'S GUIDE
TO RELATED DOCUMENTS

INTRODUCTION

Terrorism has plagued human societies for centuries. While there is no universally accepted definition of "terrorism," it is generally acknowledged to be the use of force or threats by a nonstate actor to coerce a target audience for political gain. Terrorism is typically the choice of weaker groups trying to achieve outsized influence by using fear to magnify the dangers of resistance. Stronger groups normally elect to engage in more direct confrontations, if they choose violence at all, both for reasons of legitimacy and because terrorism is a tactic that rarely achieves its objectives, for all the destruction that it might cause.

Trying to cover every facet of terrorism in a single volume would be an impossible undertaking. Instead, this encyclopedia focuses on international terrorism against the United States in the aftermath of the September 11, 2001, attacks. While some documents are from the pre-9/11 era, they have been included to clarify the American understanding of terrorism prior to the deadliest terror attack in history.

Before September 11, most Americans thought of terrorism that occurred elsewhere in the world, if they thought about it at all. If asked to name the most dangerous terror organizations in the world, they almost always focused upon Middle Eastern groups, but Al Qaeda likely was not among the first to be mentioned. Of course, everything changed on the morning of September 11. Nineteen hijackers seized control of four airplanes and transformed them into enormous suicide missiles. Two of the airplanes crashed into New York City's World Trade Center, inflicting catastrophic damage that caused the twin towers to collapse. A third was flown into the Pentagon in Washington, D.C., while the fourth aircraft crashed in a Pennsylvania field as passengers attempted to regain control from the hijackers.

The attacks represented a watershed moment in American history. Virtually every American citizen born early enough to be cognizant of current events in 2001 knows precisely where he or she was when they heard about the attacks. In this regard, 9/11 has joined other infamous dates in U.S. history that permanently scarred the psyche of the nation. Just as earlier generations were shocked by the 1941 surprise attack at Pearl Harbor, the 1963 assassination of President

John F. Kennedy, or the 1986 *Challenger* disaster, Americans found themselves confronting a host of conflicting emotions in the aftermath of the attacks.

The September 11 attacks killed nearly 3,000 civilians, the victims of a war they did not know existed. Although Al Qaeda's mysterious leader, Osama bin Laden, declared war upon the United States in 1996, to most Americans the conflict did not register much of a response until it was driven home by the deadliest terror attack in world history. Yet, if bin Laden believed he understood the United States, and by extension the West, he proved sorely mistaken. Rather than frightening the United States leadership into withdrawing military, political, and economic influence from the Middle East, the attacks provoked a terrible retribution. Rather than paving the way to the establishment of a pan-Islamic caliphate, they brought ever-greater fractures and increased conflict into the Muslim world. In the end, the September 11 attacks did not paralyze the West and trigger a retreat from conflict; they drove a U.S.-led coalition to topple the Taliban government of Afghanistan, which had sheltered Al Qaeda for years. They awoke the American public to the dangers of radicalization in the modern world, and galvanized the citizenry to fight back against those who would use wanton slaughter for political ends.

The documents in this book were chosen to illustrate the many facets of the September 11 attacks, their immediate aftermath, and the subsequent War on Terror. They are divided into four chronological periods. Part 1 contains documents from the pre-9/11 era that demonstrate the U.S. perception of terrorism and the means taken to combat it. Part 2 encompasses the September 11 attacks and the immediate aftermath. Part 3 includes documents from 2002 through 2008, when President George W. Bush worked first to build an international coalition and then to command military operations in the War on Terror. Part 4 covers 2009 through 2016, when President Barack Obama assumed the presidency and directed the U.S. military in fashioning a new strategy to combat global terrorism.

While all of the documents in this work are freely available to the reader, most are much longer and impenetrable for the lay reader. This collection is designed to pull out the most important excerpts of each document to demonstrate the long-term effects of terrorism and counterterrorism. The analysis that accompanies each document will assist readers in understanding both the context and the significance of each selection. Should a reader wish to see the entire document, most can be located on the Internet, which has proven a wonderful resource for the storage, transmission, and manipulation of information. The documents are all currently unclassified, although some of them were under security classifications at the time of their production. A few of them contain redacted portions that are still not open to public scrutiny. The vast majority of the items in the work were generated by U.S. government agencies or officials associated with the federal government. The American system of governmental transparency is a justifiable source of pride for U.S. citizens, and many of these documents have been made public, thanks to Freedom of Information Act requests. By allowing the public to scrutinize government documents, the American system proves itself a robust and effective means of government, even if it occasionally comes at the cost of tipping off the enemy regarding U.S. intentions and capabilities. A few of the documents were produced by terror organizations or their leaders. Some of these documents were never intended to be seen outside of the organizations that wrote them, while others were created to shape worldwide public opinion. While the careful reader should not automatically accept the words of a terrorist at face value, neither should they be ignored on the basis of their creator.

Readers should consider all of these documents, regardless of the source, with a critical approach. The reader should also remember that almost all of these documents are excerpts of longer pieces. While the editor has made every effort to maintain the context and original intent of the documents, it is impossible to perfectly distill every source, and for that reason, the location of each full document is provided. Finally, the reader should note that many different spellings may exist for the same person or term, largely because of differences in translations. For example, Osama bin Laden is referred to in some documents as Usama Bin Ladin, or with other similar names. The organization he founded, Al Qaeda, has been spelled as al Qa'ida, Al Qida, and in several other variations.

Terrorism over the centuries has been a cyclical activity, with periods characterized by thousands of attacks per year and entire decades when almost no attacks occurred. It may never be possible to eradicate terrorism as an activity chosen by certain groups as their method of achieving goals. However, by developing a better understanding of terrorism, and the means and methods that have developed to counter it, the possibility exists of reducing the frequency of attacks and the likelihood of their success in triggering political changes desired by the perpetrators of terrorism. In time, modern society may come to recognize terrorism as the scourge of civilization everywhere, an act so beyond the bounds of acceptable behavior as to render it abhorrent to all the citizens of the world. If so, the terrible practice of terrorism may help to weld disparate societies into a better understanding of one another, and create the opportunity to reconcile grievances without resorting to violence.

This work is humbly dedicated to the victims of the September 11 attacks. Their lives were cut short in the name of evil; their memories will live forever in the name of hope.

Paul J. Springer, PhD

1

DOCUMENTS FROM PRIOR TO SEPTEMBER 11, 2001

- **Document 1:** Executive Order 11905
- **When:** February 18, 1976
- **Where:** Washington, D.C.
- **Significance:** President Gerald Ford formally banned political assassinations by members of U.S. intelligence agencies. The ban came in the aftermath of several accusations of assassinations, or attempted assassinations, and was motivated by both a desire to adhere to international law and a desire to prevent retaliatory actions.

DOCUMENT

United States Foreign Intelligence Activities

SECTION 1. *Purpose*. The purpose of this Order is to establish policies to improve the quality of intelligence needed for national security, to clarify the authority and responsibilities of the intelligence departments and agencies, and to establish effective oversight to assure compliance with law in the management and direction of intelligence agencies and departments of the national government.

SEC. 2. *Definitions*. For the purpose of this Order, unless otherwise indicated, the following terms shall have these meanings:

(a) *Intelligence* means:

(1) *Foreign intelligence* which means information, other than foreign counterintelligence, on the capabilities, intentions and activities of foreign powers, organizations or their agents; and

(2) *Foreign counterintelligence* which means activities conducted to protect the United States and United States citizens from foreign espionage, sabotage, subversion, assassination or terrorism.

(b) *Intelligence Community* refers to the following organizations:

(1) Central Intelligence Agency;

(2) National Security Agency;

(3) Defense Intelligence Agency;

(4) Special offices within the Department of Defense for the collection of specialized intelligence through reconnaissance programs;

(5) Intelligence elements of the military services;

(6) Intelligence element of the Federal Bureau of Investigation;

(7) Intelligence element of the Department of State;

DID YOU KNOW?

Terrorism in the Roman Empire

Terrorism is not an exclusively modern phenomenon. Most experts consider the Sicarii, also called the Zealots, to be the earliest organized terror group. Their trademark attack consisted of stabbing Roman officials in Judea in public locales. They also targeted local Jewish leaders who collaborated with the Romans. To demonstrate their commitment to the cause, Zealot killers would remain with their victim and await the arrival of authorities, knowing they would be tortured and executed for their crimes. Their attacks triggered an insurrection against Roman control, which in turn provoked a massive Roman invasion and the sack of Jerusalem in 70 BCE. The Zealots retreated to Masada, an ancient mountain fortress, and were besieged by Roman legions for several months. As the Roman forces moved into position for the final assault upon their position, the Masada defenders committed mass suicide in a final act of defiance.

(8) Intelligence element of the Department of the Treasury; and

(9) Intelligence element of the Energy Research and Development Administration.

(c) Special activities in support of national foreign policy objectives means activities, other than the collection and production of intelligence and related support functions, designed to further official United States programs and policies abroad which are planned and executed so that the role of the United States Government is not apparent or publicly acknowledged.

(d) National Foreign Intelligence Program means the programs of the Central Intelligence Agency and the special offices within the Department of Defense for the collection of specialized intelligence through reconnaissance programs, the Consolidated Cryptologic Program, and those elements of the General Defense Intelligence Program and other programs of the departments and agencies, not including tactical intelligence, designated by the Committee on Foreign Intelligence as part of the Program.

. . .

SEC. 5. *Restrictions on Intelligence Activities.* Information about the capabilities, intentions and activities of other governments is essential to informed decision-making in the field of national defense and foreign relations. The measures employed to acquire such information should be responsive to the legitimate needs of our Government and must be conducted in a manner which preserves and respects our established concepts of privacy and our civil liberties.

Recent events have clearly indicated the desirability of government-wide direction which will ensure a proper balancing of these interests. This section of this Order does not authorize any activity not previously authorized and does not provide exemption from any restrictions otherwise applicable. Unless otherwise specified, the provisions of this section apply to activities both inside and outside the United States. References to law are to applicable laws of the United States.

(a) Definitions. As used in this section of this Order, the following terms shall have the meanings ascribed to them below:

(1) "Collection" means any one or more of the gathering, analysis, dissemination or storage of non-publicly available information without the informed express consent of the subject of the information.

(2) "Counterintelligence" means information concerning the protection of foreign intelligence or of national security information and its collection from detection or disclosure.

(3) "Electronic surveillance" means acquisition of a non-public communication by electronic means, without the consent of a person who is a party to, or, in the case of a non-electronic communication, visibly present at, the communication.

(4) "Employee" means a person employed by, assigned or detailed to, or acting for a United States foreign intelligence agency.

(5) "Foreign intelligence" means information concerning the capabilities, intentions and activities of any foreign power, or of any non-United States person, whether within or outside the United States, or concerning areas outside the United States.

(6) "Foreign intelligence agency" means the Central Intelligence Agency, National Security Agency, and Defense Intelligence Agency; and further includes any other department or agency of the United States Government or component thereof while it is engaged in the collection of foreign intelligence or counterintelligence, but shall not include any such department, agency or component thereof to the extent that it is engaged in its authorized civil or criminal law enforcement functions; nor shall it include in any case the Federal Bureau of Investigation.

(7) "National security information" has the meaning ascribed to it in Executive Order No. 11652, as amended.

(8) "Physical surveillance" means continuing visual observation by any means; or acquisition of a non-public communication by a person not a party thereto or visibly present thereat through any means which does not involve electronic surveillance.

(9) "United States person" means United States citizens, aliens admitted to the United States for permanent residence and corporations or other organizations incorporated or organized in the United States.

(b) Restrictions on Collection. Foreign intelligence agencies shall not engage in any of the following activities:

(1) Physical surveillance directed against a United States person, unless it is a lawful surveillance conducted pursuant to procedures approved by the head of the foreign intelligence agency and directed against any of the following:

(i) A present or former employee of such agency, its present or former contractors or their present or former employees, for the purpose of protecting foreign, intelligence or counterintelligence sources or methods or national security information from unauthorized disclosure; or

(ii) a United States person, who is in contact with either such a present or former contractor or employee or with a non-United States person who is the subject of a foreign intelligence or counterintelligence inquiry, but only to the extent necessary to identify such United States person; or

(iii) a United States person outside the United States who is reasonably believed to be acting on behalf of a foreign power or engaging in international terrorist or narcotics activities or activities threatening the national security.

(2) Electronic surveillance to intercept a communication which is made from, or is intended by the sender to be received in, the United States, or directed against United States persons abroad, except lawful electronic surveillance under procedures approved by the Attorney General; *provided,* that the Central Intelligence Agency shall not perform electronic surveillance within the United States, except for the purpose of testing equipment under procedures approved by the Attorney General consistent with law.

(3) Unconsented physical searches within the United States; or unconsented physical searches directed against United States persons abroad, except lawful searches under procedures approved by the Attorney General.

(4) Opening of mail or examination of envelopes of mail in United States postal channels except in accordance with applicable statutes and regulations.

(5) Examination of Federal tax returns or tax information except in accordance with applicable statutes and regulations.

(6) Infiltration or undisclosed participation within the United States in any organization for the purpose of reporting on or influencing its activities or members; except such infiltration or participation with respect to an organization composed primarily of non-United States persons which is reasonably believed to be acting on behalf of a foreign power.

(7) Collection of information, however acquired, concerning the domestic activities of United States persons except:

(i) Information concerning corporations or other commercial organizations which constitutes foreign intelligence or counterintelligence.

(ii) Information concerning present or former employees, present or former contractors or their present or former employees, or applicants for any such employment or contracting, necessary to protect foreign intelligence or counterintelligence sources or methods or national security information from unauthorized disclosure; and the identity of persons in contact with the foregoing or with a non-United States person who is the subject of a foreign intelligence or counterintelligence inquiry.

(iii) Information concerning persons who are reasonably believed to be potential sources or contacts, but only for the purpose of determining the suitability or credibility of such persons.

(iv) Foreign intelligence or counterintelligence gathered abroad or from electronic surveillance conducted in compliance with Section 5(b)(2); or foreign intelligence acquired from cooperating sources in the United States.

(v) Information about a United States person who is reasonably believed to be acting on behalf of a foreign power or engaging in international terrorist or narcotics activities.

(vi) Information concerning persons or activities that pose a clear threat to foreign intelligence agency facilities or personnel, *provided,* that such information is retained only by the foreign intelligence agency threatened and that proper coordination with the Federal Bureau of Investigation is accomplished.

(c) Dissemination and Storage. Nothing in this section of this Order shall prohibit:

(1) Lawful dissemination to the appropriate law enforcement agencies of incidentally gathered information indicating involvement in activities which may be in violation of law.

(2) Storage of information required by law to be retained.

(3) Dissemination to foreign intelligence agencies of information of the subject matter types listed in Section 5(b)(7).

(d) Restrictions on Experimentation. Foreign intelligence agencies shall not engage in experimentation with drugs on human subjects, except with the informed consent, in writing and witnessed by a disinterested third party, of each such human subject and in accordance with the guidelines issued by the National Commission for the Protection of Human Subjects for Biomedical and Behavioral Research.

(e) Assistance to Law Enforcement Authorities.

(1) No foreign intelligence agency shall, except as expressly authorized by law (i) provide services, equipment, personnel or facilities to the Law Enforcement Assistance Administration or to State or local police organizations of the United States or (ii) participate in or fund any law enforcement activity within the United States.

(2) These prohibitions shall not, however, preclude: (i) cooperation between a foreign intelligence agency and appropriate law enforcement agencies for the purpose of protecting the personnel and facilities of the foreign intelligence agency or preventing espionage or other criminal activity related to foreign intelligence or counterintelligence or (ii) provision of specialized equipment or technical knowledge for use by any other Federal department or agency.

(f) Assignment of Personnel. An employee of a foreign intelligence agency detailed elsewhere within the Federal Government shall be responsible to the host agency and shall not report to such employee's parent agency on the affairs of the host agency, except as may be directed by the latter. The head of the host agency, and any successor, shall be informed of the detailee's association with the parent agency.

(g) Prohibition of Assassination. No employee of the United States Government shall engage in, or conspire to engage in, political assassination.

(h) Implementation.

(1) This section of this Order shall be effective on March 1, 1976. Each department and agency affected by this section of this Order shall promptly issue internal directives to implement this section with respect to its foreign intelligence and counterintelligence operations.

(2) The Attorney General shall, within ninety days of the effective date of this section of this Order, issue guidelines relating to activities of the Federal Bureau of Investigation in the areas of foreign intelligence and counterintelligence.

GERALD R. FORD
The White House,
February 18, 1976.

Source: Weekly Compilation of Presidential Documents, Vol. 12, No. 8, February 23, 1976. Also 41 *Federal Register* 7703, February 19, 1976, available at https://www.fordlibrarymuseum.gov/library/speeches/760110e.asp.

ANALYSIS

The Vietnam War (1965–1973) included a host of activities that blurred the line between military forces and intelligence agencies, and included a significant number of killings by members of intelligence organizations. President Ford sought to establish clear limits upon the behavior of intelligence operatives by clarifying their acceptable activities. In particular, this executive order included a public prohibition upon the use of political assassinations, a tool that had characterized much of the Cold War struggle between the United States and the Soviet Union. Ford hoped that the Soviet Union would reciprocate by forgoing political assassinations as well.

- **Document 2: Executive Order 12036**
- **When:** January 24, 1978
- **Where:** Washington, D.C.

- **Significance:** President James Carter strengthened and expanded the assassination ban initially ordered by President Ford. His action demonstrated that Ford's order was not merely political theater, but rather addressed an issue that transcended political parties.

DOCUMENT

United States Intelligence Activities

2-301. Tax Information. No agency within the Intelligence Community shall examine tax returns or tax information except as permitted by applicable law.

2-302. Restrictions on Experimentation. No agency within the Intelligence Community shall sponsor, contract for, or conduct research on human subjects except in accordance with guidelines issued by the Department of Health, Education and Welfare. The subject's informed consent shall be documented as required by those guidelines.

2-303. Restrictions on Contracting. No agency within the Intelligence Community shall enter into a contract or arrangement for the provision of goods or services with private companies or institutions in the United States unless the agency sponsorship is known to the appropriate officials of the company or institution. In the case of any company or institution other than an academic institution, intelligence agency sponsorship may be concealed where it is determined, pursuant to procedures approved by the Attorney General, that such concealment is necessary to maintain essential cover or proprietary arrangements for authorized intelligence purposes.

2-304. Restrictions on Personnel Assigned to Other Agencies. An employee detailed to another agency within the federal government shall be responsible to the host agency and shall not report to the parent agency on the affairs of the host agency unless so directed by the host agency. The head of the host agency, and any successor, shall be informed of the employee's relationship with the parent agency.

2-305. Prohibition on Assassination. No person employed by or acting on behalf of the United States Government shall engage in, or conspire to engage in, assassination.

2-306. Restrictions on Special Activities. No component of the United States Government except an agency within the Intelligence Community may conduct any special activity. No such agency except the CIA (or the military services in wartime) may conduct any special activity unless the President determines, with the SCC's advice, that another agency is more likely to achieve a particular objective.

2-307. Restrictions on Indirect Participation in Prohibited Activities. No agency of the Intelligence Community shall request or otherwise encourage, directly or indirectly, any person, organization, or government agency to undertake activities forbidden by this Order or by applicable law.

2-308. Restrictions on Assistance to Law Enforcement Authorities. Agencies within the Intelligence Community other than the FBI shall not, except as expressly authorized by law:

(a) Provide services, equipment, personnel or facilities to the Law Enforcement Assistance Administration (or its successor agencies) or to state or local police organizations of the United States; or

(b) Participate in or fund any law enforcement activity within the United States.

2-309. Permissible Assistance to Law Enforcement Authorities. The restrictions in Section 2-308 shall not preclude:

(a) Cooperation with appropriate law enforcement agencies for the purpose of protecting the personnel and facilities of any agency within the Intelligence Community;

(b) Participation in law enforcement activities, in accordance with law and this Order, to investigate or prevent clandestine intelligence activities by foreign powers, international narcotics production and trafficking, or international terrorist activities; or

(c) Provision of specialized equipment, technical knowledge, or assistance of expert personnel for use by any department or agency or, when lives are endangered, to support local law enforcement agencies. Provision of assistance by expert personnel shall be governed by procedures approved by the Attorney General.

. . .

4-2. Definitions. For the purposes of this Order, the following terms shall have these meanings:

. . .

4-209. International terrorist activities means any activity or activities which:

(a) involves killing, causing serious bodily harm, kidnapping, or violent destruction of property, or an attempt or credible threat to commit such acts; and

(b) appears intended to endanger a protectee of the Secret Service or the Department of State or to further political, social or economic goals by intimidating or coercing a civilian population or any segment thereof, influencing the policy of a government or international organization by intimidation or coercion, or obtaining widespread publicity for a group or its cause; and

(c) transcends national boundaries in terms of the means by which it is accomplished, the civilian population, government, or international organization it appears intended to coerce or intimidate, or the locale in which its perpetrators operate or seek asylum.

. . .

4-212. Special activities means activities conducted abroad in support of national foreign policy objectives which are designed to further official United States programs and policies abroad and which are planned and executed so that the role of the United States Government is not apparent or acknowledged publicly, and functions in support of such activities, but not including diplomatic activity or the collection and production of intelligence or related support functions.

JIMMY CARTER
The White House,
January 24, 1978.

Source: United States Foreign Intelligence Activities. Executive Order 12036, January 24, 1978. *Public Papers of the Presidents of the United States: Jimmy Carter* (1978, Book 1). Washington, D.C.: Government Printing Office, 194–214.

ANALYSIS

By expanding upon President Ford's executive order regarding intelligence activities (see Document 1), President Carter established more thorough policies regarding intelligence collection and exploitation. This order is also noteworthy because it contains an explicit definition of "international terrorism," one of the first established by the U.S. government. That definition, provided in Section 4-209, proved extremely broad, as it essentially included almost any international attack upon the United States, to include acts perpetrated by military representatives of nations. The order renewed the formal ban on assassinations and closed the loophole by prohibiting indirect involvement in such activities. It also strictly limited intelligence agencies from conducting investigations into the activities of American citizens on U.S. soil.

- **Document 3: Foreign Intelligence Surveillance Act, 50 U.S. Code**
- **When:** October 25, 1978 (with subsequent revisions and amendments)
- **Where:** Washington, D.C.
- **Significance:** In response to wiretapping conducted by the federal government without judicial warrants, the legislature passed a series of regulations to establish the limits of federal surveillance programs.

DOCUMENT

U.S. Code, Title 50, Chapter 36, Subchapter 1—Electronic Surveillance
§1801-Definitions
As used in this subchapter:
(a) "Foreign power" means—
(1) a foreign government or any component thereof, whether or not recognized by the United States;

(2) a faction of a foreign nation or nations, not substantially composed of United States persons;

(3) an entity that is openly acknowledged by a foreign government or governments to be directed and controlled by such foreign government or governments;

(4) a group engaged in international terrorism or activities in preparation therefor;

(5) a foreign-based political organization, not substantially composed of United States persons;

(6) an entity that is directed and controlled by a foreign government or governments; or

(7) an entity not substantially composed of United States persons that is engaged in the international proliferation of weapons of mass destruction.

(b) "Agent of a foreign power" means—

(1) any person other than a United States person, who—

(A) acts in the United States as an officer or employee of a foreign power, or as a member of a foreign power as defined in subsection (a)(4) of this section, irrespective of whether the person is inside the United States;

(B) acts for or on behalf of a foreign power which engages in clandestine intelligence activities in the United States contrary to the interests of the United States, when the circumstances indicate that such person may engage in such activities, or when such person knowingly aids or abets any person in the conduct of such activities or knowingly conspires with any person to engage in such activities;

(C) engages in international terrorism or activities in preparation therefor;

(D) engages in the international proliferation of weapons of mass destruction, or activities in preparation therefor; or

(E) engages in the international proliferation of weapons of mass destruction, or activities in preparation therefor, for or on behalf of a foreign power, or knowingly aids or abets any person in the conduct of such proliferation or activities in preparation therefor, or knowingly conspires with any person to engage in such proliferation or activities in preparation therefor; or

(2) any person who—

(A) knowingly engages in clandestine intelligence gathering activities for or on behalf of a foreign power, which activities involve or may involve a violation of the criminal statutes of the United States;

(B) pursuant to the direction of an intelligence service or network of a foreign power, knowingly engages in any other clandestine intelligence activities for or on behalf of such foreign power, which activities involve or are about to involve a violation of the criminal statutes of the United States;

DID YOU KNOW?

"Terrorism" in the French Revolution

The term "terrorism" has had different connotations over the centuries. In the aftermath of the French Revolution, which began in 1789, the newly formed government of 1793 dubbed itself "le régime de la terreur" (the regime of terror). To the regime's leaders, terror was the proper mechanism for a democratic government to intimidate or eliminate enemies of the new republic, particularly those who might seek to overturn the revolution and return to the monarchy. In the words of Maximilien Robespierre, "Terror is nothing but justice, prompt, severe, and inflexible; it is therefore an emanation of virtue." Continuing on the same theme, he called for followers to uphold "virtue, without which terror is evil; terror, without which virtue is helpless." In 1794, Robespierre and his closest associates fell victim to the fear they inspired; they were denounced, convicted, and executed by rivals who preempted his plans to do the same to them.

(C) knowingly engages in sabotage or international terrorism, or activities that are in preparation therefor, for or on behalf of a foreign power;

(D) knowingly enters the United States under a false or fraudulent identity for or on behalf of a foreign power or, while in the United States, knowingly assumes a false or fraudulent identity for or on behalf of a foreign power; or

(E) knowingly aids or abets any person in the conduct of activities described in subparagraph (A), (B), or (C) or knowingly conspires with any person to engage in activities described in subparagraph (A), (B), or (C).

(c) "International terrorism" means activities that—

(1) involve violent acts or acts dangerous to human life that are a violation of the criminal laws of the United States or of any State, or that would be a criminal violation if committed within the jurisdiction of the United States or any State;

(2) appear to be intended—

(A) to intimidate or coerce a civilian population;

(B) to influence the policy of a government by intimidation or coercion; or

(C) to affect the conduct of a government by assassination or kidnapping; and

(3) occur totally outside the United States, or transcend national boundaries in terms of the means by which they are accomplished, the persons they appear intended to coerce or intimidate, or the locale in which their perpetrators operate or seek asylum.

(d) "Sabotage" means activities that involve a violation of chapter 105 of title 18, or that would involve such a violation if committed against the United States.

(e) "Foreign intelligence information" means—

(1) information that relates to, and if concerning a United States person is necessary to, the ability of the United States to protect against—

(A) actual or potential attack or other grave hostile acts of a foreign power or an agent of a foreign power;

(B) sabotage, international terrorism, or the international proliferation of weapons of mass destruction by a foreign power or an agent of a foreign power; or

(C) clandestine intelligence activities by an intelligence service or network of a foreign power or by an agent of a foreign power; or

(2) information with respect to a foreign power or foreign territory that relates to, and if concerning a United States person is necessary to—

(A) the national defense or the security of the United States; or

(B) the conduct of the foreign affairs of the United States.

(f) "Electronic surveillance" means—

(1) the acquisition by an electronic, mechanical, or other surveillance device of the contents of any wire or radio communication sent by or intended to be received by a particular, known United States person who is in the United States, if the contents are acquired by intentionally targeting that United States person, under circumstances in which a person has a reasonable expectation of privacy and a warrant would be required for law enforcement purposes;

(2) the acquisition by an electronic, mechanical, or other surveillance device of the contents of any wire communication to or from a person in the United States, without the consent of any party thereto, if such acquisition occurs in the United States, but does not include the acquisition of those communications

of computer trespassers that would be permissible under section 2511(2)(i) of title 18;

(3) the intentional acquisition by an electronic, mechanical, or other surveillance device of the contents of any radio communication, under circumstances in which a person has a reasonable expectation of privacy and a warrant would be required for law enforcement purposes, and if both the sender and all intended recipients are located within the United States; or

(4) the installation or use of an electronic, mechanical, or other surveillance device in the United States for monitoring to acquire information, other than from a wire or radio communication, under circumstances in which a person has a reasonable expectation of privacy and a warrant would be required for law enforcement purposes.

(g) "Attorney General" means the Attorney General of the United States (or Acting Attorney General), the Deputy Attorney General, or, upon the designation of the Attorney General, the Assistant Attorney General designated as the Assistant Attorney General for National Security under section 507A of title 28.

(h) "Minimization procedures," with respect to electronic surveillance, means—

(1) specific procedures, which shall be adopted by the Attorney General, that are reasonably designed in light of the purpose and technique of the particular surveillance, to minimize the acquisition and retention, and prohibit the dissemination, of nonpublicly available information concerning unconsenting United States persons consistent with the need of the United States to obtain, produce, and disseminate foreign intelligence information;

(2) procedures that require that nonpublicly available information, which is not foreign intelligence information, as defined in subsection (e)(1) of this section, shall not be disseminated in a manner that identifies any United States person, without such person's consent, unless such person's identity is necessary to understand foreign intelligence information or assess its importance;

(3) notwithstanding paragraphs (1) and (2), procedures that allow for the retention and dissemination of information that is evidence of a crime which has been, is being, or is about to be committed and that is to be retained or disseminated for law enforcement purposes; and

(4) notwithstanding paragraphs (1), (2), and (3), with respect to any electronic surveillance approved pursuant to section 1802(a) of this title, procedures that require that no contents of any communication to which a United States person is a party shall be disclosed, disseminated, or used for any purpose or retained for longer than 72 hours unless a court order under section 1805 of this title is obtained or unless the Attorney General determines that the information indicates a threat of death or serious bodily harm to any person.

(i) "United States person" means a citizen of the United States, an alien lawfully admitted for permanent residence (as defined in section 1101(a)(20) of title 8), an unincorporated association a substantial number of members of which are citizens of the United States or aliens lawfully admitted for permanent residence, or a corporation which is incorporated in the United States, but does not include a corporation or an association which is a foreign power, as defined in subsection (a)(1), (2), or (3) of this section.

(j) "United States," when used in a geographic sense, means all areas under the territorial sovereignty of the United States and the Trust Territory of the Pacific Islands.

(k) "Aggrieved person" means a person who is the target of an electronic surveillance or any other person whose communications or activities were subject to electronic surveillance.

(l) "Wire communication" means any communication while it is being carried by a wire, cable, or other like connection furnished or operated by any person engaged as a common carrier in providing or operating such facilities for the transmission of interstate or foreign communications.

(m) "Person" means any individual, including any officer or employee of the Federal Government, or any group, entity, association, corporation, or foreign power.

(n) "Contents," when used with respect to a communication, includes any information concerning the identity of the parties to such communication or the existence, substance, purport, or meaning of that communication.

(o) "State" means any State of the United States, the District of Columbia, the Commonwealth of Puerto Rico, the Trust Territory of the Pacific Islands, and any territory or possession of the United States.

(p) "Weapon of mass destruction" means—

(1) any explosive, incendiary, or poison gas device that is designed, intended, or has the capability to cause a mass casualty incident;

(2) any weapon that is designed, intended, or has the capability to cause death or serious bodily injury to a significant number of persons through the release, dissemination, or impact of toxic or poisonous chemicals or their precursors;

(3) any weapon involving a biological agent, toxin, or vector (as such terms are defined in section 178 of title 18) that is designed, intended, or has the capability to cause death, illness, or serious bodily injury to a significant number of persons; or

(4) any weapon that is designed, intended, or has the capability to release radiation or radioactivity causing death, illness, or serious bodily injury to a significant number of persons.

§1802—Electronic surveillance authorization without court order; certification by Attorney General; reports to Congressional commitees; transmittal under seal; duties and compensation of communication common carrier; applications; jurisdiction of court

(a)(1) Notwithstanding any other law, the President, through the Attorney General, may authorize electronic surveillance without a court order under this subchapter to acquire foreign intelligence information for periods of up to one year if the Attorney General certifies in writing under oath that—

(A) the electronic surveillance is solely directed at—

(i) the acquisition of the contents of communications transmitted by means of communications used exclusively between or among foreign powers, as defined in section 1801(a)(1), (2), or (3) of this title; or

(ii) the acquisition of technical intelligence, other than the spoken communications of individuals, from property or premises under the open and exclusive control of a foreign power, as defined in section 1801(a)(1), (2), or (3) of this title;

(B) there is no substantial likelihood that the surveillance will acquire the contents of any communication to which a United States person is a party; and

(C) the proposed minimization procedures with respect to such surveillance meet the definition of minimization procedures under section 1801(h) of this title; and

if the Attorney General reports such minimization procedures and any changes thereto to the House Permanent Select Committee on Intelligence and the Senate Select Committee on Intelligence at least thirty days prior to their effective date, unless the Attorney General determines immediate action is required and notifies the committees immediately of such minimization procedures and the reason for their becoming effective immediately.

(2) An electronic surveillance authorized by this subsection may be conducted only in accordance with the Attorney General's certification and the minimization procedures adopted by him. The Attorney General shall assess compliance with such procedures and shall report such assessments to the House Permanent Select Committee on Intelligence and the Senate Select Committee on Intelligence under the provisions of section 1808(a) of this title.

(3) The Attorney General shall immediately transmit under seal to the court established under section 1803(a) of this title a copy of his certification. Such certification shall be maintained under security measures established by the Chief Justice with the concurrence of the Attorney General, in consultation with the Director of National Intelligence, and shall remain sealed unless—

(A) an application for a court order with respect to the surveillance is made under sections 1801(h)(4) and 1804 of this title; or

(B) the certification is necessary to determine the legality of the surveillance under section 1806(f) of this title.

(4) With respect to electronic surveillance authorized by this subsection, the Attorney General may direct a specified communication common carrier to—

(A) furnish all information, facilities, or technical assistance necessary to accomplish the electronic surveillance in such a manner as will protect its secrecy and produce a minimum of interference with the services that such carrier is providing its customers; and

(B) maintain under security procedures approved by the Attorney General and the Director of National Intelligence any records concerning the surveillance or the aid furnished which such carrier wishes to retain.

The Government shall compensate, at the prevailing rate, such carrier for furnishing such aid.

(b) Applications for a court order under this subchapter are authorized if the President has, by written authorization, empowered the Attorney General to approve applications to the court having jurisdiction under section 1803 of this title, and a judge to whom an application is made may, notwithstanding any other law, grant an order, in conformity with section 1805 of this title, approving electronic surveillance of a foreign power or an agent of a foreign power for the purpose of obtaining foreign intelligence information, except that the court shall not have jurisdiction to grant any order approving electronic surveillance directed solely as described in paragraph (1)(A) of subsection (a) of this section unless such surveillance may involve the acquisition of communications of any United States person.

§1803—Designation of judges

(a) Court to hear applications and grant orders; record of denial; transmittal to court of review

(1) The Chief Justice of the United States shall publicly designate 11 district court judges from at least seven of the United States judicial circuits of whom no fewer than 3 shall reside within 20 miles of the District of Columbia who shall constitute a court which shall have jurisdiction to hear applications for and grant orders approving electronic surveillance anywhere within the United States under the procedures set forth in this chapter, except that no judge designated under this subsection (except when sitting en banc under paragraph (2)) shall hear the same application for electronic surveillance under this chapter which has been denied previously by another judge designated under this subsection. If any judge so designated denies an application for an order authorizing electronic surveillance under this chapter, such judge shall provide immediately for the record a written statement of each reason of his decision and, on motion of the United States, the record shall be transmitted, under seal, to the court of review established in subsection (b) of this section.

(2)(A) The court established under this subsection may, on its own initiative, or upon the request of the Government in any proceeding or a party under section 1861(f) of this title or paragraph (4) or (5) of section 1881a(h) of this title, hold a hearing or rehearing, en banc, when ordered by a majority of the judges that constitute such court upon a determination that—

(i) en banc consideration is necessary to secure or maintain uniformity of the court's decisions; or

(ii) the proceeding involves a question of exceptional importance.

(B) Any authority granted by this chapter to a judge of the court established under this subsection may be exercised by the court en banc. When exercising such authority, the court en banc shall comply with any requirements of this chapter on the exercise of such authority.

(C) For purposes of this paragraph, the court en banc shall consist of all judges who constitute the court established under this subsection.

(b) Court of review; record, transmittal to Supreme Court

The Chief Justice shall publicly designate three judges, one of whom shall be publicly designated as the presiding judge, from the United States district courts or courts of appeals who together shall comprise a court of review which shall have jurisdiction to review the denial of any application made under this chapter. If such court determines that the application was properly denied, the court shall immediately provide for the record a written statement of each reason for its decision and, on petition of the United States for a writ of certiorari, the record shall be transmitted under seal to the Supreme Court, which shall have jurisdiction to review such decision.

(c) Expeditious conduct of proceedings; security measures for maintenance of records

Proceedings under this chapter shall be conducted as expeditiously as possible. The record of proceedings under this chapter, including applications made and orders granted, shall be maintained under security measures established by the Chief Justice in consultation with the Attorney General and the Director of National Intelligence.

Source: Foreign Intelligence Surveillance Act of 1978. Public Law 95-511, U.S. Statutes at Large, 92 (1980): 1783.

ANALYSIS

The Foreign Intelligence Surveillance Act (FISA) was primarily created in response to the wiretapping behaviors of the Nixon White House. However, when Congress took up the question of what types of surveillance activities should be permitted for the federal government, it established that the judicial branch of the government should review and approve executive actions regarding surveillance. It also recognized that, under certain circumstances, such a review may not be possible, and as such, the executive branch can conduct electronic and physical surveillance without permission from the FISA court so long as it subjects its activities for review at the earliest possible time. The FISA was repeatedly revised and amended in the aftermath of the September 11 attacks, in recognition of the inherent difficulties associated with identifying and tracking members of terror organizations. However, it still sets important limits upon the types of surveillance the federal government may conduct, particularly of U.S. citizens.

- **Document 4: Executive Order 12333**
- **When:** December 4, 1981
- **Where:** Washington, D.C.
- **Significance:** President Ronald Reagan, despite his tough stances on terror organizations, continued the ban on political assassinations initially placed by his predecessors. This document revoked and replaced Executive Order 12036 (see Document 2), but kept many of its provisions intact.

DOCUMENT

United States Intelligence Activities

PART 2—CONDUCT OF INTELLIGENCE ACTIVITIES
2.1 NEED
   Accurate and timely information about the capabilities, intentions and activities of foreign powers, organizations, or persons and their agents is essential to informed decisionmaking in the areas of national defense and foreign relations.

Collection of such information is a priority objective and will be pursued in a vigorous, innovative and responsible manner that is consistent with the Constitution and applicable law and respectful of the principles upon which the United States was founded.

2.2 PURPOSE

This Order is intended to enhance human and technical collection techniques, especially those undertaken abroad, and the acquisition of significant foreign intelligence, as well as the detection and countering of international terrorist activities and espionage conducted by foreign powers. Set forth below are certain general principles that, in addition to and consistent with applicable laws, are intended to achieve the proper balance between the acquisition of essential information and protection of individual interests. Nothing in this Order shall be construed to apply to or interfere with any authorized civil or criminal law enforcement responsibility of any department or agency.

2.3 COLLECTION OF INFORMATION

Agencies within the Intelligence Community are authorized to collect, retain or disseminate information concerning United States persons only in accordance with procedures established by the head of the agency concerned and approved by the Attorney General, consistent with the authorities provided by Part 1 of this Order. Those procedures shall permit collection, retention and dissemination of the following types of information:

(a) Information that is publicly available or collected with the consent of the person concerned;

(b) Information constituting foreign intelligence or counterintelligence, including such information concerning corporations or other commercial organizations. Collection within the United States of foreign intelligence not otherwise obtainable shall be undertaken by the FBI or, when significant foreign intelligence is sought, by other authorized agencies of the Intelligence Community, provided that no foreign intelligence collection by such agencies may be undertaken for the purpose of acquiring information concerning the domestic activities of United States persons;

(c) Information obtained in the course of a lawful foreign intelligence, counterintelligence, international narcotics or international terrorism investigation;

(d) Information needed to protect the safety of any persons or organizations, including those who are targets, victims or hostages of international terrorist organizations;

DID YOU KNOW?

The Beirut Barracks Bombing

Prior to the September 11 attacks, the bloodiest act of international terrorism to target the United States came on October 23, 1983. An operative of Hezbollah drove a truck filled with explosives into the barracks housing U.S. peacekeeping forces in Beirut. A total of 241 U.S. military personnel were killed in the attack. On the same day, a second truck bomb detonated in the French peacekeepers' barracks, killing 58 French military personnel. Both the United States and France soon withdrew their personnel from Beirut. The United States has resisted the use of its troops as peacekeepers since the attack, and has not deployed units to Lebanon since the attack.

(e) Information needed to protect foreign intelligence or counterintelligence sources or methods from unauthorized disclosure. Collection within the United States shall be undertaken by the FBI except that other agencies of the Intelligence Community may also collect such information concerning present or former employees, present or former intelligence agency contractors or their present or former employees, or applicants for any such employment or contracting;

(f) Information concerning persons who are reasonably believed to be potential sources or contacts for the purpose of determining their suitability or credibility;

(g) Information arising out of a lawful personnel, physical or communications security investigation;

(h) Information acquired by overhead reconnaissance not directed at specific United States persons;

(i) Incidentally obtained information that may indicate involvement in activities that may violate federal, state, local or foreign laws; and

(j) Information necessary for administrative purposes.

In addition, agencies within the Intelligence Community may disseminate information, other than information derived from signals intelligence, to each appropriate agency within the Intelligence Community for purposes of allowing the recipient agency to determine whether the information is relevant to its responsibilities and can be retained by it.

2.4 COLLECTION TECHNIQUES

Agencies within the Intelligence Community shall use the least intrusive collection techniques feasible within the United States or directed against United States persons abroad. Agencies are not authorized to use such techniques as electronic surveillance, unconsented physical search, mail surveillance, physical surveillance, or monitoring devices unless they are in accordance with procedures established by the head of the agency concerned and approved by the Attorney General. Such procedures shall protect constitutional and other legal rights and limit use of such information to lawful governmental purposes. These procedures shall not authorize:

(a) The CIA to engage in electronic surveillance within the United States except for the purpose of training, testing, or conducting countermeasures to hostile electronic surveillance;

(b) Unconsented physical searches in the United States by agencies other than the FBI, except for:

(1) Searches by counterintelligence elements of the military services directed against military personnel within the United States or abroad for intelligence purposes, when authorized by a military commander empowered to approve physical searches for law enforcement purposes, based upon a finding of probable cause to believe that such persons are acting as agents of foreign powers; and

(2) Searches by CIA of personal property of non-United States persons lawfully in its possession.

(c) Physical surveillance of a United States person in the United States by agencies other than the FBI, except for:

(1) Physical surveillance of present or former employees, present or former intelligence agency contractors or their present or former employees, or applicants for any such employment or contracting; and

(2) Physical surveillance of a military person employed by a nonintelligence element of a military service.

(d) Physical surveillance of a United States person abroad to collect foreign intelligence, except to obtain significant information that cannot reasonably be acquired by other means.

. . .

2.9 UNDISCLOSED PARTICIPATION IN ORGANIZATIONS WITHIN THE UNITED STATES

No one acting on behalf of agencies within the Intelligence Community may join or otherwise participate in any organization in the United States on behalf of any agency within the Intelligence Community without disclosing his intelligence affiliation to appropriate officials of the organization, except in accordance with procedures established by the head of the agency concerned and approved by the Attorney General. Such participation shall be authorized only if it is essential to achieving lawful purposes as determined by the agency head or designee. No such participation may be undertaken for the purpose of influencing the activity of the organization or its members except in cases where:

(a) The participation is undertaken on behalf of the FBI in the course of a lawful investigation; or

(b) The organization concerned is composed primarily of individuals who are not United States persons and is reasonably believed to be acting on behalf of a foreign power.

. . .

2.11 PROHIBITION ON ASSASSINATION

No person employed by or acting on behalf of the United States Government shall engage in, or conspire to engage in, assassination.

2.12 INDIRECT PARTICIPATION

No agency of the Intelligence Community shall participate in or request any person to undertake activities forbidden by this Order.

. . .

3.6 REVOCATION

Executive Order No. 12036 of January 24, 1978, as amended, entitled "United States Intelligence Activities," is revoked.

Ronald Reagan

Source: Public Papers of the Presidents of the United States: Ronald Reagan (1981). Washington, D.C.: Government Printing Office, 1128–1139.

ANALYSIS

President Reagan continued many of the policies of his predecessors regarding intelligence collection. However, during the Reagan administration, one of the deadliest incidents of terror in U.S. history occurred. On October 23, 1983, a suicide bomber from Hezbollah drove a truck packed with explosives into a Beirut compound housing U.S. Marines on a peacekeeping mission. The attack killed 241 American service personnel and triggered a significant shift away from peacekeeping missions employing American troops. President Reagan had campaigned on a promise that his administration would never negotiate with terrorist organizations, a hardline stance that he believed would serve to deter any terror attacks against the United States or its interests. Although Executive Order 12036 continued and expanded the limits upon intelligence collection that had been established by his predecessors, it did not mean that Reagan took terrorism lightly. Rather, it signaled that his administration had begun to conceive of terrorism as a military problem, rather than one best tackled by law enforcement and intelligence agencies.

- **Document 5: Judge Advocate General Memorandum on Assassination**
- **When:** November 2, 1989
- **Where:** Washington, D.C.
- **Significance:** This memorandum clarified the Department of Defense position upon what constitutes assassination and is therefore banned by Executive Order 12333.

DOCUMENT

MEMORANDUM OF LAW
SUBJECT: Executive Order 12333 and Assassination

Summary. Executive Order 12333 prohibits assassination as a matter of national policy, but does not expound on its meaning or application. This memorandum explores the term and analyzes application of the ban to military operations at three levels: (a) conventional military operations; (b) counterinsurgency operations; and (c) peacetime counter-terrorist operations. It concludes that the clandestine, low visibility or overt use of military force against legitimate targets in time of war, or against similar targets in time of peace where such individuals or groups pose an immediate threat to United States citizens or the national security of the United States, as determined by competent authority, does not constitute assassination or conspiracy to engage in assassination, and would not be prohibited by the proscription in EO 12333 or by international law.

Assassination in general. Executive Order 12333 is the Reagan Administration's successor to an Executive Order renouncing assassination first promulgated in the Ford Administration. Paragraph 2.11 of EO 12333 states that "No person employed by or acting on behalf of the United States Government shall engage in, or conspire to engage in, assassination." The Bush Administration has continued Executive Order 12333 in force without change. Neither Executive Order 12333 nor its predecessors defines *assassination*.

While assassination generally is regarded as an act of murder for political purposes, its victims are not necessarily limited to persons of public office or prominence. The murder of a private person, if carried out for political purposes, may constitute an act of assassination. For example, the 1978 "poisoned-tip umbrella" killing of Bulgarian defector Georgi Markov by Bulgarian State Security agents on the streets of London falls into the category of an act of murder carried out for political purposes, and constitutes an assassination. In contrast, the murder of Leon Klinghoffer, a private U.S. citizen, by the terrorist Abu el Abbas during the 1985 hijacking of the Italian cruise ship *Achille Lauro*, though an act of murder for political purposes, would not constitute an act of assassination. The distinction lies not merely in the purpose of the act and/or its intended victim, but also under certain circumstances in its covert nature. Finally, the killing of Presidents Abraham Lincoln, James A. Garfield, William McKinley, and John F. Kennedy are regarded as assassination because each involved the murder of a public figure or national leader for political purposes accomplished through surprise attack.

Assassination in peacetime. In peacetime, the citizens of a nation—whether private individuals or public figures—are entitled to immunity from intentional acts of violence by citizens, agents, or military forces of another nation. Article 2(4) of the Charter of the United Nations provides that all Member States "shall refrain in their international relations from the threat or use of force against the territorial integrity or political independence of any state, or in any manner inconsistent with the Purpose of the United Nations."

Peacetime assassination, then, would seem to encompass the murder of a private individual or public figure for political purposes, and in some cases (as cited above) also require that the act constitute a covert activity, particularly when the individual is a private citizen. Assassination is unlawful killing, and would be prohibited by international law even if there was no executive order proscribing it.

Assassination in wartime. Assassination in wartime takes on a different meaning. As Clausewitz noted, war is a "continuation of political activity by

DID YOU KNOW?

Defining "Terrorism"

The U.S. government has many definitions of "terrorism." Prominent examples include:

Title 22, U.S. Code, Section 2656f (d), "Premeditated, politically motivated violence perpetrated against non-combatant targets by subnational groups or clandestine agents, usually intended to influence an audience."

Federal Bureau of Investigation, "The unlawful use of force or violence against persons or property to intimidate or coerce a Government, the civilian population, or any segment thereof, in furtherance of political or social objectives."

Department of Homeland Security, "Any activity that involves an act that: is dangerous to human life or potentially destructive of critical infrastructure or key resources; and ... must also appear to be intended (i) to intimidate or coerce a civilian population; (ii) to influence the policy of a government by intimidation or coercion; or (iii) to affect the conduct of a government by mass destruction, assassination, or kidnapping."

Department of Defense, "The calculated use of unlawful violence or threat of unlawful violence to inculcate fear; intended to coerce or to intimidate governments or societies in the pursuit of goals that are generally political, religious, or ideological objectives."

other means." In wartime the role of the military includes the legalized killing (as opposed to murder) of the enemy, whether lawful combatants or unprivileged belligerents, and may include in either category civilians who take part in the hostilities.

The term *assassination* when applied to wartime military activities against enemy combatants or military objectives does not preclude acts of violence involving the element of surprise. Combatants are liable to attack at any time or place, regardless of their activity when attacked. Nor is a distinction made between combat and combat service support with regard to the right to be attacked as combatants; combatants are subject to attack if they are participating in hostilities through fire, maneuver, and assault; providing logistic, communications, administrative, or other support; or functioning as staff planners. An individual combatant's vulnerability to lawful targeting (as opposed to assassination) is not dependent upon his or her military duties, or proximity to combat as such. Nor does the prohibition on assassination limit means that otherwise are lawful; no distinction is made between an attack accomplished by aircraft, missile, naval gunfire, artillery, mortar, infantry assault, ambush, landmine or booby trap, a single shot by a sniper, a commando attack, or other, similar means. All are lawful means for attacking the enemy and the choice of one *vis-à-vis* another has no bearing on the legality of the attack. If the person attacked is a combatant, the use of a particular lawful means for attack (as opposed to another) cannot make an otherwise lawful attack either unlawful or assassination.

Likewise, the death of noncombatants ancillary to the lawful attack of a military objective is neither assassination nor otherwise unlawful. Civilians and other noncombatants who are within or in close proximity to a military objective assume a certain risk through their presence in or proximity to such targets; this is not something about which an attacking military force normally would have knowledge or over which it would have control.

The scope of assassination in the U.S. military was first outlined in U.S. Army General Orders No. 100 (1863). Paragraph 148 states:

Assassination. The law of war does not allow proclaiming either an individual belonging to the hostile army, or a citizen, or a subject of the hostile government, an outlaw, who may be slain without trial by any captor, any more than the modern law of peace allows such international outlawry; on the contrary, it abhors such outrage. . . .

This provision, consistent with the earlier writings of Hugo Grotius, was continued in U.S. Army Field Manual 27-10 (1956), which provides (paragraph 31):

[Article 23(b), Annex to Hague Convention IV, 1907] is construed as prohibiting assassination, proscription, or outlawry of an enemy, or putting a price upon an enemy's head, as well as offering a reward for an enemy "dead or alive."

The foregoing has endeavored to define *assassination* in the sense of what the term normally encompasses, as well as those lawful acts carried out by military forces in time of war that do not constitute assassination. The following is a discussion of assassination in the context of specific levels of conflict.

Peacetime operations. The use of force in peacetime is limited by the previously cited article 2(4) of the Charter of the United Nations. However, article 51 of the Charter recognizes the inherent right of self defense of nations. Historically, the United States has resorted to the use of military force in peacetime where another nation has failed to discharge its international responsibilities in protecting U.S. citizens from acts of violence originating in or launched from its sovereign territory, or has been culpable in aiding and abetting international criminal activities. For example:

1804–1805: Marine First Lieutenant Presley O'Bannon led an expedition into Libya to capture or kill the Barbary pirates.

1916: General "Blackjack" Pershing led a year-long campaign into Mexico to capture or kill the Mexican bandit Pancho Villa following Villa's attack on Columbus, New Mexico.

1928–1932: U.S. Marines conducted a successful campaign to capture or kill the Nicaraguan bandit leader Augusto Cesar Sandino.

1967: U.S. Army personnel assisted the Bolovian Army in its campaign to capture or kill Ernesto "Che" Guevara.

1985: U.S. naval forces were used to force an Egypt Air airliner to land at Sigonella, Sicily, in an attempt to prevent the escape of the *Achille Lauro* hijackers.

1986: U.S. naval and air forces attacked terrorist-related targets in Libya in response to the Libyan government's continued employment of terrorism as a foreign policy means.

Hence there is historical precedent for the use of military force to capture or kill individuals whose peacetime actions constitute a direct threat to U.S. citizens or national security.

The Charter of the United Nations recognizes the inherent right of self defense and does not preclude unilateral action against an immediate threat. In general terms, the United States recognizes three forms of self defense:

Against an actual use of force, or hostile act;

Pre-emptive self defense against an imminent use of force; and

Self defense against a continuing threat.

A national decision to employ military force in self defense against a legitimate terrorist threat would not be unlike the employment of force in response to a threat by conventional forces; only the nature of the threat has changed, rather than the international legal right of self defense. The terrorist organizations envisaged as appropriate to necessitate or warrant an armed response by U.S. military forces are well-financed, highly organized paramilitary structures engaged in the illegal use of force.

Summary. Assassination constitutes an act of murder that is prohibited by international law and Executive Order 12333. The purpose of Executive Order 12333 and its predecessors was to preclude unilateral actions by individual agents or agencies against selected foreign public officials, and to establish beyond any doubt that the United States does not condone assassination as an instrument of national policy. Its intent was not to limit lawful self defense options against legitimate threats to the national security of the United States or individual U.S. citizens. Acting consistent with the Charter of the United Nations, a decision by the President to employ clandestine, low visibility or overt military force would not constitute assassination if U.S. military forces were employed against the combatant forces of another nation, a guerrilla force, or a terrorist or other organization whose actions pose a threat to the security of the United States.

W. Hays Parks
Chief, International Law Branch
International Affairs Division

Source: This memorandum was sent to all army JAG lawyers via *The Army Lawyer*, Department of the Army Pamphlet 27-50-204 (December 1989), 4–9. It has been digitized and is available at https://www.loc.gov/rr/frd/Military_Law/AL-1989.html.

ANALYSIS

This memorandum clarified the working definition of "assassination" for U.S. military personnel. The executive orders banning assassination had left the definition somewhat open-ended, which led to the question of what types of activities in wartime and peacetime might be banned by them. This explanation has the key elements of assassination established, limiting the ban to acts of murder carried out for political purposes in a treacherous fashion. In other words, killing enemy leaders was not inherently banned, though the method of approach to facilitate an attack might be banned. Killing potential enemies without a declaration of war was also potentially legal, so long as the killing was conducted to thwart a terrorist organization. In the aftermath of the September 11 attacks, the United States used both covert and conventional organizations to engage in targeted killings, and clearly broadened the categories of targets that might be considered a threat to U.S. security. By 2015, that category essentially included all members of Al Qaeda, the Islamic State, organizations allied with either group, and any other terrorists who professed a desire to attack the United States, its citizenry, its interests, or its allies.

- **Document 6: Executive Order 12947**
- **When:** January 23, 1995
- **Where:** Washington, D.C.
- **Significance:** President William Clinton, concerned about the proliferation of terror organizations in the post–Cold War period, sought to prohibit all economic and social transactions between U.S. citizens and specially designated terror organizations. In order

to do so, he had to declare a formal state of national emergency, as contained in the order.

DOCUMENT

Prohibiting Transactions with Terrorists Who Threaten to Disrupt the Middle East Peace Process

I, WILLIAM J. CLINTON, President of the United States of America, find that grave acts of violence committed by foreign terrorists that disrupt the Middle East peace process constitute an unusual and extraordinary threat to the national security, foreign policy, and economy of the United States, and hereby declare a national emergency to deal with that threat.

I hereby order:

Section 1. Except to the extent provided in section 203(b)(3) and (4) of IEEPA (50 U.S.C. 1702(b)(3) and (4)) and in regulations, orders, directives, or licenses that may be issued pursuant to this order, and notwithstanding any contract entered into or any license or permit granted prior to the effective date: (a) all property and interests in property of:

(i) the persons listed in the Annex to this order;

(ii) foreign persons designated by the Secretary of State, in coordination with the Secretary of the Treasury and the Attorney General, because they are found:

(A) to have committed, or to pose a significant risk of committing, acts of violence that have the purpose or effect of disrupting the Middle East peace process, or

(B) to assist in, sponsor, or provide financial, material, or technological support for, or services in support of, such acts of violence; and

(iii) persons determined by the Secretary of the Treasury, in coordination with the Secretary of State and the Attorney General, to be owned or controlled by, or to act for or on behalf of, any of the foregoing persons, that are in the United States, that hereafter come within the United States, or that hereafter come within the possession or control of United States persons, are blocked;

(b) any transaction or dealing by United States persons or within the United States in property or interests in property of the persons designated in or pursuant to this order is prohibited, including the making or receiving of any contribution of funds, goods, or services to or for the benefit of such persons;

(c) any transaction by any United States person or within the United States that evades or avoids, or has the purpose of evading or avoiding, or attempts to violate, any of the prohibitions set forth in this order, is prohibited.

Sec. 2. For the purposes of this order: (a) the term "person" means an individual or entity;

(b) the term "entity" means a partnership, association, corporation, or other organization, group, or subgroup;

(c) the term "United States person" means any United States citizen, permanent resident alien, entity organized under the laws of the United States (including foreign branches), or any person in the United States; and

(d) the term "foreign person" means any citizen or national of a foreign state (including any such individual who is also a citizen or national of the United States) or any entity not organized solely under the laws of the United States or existing solely in the United States, but does not include a foreign state.

Sec. 3. I hereby determine that the making of donations of the type specified in section 203(b)(2)(A) of IEEPA (50 U.S.C. 1702(b)(2)(A)) by United States persons to persons designated in or pursuant to this order would seriously impair my ability to deal with the national emergency declared in this order, and hereby prohibit such donations as provided by section 1 of this order.

Sec. 4. (a) The Secretary of the Treasury, in consultation with the Secretary of State and, as appropriate, the Attorney General, is hereby authorized to take such actions, including the promulgation of rules and regulations, and to employ all powers granted to me by IEEPA as may be necessary to carry out the purposes of this order. The Secretary of the Treasury may redelegate any of these functions to other officers and agencies of the United States Government. All agencies of the United States Government are hereby directed to take all appropriate measures within their authority to carry out the provisions of this order.

(b) Any investigation emanating from a possible violation of this order, or of any license, order, or regulation issued pursuant to this order, shall first be coordinated with the Federal Bureau of Investigation (FBI), and any matter involving evidence of a criminal violation shall be referred to the FBI for further investigation. The FBI shall timely notify the Department of the Treasury of any action it takes on such referrals.

Sec. 5. Nothing contained in this order shall create any right or benefit, substantive or procedural, enforceable by any party against the United States, its agencies or instrumentalities, its officers or employees, or any other person.

Sec. 6. (a) This order is effective at 12:01 a.m., eastern standard time on January 24, 1995.

(b) This order shall be transmitted to the Congress and published in the **Federal Register**.

The White House
January 23, 1995
ANNEX
TERRORIST ORGANIZATIONS WHICH THREATEN TO DISRUPT THE MIDDLE EAST PEACE PROCESS

Abu Nidal Organization (ANO)
Democratic Front for the Liberation of Palestine (DFLP)
Hizballah
Islamic Gama'at (IG)
Islamic Resistance Movement (HAMAS)
Jihad

Kach
Kahane Chai
Palestinian Islamic Jihad-Shiqaqi Faction (PIJ)
Palestinian Liberation Front-Abu Abbas Faction (PLF-Abu Abbas)
Popular Front for the Liberation of Palestine (PFLP)
Popular Front for the Liberation of Palestine-General Command (PFLP-GC)

Source: 60 *Federal Register* 5079.

ANALYSIS

President Clinton recognized that one of the primary funding sources for terror organizations was the creation of false charity organizations. Through an executive order, he sought to eliminate this key sponsorship by formally banning all transactions with specially designated terror organizations. This was an important step, in that the U.S. government served formal notice that it would define each of these groups as terrorists, and hence beyond the pale of diplomatic discourse. Over time, the federal government has expanded the list of terror organizations, which is maintained by the Department of State (see Document 33 for the 2001 list). The document is also noteworthy because it acknowledged the growing power of terror organizations, and the possibility that their activities might threaten ongoing peace talks in the Middle East. Not only was President Clinton signifying the increased risk of terror attacks, but he was also demonstrating that the United States considered the Middle East peace process to be vitally important to U.S. national security. Although the United States had been subjected to relatively few terror attacks originating in the Middle East, it is clear that President Clinton considered such attacks in the future to be a strong possibility.

- **Document 7: Osama bin Laden's Declaration of War upon the United States**
- **When:** August 23, 1996
- **Where:** Khartoum, Sudan
- **Significance:** This document laid out Osama bin Laden's grievances against the West, and against the United States in particular. He formally declared his intention that his followers should engage in acts of terrorism and other violence as a means to expel Western influence from the Arabian Peninsula.

DOCUMENT

It should not be hidden from you that the people of Islam had suffered from aggression, iniquity and injustice imposed on them by the Zionist-Crusaders alliance and their collaborators; to the extent that the Muslims blood became the cheapest and their wealth as loot in the hands of the enemies. Their blood was spilled in Palestine and Iraq. The horrifying pictures of the massacre of Qana, in Lebanon are still fresh in our memory. Massacres in Tajakestan, Burma, Cashmere, Assam, Philippine, Fatani, Ogadin, Somalia, Erithria, Chechnia and in Bosnia-Herzegovina took place, massacres that send shivers in the body and shake the conscience. All of this and the world watch and hear, and not only didn't respond to these atrocities, but also with a clear conspiracy between the USA and its allies and under the cover of the iniquitous United Nations, the dispossessed people were even prevented from obtaining arms to defend themselves.

The people of Islam awakened and realised that they are the main target for the aggression of the Zionist-Crusaders alliance. All false claims and propaganda about "Human Rights" were hammered down and exposed by the massacres that took place against the Muslims in every part of the world.

The latest and the greatest of these aggressions, incurred by the Muslims since the death of the Prophet (ALLAH'S BLESSING AND SALUTATIONS ON HIM) is the occupation of the land of the two Holy Places—the foundation of the house of Islam, the place of the revelation, the source of the message and the place of the noble Ka'ba, the Qiblah of all Muslims—by the armies of the American Crusaders and their allies. (We bemoan this and can only say: "No power and power acquiring except through Allah").

Under the present circumstances, and under the banner of the blessed awakening which is sweeping the world in general and the Islamic world in particular, I meet with you today. And after a long absence, imposed on the scholars (Ulama) and callers (Da'ees) of Islam by the iniquitous crusaders movement under the leadership of the USA; who fears that they, the scholars and callers of Islam, will instigate the Ummah of Islam against its enemies as their ancestor scholars—may Allah be pleased with them—like Ibn Taymiyyah and Al'iz Ibn Abdes-Salaam did. And therefore the Zionist-Crusader alliance resorted to killing and arresting the truthful Ulama and the working Da'ees (We are not praising or sanctifying them; Allah sanctify whom He pleased). They killed the Mujahid Sheikh Abdullah Azzaam, and they arrested the Mujahid Sheikh Ahmad Yaseen and the Mujahid Sheikh Omar Abdur Rahman (in America).

Quick efforts were made by each group to contain and to correct the situation. All agreed that the country is heading toward a great catastrophe, the depth of which is not known except by Allah. One big merchant commented: "the king is leading the state into 'sixty-six' folded disaster," (We bemoan this and can only say: "No power and power acquiring except through Allah"). Numerous princes share with the people their feelings, privately expressing their concerns and objecting to the corruption, repression and the intimidation taking place in the country. But the competition between influential princes for personal gains and interest had destroyed the country. Through its course of actions the regime has torn off its legitimacy:

(1) Suspension of the Islamic Shari'ah law and exchanging it with man made civil law. The regime entered into a bloody confrontation with the truthful Ulamah and the righteous youths (we sanctify nobody; Allah sanctify Whom He pleaseth).

(2) The inability of the regime to protect the country, and allowing the enemy of the Ummah—the American crusader forces—to occupy the land for the longest of years. The crusader forces became the main cause of our disastrous condition, particularly in the economical aspect of it due to the unjustified heavy spending on these forces. As a result of the policy imposed on the country, especially in the field of oil industry where production is restricted or expanded and prices are fixed to suit the American economy ignoring the economy of the country. Expensive deals were imposed on the country to purchase arms. People asking what is the justification for the very existence of the regime then?

But—to our deepest regret—the regime refused to listen to the people accusing them of being ridiculous and imbecile. The matter got worse as previous wrong doings were followed by mischiefs of greater magnitudes. All of this taking place in the land of the two Holy Places! It is no longer possible to be quiet. It is not acceptable to give a blind eye to this matter.

But with the grace of Allah, the majority of the nation, both civilians and military individuals are aware of the wicked plan. They refused to be played against each other and to be used by the regime as a tool to carry out the policy of the American-Israeli alliance through their agent in our country: the Saudi regime.

If there are more than one duty to be carried out, then the most important one should receive priority. Clearly after Belief (Imaan) there is no more important duty than pushing the American enemy out of the holy land. No other priority, except Belief, could be considered before it; the people of knowledge, Ibn Taymiyyah, stated: "to fight in defence of religion and Belief is a collective duty; there is no other duty after Belief than fighting the enemy who is corrupting the life and the religion." There is no preconditions for this duty and the enemy should be fought with one best abilities. (ref: supplement of Fatawa). If it is not possible to push back the enemy except by the collective movement of the Muslim people, then there is a duty on the Muslims to ignore the minor differences among themselves; the ill effect of ignoring these differences, at a given period of time, is much less than the ill effect of the occupation of the Muslims' land by the main Kufr. Ibn Taymiyyah had explained this issue and emphasized the importance of dealing with the major threat on the expense of the minor one. He described the situation of the Muslims and the Mujahideen and stated that even the military personnel who are not practicing Islam are not exempted from the duty of Jihad against the enemy.

Under such circumstances, to push the enemy—the greatest Kufr—out of the country is a prime duty. No other duty after Belief is more important than the duty of had. Utmost effort should be made to prepare and instigate the Ummah against the enemy, the American-Israeli alliance—occupying the country of the two Holy Places and the route of the Apostle (Allah's Blessings and Salutations may be on him) to the Furthest Mosque (Al-Aqsa Mosque). Also to remind the Muslims not to be engaged in an internal war among themselves, as that will have grieve consequences namely:

1-consumption of the Muslims human resources as most casualties and fatalities will be among the Muslims people.

2-Exhaustion of the economic and financial resources.

3-Destruction of the country infrastructures.

4-Dissociation of the society.

5-Destruction of the oil industries. The presence of the USA Crusader military forces on land, sea and air of the states of the Islamic Gulf is the greatest danger threatening the largest oil reserve in the world. The existence of these forces in the area will provoke the people of the country and induces aggression on their religion, feelings and prides and push them to take up armed struggle against the invaders occupying the land; therefore spread of the fighting in the region will expose the oil wealth to the danger of being burned up. The economic interests of the States of the Gulf and the land of the two Holy Places will be damaged and even a greater damage will be caused to the economy of the world. I would like here to alert my brothers, the Mujahideen, the sons of the nation, to protect this (oil) wealth and not to include it in the battle as it is a great Islamic wealth and a large economical power essential for the soon to be established Islamic state, by Allah's Permission and Grace. We also warn the aggressors, the USA, against burning this Islamic wealth (a crime which they may commit in order to prevent it, at the end of the war, from falling in the hands of its legitimate owners and to cause economic damages to the competitors of the USA in Europe or the Far East, particularly Japan which is the major consumer of the oil of the region).

6-Division of the land of the two Holy Places, and annexing of the northerly part of it by Israel. Dividing the land of the two Holy Places is an essential demand of the Zionist-Crusader alliance. The existence of such a large country with its huge resources under the leadership of the forthcoming Islamic State, by Allah's Grace, represent a serious danger to the very existence of the Zionist state in Palestine. The Nobel Ka'ba,—the Qiblah of all Muslims—makes the land of the two Holy Places a symbol for the unity of the Islamic world. Moreover, the presence of the world largest oil reserve makes the land of the two Holy Places an important economical power in the Islamic world. The sons of the two Holy Places are directly related to the life style (Seerah) of their forefathers, the companions, may Allah be pleased with them. They consider the Seerah of their forefathers as a source and an example for re-establishing the greatness of this Ummah and to raise the word of Allah again. Furthermore the presence of a population of fighters in the south of Yemen, fighting in the cause of Allah, is a strategic threat to the Zionist-Crusader alliance in the area. The Prophet (ALLAH'S BLESSING AND SALUTATIONS ON HIM) said: (around twelve thousands will emerge from Aden/Abian helping—the cause of—Allah and His messenger, they are the best, in the time, between me and them) narrated by Ahmad with a correct trustworthy reference.

7-An internal war is a great mistake, no matter what reasons are there for it. The presence of the occupier—the USA—forces will control the outcome of the battle for the benefit of the international Kufr.

Muslims Brothers of land of the two Holy Places:

It is incredible that our country is the world largest buyer of arms from the USA and the area biggest commercial partners of the Americans who are assisting their Zionist brothers in occupying Palestine and in evicting and killing the Muslims there, by providing arms, men and financial supports.

To deny these occupiers from the enormous revenues of their trading with our country is a very important help for our Jihad against them. To express our anger and hate to them is a very important moral gesture. By doing so we would have taken part in (the process of) cleansing our sanctities from the crusaders and the Zionists and forcing them, by the Permission of Allah, to leave disappointed and defeated.

We expect the woman of the land of the two Holy Places and other countries to carry out their role in boycotting the American goods.

If economical boycotting is intertwined with the military operations of the Mujahideen, then defeating the enemy will be even nearer, by the Permission of Allah. However if Muslims don't co-operate and support their Mujahideen brothers then, in effect, they are supplying the army of the enemy with financial help and extending the war and increasing the suffering of the Muslims.

The security and the intelligence services of the entire world can not force a single citizen to buy the goods of his/her enemy. Economical boycotting of the American goods is a very effective weapon of hitting and weakening the enemy, and it is not under the control of the security forces of the regime.

Few days ago the news agencies had reported that the Defense Secretary of the Crusading Americans had said that "the explosion at Riyadh and Al-Khobar had taught him one lesson: that is not to withdraw when attacked by coward terrorists."

We say to the Defence Secretary that his talk can induce a grieving mother to laughter! and shows the fears that had enshrined you all. Where was this false courage of yours when the explosion in Beirut took place on 1983 AD (1403 A.H). You were turned into scattered pits and pieces at that time; 241 mainly marines soldiers were killed. And where was this courage of yours when two explosions made you to leave Aden in less than twenty four hours!

But your most disgraceful case was in Somalia; where—after vigorous propaganda about the power of the USA and its post cold war leadership of the new world order —you moved tens of thousands of international force, including twenty eight thousands American soldiers into Somalia. However, when tens of your solders were killed in minor battles and one American pilot was dragged in the streets of Mogadishu you left the area carrying disappointment, humiliation, defeat and your dead with you. Clinton appeared in front of the whole world threatening and promising revenge, but these threats were merely a preparation for withdrawal. You have been disgraced by Allah and you withdrew; the extent of your impotence and weaknesses became very clear. It was a pleasure for the "heart" of every Muslim and a remedy to the "chests" of believing nations to see you defeated in the three Islamic cities of Beirut, Aden and Mogadishu.

I say to the Secretary of Defense: The sons of the land of the two Holy Places had come out to fight against the Russian in Afghanistan, the Serb in Bosnia-Herzegovina and today they are fighting in Chechenia and—by the Permission of Allah—they have been made victorious over your partner, the Russians. By the command of Allah, they are also fighting in Tajakistan.

I say: Since the sons of the land of the two Holy Places feel and strongly believe that fighting (Jihad) against the Kuffar in every part of the world, is absolutely essential; then they would be even more enthusiastic, more powerful and larger in number upon fighting on their own land—the place of their births—defending the greatest of their sanctities, the noble Ka'ba (the Qiblah of all Muslims). They know that the Muslims of the world will assist and help them to victory. To liberate their sanctities is the greatest of issues concerning all Muslims; It is the duty of every Muslims in this world.

I say to you William (Defense Secretary) that: These youths love death as you love life. They inherit dignity, pride, courage, generosity, truthfulness and sacrifice from father to father. They are most delivering and steadfast at war. They inherit these values from their ancestors (even from the time of the Jaheliyyah, before Islam). These values were approved and completed by the arriving Islam as stated by the messenger of Allah (Allah's Blessings and Salutations may be on him): "I have been send to perfecting the good values." (Saheeh Al-Jame' As-Sagheer).

Those youths know that their rewards in fighting you, the USA, is double than their rewards in fighting some one else not from the people of the book. They have no intention except to enter paradise by killing you. An infidel, and enemy of God like you, cannot be in the same hell with his righteous executioner.

Terrorising you, while you are carrying arms on our land, is a legitimate and morally demanded duty. It is a legitimate right well known to all humans and other creatures. Your example and our example is like a snake which entered into a house of a man and got killed by him. The coward is the one who lets you walk, while carrying arms, freely on his land and provides you with peace and security.

The youths hold you responsible for all of the killings and evictions of the Muslims and the violation of the sanctities, carried out by your Zionist brothers in Lebanon; you openly supplied them with arms and finance. More than 600,000 Iraqi children have died due to lack of food and medicine and as a result of the unjustifiable aggression (sanction) imposed on Iraq and its nation. The children of Iraq are our children. You, the USA, together with the Saudi regime are responsible for the shedding of the blood of these innocent children. Due to all of that, whatever treaty you have with our country is now null and void.

Source: This document was originally published in Arabic in London newspaper *Al Quds al Arabi*. This translation can be found at http://www.pbs.org/newshour/updates/military-july-dec96-fatwa_1996/.

ANALYSIS

With this message, Osama bin Laden declared his intention to engage in terrorism, and any other form of resistance, until all nonbelievers were forced to depart from the Arabian Peninsula. The full document, which is more than 30 pages long when translated into English, contains a list of grievances along with a series of justifications for engaging in violence. Many of his complaints revolved around the Saudi government, which he felt was complicit in allowing an invasion and occupation of the Holy Land of Islam. By attempting to lay the blame for the subsequent violence upon the United States and Saudi Arabia, he sought to absolve his followers for any of their misdeeds. Unfortunately, the document was not taken seriously by many American officials, who believed that Al Qaeda had very limited reach and little chance of striking a major blow against American interests.

Even the bombing of two U.S. embassies in sub-Saharan Africa and the attack upon the USS *Cole* did little to move the American government to significant action, and American domestic security measures were woefully inadequate on September 11, 2001, even in the face of this naked declaration of intent to engage in hostilities.

- **Document 8: Central Intelligence Agency's 1996 Profile of Osama bin Laden**
- **When:** 1996
- **Where:** Langley, VA
- **Significance:** This document demonstrates that the U.S. Central Intelligence Agency had conducted extensive research into the background and previous behaviors of Osama bin Laden, and considered him a significant risk to U.S. national security, primarily as a financier of terror activities.

DOCUMENT

Usama Bin Ladin: Islamic Extremist Financier

Usama bin Muhammad bin Awad Bin Ladin is one of the most significant financial sponsors of Islamic extremist activities in the world today. One of some 20 sons of wealthy Saudi construction magnate Muhammed Bin Ladin—founder of the Kingdom's Bin Ladin Group business empire—Usama joined the Afghan resistance movement following the 26 December 1979 Soviet invasion of Afghanistan. "I was enraged and went there at once," he claimed in a 1993 interview, "I arrived within days, before the end of 1979."

Bin Ladin gained prominence during the Afghan war for his role in financing the recruitment, transportation, and training of Arab nationals who volunteered to fight alongside the Afghan mujahedin. By 1985, Bin Ladin had drawn on his family's wealth, plus donations received from sympathetic merchant families in the Gulf region, to organize the Islamic Salvation Foundation, or al-Qaida, for this purpose.

A network of al-Qaida recruitment centers and guesthouses in Egypt, Saudi Arabia, and Pakistan has enlisted and sheltered thousands of Arab recruits. This network remains active.

Working in conjunction with extremist groups like the Egyptian al-Gama'at al-Islamiyyah, also known as the Islamic Group, al-Qaida organized and funded camps in Afghanistan and Pakistan that provided new recruits paramilitary training in preparation for the fighting in Afghanistan.

Under al-Qaida auspices, Bin Ladin imported bulldozers and other heavy equipment to cut roads, tunnels, hospitals, and storage depots through Afghanistan's mountainous terrain to move and shelter fighters and supporters.

After the Soviets withdrew from Afghanistan in 1989, Bin Ladin returned to work in the family's Jeddah-based construction business. However, he continued to support militant Islamic groups that had begun targeting moderate Islamic governments in the region. Saudi officials held Bin Ladin's passport during 1989–1991 in a bid to prevent him from solidifying contacts with extremists whom he had befriended during the Afghan war.

Bin Ladin relocated to Sudan in 1991, where he was welcomed by National Islamic Front (NIF) leader Hasan al-Turabi. In a 1994 interview, Bin Ladin claimed to have surveyed business and agricultural investment opportunities in Sudan as early as 1983. He embarked on several business ventures in Sudan in 1990, which began to thrive following his move to Khartoum. Bin Ladin also formed symbiotic business relationships with wealthy NIF members by undertaking civil infrastructure development projects on the regime's behalf.

Bin Ladin's company, Al-Hijrah for Construction and Development, Ltd., built the tahaddi (challenge) road linking Khartoum with Port Sudan, as well as the modern international airport near Port Sudan.

Bin Ladin's import-export firm Wadi al-Aqiq Company, Ltd., in conjunction with his Taba Investment Company, Ltd., acquired a near monopoly over Sudan's major agricultural exports of gum, corn, sunflower, and sesame products in cooperation with prominent NIF members. At the same time, Bin Ladin's Al-Themar al-Mubarakah Agriculture Company, Ltd. Grew to encompass large tracts of land near Khartoum and in eastern Sudan.

Bin Ladin and wealthy NIF members capitalized Al-Shamal Islamic Bank in Khartoum. Bin Ladin invested $50 million in the bank.

Bin Ladin's work force grew to include militant Afghan war veterans seeking to avoid a return to their own countries, where many stood accused of subversive and terrorist activities. In May 1993, for example, Bin Ladin financed the travel of 300 to 450 Afghan war veterans to Sudan after Islamabad launched a crackdown against extremists lingering in Pakistan. In addition to safe haven in Sudan, Bin Ladin has provided financial support to militants actively opposed to moderate Islamic governments and the West.

Islamic extremists who perpetrated the December 1992 attempted bombings against some 100 U.S. servicemen in Aden—billeted there to support U.N. relief operations in Somalia—claimed that Bin Ladin financed their group.

A joint Egyptian-Saudi investigation revealed in May 1993 that Bin Ladin's business interests helped funnel money to Egyptian extremists, who used the cash to buy unspecified equipment, printing presses, and weapons.

By January 1994, Bin Ladin had begun financing at least three terrorist training camps in north Sudan—camp residents included Egyptian, Algerian, Tunisian, and Palestinian extremists—in cooperation with the NIF. Bin Ladin's Al-Hijrah for Construction and Development works directly with Sudanese military officials to transport and provision terrorists training in such camps.

Pakistani investigators have said that Ramzi Ahmed Yousef, the alleged mastermind of the February 1993 World Trade Center bombing, resided at the Bin Ladin-funded Bayt Ashuhada (house of martyrs) guesthouse in Peshawar during most of the three years before his apprehension in February 1995.

A leading member of the Egyptian extremist group al-Jihad claimed in a July 1995 interview that Bin Ladin helped fund the group and was at times writing of specific terrorist operations mounted by the group against Egyptian interests.

Bin Ladin remains the key financier behind the "Kumar" camp in Afghanistan, which provides terrorist training to al-Jihad and al-Gama'at al-Islamiyyah members, according to suspect terrorists captured recently by Egyptian authorities.

Bin Ladin's support for extremist causes continues despite criticisms from regional governments and his family. Algeria, Egypt, and Yemen have accused Bin Ladin of financing military Islamic groups on their soil (Yemen reportedly sought INTERPOL's assistance to apprehend Bin Ladin during 1994). In February 1994, Riyadh revoked Bin Ladin's Saudi citizenship for behavior that "contradicts the Kingdom's interests and risks harming its relations with fraternal countries." The move prompted Bin Ladin to form the Advisory and Reformation Committee, a London-based dissident organization that by July 1995 had issued over 350 pamphlets critical of the Saudi Government. Bin Ladin has not responded to condemnation leveled against him in March 1994 by his eldest brother, Hakr Bin Ladin, who expressed through the Saudi media his family's "regret, denunciation, and condemnation" of Bin Ladin's extremist activities.

Source: Central Intelligence Agency, available online at National Security Archive Electronic Briefing Book No. 343, 2011. http://nsarchive.gwu.edu/ NSAEBB/NSAEBB343/.

ANALYSIS

Although Osama bin Laden had come to the attention of the CIA by the mid-1990s, he was primarily considered a financier and logistical organizer, rather than a direct threat to U.S. interests. As such, bin Laden's ideological influence was largely overlooked and there was no specific call to capture or kill the rising terrorist leader. This document also mentions bin Laden's exile by the Saudi government, a move that he largely blamed on U.S. influence. The revocation of his citizenship led bin Laden to target the Saudi royal family and government, as he came to believe that it had adopted secular ways and stood in the way of the creation of an Islamist state that might grow into a pan-Islamic caliphate.

- **Document 9: International Convention for the Suppression of Terrorist Bombing**
- **When:** November 25, 1997
- **Where:** United Nations, New York City
- **Significance:** The UN General Assembly adopted this convention, and urged all member states to sign it, as a recognition that terrorism and terrorist bombing are common enemies of the civilized world, and thus require a collective response.

DOCUMENT

International Convention for the Suppression of Terrorist Bombings
The States Parties to this Convention,

Deeply concerned about the worldwide escalation of acts of terrorism in all its forms and manifestations,

Noting also that terrorist attacks by means of explosives or other lethal devices have become increasingly widespread,

Noting further that existing multilateral legal provisions do not adequately address these attacks,

Being convinced of the urgent need to enhance international cooperation between States in devising and adopting effective and practical measures for the prevention of such acts of terrorism, and for the prosecution and punishment of their perpetrators,

Considering that the occurrence of such acts is a matter of grave concern to the international community as a whole,

Noting that the activities of military forces of States are governed by rules of international law outside the framework of this Convention and that the exclusion of certain actions from the coverage of this Convention does not condone or make lawful otherwise unlawful acts, or preclude prosecution under other laws,

Have agreed as follows:

Article 1

For the purposes of this Convention:

1. "State or government facility" includes any permanent or temporary facility or conveyance that is used or occupied by representatives of a State, members of Government, the legislature or the judiciary or by officials or employees of a State or any other public authority or entity or by employees or officials of an intergovernmental organization in connection with their official duties.

2. "Infrastructure facility" means any publicly or privately owned facility providing or distributing services for the benefit of the public, such as water, sewage, energy, fuel or communications.

3. "Explosive or other lethal device" means:

(a) An explosive or incendiary weapon or device that is designed, or has the capability, to cause death, serious bodily injury or substantial material damage; or

(b) A weapon or device that is designed, or has the capability, to cause death, serious bodily injury or substantial material damage through the release, dissemination or impact of toxic chemicals, biological agents or toxins or similar substances or radiation or radioactive material.

Article 2

1. Any person commits an offence within the meaning of this Convention if that person unlawfully

---

DID YOU KNOW?

Was Timothy McVeigh a Terrorist?

Some scholars of terrorism do not classify Timothy McVeigh as a terrorist because he did not belong to a terror organization. These experts argue that so-called lone-wolf attacks only constitute terrorism if they are conducted in the furtherance of an organization's objectives. Others argue that because McVeigh identified with the broad ideology of a number of groups, even though he had not formally joined them, and because he desired to incite fear in the federal government and coerce its future behavior, he should be considered a terrorist. His situation illustrates the problems that arise due to the lack of consensus regarding the definition of "terrorism."

and intentionally delivers, places, discharges or detonates an explosive or other lethal device in, into or against a place of public use, a State or government facility, a public transportation system or an infrastructure facility:

(a) With the intent to cause death or serious bodily injury; or

(b) With the intent to cause extensive destruction of such a place, facility or system, where such destruction results in or is likely to result in major economic loss.

Article 3

This Convention shall not apply where the offence is committed within a single State, the alleged offender and the victims are nationals of that State, the alleged offender is found in the territory of that State and no other State has a basis under article 6, paragraph 1, or article 6, paragraph 2, of this Convention to exercise jurisdiction, except that the provisions of articles 10 to 15 shall, as appropriate, apply in those cases.

Article 4

Each State Party shall adopt such measures as may be necessary:

(a) To establish as criminal offences under its domestic law the offences set forth in article 2 of this Convention;

(b) To make those offences punishable by appropriate penalties which take into account the grave nature of those offences.

Article 5

Each State Party shall adopt such measures as may be necessary, including, where appropriate, domestic legislation, to ensure that criminal acts within the scope of this Convention, in particular where they are intended or calculated to provoke a state of terror in the general public or in a group of persons or particular persons, are under no circumstances justifiable by considerations of a political, philosophical, ideological, racial, ethnic, religious or other similar nature and are punished by penalties consistent with their grave nature.

Article 6

1. Each State Party shall take such measures as may be necessary to establish its jurisdiction over the offences set forth in article 2 when:

(a) The offence is committed in the territory of that State; or

(b) The offence is committed on board a vessel flying the flag of that State or an aircraft which is registered under the laws of that State at the time the offence is committed; or

(c) The offence is committed by a national of that State.

2. A State Party may also establish its jurisdiction over any such offence when:

(a) The offence is committed against a national of that State; or

(b) The offence is committed against a State or government facility of that State abroad, including an embassy or other diplomatic or consular premises of that State; or

(c) The offence is committed by a stateless person who has his or her habitual residence in the territory of that State; or

(d) The offence is committed in an attempt to compel that State to do or abstain from doing any act; or

(e) The offence is committed on board an aircraft which is operated by the Government of that State.

Article 7

    1. Upon receiving information that a person who has committed or who is alleged to have committed an offence as set forth in article 2 may be present in its territory, the State Party concerned shall take such measures as may be necessary under its domestic law to investigate the facts contained in the information.

    2. Upon being satisfied that the circumstances so warrant, the State Party in whose territory the offender or alleged offender is present shall take the appropriate measures under its domestic law so as to ensure that person's presence for the purpose of prosecution or extradition.

Article 8

    1. The State Party in the territory of which the alleged offender is present shall, in cases to which article 6 applies, if it does not extradite that person, be obliged, without exception whatsoever and whether or not the offence was committed in its territory, to submit the case without undue delay to its competent authorities for the purpose of prosecution, through proceedings in accordance with the laws of that State. Those authorities shall take their decision in the same manner as in the case of any other offence of a grave nature under the law of that State.

    2. Whenever a State Party is permitted under its domestic law to extradite or otherwise surrender one of its nationals only upon the condition that the person will be returned to that State to serve the sentence imposed as a result of the trial or proceeding for which the extradition or surrender of the person was sought, and this State and the State seeking the extradition of the person agree with this option and other terms they may deem appropriate, such a conditional extradition or surrender shall be sufficient to discharge the obligation set forth in paragraph 1.

. . .

Article 10

    1. States Parties shall afford one another the greatest measure of assistance in connection with investigations or criminal or extradition proceedings brought in respect of the offences set forth in article 2, including assistance in obtaining evidence at their disposal necessary for the proceedings.

    2. States Parties shall carry out their obligations under paragraph 1 in conformity with any treaties or other arrangements on mutual legal assistance that may exist between them. In the absence of such treaties or arrangements, States Parties shall afford one another assistance in accordance with their domestic law.

. . .

Article 14

Any person who is taken into custody or regarding whom any other measures are taken or proceedings are carried out pursuant to this Convention shall be guaranteed fair treatment, including enjoyment of all rights and guarantees in conformity with the law of the State in the territory of which that person is present and applicable provisions of international law, including international law of human rights.

Article 15

States Parties shall cooperate in the prevention of the offences set forth in article 2, particularly:

(a) By taking all practicable measures, including, if necessary, adapting their domestic legislation, to prevent and counter preparations in their respective territories for the commission of those offences within or outside their territories, including measures to prohibit in their territories illegal activities of persons, groups and organizations that encourage, instigate, organize, knowingly finance or engage in the perpetration of offences as set forth in article 2;

(b) By exchanging accurate and verified information in accordance with their national law, and coordinating administrative and other measures taken as appropriate to prevent the commission of offences as set forth in article 2;

(c) Where appropriate, through research and development regarding methods of detection of explosives and other harmful substances that can cause death or bodily injury, consultations on the development of standards for marking explosives in order to identify their origin in post-blast investigations, exchange of information on preventive measures, cooperation and transfer of technology, equipment and related materials.

. . .

Article 18

Nothing in this Convention entitles a State Party to undertake in the territory of another State Party the exercise of jurisdiction and performance of functions which are exclusively reserved for the authorities of that other State Party by its domestic law.

Article 19

1. Nothing in this Convention shall affect other rights, obligations and responsibilities of States and individuals under international law, in particular the purposes and principles of the Charter of the United Nations and international humanitarian law.

2. The activities of armed forces during an armed conflict, as those terms are understood under international humanitarian law, which are governed by that law, are not governed by this Convention, and the activities undertaken by military forces of a State in the exercise of their official duties, inasmuch as

they are governed by other rules of international law, are not governed by this Convention.

Source: United Nations, International Convention for the Suppression of Terrorist Bombings. A/52/653, November 25, 1997. Available online at http://www.un.org /law/cod/terroris.htm. Used by permission of the United Nations.

ANALYSIS

The United Nations had previously undertaken measures to deter terrorism and bombing attacks, but the 1997 convention was a stronger declaration of the common understanding that terrorism and terror bombings represent a common threat to all of the member states if they became an acceptable act. Interestingly, this convention does not apply if the target and perpetrators are all in and from the same nation, meaning that only international terror organizations faced sanction and punishment under this convention. Likewise, the convention did not absolutely require extradition of accused bombers, although it encouraged states to cooperate with one another regarding investigations, prosecutions, and incarcerations. In many ways, the UN convention regarding international bombing followed the established precedents of piracy law, in that it regarded the act, not the motivation, as the key determinant of guilt; and further, it allowed the punishment of perpetrators by any state that acceded to the convention. Thus, in theory, international terrorists who engaged in bombing attacks would not remain immune from arrest and prosecution by hiding in a different nation, and could even theoretically be put through the justice system of a third, otherwise uninvolved, nation that agreed to abide by the convention.

- **Document 10: "Jihad against Jews and Crusaders"**
- **When:** February 23, 1998
- **Where:** Jalalabad, Afghanistan
- **Significance:** This is the second fatwa issued by Osama bin Laden, the first was his 1996 Declaration of War (Document 7), in this case on behalf of the World Islamic Front. Like his first declaration, this communique called for faithful Muslims around the globe to engage in jihad against the United States until it evacuated the Arabian Peninsula and ceased meddling in the Middle East.

DOCUMENT

Declaration of the World Islamic Front

Praise be to God, who revealed the Book, controls the clouds, defeats factionalism, and says in His Book: "But when the forbidden months are past, then fight and slay the pagans wherever ye find them, seize them, beleaguer them, and lie in wait for them in every stratagem (of war)"; and peace be upon our Prophet, Muhammad Bin-'Abdallah, who said: I have been sent with the sword between my hands to ensure that no one but God is worshipped, God who put my livelihood under the shadow of my spear and who inflicts humiliation and scorn on those who disobey my orders.

The Arabian Peninsula has never—since God made it flat, created its desert, and encircled it with seas—been stormed by any forces like the crusader armies spreading in it like locusts, eating its riches and wiping out its plantations. All this is happening at a time in which nations are attacking Muslims like people fighting over a plate of food. In the light of the grave situation and the lack of support, we and you are obliged to discuss current events, and we should all agree on how to settle the matter.

No one argues today about three facts that are known to everyone; we will list them, in order to remind everyone:

First, for over seven years the United States has been occupying the lands of Islam in the holiest of places, the Arabian Peninsula, plundering its riches, dictating to its rulers, humiliating its people, terrorizing its neighbors, and turning its bases in the Peninsula into a spearhead through which to fight the neighboring Muslim peoples.

If some people have in the past argued about the fact of the occupation, all the people of the Peninsula have now acknowledged it. The best proof of this is the Americans' continuing aggression against the Iraqi people using the Peninsula as a staging post, even though all its rulers are against their territories being used to that end, but they are helpless.

Second, despite the great devastation inflicted on the Iraqi people by the crusader-Zionist alliance, and despite the huge number of those killed, which has exceeded 1 million . . . despite all this, the Americans are once again trying to repeat the horrific massacres, as though they are not content with the protracted blockade imposed after the ferocious war or the fragmentation and devastation.

So here they come to annihilate what is left of this people and to humiliate their Muslim neighbors. Third, if the Americans' aims behind these wars are religious and economic, the aim is also to serve the Jews' petty state and divert attention from its occupation of Jerusalem and murder of Muslims there. The best proof of this is their eagerness to destroy Iraq, the strongest neighboring Arab state, and their endeavor to fragment all the states of the region such as Iraq, Saudi Arabia, Egypt, and Sudan into paper statelets and through their disunion and weakness to guarantee Israel's survival and the continuation of the brutal crusade occupation of the Peninsula.

All these crimes and sins committed by the Americans are a clear declaration of war on God, his messenger, and Muslims. And ulema have throughout Islamic history unanimously agreed that the jihad is an individual duty if the enemy destroys the Muslim countries. This was revealed by Imam Bin-Qadamah in "Al-Mughni," Imam al-Kisa'i in "Al-Bada'i," al-Qurtubi in his interpretation, and the shaykh of al-Islam in his books, where he said: "As for the fighting to repulse [an enemy], it is aimed at defending sanctity and religion, and it is a duty as agreed [by the ulema]. Nothing is more sacred than belief except repulsing an enemy who is attacking religion and life." On that basis, and in compliance with God's order, we issue the following fatwa to all Muslims:

The ruling to kill the Americans and their allies—civilians and military—is an individual duty for every Muslim who can do it in any country in which it is possible to do it, in order to liberate the al-Aqsa Mosque and the holy mosque [Mecca] from their grip, and in order for their armies to move out of all the lands of Islam, defeated and unable to threaten any Muslim. This is in accordance with the words of Almighty God, "and fight the pagans all together as they fight you all together," and "fight them until there is no more tumult or oppression, and there prevail justice and faith in God."

This is in addition to the words of Almighty God: "And why should ye not fight in the cause of God and of those who, being weak, are ill-treated (and oppressed)?—women and children, whose cry is: 'Our Lord, rescue us from this town, whose people are oppressors; and raise for us from thee one who will help!'"

We—with God's help—call on every Muslim who believes in God and wishes to be rewarded to comply with God's order to kill the Americans and plunder their money wherever and whenever they find it. We also call on Muslim ulema, leaders, youths, and soldiers to launch the raid on Satan's U.S. troops and the devil's supporters allying with them, and to displace those who are behind them so that they may learn a lesson.

Almighty God said: "O ye who believe, give your response to God and His Apostle, when He calleth you to that which will give you life. And know that God cometh between a man and his heart, and that it is He to whom ye shall all be gathered."

Almighty God also says: "O ye who believe, what is the matter with you, that when ye are asked to go forth in the cause of God, ye cling so heavily to the earth! Do ye prefer the life of this world to the hereafter? But little is the comfort of this life, as compared with the hereafter. Unless ye go forth, He will punish you with a grievous penalty, and put others in your place; but Him ye would not harm in the least. For God hath power over all things."

Almighty God also says: "So lose no heart, nor fall into despair. For ye must gain mastery if ye are true in faith."

Source: This document was originally published in Arabic in London newspaper *Al Quds al Arabi*. Translation by the Federation of American Scientists. Available at http://www.fas.org/irp/world/para/docs/980223-fatwa.htm.

ANALYSIS

In 1996, international pressure upon the government of Sudan led it to expel Osama bin Laden and his followers. However, the Saudi government had already revoked his citizenship, leaving him very few locations in which to regroup. An invitation from the Taliban, the theocracy ruling Afghanistan, drew bin Laden and his followers back to the site of his earlier activities as a mujahideen fighting against Soviet occupation. This declaration was issued by bin Laden, but signed by many other prominent radical Islamists, suggesting that a rudimentary alliance was forming between various factions opposed to Western influence in Saudi Arabia. Once again, bin Laden presented his position as a logical and defensible reaction to the U.S. presence in Saudi Arabia. He also suggests that his call for jihad was motivated by the sufferings of other Arab Muslims, specifically the people of Iraq who were subjected to occasional attack as part of the enforcement of a no-fly zone, and who had lived under the effects of a de facto blockade for nearly a decade. By bin Laden's reckoning, more than one million Iraqi children died as a result of American actions, and thus, any casualties inflicted by Al Qaeda's terror attacks would pale in comparison to the scale of lives lost in Iraq.

- Document 11: Testimony of J. Gilmore Childers and Henry J. DePippo before the Senate Committee on the Judiciary, Subcommittee on Technology, Terrorism, and Government Information, Hearing on "Foreign Terrorists in America: Five Years after the World Trade Center"
- When: February 24, 1998
- Where: Washington, D.C.
- Significance: Childers and DePippo were part of the trial of several conspirators in the February 26, 1993 bombing of the World Trade Center. They offered a thorough summary of the case for the Senate Judiciary Committee.

DOCUMENT

As you know, we are here to discuss the trial of the terrorists who bombed the World Trade Center. The trial of four of the conspirators began approximately six months after the bombing.

After a six-month jury trial, each defendant was found guilty on all counts. Last fall, Ramzi Yousef, who was a fugitive during the first trial, was also tried and convicted for the World Trade Center bombing. Each defendant was sentenced to a total of 240 years' imprisonment.

The defendants' respective roles in the terrorist plot—and their participation in the World Trade Center bombing—were reconstructed using over 1,000 exhibits and the testimony of more than 200 witnesses. In the end, the evidence overwhelmingly established that Ramzi Yousef, Mohammed Salameh, Nidal Ayyad, Mahmud Abouhalima, Ahmad Ajaj and Abdul Rahman Yasin conspired to bomb targets in the United States and that, as part of their terrorist scheme, they participated in the February 26, 1993 bombing of the World Trade Center.

The February 26, 1993 Bombing of The World Trade Center Complex

The day before the bombing the conspirators loaded the bomb into the cargo area of the Ryder van. The completed bomb contained a urea nitrate main charge laced with aluminum powder, magnesium powder and ferric oxide for extra potency; ammonium nitrate dynamite and lead azide boosters; a smokeless powder booster; and hobby fuse inside rubber-tubing to prevent early detonation. Further to enhance the bomb's destructive impact, the conspirators also placed the AGL hydrogen tanks inside the cargo area of the Ryder van.

The conspirators then drove the van and its deadly cargo from Jersey City to Manhattan, eventually making their way into the red parking lot on the B-2 level of the World Trade Center Complex, where they parked the van. The conspirators then exited the van, with the bomb set to explode in the middle of a busy work day, and fled the World Trade Center Complex.

At approximately 12:18 p.m., the bomb in the Ryder van exploded, killing six people inside the World Trade Center Complex. The violent blast injured more than a thousand others, who suffered injuries ranging from crushed limbs to smoke inhalation.

The blast blew a huge crater in the B-2 level and destroyed portions of the B-1 level above it. A steel beam weighing approximately 3,000 pounds, that was immediately adjacent to the point of the explosion, was propelled 30 feet inside Tower One, into a room where four people were killed. The Visit Hotel, located directly above the blast area, was almost toppled. The explosion so badly damaged the water system for the World Trade Center Complex that two million gallons of water gushed from severed pipes into the sub-grade levels. In addition, almost all electricity to the World Trade Center was cut, and the remaining lines had to be severed to avoid electrocution. Thus, as of the bombing, there was no lighting, heat, emergency power or running water, and no way to communicate with the Complex's numerous tenants. The explosion also caused approximately $300 million in property damage to the World Trade Center Complex.

On February 27, 1993, the day after the bombing, Ayyad called the Daily News "tips line" to claim responsibility on behalf of the "Liberation Army." Specifically, in his spoken message, which the Daily News tape recorded, Ayyad proclaimed:

This is the Liberation Army. We conducted the explosion at the World Trade Center. You will get our demands by mail. This is the Liberation Army.

Consistent with Ayyad's announcement to the Daily News that the demands of the "Liberation Army" would be sent by mail, the conspirators sent a letter to the New York Times. The conspirators' letter stated that the World Trade Center was bombed in retaliation for American support of Israel, demanded changes in United States foreign policy in the Middle East, and threatened that, if these demands were not met, more terrorist "missions" would be carried out against military and civilian targets in America and abroad. Specifically, the letter declared:

We are, the fifth battalion in the LIBERATION ARMY, declare our responsibility for the

DID YOU KNOW?

World Trade Center Bombing of 1993

On February 26, 1993, terrorists detonated a truck filled with 1,500 pounds of explosives in the underground parking structure of the World Trade Center. The lead plotter of the attacks, Ramzi Yousef, hoped the explosion would collapse the entire World Trade Center complex, a consequence that might kill more than 100,000 victims. Instead, while the bomb did major damage to the parking structure, it narrowly missed inflicting fatal damage to the building. Had it been placed in a more dangerous location, it might have either cut through a portion of the buildings' foundation or breached the watertight structure keeping the Hudson River from flooding the subbasements of the complex. Either form of damage would likely have triggered a full collapse. In the end, 6 people were killed and 1,000 injured in the explosion, far fewer than Yousef expected. Eight years later, Yousef's uncle, Khalid Sheikh Mohammed, masterminded the plot that destroyed the towers on September 11, 2001.

explosion on the mentioned building. This action was done in response for the American political, economical, and military support to Israel the state of terrorism and to the rest of the dictator countries in the region.

OUR DEMANDS ARE:

1. Stop all military, economical, and political aid to Israel.
2. All diplomatic relations with Israel must stop.
3. Not to interfere with any of the Middle East countries interior affairs.

If our demands are not met, all of our functional groups in the army will continue to execute our missions against the military and civilian targets in and out the United States. For your own information, our army has more than hundred and fifty suicidal soldiers ready to go ahead. The terrorism that Israel practices (Which is supported by America) must be faced with a similar one. The dictatorship and terrorism also supported by America that some countries are practicing against their own people must also be faced with terrorism.

The American people must know, that their civilians who got killed are not better than those who are getting killed by the American weapons and support.

The American people are responsible for the actions of their government and they must question all of the crimes that their government is committing against other people. Or they—Americans—will be the targets of our operations that could diminish them.

LIBERATION ARMY
FIFTH BATTALION

Source: U.S. Senate, Committee on the Judiciary, Subcommittee on Technology, Terrorism, and Government Information, Hearing on "Foreign Terrorists in America: Five Years after the World Trade Center," available at http://fas.org/irp/congress/1998_hr/s980224c.htm.

ANALYSIS

The World Trade Center bombing of 1993 shocked the U.S. government and population, in part because it was an international act of terrorism on American soil, a relatively rare occurrence, and in part because of the catastrophic damage that might have resulted had the attackers created a larger bomb or placed it more efficiently in the subbasement of the World Trade Center. Yet, the attack also confirmed many assumptions regarding the nature of the greatest terror threats to American citizens and structures, namely that they would take the form of homemade bombs delivered by vehicles. The fact that the bombers sought to destroy the tallest buildings in the United States, an act that could potentially cost thousands of lives, seems to have gone largely ignored by federal officials. The law enforcement community took heart from the FBI's ability to quickly piece together the remnants of the bomb and the truck that carried it, allowing the arrest of one of the conspirators. Many assumed that future attacks would also be carried out in an inept fashion, and thus terrorism might prove irritating but not particularly dangerous to the nation.

- **Document 12: Executive Order 13099**
- **When:** August 20, 1998
- **Where:** Washington, D.C.
- **Significance:** With this order, President William Clinton added Al Qaeda and its leader, Osama bin Laden, to the list of designated terror organizations that represented a threat to peace in the Middle East. By being placed on the list, Al Qaeda and bin Laden joined the group of international terrorists that could not benefit from the activities of American citizens, to include contracting and trade relationships or the receipt of material support.

DOCUMENT

Prohibiting Transactions with Terrorists Who Threaten to Disrupt the Middle East Peace Process

I, WILLIAM J. CLINTON, President of the United States of America, in order to take additional steps with respect to grave acts of violence committed by foreign terrorists that disrupt the Middle East peace process and the national emergency described and declared in Executive Order 12947 of January 23, 1995, hereby order:

Section 1. The title of the Annex to Executive Order 12947 of January 23, 1995, is revised to read "TERRORISTS WHO THREATEN TO DISRUPT THE MIDDLE EAST PEACE PROCESS."

Sec. 2. The Annex to Executive Order 12947 of January 23, 1995, is amended by adding thereto the following persons in appropriate alphabetical order:

Usama bin Muhammad bin Awad bin Ladin (a.k.a. Usama bin Ladin)

Islamic Army (a.k.a. Al-Qaida, Islamic Salvation Foundation, The Islamic Army for the Liberation of the Holy Places, The World Islamic Front for Jihad Against Jews and Crusaders, and The Group for the Preservation of the Holy Sites)

Abu Hafs al-Masri

Rifa'i Ahmad Taha Musa

Sec. 3. Nothing contained in this order shall create any right or benefit, substantive or procedural,

DID YOU KNOW?

1998 Bombing of U.S. Embassy in Africa

Prior to the September 11 attacks, the bloodiest Al Qaeda terrorist acts against the United States were twin bombings of two American embassies in sub-Saharan Africa. On August 7, 1998, vehicular-borne bombs exploded outside of the embassies in Nairobi, Kenya, and Dar es Salaam, Tanzania. The Nairobi bomb killed 12 Americans and 201 Kenyans, and wounded 4,000 victims. In Tanzania, the bomb placement and the hardened defenses of the embassy minimized casualties. There, the explosion left 11 Tanzanians dead and dozens wounded. The United States retaliated against Al Qaeda by firing dozens of Tomahawk cruise missiles against Al Qaeda targets in Afghanistan and Sudan. Local intelligence agencies tipped off Al Qaeda leaders to the likely counterattack, providing them time to evacuate most of the sites and minimize the damages.

enforceable by any party against the United States, its agencies or instrumentalities, its officers or employees, or any other person.

Sec. 4. (a) This order is effective at 12:01 a.m., eastern daylight time on August 21, 1998.

(b) This order shall be transmitted to the Congress and published in the Federal Register.

WILLIAM J. CLINTON
THE WHITE HOUSE,
August 20, 1998

Source: 63 *Federal Register* 45167, August 25, 1998.

ANALYSIS

This expansion of Executive Order 12947 came only two weeks after the twin bombing attacks at U.S. embassies in Nairobi, Kenya, and Dar es Salaam, Tanzania. When Al Qaeda claimed responsibility for the attacks, one of the first actions that President Clinton undertook was to add it to the specially designated list of terrorists who threatened the Middle East peace process, even though the attacks had occurred in sub-Saharan Africa.

- **Document 13: A National Security Strategy for a New Century**
- **When:** October 1, 1998
- **Where:** Washington, D.C.
- **Significance:** The National Security Strategy is a public document that explains the broad parameters of U.S. military preparedness and defense policies.

DOCUMENT

Threats to U.S. Interests

Transnational threats: Terrorism, international crime, drug trafficking, illicit arms trafficking, uncontrolled refugee migrations and environmental damage threaten U.S. interests, citizens and the U.S. homeland itself. The possibility of terrorists and other criminals using WMD—nuclear, biological and chemical weapons—is of special concern. Threats to the national information infrastructure, ranging from cyber-crime to a strategic information attack on the United States via the global information network, present a dangerous new threat to our national security. We must also guard against threats to our other critical national infrastructures—such as electrical power and transportation—which increasingly could take the form of a cyber-attack in addition to physical attack or sabotage, and could originate from terrorist or criminal groups as well as hostile states. International drug trafficking organizations have become the most powerful and dangerous organized crime groups the United States has ever confronted due to their sophisticated production, shipment, distribution and financial systems, and the violence and corruption they promote everywhere they operate.

Terrorism

To meet the growing challenge of terrorism, President Clinton signed Presidential Directive 62 in May 1998. This Directive creates a new and more systematic approach to fighting the terrorist threat of the next century. It reinforces the mission of the many U.S. agencies charged with roles in defeating terrorism; it also codifies and clarifies their activities in the wide range of U.S. counter-terrorism programs, including apprehension and prosecution of terrorists, increasing transportation security, and enhancing incident response capabilities. The Directive will help achieve the President's goal of ensuring that we meet the threat of terrorism in the 21st century.

Our policy to counter international terrorists rests on the following principles: (1) make no concessions to terrorists; (2) bring all pressure to bear on all state sponsors of terrorism; (3) fully exploit all available legal mechanisms to punish international terrorists; and (4) help other governments improve their capabilities to combat terrorism. Following these principles, we seek to uncover and eliminate foreign terrorists and their support networks in our country; eliminate terrorist sanctuaries; and counter state-supported terrorism and subversion of moderate regimes through a comprehensive program of diplomatic, law enforcement, economic, military and intelligence activities. We are working to improve aviation security at airports in the United States and worldwide, to ensure better security for all U.S. transportation systems, and to improve protection for our personnel assigned overseas.

Countering terrorism effectively requires day-to-day coordination within the U.S. Government and close cooperation with other governments and international organizations. Foreign terrorists will not be allowed to enter the United States, and the full force of legal authorities will be used to remove foreign terrorists from the United States and prevent fundraising within the United States to support foreign terrorist activity. We have seen positive results from the increasing integration of intelligence, diplomatic, military and law enforcement activities among the Departments of State, Justice, Defense, Treasury, Energy, Transportation, the CIA and other intelligence agencies. The Administration is working with Congress to increase the ability of these agencies to combat terrorism through augmented funding and manpower.

The United States has made concerted efforts to deter and punish terrorists and remains determined to apprehend and bring to justice those who terrorize American citizens. In January 1998, the United States signed the International Convention for the Suppression of Terrorist Bombings. The Convention fills an important gap in international law by expanding the legal framework for international cooperation in the investigation, prosecution and extradition of persons who engage in such bombings. Whenever possible, we use law enforcement and diplomatic tools to wage the fight against terrorism. But there have been, and will be, times when law enforcement and diplomatic tools are simply not enough, when our very national security is challenged, and when we must take extraordinary steps to protect the safety of our citizens. As long as terrorists continue to target American citizens, we reserve the right to act in self defense by striking at their bases and those who sponsor, assist or actively support them. We exercised that right in 1993 with the attack against Iraqi intelligence headquarters in response to Baghdad's assassination attempt against former President Bush. We exercised that right again in August 1998.

On August 7, 1998, 12 Americans and nearly 300 Kenyans and Tanzanians lost their lives, and another 5,000 were wounded when our embassies in Nairobi and Dar es Salaam were bombed. Soon afterward, our intelligence community acquired convincing information from a variety of reliable sources that the network of radical groups affiliated with Osama bin Laden, perhaps the preeminent organizer and financier of international terrorism in the world today, planned, financed and carried out the bombings. The groups associated with bin Laden come from diverse places, but share a hatred for democracy, a fanatical glorification of violence and a horrible distortion of their religion to justify the murder of innocents. They have made the United States their adversary precisely because of what we stand for and what we stand against.

On August 20, 1998, our Armed Forces carried out strikes against terrorist facilities and infrastructure in Afghanistan. Our forces targeted one of the most active terrorist bases in the world. It contained key elements of the bin Laden network's infrastructure and has served as a training camp for literally thousands of terrorists from around the globe. Our forces also attacked a factory in Sudan associated with the bin Laden network that was involved in the production of materials for chemical weapons. The strikes were a necessary and proportionate response to the imminent threat of further terrorist attacks against U.S. personnel and facilities. Afghanistan and Sudan had been warned for years to stop harboring and supporting these terrorist groups. Countries that persistently host terrorists have no right to be safe havens.

Placing terrorism at the top of the diplomatic agenda has increased international information sharing and law enforcement efforts. At the June 1997 Denver Summit of the Eight, the leaders of Canada, France, Germany, Italy, Japan, Russia, the United Kingdom and the United States reaffirmed their determination to combat terrorism in all forms, their opposition to concessions to terrorist demands and their determination to deny hostage-takers any benefits from their acts. They agreed to intensify diplomatic efforts to ensure that by the year 2000 all States have joined the international counterterrorism conventions specified in the 1996 UN resolution on measures to counter terrorism. The eight leaders also agreed to strengthen the capability of hostage negotiation experts and counterterrorism response units, to exchange information on technologies to detect and deter the use of weapons of mass destruction in terrorist attacks, to develop means to deter terrorist attacks on electronic and computer infrastructure, to strengthen maritime security, to exchange information on security practices for international special events, and to strengthen and expand international cooperation and consultation on terrorism.

Military Activities

While our overall deterrence posture—nuclear and conventional—has been effective against most potential adversaries, a range of terrorist and criminal organizations may not be deterred by traditional deterrent threats. For these actors to be deterred, they must believe that any type of attack against the United States or its citizens will be attributed to them and that we will respond effectively and decisively to protect our national interests and ensure that justice is done.

Source: William J. Clinton, "A National Security Strategy for a New Century," http://nssarchive.us/national-security-strategy-1998/.

ANALYSIS

In 1998, the U.S. National Security Strategy focused upon a wide range of potential threats, particularly the proliferation of nuclear weapons and the possibility of renewed conflict with Iraq. Although it identified terrorism as one threat among many, and recounted a series of terror attacks that had struck U.S. forces in the preceding year, it offered little insight into how the U.S. military and other government agencies might seek to deter or defeat terror organizations, beyond broad pronouncements of the need to promote democracy and economic partnerships. Compare this document with later national security strategies to see the rapid evolution of U.S. national defense policies regarding terrorism in the aftermath of the September 11 attacks.

- **Document 14: Convention of the Organisation of the Islamic Conference on Combating International Terrorism**
- **When:** July 1, 1999
- **Where:** Ouagadougou, Burkina Faso
- **Significance:** This convention, passed two years before the September 11 attacks, was hailed by some observers as a positive step toward a global agreement regarding the definition of "terrorism" and the key mechanisms to combat it. By this time, terrorism had come to be inextricably linked with Islamic radicalism, despite its prevalence around the globe.

DOCUMENT

Convention of the Organisation of the Islamic Conference on Combating International Terrorism

The Member States of the Organisation of the Islamic Conference,
Pursuant to the tenets of the tolerant Islamic Sharia which reject all forms of violence and terrorism, and in particular specially those based on extremism and call for

protection of human rights, which provisions are parallelled by the principles and rules of international law founded on cooperation between peoples for the establishment of peace;

Abiding by the lofty, moral and religious principles particularly the provisions of the Islamic Sharia as well as the human heritage of the Islamic Ummah.

Desiring to promote cooperation among them for combating terrorist crimes that threaten the security and stability of the Islamic States and endanger their vital interests;

Being committed to combating all forms and manifestations of terrorism and eliminating its objectives and causes which target the lives and properties of people;

Confirming the legitimacy of the right of peoples to struggle against foreign occupation and colonialist and racist regimes by all means, including armed struggle to liberate their territories and attain their rights to self-determination and independence in compliance with the purposes and principles of the Charter and resolutions of the United Nations;

Believing that terrorism constitutes a gross violation of human rights, in particular the right to freedom and security, as well as an obstacle to the free functioning of institutions and socio-economic development, as it aims at destabilizing States;

Convinced that terrorism cannot be justified in any way, and that it should therefore be unambiguously condemned in all its forms and manifestations, and all its actions, means and practices, whatever its origin, causes or purposes, including direct or indirect actions of States;

Recognizing the growing links between terrorism and organized crime, including illicit trafficking in arms, narcotics, human beings and money laundering;

Have agreed to conclude this Convention, calling on all Member States of the Organization of the Islamic Conference to accede to it.

PART I
Definition and General Provisions
Article 1
For the purposes of this Convention:

1. "Contracting State" or "Contracting Party" means every Member State in the Organisation of the Islamic Conference that has ratified or adhered to this Convention and deposited its instruments of ratification or adherence with the General Secretariat of the Organisation.

2. "Terrorism" means any act of violence or threat thereof notwithstanding its motives or intentions perpetrated to carry out an individual or collective criminal plan with the aim of terrorizing people or threatening to harm them or imperiling their lives, honour, freedoms, security or rights or exposing the environment or any facility or public or private property to hazards or occupying or seizing them, or endangering a national resource, or international facilities, or threatening the stability, territorial integrity, political unity or sovereignty of independent States.

3. "Terrorist Crime" means any crime executed, started or participated in to realize a terrorist objective in any of the Contracting States or against its

nationals, assets or interests or foreign facilities and nationals residing in its territory punishable by its internal law.

Article 2

    a. Peoples' struggle including armed struggle against foreign occupation, aggression, colonialism, and hegemony, aimed at liberation and self-determination in accordance with the principles of international law shall not be considered a terrorist crime.

    b. None of the terrorist crimes mentioned in the previous article shall be considered political crimes.

    c. In the implementation of the provisions of this Convention the following crimes shall not be considered political crimes even when politically motivated:

        1. Aggression against kings and heads of state of Contracting States or against their spouses, their ascendants or descendants.

        2. Aggression against crown princes or vice-presidents or deputy heads of government or ministers in any of the Contracting States.

        3. Aggression against persons enjoying international immunity including Ambassadors and diplomats in Contracting States or in countries of accreditation.

        4. Murder or robbery by force against individuals or authorities or means of transport and communications.

        5. Acts of sabotage and destruction of public properties and properties geared for public services, even if belonging to another Contracting State.

        6. Crimes of manufacturing, smuggling or possessing arms and ammunition or explosives or other materials prepared for committing terrorist crimes.

    d. All forms of international crimes, including illegal trafficking in narcotics and human beings money laundering aimed at financing terrorist objectives shall be considered terrorist crimes.

PART II
Foundations of Islamic Cooperation for Combating Terrorism
Chapter I
In the Field of Security
Division I
Measures to Prevent and Combat Terrorist Crimes.
Article 3

    I. The Contracting States are committed not to execute, initiate or participate in any form in organizing or financing or committing or instigating or supporting terrorist acts whether directly or indirectly.

    II. Committed to prevent and combat terrorist crimes in conformity with the provisions of this Convention and their respective domestic rules and regulations the contracting States shall see to:

(A) *Preventive Measures:*

1. Barring their territories from being used as an arena for planning, organizing, executing terrorist crimes or initiating or participating in these crimes in any form; including preventing the infiltration of terrorist elements or their gaining refuge or residence therein individually or collectively, or receiving hosting, training, arming, financing or extending any facilities to them.

2. Cooperating and coordinating with the rest of the Contracting States, particularly neighbouring countries which suffer from similar or common terrorist crimes.

3. Developing and strengthening systems relating to detecting transportation, importing, exporting stockpiling, and using of weapons, ammunition and explosives as well as other means of aggression, killing and destruction in addition to strengthening trans-border and custom controls in order to intercept their transfer from one Contracting State to another or to other States unless they are intended for specific legitimate purposes.

4. Developing and strengthening systems related to surveillance procedures, securing borders, and land, sea and air passages in order to prevent infiltration through them.

5. Strengthening systems for ensuring the safety and protection of personalities, vital installations and means of public transport.

6. Re-enforcing protection, security and safety of diplomatic and consular persons and missions; and regional and international organizations accredited in the Contracting State in accordance with the conventions and rules of international law which govern this subject.

7. Promoting security intelligence activities and coordinating them with the intelligence activities of each Contracting State pursuant to their respective intelligence policies, aimed at exposing the objectives of terrorist groups and organisations, thwarting their designs and revealing the extent of their danger to security and stability.

8. Establishing a data base by each Contracting State to collect and analyze data on terrorist elements, groups, movements and organizations and monitor developments of the phenomenon of terrorism and successful experiences in combating it. Moreover, the Contracting State shall update this information and exchange them with competent authorities in other Contracting States within the limits of the laws and regulations in every State.

9. To take all necessary measures to eliminate and prevent the establishment of webs supporting all kinds of terrorist crimes.

(B) *Combating Measures:*

1. Arresting perpetrators of terrorists' crimes and prosecuting them according to the national law or extraditing them in accordance with the provisions of this Convention or existing Conventions between the requesting and requested States.

2. Ensuring effective protection of persons working in the field of criminal justice as well as to witnesses and investigators.

3. Ensuring effective protection of information sources and witnesses on terrorist crimes.

4. Extending necessary assistance to victims of terrorism.

5. Establishing effective cooperation between the concerned organs in the contracting States and the citizens for combating terrorism including extending appropriate guarantees and appropriate incentives to encourage informing on terrorist acts and submitting information to help uncover them and cooperating in arresting the perpetrators.

Source: Organisation of Islamic Cooperation, OIC Convention to Combat Terrorism (1999-1420H). Available online at http://www.oic-oci.org/english/convenion/terrorism_convention.htm. Used by permission of the United Nations.

ANALYSIS

The Organisation of the Islamic Conference (OIC) is a coordinating body of Islamic representatives at the United Nations. Knowing that the global conception of terrorism had become linked to Islamic radicalism, the OIC sought to reassure the world that Islamic states recognized the dangers of terrorism. The convention is noteworthy in that it contains an extremely broad definition of "terrorism," to include virtually any form of international criminal activity. However, the convention also distinctly reserves the right of all adherents to engage in any form of violence as a matter of anti-colonialism and self-determination. Thus, the adage "one man's terrorist is another man's freedom fighter" is firmly ensconced in the convention, and as long as a terrorist act might plausibly be defended as an attempt to throw off the yoke of external control or influence, it might be considered a perfectly acceptable form of political expression. Thus, the convention is both extremely broad and riddled with loopholes that make it little more than a transparent attempt at global opinion-shaping and public relations.

- **Document 15: Executive Order 13129**
- **When:** July 4, 1999
- **Where:** Washington, D.C.
- **Significance:** This order prohibited all transactions with the Taliban, the de facto government of Afghanistan, because it supported and hosted Al Qaeda and Osama Bin Laden.

DOCUMENT

Executive Order 13129 of July 4, 1999
Blocking Property and Prohibiting Transactions With the Taliban

By the authority vested in me as President by the Constitution and the laws of the United States of America, including the International Emergency Economic Powers Act (50 U.S.C. 1701 et seq.)("IEEPA"), the National Emergencies Act (50 U.S.C. 1601 et seq.), and section 301 of title 3, United States Code,

I, WILLIAM J. CLINTON, President of the United States of America, find that the actions and policies of the Taliban in Afghanistan, in allowing territory under its control in Afghanistan to be used as a safe haven and base of operations for Usama bin Ladin and the Al-Qaida organization who have committed and threaten to continue to commit acts of violence against the United States and its nationals, constitute an unusual and extraordinary threat to the national security and foreign policy of the United States, and hereby declare a national emergency to deal with that threat.

I hereby order:

Section 1. Except to the extent provided in section 203(b) of IEEPA (50 U.S.C. 1702(b)) and in regulations, orders, directives, or licenses that may be issued pursuant to this order, and notwithstanding any contract entered into or any license or permit granted prior to the effective date:

(a) all property and interests in property of the Taliban; and

(b) all property and interests in property of persons determined by the Secretary of the Treasury, in consultation with the Secretary of State and the Attorney General:

(i) to be owned or controlled by, or to act for or on behalf of, the Taliban; or

(ii) to provide financial, material, or technological support for, or services in support of, any of the foregoing, that are in the United States, that hereafter come within the United States, or that are or hereafter come within the possession or control of United States persons, are blocked.

Sec. 2. Except to the extent provided in section 203 (b) of IEEPA (50 U.S.C. 1702(b)) and in regulations, orders, directives, or licenses that may be issued pursuant to this order, and notwithstanding any contract entered into or any license or permit granted prior to the effective date:

(a) any transaction or dealing by United States persons or within the United States in property or interests in property blocked pursuant to this order is prohibited, including the making or receiving of any contribution of funds, goods, or services to or for the benefit of the Taliban or persons designated pursuant to this order;

(b) the exportation, reexportation, sale, or supply, directly or indirectly, from the United States, or by a United States person, wherever located, of any goods, software, technology (including technical data), or services to the

DID YOU KNOW?

Mujahideen

"Mujahideen" is an Arabic term that translates to "holy warrior." During the Soviet invasion of Afghanistan (1979–1989), resistance fighters from Arabic countries used the term to explain their presence in Afghanistan. Osama bin Laden proudly declared himself a mujahideen, as did many of the future leaders of Al Qaeda and other terror organizations. In 1990, bin Laden offered a self-financed army of mujahideen, allegedly numbering in the tens of thousands, to defend Saudi Arabia from potential Iraqi aggression, but was rejected in favor of a U.S.-led coalition. Many of the Afghan mujahideen contributed to the formation of the Taliban, which seized power in Afghanistan in 1996. The term has also been used by foreign fighters facing the U.S.-led coalitions in Afghanistan and Iraq in the 21st century.

territory of Afghanistan controlled by the Taliban or to the Taliban or persons designated pursuant to this order is prohibited;

(c) the importation into the United States of any goods, software, technology, or services owned or controlled by the Taliban or persons designated pursuant to this order or from the territory of Afghanistan controlled by the Taliban is prohibited;

(d) any transaction by any United States person or within the United States that evades or avoids, or has the purpose of evading or avoiding, or attempts to violate, any of the prohibitions set forth in this order is prohibited; and

(e) any conspiracy formed to violate any of the prohibitions set forth in this order is prohibited.

Sec. 3. The Secretary of the Treasury, in consultation with the Secretary of State, is hereby directed to authorize commercial sales of agricultural commodities and products, medicine, and medical equipment for civilian end use in the territory of Afghanistan controlled by the Taliban under appropriate safeguards to prevent diversion to military, paramilitary, or terrorist end users or end use or to political end use.
Sec. 4. For the purposes of this order:

(a) the term "person" means an individual or entity;

(b) the term "entity" means a partnership, association, corporation, or other organization, group, or subgroup;

(c) the term "the Taliban" means the political/military entity headquartered in Kandahar, Afghanistan that as of the date of this order exercises de facto control over the territory of Afghanistan described in paragraph (d) of this section, its agencies and instrumentalities, and the Taliban leaders listed in the Annex to this order or designated by the Secretary of State in consultation with the Secretary of the Treasury and the Attorney General. The Taliban is also known as the "Taleban," "Islamic Movement of Taliban," "the Taliban Islamic Movement," "Talibano Islami Tahrik," and "Tahrike Islami'a Taliban";

(d) the term "territory of Afghanistan controlled by the Taliban" means the territory referred to as the "Islamic Emirate of Afghanistan," known in Pashtun as "de Afghanistan Islami Emarat" or in Dari as "Emarat Islami-e Afghanistan," including the following provinces of the country of Afghanistan: Kandahar, Farah, Helmund, Nimruz, Herat, Badghis, Ghowr, Oruzghon, Zabol, Paktiha, Ghazni, Nangarhar, Lowgar, Vardan, Faryab, Jowlan, Balkh, and Paktika. The Secretary of State, in consultation with the Secretary of the Treasury, is hereby authorized to modify the description of the term "territory of Afghanistan controlled by the Taliban";

(e) the term "United States person" means any United States citizen, permanent resident alien, entity organized under the laws of the United States (including foreign branches), or any person in the United States.

Sec. 5. The Secretary of the Treasury, in consultation with the Secretary of State and the Attorney General, is hereby authorized to take such actions, including the promulgation of rules and regulations, and to employ all powers granted to me by IEEPA as may be necessary to carry out the purposes of this order. The Secretary of the Treasury may redelegate any of these functions to other officers and agencies of the United States Government. All agencies of the United States Government are hereby directed to take all appropriate measures within their authority to carry out the provisions of this order.

Sec. 6. Nothing contained in this order shall create any right or benefit, substantive or procedural, enforceable by any party against the United States, its agencies or instrumentalities, its officers or employees, or any other person.

Sec. 7. (a) This order is effective at 12:01 a.m. Eastern Daylight Time on July 6, 1999.

(b) This order shall be transmitted to the Congress and published in the Federal Register.

[signed] William J. Clinton
THE WHITE HOUSE
July 4, 1999

Source: Bill Clinton, Executive Order 13129, Blocking Property and Prohibiting Transactions with the Taliban. Signed July 4, 1999. 64 *Federal Register* 36759, July 7, 1999.

ANALYSIS

With this executive order, President Clinton sought to apply diplomatic and economic pressure upon the Taliban, a theocracy controlling Afghanistan that had offered shelter and assistance to Al Qaeda and its leader, Osama Bin Laden. President Clinton hoped that this order would cause the Taliban to either expel Al Qaeda or capture and extradite its leadership in exchange for greater legitimacy in world affairs. This represented a fundamental misunderstanding of the Taliban and its relationship with Al Qaeda. It also reflected that the U.S. government did not yet recognize the danger represented by Al Qaeda, which used the hinterlands of Afghanistan as a safe haven in which to train new members and plan terror attacks upon Western targets.

- **Document 16: United Nations Security Council Resolution 1267**
- **When:** October 15, 1999
- **Where:** United Nations, New York City
- **Significance:** This resolution demanded that the Taliban government of Afghanistan turn Osama bin Laden over to international authorities within 30 days so that he could be tried for terrorist activities.

DOCUMENT

The Security Council,

Strongly condemning the continuing use of Afghan territory, especially areas controlled by the Taliban, for the sheltering and training of terrorists and planning of terrorist acts, and *reaffirming* its conviction that the suppression of international terrorism is essential for the maintenance of international peace and security,

Deploring the fact that the Taliban continues to provide safe haven to Usama bin Laden and to allow him and others associated with him to operate a network of terrorist training camps from Taliban-controlled territory and to use Afghanistan as a base from which to sponsor international terrorist operations,

Noting the indictment of Usama bin Laden and his associates by the United States of America for, *inter alia,* the 7 August 1998 bombings of the United States embassies in Nairobi, Kenya, and Dar es Salaam, Tanzania, and for conspiring to kill American nationals outside the United States, and noting also the request of the United States of America to the Taliban to surrender them for trial (S/1999/1021),

Determining that the failure of the Taliban authorities to respond to the demands in paragraph 13 of resolution 1214 (1998) constitutes a threat to international peace and security,

1. *Insists* that the Afghan faction known as the Taliban, which also calls itself the Islamic Emirate of Afghanistan, comply promptly with its previous resolutions and in particular cease the provision of sanctuary and training for international terrorists and their organizations, take appropriate effective measures to ensure that the territory under its control is not used for terrorist installations and camps, or for the preparation or organization of terrorist acts against other States or their citizens, and cooperate with efforts to bring indicted terrorists to justice;

2. *Demands* that the Taliban turn over Usama bin Laden without further delay to appropriate authorities in a country where he has been indicted, or to appropriate authorities in a country where he will be returned to such a country, or to appropriate authorities in a country where he will be arrested and effectively brought to justice;

3. *Decides* that on 14 November 1999 all States shall impose the measures set out in paragraph 4 below, unless the Council has previously decided, on the basis of a report of the Secretary-General, that the Taliban has fully complied with the obligation set out in paragraph 2 above;

4. *Decides further* that, in order to enforce paragraph 2 above, all States shall:

(a) Deny permission for any aircraft to take off from or land in their territory if it is owned, leased or operated by or on behalf of the Taliban as designated by the Committee established by paragraph 6 below, unless the particular flight has been approved in advance by the Committee on the grounds of humanitarian need, including religious obligation such as the performance of the Hajj;

(b) Freeze funds and other financial resources, including funds derived or generated from property owned or controlled directly or indirectly by the Taliban, or by any undertaking owned or controlled by the Taliban, as designated by the

Committee established by paragraph 6 below, and ensure that neither they nor any other funds or financial resources so designated are made available, by their nationals or by any persons within their territory, to or for the benefit of the Taliban or any undertaking owned or controlled, directly or indirectly, by the Taliban, except as may be authorized by the Committee on a case-by-case basis on the grounds of humanitarian need;

5. *Urges* all States to cooperate with efforts to fulfil the demand in paragraph 2 above, and to consider further measures against Usama bin Laden and his associates.

Source: United Nations, Resolution 1267. S/Res/1267, October 15, 1999. Available online at http://daccess-dds-ny.un.org/doc/UNDOC/GEN/N99/300/44/PDF/N9930044.pdf?OpenElement. Used by permission of the United Nations.

ANALYSIS

When the United States determined that Al Qaeda was behind the bombings of the U.S. embassies in Nairobi, Kenya, and Dar es Salaam, Tanzania, the federal government indicted Osama bin Laden in absentia on charges of terrorism and murder. It also took the case to the UN Security Council and demanded that all member states condemn the attacks, and the activities of Al Qaeda in general, and move to capture and extradite the terrorist leader. The Taliban, which had essentially become an outcast state by 1999, felt little obligation to comply with UN demands, particularly because Al Qaeda was a strong supporter of the regime with both financial and military resources. Although this document clarified that the world stood with the United States in its determination to capture bin Laden, it did little to compel the Taliban to surrender his person. The resolution did signify that the United States intended to use all means at its disposal, to include legal actions, to eliminate the Al Qaeda threat, but it also indicated to bin Laden that the U.S. resolve was not strong enough to include the use of ground forces in Afghanistan to effect his capture.

- **Document 17: International Convention for the Suppression of the Financing of Terrorism**
- **When:** December 9, 1999
- **Where:** United Nations, New York City
- **Significance:** Recognizing that the reach and capacity of terrorist organizations are largely dependent upon their ability to acquire resources, particularly financial support, the UN General Assembly adopted a convention designed to hinder the ability of terror organizations to obtain and internationally transfer finances.

DOCUMENT

International Convention for the Suppression of the Financing of Terrorism

The States Parties to this Convention,

Deeply concerned about the worldwide escalation of acts of terrorism in all its forms and manifestations,

Noting that the Declaration on Measures to Eliminate International Terrorism also encouraged States to review urgently the scope of the existing international legal provisions on the prevention, repression and elimination of terrorism in all its forms and manifestations, with the aim of ensuring that there is a comprehensive legal framework covering all aspects of the matter,

Considering that the financing of terrorism is a matter of grave concern to the international community as a whole,

Noting that the number and seriousness of acts of international terrorism depend on the financing that terrorists may obtain,

Noting also that existing multilateral legal instruments do not expressly address such financing,

Being convinced of the urgent need to enhance international cooperation among States in devising and adopting effective measures for the prevention of the financing of terrorism, as well as for its suppression through the prosecution and punishment of its perpetrators,

Have agreed as follows:

Article 2

1. Any person commits an offence within the meaning of this Convention if that person by any means, directly or indirectly, unlawfully and willfully, provides or collects funds with the intention that they should be used or in the knowledge that they are to be used, in full or in part, in order to carry out:

   (a) An act which constitutes an offence within the scope of and as defined in one of the treaties listed in the annex; or

   (b) Any other act intended to cause death or serious bodily injury to a civilian, or to any other person not taking an active part in the hostilities in a situation of armed conflict, when the purpose of such act, by its nature or context, is to intimidate a population, or to compel a government or an international organization to do or to abstain from doing any act.

   . . .

Article 4

Each State Party shall adopt such measures as may be necessary:

   (a) To establish as criminal offences under its domestic law the offences set forth in article 2;

   (b) To make those offences punishable by appropriate penalties which take into account the grave nature of the offences.

. . .

Article 6

Each State Party shall adopt such measures as may be necessary, including, where appropriate, domestic legislation, to ensure that criminal acts within the scope of this Convention are under no circumstances justifiable by considerations of a political, philosophical, ideological, racial, ethnic, religious or other similar nature.

Article 7

1. Each State Party shall take such measures as may be necessary to establish its jurisdiction over the offences set forth in article 2 when:

   (a) The offence is committed in the territory of that State;
   (b) The offence is committed on board a vessel flying the flag of that State or an aircraft registered under the laws of that State at the time the offence is committed;
   (c) The offence is committed by a national of that State.

. . .

Article 12

1. States Parties shall afford one another the greatest measure of assistance in connection with criminal investigations or criminal or extradition proceedings in respect of the offences set forth in article 2, including assistance in obtaining evidence in their possession necessary for the proceedings.
2. States Parties may not refuse a request for mutual legal assistance on the ground of bank secrecy.
3. The requesting Party shall not transmit nor use information or evidence furnished by the requested Party for investigations, prosecutions or proceedings other than those stated in the request without the prior consent of the requested Party.

Source: International Convention for the Suppression of the Financing of Terrorism, A/RES/54/109, Annex. Available at: https://www.unodc.org/tldb/en/ 1999_Convention_Financing%20of%20Terrorism.html. Used by permission of the United Nations.

ANALYSIS

This convention was hailed as a specific, measurable way to take action against terror organizations. Once again, the UN General Assembly recognized the danger that terror organizations might represent to civilized society, and attempted to enable member states to cooperate in reducing or eliminating international financing of terrorism. As had been true in virtually every UN resolution regarding terrorism, this convention required an international aspect before it could be considered applicable to any given financial transaction. Thus, terror organizations were still free to obtain financing from domestic sources, at least from the UN perspective, although presumably such financing would still be illegal under domestic law. Perhaps most importantly, this convention required states to share banking information with one another, and prohibited adherents from shielding information under banking secrecy laws. However, any information shared under the provisions of this convention could only be used to counteract terror organizations, offering some degree of protection to members of the international banking community who expressed objections to sharing their information.

- **Document 18: Report of the National Commission on Terrorism, "Countering the Changing Threat of International Terrorism"**
- **When:** June 5, 2000
- **Where:** Washington, D.C.
- **Significance:** This commission, chaired by Ambassador L. Paul Bremer III, illustrated the rising threat of international terrorism. The authors perceived terrorism primarily as a problem for intelligence agencies, rather than one that should be tackled by military or law enforcement authorities.

DOCUMENT

Good Intelligence Is the Best Weapon against International Terrorism

Obtaining information about the identity, goals, plans, and vulnerabilities of terrorists is extremely difficult. Yet, no other single policy effort is more important for preventing, preempting, and responding to attacks.

The Commission has identified significant obstacles to the collection and distribution of reliable information on terrorism to analysts and policymakers. These obstacles must be removed.

In addition, this information, often collected at great risk to agents and officers in the field, must be safeguarded. Leaks of intelligence and law enforcement information reduce its value, endanger sources, alienate friendly nations and inhibit their cooperation, and jeopardize the U.S. Government's ability to obtain further information.

Eliminate Barriers to Aggressive Collection of Information on Terrorists

Complex bureaucratic procedures now in place send an unmistakable message to Central Intelligence Agency (CIA) officers in the field that recruiting clandestine sources of terrorist information is encouraged in theory but discouraged in practice.

Inside information is the key to preventing attacks by terrorists. The CIA must aggressively recruit informants with unique access to terrorists' plans. That sometimes requires recruiting those who have committed terrorist acts or related crimes, just as domestic law enforcement agencies routinely recruit criminal informants in order to pursue major criminal figures.

CIA has always had a process for assessing a potential informant's reliability, access, and value. However, the CIA issued new guidelines in 1995 in response to concern about alleged serious acts of violence by Agency sources. The guidelines set up complex procedures for seeking approval to recruit informants who may have been involved in human rights violations. In practice, these procedures have deterred and delayed vigorous efforts to recruit potentially useful informants. The CIA has created a climate that is overly risk averse. This has inhibited the recruitment of essential, if sometimes unsavory, terrorist informants and forced the United States to rely too heavily on foreign intelligence services. The adoption of the guidelines contributed to a marked decline in Agency morale unparalleled since the 1970s, and a significant number of case officers retired early or resigned.

Recruiting informants is not tantamount to condoning their prior crimes, nor does it imply support for crimes they may yet commit. The long-standing process in place before 1995 provided managers with adequate guidance to judge the risks of going forward with any particular recruitment.

Recommendations:

- The Director of Central Intelligence should make it clear to the Central Intelligence Agency that the aggressive recruitment of human intelligence sources on terrorism is one of the intelligence community's highest priorities.
- The Director of Central Intelligence should issue a directive that the 1995 guidelines will no longer apply to recruiting terrorist informants. That directive should notify officers in the field that the pre-existing process of assessing such informants will apply.

The Federal Bureau of Investigation (FBI), which is responsible for investigating terrorism in the United States, also suffers from bureaucratic and cultural obstacles to obtaining terrorism information.

The World Trade Center bombers and the foreign nationals arrested before the millennium sought to inflict mass casualties on the American people. These incidents highlight the importance of ensuring that

---

DID YOU KNOW?

The Other 10 Deadliest Terror Attacks in the United States

The 10 deadliest terror attacks on American soil aside from the September 11 attacks were:

1. Oklahoma City bombing, April 19, 1995; 169 killed, 675 wounded.
2. Orlando nightclub shooting, June 12, 2016, 49 killed, 53 wounded.
3. Wall Street bombing, September 16, 1920; 38 killed, 300 wounded.
4. *Los Angeles Times* bombing, October 1, 1910; 21 killed, 20 wounded.
5. San Bernardino mass shooting, December 2, 2015; 14 killed, 22 wounded.
6. Haymarket Square bombing, May 4, 1886; 12 killed, 60 wounded.
7. La Guardia Airport bombing, December 29, 1975; 11 killed, 75 wounded.
8. San Francisco Preparedness Day Parade bombing; July 22, 1916; 10 killed, 44 wounded.
9. Milwaukee Police Station bombing, November 24, 1917; 10 killed, 2 wounded.
10. New Orleans mass shooting, January 7, 1973; 9 killed, 13 wounded.

All told, 343 victims died in these 10 attacks. The official death toll for the September 11 attacks stands at 2,996 victims.

the FBI's investigations of international terrorism are as vigorous as the Constitution allows.

The FBI's terrorism investigations are governed by two sets of Attorney General guidelines. The guidelines for Foreign Intelligence Collection and Foreign Counterintelligence Investigations (FI guidelines), which are classified, cover the FBI's investigations of international terrorism, defined as terrorism occurring outside the United States or transcending national boundaries. Domestic terrorism is governed by the Attorney General guidelines on General Crimes, Racketeering Enterprise and Domestic Security/Terrorism Investigations (domestic guidelines).

Both guidelines set forth the standards that must be met before the FBI can open a preliminary inquiry or full investigation. The domestic guidelines authorize a preliminary inquiry where there is information or an allegation indicating possible criminal activity. A full investigation may be opened where there is a reasonable indication of a criminal violation, which is described as a standard "substantially lower than probable cause."

The domestic and FI guidelines provide the FBI with sufficient legal authority to conduct its investigations. In many situations, however, agents are unsure as to whether the circumstances of a particular case allow the authority to be invoked. This lack of clarity contributes to a risk-averse culture that causes some agents to refrain from taking prompt action against suspected terrorists.

In 1995, largely in response to the Oklahoma City bombing and indications that confusion was inhibiting investigations, the Department of Justice (DoJ) issued a memorandum to the FBI field offices attempting to clarify the circumstances that would merit opening a preliminary inquiry and full investigation under the domestic guidelines. Nonetheless, there is still considerable confusion among the FBI field agents about the application of the guidelines. Neither the DoJ nor the FBI has attempted to clarify the FI guidelines for international terrorism investigations.

Recommendation:

- The Attorney General and the Director of the Federal Bureau of Investigation should develop guidance to clarify the application of both sets of guidelines. This guidance should specify what facts and circumstances merit the opening of a preliminary inquiry or full investigation and should direct agents in the field to investigate terrorist activity vigorously, using the full extent of their authority.

The Department of Justice applies the statute governing electronic surveillance and physical searches of international terrorists in a cumbersome and overly cautious manner.

Pursuant to the Foreign Intelligence Surveillance Act (FISA), the FBI can obtain a court order for electronic surveillance and physical searches of foreign powers, including groups engaged in international terrorism, and agents of foreign powers.

Applications from the FBI for FISA orders are first approved by the Office of Intelligence Policy and Review (OIPR) in the Department of Justice before being presented to a judge of the FISA Court for approval. OIPR has not traditionally viewed its role as assisting the FBI to meet the standards for FISA applications in the same way that the Criminal Division of DoJ assists the FBI investigators to meet the standards for a wiretap. For instance, the Criminal Division works with the investigating agents to identify and develop ways to obtain the type of information needed for a particular application to satisfy statutory requirements. OIPR has traditionally not been that proactive.

The Commission heard testimony that, under ordinary circumstances, the FISA process can be slow and burdensome, requiring information beyond the minimum required by the statute. For example, to obtain a FISA order, the statute requires only probable cause to believe that someone who is not a citizen or legal permanent resident of the United States is a member of an international terrorist organization. In practice, however, OIPR requires evidence of wrongdoing or specific knowledge of the group's terrorist intentions in addition to the person's membership in the organization before forwarding the application to the FISA Court. Also, OIPR does not generally consider the past activities of the surveillance target relevant in determining whether the FISA probable cause test is met.

During the period leading up to the millennium, the FISA application process was streamlined. Without lowering the FISA standards, applications were submitted to the FISA Court by DoJ promptly and with enough information to establish probable cause.

Recommendations:

- The Attorney General should direct that the Office of Intelligence Policy and Review not require information in excess of that actually mandated by the probable cause standard in the Foreign Intelligence Surveillance Act statute.
- To ensure timely review of the Foreign Intelligence Surveillance Act applications, the Attorney General should substantially expand the Office of Intelligence Policy and Review staff and direct it to cooperate with the Federal Bureau of Investigation.

The risk of personal liability arising from actions taken in an official capacity discourages law enforcement and intelligence personnel from taking bold actions to combat terrorism.

FBI special agents and CIA officers in the field should be encouraged to take reasonable risks to combat terrorism without fear of being sued individually for officially authorized activities. However, government representation is not always available to such agents and officers when they are sued. As a result, FBI special agents and CIA officers are buying personal liability insurance, which provides for private representation in such suits. By recent statute, federal agencies must reimburse up to one half of the cost of personal liability insurance to law enforcement officers and managers or supervisors.

Recommendation:

- Congress should amend the statute to mandate full reimbursement of the costs of personal liability insurance for Federal Bureau of Investigation special agents and Central Intelligence Agency officers in the field who are combating terrorism.

Source: Countering the Changing Threat of International Terrorism, Report of the National Commission on Terrorism, pursuant to Public Law 277, 105th Congress. Washington, D.C.: Government Printing Office, 2000.

ANALYSIS

The National Commission on Terrorism was chartered to investigate U.S. laws, policies, and practices for preventing, investigating, and punishing acts of terrorism. It included former federal officials and private citizens who had expertise in terrorism and counterterrorism studies. It was created in the aftermath of the twin bombings of U.S. embassies in Nairobi, Kenya, and Dar es Salaam, Tanzania. L. Paul Bremer, its chair, had previously served as the U.S. State Department's top-ranking official in the Counterterrorism Office. The commission's key recommendations included formally designating Afghanistan as a state sponsor of terrorism, reducing or eliminating barriers to effective intelligence collection on terror organizations, better mechanisms for the various intelligence agencies to share information with one another, and a system to track foreign students in the U.S. educational system. Some contemporary critics of the commission argued that its recommendations would infringe upon American civil liberties, a persistent theme in the struggle between the United States and terrorism.

- **Document 19: Memorandum, Richard Clarke to Condoleezza Rice**
- **When:** January 25, 2001
- **Where:** Washington, D.C.
- **Significance:** Richard Clarke served as the chief counterterrorism adviser to President William Clinton. As the administration of President George W. Bush came into the White House in 2001, Clarke sought to inform incoming National Security Advisor Condoleezza Rice of the dangers presented by Al Qaeda.

DOCUMENT

MEMORANDUM FOR CONDOLEEZA RICE
FROM: RICHARD A. CLARKE
SUBJECT: Presidential Policy Initiative/Review—The Al-Qida Network
Just Some Terrorist Group?

As we noted in our briefings for you, *al Qida* is not some narrow, little terrorist issue that needs to be included in broader regional policy. Rather, several of our regional policies need to address centrally the transnational challenge to the US and our interests posed by the *al Qida* network. By proceeding with separate policy reviews on Central Asia, the GCC, North Africa, etc. we would deal inadequately with the need for a comprehensive multi-regional policy on *al Qida*.

al Qida is the active, organized, major force that is using a distorted version of Islam as its vehicle to achieve two goals:

- to drive the US out of the Muslim world, forcing the withdrawal of our military and economic presence in countries from Morocco to Indonesia;
- to replace moderate, modern, Western regimes in Muslim countries with theocracies modeled along the lines of the Taliban.

al Qida affects centrally our policies on Pakistan, Afghanistan, Central Asia, North Africa and the GCC. Leaders in Jordan and Saudi Arabia see *al Qida* as a direct threat to them. The strength of the network of organizations limits the scope of support friendly Arab regimes can give to a range of US policies, including Iraq policy and the Peace Process. We would make a major error if we underestimated the challenge *al Qida* poses, or over estimated the stability of the moderate, friendly regimes *al Qida* threatens.

Pending Time Sensitive Decisions

At the close of the Clinton Administration, two decisions about *al Qida* were deferred to the Bush Administration.

- *First, should we provide the Afghan Northern Alliance enough assistance to maintain it as a viable opposition force to the Taliban/al Qida?* If we do not, I believe that the Northern Alliance may be effectively taken out of action this Spring when fighting resumes after the winter thaw. The al Qida 55th Brigade, which has been a key fighting force for the Taliban, would then be freed to send its personnel elsewhere, where they would likely threaten US interests. For any assistance to get there in time to effect the Spring fighting, a decision is needed now.
- *Second, should we increase assistance to Uzbekistan to allow them to deal with the al Qida/IMU threat?* [REDACTED]

Three other issues awaiting addressal now are:

- First, what the new Administration says to the Taliban and Pakistan about the importance we attach to ending the al Qida sanctuary in Afghanistan. We are separately proposing early, strong messages to both.
- Second, do we propose significant program growth in the FY02 budget for anti-al Qida operations by CIA and counterterrorism training and assistance by State and CIA?
- Third, when and how does the Administration choose to respond to the attack on the USS Cole. That decision is obviously complex. We can make some decisions, such as those above, now without yet coming to grips with the harder decision about the Cole. On the Cole, we should take advantage

of the policy that we "will respond at a time, place, and manner of our own choosing" and not be forced into knee jerk responses.

Attached is the year-end 2000 strategy on al Qida developed by the last Administration to give to you. Also attached is the 1998 strategy. Neither was a "covert action only" approach. Both incorporated diplomatic, economic, military, public diplomacy and intelligence tools. Using the 2000 paper as background, we could prepare a decision paper/guide for a PC review.

I recommend that you have a Principals discussion of *al Qida* soon and address the following issues:

1. *Threat Magnitude*: Do the Principals agree that the *al Qida* network poses a first order threat to US interests in a number of regions, or is this analysis a "chicken little" over reaching and can we proceed without new major initiatives and by handling this issue in a more routine manner?

2. *Strategy*: If it is a first order issue, how should the existing strategy be modified or strengthened?
   Two elements of the existing strategy that have not been made to work effectively are a) going after *al Qida's* money and b) public information to counter *al Qida* propaganda.

3. *FY02 Budget*: Should we continue the funding increases into FY02 for State and CIA programs designed to implement the *al Qida* strategy?

4. *Immediate Decisions*: Should we initiate [REDACTED] funding to the Northern Alliance and to the Uzbek's?

Please let us know if you would like such a decision/discussion paper or any modifications to the background paper.

Source: Barbara Elias (ed.), "National Security Archive Electronic Briefing Book, no. 147," http://www.gwu.edu/~nsarchiv/NSAEBB/NSAEBB147/clarke%20 memo.pdf.

ANALYSIS

This memorandum illustrates the challenges associated with changing administrations in the United States. Often, incoming administrations do not have the necessary background information to make rapid decision, as they are consumed by the effort associated with staffing offices. In this particular case, the attack upon the USS *Cole* came in the last three months of the Clinton administration, and shortly before the 2000 election, making President Clinton somewhat hesitant to bind his successor to a certain course of action. Clarke was often perceived as an alarmist regarding the threat posed by terrorism, and Al Qaeda in particular, a fact that probably caused Rice and other inbound officials to discount some of his warnings. In any event, the Bush administration did not make Al Qaeda a top priority prior to the September 11 attacks.

- **Document 20: George Tenet, Testimony before the Senate Select Committee on Intelligence**
- **When:** February 7, 2001
- **Where:** Washington, D.C.
- **Significance:** Tenet, the director of the Central Intelligence Agency, laid out the current threats to national security at the beginning of the Bush administration. Four months earlier, the USS *Cole* had taken heavy damage from a suicide bombing attack in Aden, Yemen. Tenet placed special emphasis upon regional threats in the Middle East, particularly those created by Al Qaeda.

DOCUMENT

As I reflect this year, Mr. Chairman, on the threats to American security, what strikes me most forcefully is the accelerating pace of change in so many arenas that affect our nation's interests. Numerous examples come to mind: new communications technology that enables the efforts of terrorists and narcotraffickers as surely as it aids law enforcement and intelligence, rapid global population growth that will create new strains in parts of the world least able to cope, the weakening internal bonds in a number of states whose cohesion can no longer be taken for granted, the breaking down of old barriers to change in places like the Koreas and Iran, the accelerating growth in missile capabilities in so many parts of the world—to name just a few.

Never in my experience, Mr. Chairman, has American intelligence had to deal with such a dynamic set of concerns affecting such a broad range of US interests. Never have we had to deal with such a high quotient of uncertainty. With so many things on our plate, it is important always to establish priorities. For me, the highest priority must invariably be on those things that threaten the lives of Americans or the physical security of the United States. With that in mind, let me turn first to the challenges posed by international terrorism.

TRANSNATIONAL ISSUES

We have made considerable progress on terrorism against US interests and facilities, Mr. Chairman, but it persists. The most dramatic and recent evidence, of course, is the loss of 17 of our men and women on the USS Cole at the hands of terrorists.

The threat from terrorism is real, it is immediate, and it is evolving. State sponsored terrorism appears

---

DID YOU KNOW?

Transitioning to Legitimacy

Some terror organizations have sought to transition from unlawful combatant groups terrorizing the civilian population to legitimate political movements within the mainstream. The Irish Republican Army forswore acts of terror and largely disarmed as part of a 1990s peace process. Splinter factions such as the Real Irish Republican Army have vowed to continue the fight to pry Northern Ireland out of the United Kingdom and unite it with the Republic of Ireland.

In the Middle East, Hamas became the de facto ruling party of the Gaza Strip in 2006, seizing control from Fatah in the local elections. In Lebanon, Hezbollah has continued attacks against Israel while simultaneously running candidates for public office. In the 2009 Lebanese parliamentary elections, 12 Hezbollah candidates were elected to the Lebanese parliament.

to have declined over the past five years, but transnational groups—with decentralized leadership that makes them harder to identify and disrupt—are emerging. We are seeing fewer centrally controlled operations, and more acts initiated and executed at lower levels.

Terrorists are also becoming more operationally adept and more technically sophisticated in order to defeat counterterrorism measures. For example, as we have increased security around government and military facilities, terrorists are seeking out "softer" targets that provide opportunities for mass casualties. Employing increasingly advanced devices and using strategies such as simultaneous attacks, the number of people killed or injured in international terrorist attacks rose dramatically in the 1990s, despite a general decline in the number of incidents. Approximately one-third of these incidents involved US interests.

Usama bin Ladin and his global network of lieutenants and associates remain the most immediate and serious threat. Since 1998, Bin Ladin has declared all US citizens legitimate targets of attack. As shown by the bombing of our Embassies in Africa in 1998 and his Millennium plots last year, he is capable of planning multiple attacks with little or no warning.

His organization is continuing to place emphasis on developing surrogates to carry out attacks in an effort to avoid detection, blame, and retaliation. As a result it is often difficult to attribute terrorist incidents to his group, Al Qa'ida.

Beyond Bin Ladin, the terrorist threat to Israel and to participants in the Middle East peace negotiations has increased in the midst of continuing Palestinian-Israeli violence. Palestinian rejectionists—including HAMAS and the Palestine Islamic Jihad (PIJ)—have stepped up violent attacks against Israeli interests since October. The terrorist threat to US interests, because of our friendship with Israel has also increased.

At the same time, Islamic militancy is expanding, and the worldwide pool of potential recruits for terrorist networks is growing. In central Asia, the Middle East, and South Asia, Islamic terrorist organizations are trying to attract new recruits, including under the banner of anti-Americanism.

International terrorist networks have used the explosion in information technology to advance their capabilities. The same technologies that allow individual consumers in the United States to search out and buy books in Australia or India also enable terrorists to raise money, spread their dogma, find recruits, and plan operations far afield. Some groups are acquiring rudimentary cyberattack tools. Terrorist groups are actively searching the internet to acquire information and capabilities for chemical, biological, radiological, and even nuclear attacks. Many of the 29 officially designated terrorist organizations have an interest in unconventional weapons, and Usama bin Ladin in 1998 even declared their acquisition a "religious duty."

Nevertheless, we and our Allies have scored some important successes against terrorist groups and their plans, which I would like to discuss with you in closed session later today. Here, in an open session, let me assure you that the Intelligence Community has designed a robust counterterrorism program that has preempted, disrupted, and defeated international terrorists and their activities. In most instances, we have kept terrorists off-balance, forcing them to worry about their own security and degrading their ability to plan and conduct operations.

THE MIDDLE EAST

Mr. Chairman, I would like to turn now to the Middle East. We are all aware of the violence between the Israelis and the Palestinians, and the uncertainty it has cast on the prospects for a near-term peace agreement. So let me take this time to look at the less obvious trends in the region—such as population pressures, growing public access to information, and the limited prospects for economic development—that will have a profound effect on the future of the Middle East.

The recent popular demonstrations in several Arab countries—including Egypt, Saudi Arabia, Oman, and Jordan—in support of the Palestinian intifada demonstrate the changing nature of activism of the Arab street. In many places in the Arab world, Mr. Chairman, average citizens are becoming increasingly restive and getting louder. Recent events show that the right catalyst—such as the outbreak of Israeli-Palestinian violence—can move people to act. Through access to the Internet and other means of communication, a restive public is increasingly capable of taking action without any identifiable leadership or organizational structure.

Mr. Chairman, balanced against an energized street is a new generation of leaders, such as Bashar al Asad in Syria. These new leaders will have their mettle tested both by populations demanding change and by entrenched bureaucracies willing to fight hard to maintain the status quo.

Compounding the challenge for these leaders are the persistent economic problems throughout the region that prevent them from providing adequately for the economic welfare of many of their citizens. The region's legacy of statist economic policies and an inadequate investment climate in most countries present big obstacles. Over the past 25 years, Middle Eastern economies have averaged only 2.8 percent GDP growth—far less than Asia and only slightly more than sub-Saharan Africa. The region has accounted for a steadily shrinking share of world GDP, trade, and foreign direct investment since the mid-1970s, and real wages and labor productivity today are about the same as 30 years ago. As the region falls behind in competitive terms, governments will find it hard over the next 5 to 10 years to maintain levels of state sector employment and government services that have been key elements of their strategy for domestic stability.

Adding to this is the challenge of demographics. Many of the countries of the Middle East still have population growth rates among the highest in the world, significantly exceeding 3 percent—compare that with 0.85 percent in the United States and 0.2 percent in Japan. Job markets will be severely challenged to create openings for the large mass of young people entering the labor force each year.

One-fourth of Jordanians, for example, are unemployed, and annual economic growth is well below the level needed to absorb some 60,000 new labor market entrants each year.

In Egypt the disproportionately young population adds 600,000 new job applicants a year in a country where unemployment is already near 20 percent.

Mr. Chairman, the inability of traditional sources of income such as oil, foreign aid, and worker remittances to fund an increasingly costly system of subsidies, education, health care, and housing for rapidly growing populations has motivated governments to implement economic reforms. The question is whether these reforms will go far enough for the long term. Reform thus far has been deliberately gradual and slow, to avoid making harsh economic choices that could lead to short term spikes in high unemployment.

Arab governments will soon face the dilemma of choosing between a path of gradual reform that is unlikely to close the region's widening gap with the rest of the world, and the path of comprehensive change that risks fueling independent political activity. Choosing the former risks building tension among a younger, poorer, and more politically assertive population.

IRAQ

Mr. Chairman, in Iraq Saddam Hussein has grown more confident in his ability to hold on to his power. He maintains a tight handle on internal unrest, despite the erosion of his overall military capabilities. Saddam's confidence has been buoyed by his success in quieting the Shia insurgency in the south, which last year had reached a level unprecedented since the domestic uprising in 1991. Through brutal suppression, Saddam's multilayered security apparatus has continued to enforce his authority and cultivate a domestic image of invincibility.

High oil prices and Saddam's use of the oil-for-food program have helped him manage domestic pressure. The program has helped meet the basic food and medicine needs of the population. High oil prices buttressed by substantial illicit oil revenues have helped Saddam ensure the loyalty of the regime's security apparatus operating and the few thousand politically important tribal and family groups loyal.

There are still constraints on Saddam's power. His economic infrastructure is in long-term decline, and his ability to project power outside Iraq's borders is severely limited, largely because of the effectiveness and enforcement of the No-Fly Zones. His military is roughly half the size it was during the Gulf War and remains under a tight arms embargo. He has trouble efficiently moving forces and supplies—a direct result of sanctions. These difficulties were demonstrated most recently by his deployment of troops to western Iraq last fall, which were hindered by a shortage of spare parts and transport capability.

Despite these problems, we are likely to see greater assertiveness—largely on the diplomatic front—over the next year. Saddam already senses improved prospects for better relations with other Arab states. One of his key goals is to sidestep the 10-year-old economic sanctions regime by making violations a routine occurrence for which he pays no penalty.

Saddam has had some success in ending Iraq's international isolation. Since August, nearly 40 aircraft have flown to Baghdad without obtaining UN approval, further widening fissures in the UN air embargo. Moreover, several countries have begun to upgrade their diplomatic relations with Iraq. The number of Iraqi diplomatic missions abroad are approaching pre-Gulf War levels, and among the states of the Gulf Cooperation Council, only Kuwait and Saudi Arabia have not reestablished ties.

Our most serious concern with Saddam Hussein must be the likelihood that he will seek a renewed WMD capability both for credibility and because every other strong regime in the region either has it or is pursuing it. For example, the Iraqis have rebuilt key portions of their chemical production infrastructure for industrial and commercial use. The plants he is rebuilding were used to make chemical weapons precursors before the Gulf War and their capacity exceeds Iraq's needs to satisfy its civilian requirements.

We have similar concerns about other dual-use research, development, and production in the biological weapons and ballistic missile fields; indeed, Saddam has rebuilt several critical missile production complexes.

IRAN

Turning now to Iraq's neighbor: events of the past year have been discouraging for positive change in Iran. Several years of reformist gains in national elections and a strong populist current for political change all threaten the political and economic privileges that authoritarian interests have enjoyed for years under the Islamic Republic—and they have begun to push back hard against the reformers.

Prospects for near-term political reform are now fading. Opponents of reform have not only muzzled the open press, they have also arrested prominent activists and blunted the legislature's powers. Over the Summer, Supreme Leader Khamenei ordered the new legislature not to ease press restrictions, a key reformist pursuit. This signaled the narrow borders within which he would allow the legislature to operate.

The reformist movement is still young, however, and it reflects on the deep sentiments of the Iranian people. Although frustrated and in part muzzled, the reformers have persisted in their demands for change. And the Iranian people will have another opportunity to demonstrate their support for reform in the presidential election scheduled for June. Although Khatami has not announced his candidacy, and has voiced frustration with the limitations placed on his office, opinion polls published in Iran show him to remain by far the most popular potential candidate for president.

The short-term gains made by shutting down the pro-reform press and prosecuting some of its most outspoken members is not a formula for long-term success. A strategy of suppressing the demands of the new generation coming of age risks a political explosion down the road. Some advocates of the status quo are beginning to recognize this danger as more conservatives—to include Khamenei—have endorsed the principle, if not the substance, of reform.

Despite Iran's uncertain domestic prospects, Mr. Chairman, it is clear that Khatami's appeal and promise of reform thus far, as well as the changing world economy, have contributed to a run of successes for Iran in the foreign arena over the past year. Some Western ambassadors have returned to Tehran, and Iranian relations with EU countries and Saudi Arabia are at their highest point since the revolution in 1979. Higher oil prices, meanwhile, have temporarily eased the government's need to address difficult and politically controversial economic problems. They have also taken more of the sting out of US sanctions. Iran's desire to end its isolation has not resulted in a decline in its willingness to use terrorism to pursue strategic foreign policy agendas—Tehran, in fact, has increased its support to terrorist groups opposed to the peace process over the past two years.

FRAGMENTATION AND FAILURE

The final point that I would like to discuss today is the growing in potential for state fragmentation and failure that we have observed this past year.

Mr. Chairman, Afghanistan obviously falls into this category. The Afghan civil war will continue into the foreseeable future, leaving the country fragmented and unstable. The Taliban remains determined to impose its radical form of Islam on all of Afghanistan, even in the face of resistance from other ethnic groups and the Shia minority.

Mr. Chairman, what we have in Afghanistan is a stark example of the potential dangers of allowing states—even those far from the US—to fail. The chaos here is providing an incubator for narcotics traffickers and militant Islamic groups operating in such places as Kashmir, Chechnya, and Central Asia. Meanwhile the Taliban shows no sign of relinquishing terrorist Usama Bin Ladin, despite strengthened UN sanctions and prospects that Bin Ladin's terrorist operations could lead to retaliatory strikes against Afghanistan. The Taliban and Bin Ladin have a symbiotic relationship—Bin Ladin gets safe haven and in return, he gives the Taliban help in fighting its civil war.

Mr. Chairman, events of the last few years in Indonesia paint a vivid picture of a state struggling to regain stability. Last year I described the difficult political transition that Indonesian President Wahid was trying to manage. He has managed to stay one step ahead of his opponents, mostly because they are unable to work together. He has survived several confrontations with the legislature, but efforts to impeach him on corruption charges will continue.

Separatist violence is rampant in Aceh and rising in two other key provinces. Muslim-Christian violence continues, and resulted in several thousand deaths last year. The country's security forces are poorly equipped, and either back away from challenges or respond too forcefully.

Mr. Chairman, Indonesia's problems are worrying neighboring countries that have long considered it as the pillar of regional stability. Some Southeast Asian leaders fear a power vacuum in Indonesia would create fertile ground for international terrorist groups and Islamic activists, drug trafficking, and organized crime.

My final case study, Mr. Chairman, is Africa, a land of chronic turbulence and crises that are among the most brutal and intractable in the world. Left behind by globalization and plagued by ethnic conflicts, several African states appear to be the first of the wave of failed nations predicted by the Global Trends 2015 Report.

We are especially concerned because hotspots often set off chain reactions across the region. The brutal civil war in Sierra Leone, for example, started as an offshoot of fighting in Liberia and has now spread into Guinea. These waves of violent instability bring even worse woes in their wake, including the ethnically-based killings that are now routine in the wars in Sudan, Congo (Kinshasa), and Burundi. Coping with this unrest depletes the scant resources available to the region's governments for fighting HIV/AIDS and other epidemics.

One immediate challenge in Africa, Mr. Chairman, is the protection of US diplomats, military personnel, citizens, and other interests in the region. Violent unrest has necessitated a half-dozen evacuations of Embassy employees, other citizens, and Allied nationals in recent years.

CONCLUSION

Mr. Chairman, I have spoken at some length about the threats we face to our national security. It is inevitable given our position as the world's sole superpower that we would attract the opposition of those who do not share our vision or our goals, and those who feel intimidated by our strength. Many of the threats I've outlined are familiar to you. Many of the trends I've described are not new. The complexity, intricacy, and confluence of these threats, however, is necessitating a fundamental change in the way we, in the Intelligence Community, do our business. To keep pace with these challenges:

We must aggressively challenge our analytic assumptions, avoid old-think, and embrace alternate analysis and viewpoints.

We must constantly push the envelope on collection beyond the traditional to exploit new systems and operational opportunities to gain the intelligence needed by our senior policymakers.

And we must continue to stay ahead on the technology and information fronts by seeking new partnerships with private industry as demonstrated by our IN-Q-TEL initiative.

Our goal is simple. It is to ensure that our nation has the intelligence it needs to anticipate and counter threats I have discussed here today.

Thank you Mr. Chairman, I would welcome any questions you and your fellow Senators may have for me.

Source: Current and Projected National Security Threats to the United States, Hearing before the Select Committee on Intelligence. February 7, 2001. S. Hrg. 107-2. Washington, D.C.: Government Printing Office, 2001. Available online at https://www.gpo.gov/fdsys/pkg/CHRG-107shrg31286/pdf/CHRG-107shrg31286.pdf.

ANALYSIS

As the director of the CIA, George Tenet had a better understanding of the threats facing the United States than almost anyone in the nation. However, he, like most American officials, considered the activities of peer competitors to remain by far the greatest threat confronting the United States, effectively minimizing the threat of terror attacks upon the homeland. The presumption at the time was that terror attacks are simply something that occur outside the national boundaries, regardless of the intentions of Al Qaeda or other terror organizations. Such a presumption left the United States vulnerable to a surprise attack carried out in an innovative manner unlike any previous act of terrorism.

- **Document 21: Letter, Michael Canavan to FAA Federal Security Managers**
- **When:** May 30, 2001
- **Where:** Washington, D.C.

• **Significance:** Michael Canavan served as the Associate Administrator for Civil Aviation Security at the Federal Aviation Administration (FAA). Less than four months before the September 11 attacks, he tried to encourage regional security managers to get civil air carriers to comply with improved security measures in the face of known terrorist threats.

DOCUMENT

Action: Compliance and enforcement philosophy
From: Associate Administrator for Civil Aviation Security, ACS-1
To: Managers, Civil Aviation Security Division 700's, Federal Security Managers

As we work with the aviation industry, it is important to remember that our primary goal as a regulatory agency is to gain compliance. While I know there are circumstances that present difficult choices, it would be helpful to explain our approach to compliance and enforcement issues.

As I outlined in the ACS strategic plan, the safety and security of the flying public will depend upon the FAA and industry maintaining a candid, respectful, and mutually responsive business relationship. To be effective in this relationship, we need to be flexible. While I expect regulated parties to comply with regulatory requirements, there will be times when we find areas of noncompliance. When we do, I want to fully consider the actions the party has taken to fix the problem. I want to work with industry to develop action plans to permanently correct problems that have resulted in violations. To encourage industry to join us in this effort I do not expect us to impose a civil penalty against a regulated party for certain unaggravated violations, if we believe the party has successfully implemented a permanent fix that will resolve violations. To answer questions you may have about this new philosophy and how it will work, detailed guidance will be provided to you shortly.

I want to continue to give our partners a realistic opportunity to comply with the regulations and to work with us.

Source: Andrew R. Thomas, *Aviation Insecurity: The New Challenges of Air Travel* (Amherst, NY: Prometheus Books, 2003), 227. Letter from Canavan is in the possession of Brian F. Sullivan, who has given permission to reprint this government document.

ANALYSIS

In the few years prior to the September 11 attacks, it became increasingly obvious that Al Qaeda would seek to strike at the United States in any manner

---

DID YOU KNOW?

Mao Zedong's Phases of Insurgency

The founder of the Chinese Communist Party, Mao Zedong, considered acts of terrorism to be a key aspect in the earliest phase of an insurgency against government control. He divided a successful "peoples' war" into three periods. In Phase I, insurgents commit terror attacks against public figures to raise awareness of the cause and trigger government overreactions. Those oppressive activities by the government in turn will inflame the populace, raising the level of support for the insurgents. Phase II encompassed guerrilla attacks of mounting size and sophistication. In Phase III, insurgents will shift to conventional operations in a general civil war, and wrest final control of the society.

possible, and Osama bin Laden coveted a spectacular attack that would draw enormous attention to his cause. Like many government agencies, the FAA was slow to respond to the threat. Most intelligence agencies had a cultural habit of withholding information from their peer organizations, which meant that the gravity of the threats facing the nation was often not grasped by federal officials. While airliners had been subjected to hijackings for more than three decades, none had ever been deliberately used in a suicide attack to date, although a handful of planes had been brought down by bombs snuck into the cargo compartment. Thus, most airline security measures were designed to detect explosives and prevent hijackings, which often led to hostage situations. Yet, but 2001, many airline officials considered hijackings and bombings to be a relic of the past rather than a likely future threat, and thus airline compliance with security directives had gradually fallen off, in part because resources spent on security tended to reduce total revenues and elicit complaints from customers. Unfortunately, the FAA refused to take a hard stance on security failures, and thus became a complicit partner in allowing those known vulnerabilities to continue.

- **Document 22: President's Daily Brief from Central Intelligence Agency**
- **When:** August 6, 2001 (declassified April 10, 2004)
- **Where:** Washington, D.C.
- **Significance:** The Central Intelligence Agency routinely prepares daily briefings for the president regarding international threats to the United States and its interests. Such briefings typically focus upon broad strategic dangers, such as the activities of peer competitor nations, and more specific concerns regarding the activities of nonstate actors, including terrorist organizations. This briefing, which included significant discussion of Al Qaeda, was delivered to President George W. Bush just five weeks before the September 11 attacks. Portions of the document were redacted when it was declassified.

DOCUMENT

Bin Ladin Determined to Strike in US

Clandestine, foreign government, and media reports indicate Bin Ladin since 1997 has wanted to conduct terrorist attacks in the US. Bin Ladin implied in US television interviews in 1997 and 1998 that his followers would follow the example of World Trade Center bomber Ramzi Yousef and "bring the fighting to America."

After US missile strikes on his base in Afghanistan in 1998, Bin Ladin told his followers he wanted to retaliate in Washington, according to a [REDACTED] service.

An Egyptian Islamic Jihad (EIJ) operative told an [REDACTED] service at the same time that Bin Ladin was planning to exploit the operative's access to the US to mount a terrorist strike.

The millennium plotting in Canada in 1999 may have been part of Bin Ladin's first serious attempt to implement a terrorist strike in the US. Convicted plotter Ahmed Ressam has told the FBI that he conceived the idea to attack Los Angeles International Airport himself, but that Bin Ladin lieutenant Abu Zubaydah encouraged him and helped facilitate the operation. Ressam also said that in 1998 Abu Zubaydah was planning his own US attack.

Ressam says Bin Ladin was aware of the Los Angeles operation.

Although Bin Ladin has not succeeded, his attacks against the US Embassies in Kenya and Tanzania in 1998 demonstrate that he prepares operations years in advance and is not deterred by setbacks. Bin Ladin associates surveilled our Embassies in Nairobi and Dar es Salaam as early as 1993, and some members of the Nairobi cell planning the bombings were arrested and deported in 1997.

Al-Qa'ida members—including some who are US citizens—have resided in or traveled to the US for years, and the group apparently maintains a support structure that could aid attacks. Two al-Qa'ida members found guilty in the conspiracy to bomb our Embassies in East Africa were US citizens, and a senior EIJ member lived in California in the mid-1990s.

A clandestine source said in 1998 that a Bin Ladin cell in New York was recruiting Muslim-American youth for attacks.

We have not been able to corroborate some of the more sensational threat reporting, such as that from a [REDACTED] service in 1998 saying that Bin Ladin wanted to hijack a US aircraft to gain the release of "Blind Shaykh" 'Umar 'Abd al-Rahman and other US-held extremists.

Nevertheless, FBI information since that time indicates a pattern of suspicious activity in this country consistent with preparations for hijackings or other types of attacks, including recent surveillance of federal buildings in New York.

The FBI is conducting approximately 70 full filed investigations throughout the US that it considers Bin Ladin-related. CIA and the FBI are investigating a call to our Embassy in the UAF in May saying that a group of Bin Ladin supporters was in the US planning attacks with explosives.

Source: Central Intelligence Agency, President's Daily Brief, August 6, 2001, available online at National Security Archive Electronic Briefing Book No. 343, 2011, http://nsarchive.gwu.edu/NSAEBB/NSAEBB343/.

ANALYSIS

While this document drew the president's attention toward the threat represented by Osama bin Laden and Al Qaeda, it contained very little specific information, and no specific recommendations for action on the president's part. The document does illustrate some of the collaboration between the CIA and the FBI, but there is nothing in the brief to warn of the nature of the September 11 attacks, beyond a vague threat of an airliner hijacking to negotiate a hostage exchange.

It is noteworthy that the brief contains references to previous Al Qaeda attacks and attempted actions against the United States, but does not mention the bombing of the USS *Cole*, which had occurred on October 12, 2000, and was the most recent large-scale Al Qaeda attack against the United States. It is possible that the mention of bin Laden's interest in hijacking an aircraft to negotiate a prisoner release may have influenced the immediate federal response to the September 11 hijackings.

2

DOCUMENTS FROM 9/11 AND THE IMMEDIATE AFTERMATH

- **Document 23: Mohamed Atta's Letter to Fellow Attackers**
- **When:** September 2001
- **Where:** Boston, MA
- **Significance:** This letter was found in a suitcase belonging to Mohamed Atta that did not make his final flight connection. Copies were also found in the personal effects of two of the other September 11 attackers.

DOCUMENT

The Last Night

1) Making an oath to die and renew your intentions.
Shave excess hair from the body and wear cologne.
Shower.

2) Make sure you know all aspects of the plan well, and expect the response, or a reaction, from the enemy.

3) Read al-Tawba and Anfal [traditional war chapters from the Qur'an] and reflect on their meanings and remember all of the things God has promised for the martyrs.

4) Remind your soul to listen and obey [all divine orders] and remember that you will face decisive situations that might prevent you from 100 per cent obedience, so tame your soul, purify it, convince it, make it understand, and incite it. God said: "Obey God and His Messenger, and do not fight amongst yourselves or else you will fail. And be patient, for God is with the patient."

5) Pray during the night and be persistent in asking God to give you victory, control and conquest, and that He may make your task easier and not expose us.

6) Remember God frequently, and the best way to do it is to read the Holy Qur'an, according to all scholars, as far as I know. It is enough for us that it [the Qur'an] are the words of the Creator of the Earth and the plants, the One that you will meet [on the Day of Judgment].

7) Purify your soul from all unclean things. Completely forget something called "this world" [or "this life"]. The time for play is over and the serious time is upon us. How much time have we wasted in our lives? Shouldn't we take advantage of these last hours to offer good deeds and obedience?

8) You should feel complete tranquility, because the time between you and your marriage [in heaven]

is very short. Afterwards begins the happy life, where God is satisfied with you, and eternal bliss "in the company of the prophets, the companions, the martyrs and the good people, who are all good company." Ask God for his mercy and be optimistic, because [the Prophet], peace be upon him, used to prefer optimism in all his affairs.

9) Keep in mind that, if you fall into hardship, how will you act and how will you remain steadfast and remember that you will return to God and remember that anything that happens to you could never be avoided, and what did not happen to you could never have happened to you. This test from Almighty God is to raise your level [levels of heaven] and erase your sins. And be sure that it is a matter of moments, which will then pass, God willing, so blessed are those who win the great reward of God. Almighty God said: "Did you think you could go to heaven before God knows whom amongst you have fought for Him and are patient?"

10) Remember the words of Almighty God: "You were looking to the battle before you engaged in it, and now you see it with your own two eyes." Remember: "How many small groups beat big groups by the will of God." And His words: "If God gives you victory, no one can beat you. And if He betrays you, who can give you victory without Him? So the faithful put their trust in God."

11) Remind yourself of the supplications and of your brethren and ponder their meanings. (The morning and evening supplications, and the supplications of [entering] a town, and the [unclear] supplications, and the supplications said before meeting the enemy.)

12) Bless your body with some verses of the Qur'an [done by reading verses into one's hands and then rubbing the hands over whatever is to be blessed], the luggage, clothes, the knife, your personal effects, your ID, passport, and all your papers.

13) Check your weapon before you leave and long before you leave. (You must make your knife sharp and must not discomfort your animal during the slaughter).

14) Tighten your clothes [a reference to making sure his clothes will cover his private parts at all times], since this is the way of the pious generations after the Prophet. They would tighten their clothes before battle. Tighten your shoes well, wear socks so that your feet will be solidly in your shoes. All of these are worldly things [that humans can do to control their fate, although God decrees what will work and what won't] and the rest is left to God, the best One to depend on.

15) Pray the morning prayer in a group and ponder the great rewards of that prayer. Make supplications afterwards, and do not leave your apartment unless you have performed ablution before leaving, because the angels will ask for your forgiveness as long as you are in a state of ablution, and will pray for you. This saying of the Prophet was mentioned by An-Nawawi in his book, The Best of Supplications. Read the words of God: "Did you think that We created you for no reason . . ." from the Al-Mu'minun Chapter.

The Second Step

When the taxi takes you to (M) [this initial could stand for matar, airport in Arabic] remember God constantly while in the car. (Remember the supplication for entering a car, for entering a town, the supplication of place and other supplications.)

When you have reached (M) and have left the taxi, say a supplication of place ["Oh Lord, I ask you for the best of this place, and ask you to protect me from its evils"], and everywhere you go say that prayer and smile and be calm, for God is with the believers. And the angels protect you without you feeling anything. Say this supplication: "God is more dear than all of His creation." And say: "Oh Lord, protect me from them as You wish." And say: "Oh Lord, take your anger out on [the enemy] and we ask You to protect us from their evils." And say: "Oh Lord, block their vision from in front of them, so that they may not see." And say: "God is all we need, He is the best to rely upon." Remember God's words: "Those to whom the people said, 'The people have gathered to get you, so fear them,' but that only increased their faith and they said, God is all we need, He is the best to rely upon." After you say that, you will find [unclear] as God promised this to his servants who say this supplication:

1. They will come back [from battle] with God's blessings
2. They were not harmed
3. And God was satisfied with them.

God says: "They came back with God's blessings, were not harmed, and God was satisfied with them, and God is ever-blessing."

All of their equipment and gates and technology will not prevent, nor harm, except by God's will. The believers do not fear such things. The only ones that fear it are the allies of Satan, who are the brothers of the devil. They have become their allies, God save us, for fear is a great form of worship, and the only one worthy of it is God. He is the only one who deserves it. He said in the verses: "This is only the Devil scaring his allies" who are fascinated with Western civilisation, and have drank the love [of the West] like they drink water [unclear] and have become afraid of their weak equipment, "so fear them not, and fear Me, if you are believers."

Fear is a great worship. The allies of God do not offer such worship except for the one God, who controls everything. [unclear] with total certainty that God will weaken the schemes of non-believers. God said: "God will weaken the schemes of the non-believers."

You must remember your brothers with all respect. No one should notice that you are making the supplication, "There is no God but God," because if you say it 1,000 times no one will be able to tell whether you are quiet or remember God. And among its miracles is what the Prophet, peace be upon him, said: "Whoever says, 'There is no God but God,' with all his heart, goes to heaven." The Prophet, peace be upon him, said: "If you put all the worlds and universes on one side of the balance, and 'No God but God' on the other, 'No God but God' will weigh more heavily." You can repeat these words confidently, and this is just one of the strengths of these words. Whoever thinks deeply about these words will find that they have no dots [in the Arabic letter] and this is just one of its greatnesses, for words that have dots in them carry less weight than those that do not. And it is enough that these are the words of monotheism, which will make you steadfast in battle [unclear] as the Prophet, peace be upon him, and his companions, and those who came after them, God willing, until the Day of Judgment.

Do not seem confused or show signs of nervous tension. Be happy, optimistic, calm because you are heading for a deed that God loves and will accept. It will be the day, God willing, you spend with the women of paradise.

[poetry] Smile in the face of hardship young man/For you are heading toward eternal paradise

You must remember to make supplications wherever you go, and anytime you do anything, and God is with his faithful servants, He will protect them and make their tasks easier, and give them success and control, and victory, and everything . . .

The Third Phase

When you ride the (T) [probably for tayyara, aeroplane in Arabic], before your foot steps in it, and before you enter it, you make a prayer and supplications. Remember that this is a battle for the sake of God. As the Prophet, peace be upon him, said, "An action for the sake of God is better than all of what is in this world." When you step inside the (T), and sit in your seat, begin with the known supplications that we have mentioned before. Be busy with the constant remembrance of God. God said: "Oh ye faithful, when you find the enemy be steadfast, and remember God constantly so that you may be successful." When the (T) moves, even slightly, toward (Q) [unknown reference], say the supplication of travel. Because you are traveling to Almighty God, so be attentive on this trip.

Then [unclear] it takes off. This is the moment that both groups come together. So remember God, as He said in His book: "Oh Lord, pour your patience upon us and make our feet steadfast and give us victory over the infidels." And His words: "And the only thing they said Lord, forgive our sins and excesses and make our feet steadfast and give us victory over the infidels." And His prophet said: "Oh Lord, You have revealed the book, You move the clouds, You gave us victory over the enemy, conquer them and give us victory over them." Give us victory and make the ground shake under their feet. Pray for yourself and all your brothers that they may be victorious and hit their targets and ask God to grant you martyrdom facing the enemy, not running away from it, and for Him to grant you patience and the feeling that anything that happens to you is for Him.

Then every one of you should prepare to carry out his role in a way that would satisfy God. You should clench your teeth, as the pious early generations did.

When the confrontation begins, strike like champions who do not want to go back to this world. Shout, "Allahu Akbar," because this strikes fear in the hearts of the non-believers. God said: "Strike above the neck, and strike at all of their extremities." Know that the gardens of paradise are waiting for you in all their beauty, and the women of paradise are waiting, calling out, "Come hither, friend of God." They have dressed in their most beautiful clothing.

If God decrees that any of you are to slaughter, dedicate the slaughter to your fathers and [unclear], because you have obligations toward them. Do not disagree, and obey. If you slaughter, do not cause the discomfort of those you are killing, because this is one of the practices of the Prophet, peace be upon him. On one condition: that you do not become distracted by [unclear] and neglect what is greater, paying attention to the enemy. That would be treason, and would do more damage than good. If this happens, the deed at hand is more important than doing that, because the deed is an obligation, and [the other thing] is optional. And an obligation has priority over an option.

Do not seek revenge for yourself. Strike for God's sake. One time Ali bin Abi Talib [a companion and close relative of the Prophet Muhammad], fought with a non-believer. The non-believer spit on Ali, may God bless him. Ali [unclear] his sword, but did not strike him. When the battle was over, the companions of the Prophet asked him why he had not smitten the non-believer. He said, "After he spat at me, I was afraid I would be striking at him in revenge for myself, so I lifted my sword." After he renewed his intentions, he went back and killed the man. This means that before you do anything, make sure your soul is prepared to do everything for God only.

Then implement the way of the Prophet in taking prisoners. Take prisoners and kill them. As Almighty God said: "No prophet should have prisoners until he has soaked the land with blood. You want the bounties of this world [in exchange for prisoners] and God wants the other world [for you], and God is all-powerful, all-wise."

If everything goes well, every one of you should pat the other on the shoulder in confidence that (M) and (T) number (K). Remind your brothers that this act is for Almighty God. Do not confuse your brothers or distract them. He should give them glad tidings and make them calm, and remind them [of God] and encourage them. How beautiful it is for one to read God's words, such as: "And those who prefer the afterlife over this world should fight for the sake of God." And His words: "Do not suppose that those who are killed for the sake of God are dead; they are alive..." And others. Or they should sing songs to boost their morale, as the pious first generations did in the throes of battle, to bring calm, tranquility and joy to the hearts of his brothers.

Do not forget to take a bounty, even if it is a glass of water to quench your thirst or that of your brothers, if possible. When the hour of reality approaches, the zero hour, [unclear] and wholeheartedly welcome death for the sake of God. Always be remembering God. Either end your life while praying, seconds before the target, or make your last words: "There is no God but God, Muhammad is His messenger."

Afterwards, we will all meet in the highest heaven, God willing.

If you see the enemy as strong, remember the groups [that had formed a coalition to fight the Prophet Muhammad]. They were 10,000. Remember how God gave victory to his faithful servants. He said: "When the faithful saw the groups, they said, this is what God and the prophet promised, they said the truth. It only increased their faith."

And may the peace of God be upon the Prophet.

Source: Scans of the original letter (in Arabic) were released by the FBI at https://www.fbi.gov/news/pressrel/press-releases/fbi-releases-copy-of-four-page-letter-linked-to-hijackers. This translation was published by *The New York Times*, September 29, 2001. Available online at http://www.nytimes.com/2001/09/29/national/29SFULL-TEXT.html?pagewanted=all.

ANALYSIS

In this letter, Atta sought to provide specific instructions to his fellow hijackers and at the same time provide them with religious justification for the murder of thousands of people. The letter indicates that Atta fervently believed he acted in the name of God in undertaking the attacks, and believed that he and his followers would be rewarded for making a religious sacrifice. The letter also provided cues for how to detect an impending attack, to include the continual references to repetitive prayer. It indicated that Atta thought of his victims as animals being brought to the slaughter, not humans—they should not be made to suffer, but they also deserved no mercy from the practitioners of a holy mission.

- **Document 24: President George W. Bush, Address to the Nation**
- **When:** September 11, 2001
- **Where:** Washington, D.C.
- **Significance:** On the evening of September 11, 2001, President George W. Bush addressed the nation in an attempt to calm the citizenry. In that address, he shared the preliminary investigation's conclusions about the attacks earlier in the day, and promised a response without clarifying what form that response would take.

DOCUMENT

Good evening. Today our fellow citizens, our way of life, our very freedom came under attack in a series of deliberate and deadly terrorist acts. The victims were in airplanes or in their offices: secretaries, business men and women, military and Federal workers, moms and dads, friends and neighbors. Thousands of lives were suddenly ended by evil, despicable acts of terror.

The pictures of airplanes flying into buildings, fires burning, huge structures collapsing, have filled us with disbelief, terrible sadness, and a quiet, unyielding anger. These acts of mass murder were intended to frighten our Nation into chaos and retreat, but they have failed. Our country is strong.

A great people has been moved to defend a great nation. Terrorist attacks can shake the foundations of our biggest buildings, but they cannot touch the foundation of America. These acts shattered steel, but they cannot dent the steel of American resolve. America was targeted for attack because we're the brightest beacon for freedom and opportunity in the world. And no one will keep that light from shining.

Today our Nation saw evil, the very worst of human nature. And we responded with the best of America, with the daring of our rescue workers, with the caring for strangers and neighbors who came to give blood and help in any way they could.

Immediately following the first attack, I implemented our Government's emergency response plans. Our military is powerful, and it's prepared. Our emergency teams are working in New York City and Washington, DC, to help with local rescue efforts.

Our first priority is to get help to those who have been injured and to take every precaution to protect our citizens at home and around the world from further attacks.

The functions of our Government continue without interruption. Federal agencies in Washington which had to be evacuated today are reopening for essential personnel tonight and will be open for business tomorrow. Our financial institutions remain strong, and the American economy will be open for business, as well.

The search is underway for those who are behind these evil acts. I've directed the full resources of our intelligence and law enforcement communities to find those responsible and to bring them to justice. We will make no distinction between the terrorists who committed these acts and those who harbor them.

I appreciate so very much the Members of Congress who have joined me in strongly condemning these attacks. And on behalf of the American people, I thank the many world leaders who have called to offer their condolences and assistance.

America and our friends and allies join with all those who want peace and security in the world, and we stand together to win the war against terrorism. Tonight I ask for your prayers for all those who grieve, for the children whose worlds have been shattered, for all whose sense of safety and security has been threatened. And I pray they will be comforted by a power greater than any of us, spoken through the ages in Psalm 23: "Even though I walk through the valley of the shadow of death, I fear no evil, for You are with me."

This is a day when all Americans from every walk of life unite in our resolve for jus tice and peace. America has stood down enemies before, and we will do so this time. None of us will ever forget this day. Yet, we go forward to defend freedom and all that is good and just in our world.

Thank you. Good night, and God bless America.

Source: *Public Papers of the Presidents of the United States: George W. Bush* (2001, Book 2). Washington, D.C.: Office of the Federal Register, National Archives and Records Administration, 1099–1100.

ANALYSIS

The first eight months of President Bush's administration were rocky, to say the least. He won the 2000 election by the narrowest of margins, and there was plenty of opposition within the country to the eventual outcome, which had undergone a lengthy recount process and which was eventually decided in the U.S. Supreme Court on a 5–4 vote. The September 11 attacks, in many ways, represented an opportunity for President Bush to demonstrate his leadership capabilities, an opportunity he never desired but could not avoid. In this brief address, President Bush had a few primary goals, and did well to achieve each of them. His first objective was to reassure the American people that the government and military were continuing operations, and taking every precaution to protect the United States from further attacks. He also wished to calm the public and to demonstrate that he understood their fear and outrage at being the victims of the deadliest terror attack in history. At the same time, the president wished to show a strong resolve, to rally the nation behind the idea that the federal government could and would determine who was behind the attacks, and unleash the full fury of the American military upon the guilty party. President Bush had already begun to frame the struggle with an as-yet-unnamed opponent as a basic contest between good and evil, and he fully intended to place the United States on the side of justice and hope. While no speech could have calmed all of the American anxieties present on the evening of September 11, this brief message went a long way toward building support for the president, and also began the transition of the United States from an aggrieved victim to a resolute nation on a war footing.

- **Document 25: White House Press Briefing by Ari Fleischer, White House Spokesperson**
- **When:** September 12, 2001
- **Where:** Washington, D.C.
- **Significance:** This press briefing was the first opportunity for members of the national media to ask questions of the George W. Bush administration in the immediate aftermath of the September 11 attacks. The briefing included the most recent information cleared for public release by the White House.

DOCUMENT

MR. FLEISCHER: Good afternoon. The President today has been making a series of phone calls to leaders around the world, to rally an international coalition to combat terrorism.

He has spoken today with Prime Minister Blair, with Prime Minister Chretien, with President Chirac, with Chancellor Schroeder, with President Jiang of China, and twice with President Putin. The President will continue to reach out to leaders throughout the world to develop this coalition, send a message that the United States and the world stand united, all the freedom loving countries and others to fight terrorism.

The President is also gratified by the action taken today by the North Atlantic Treaty Organization, NATO, in which they invoked Article 5, saying that an attack on one NATO nation is an attack on all NATO nations.

The President is also gratified by the United Nations Security Council Resolution that passed today condemning this attack and saying that it was a threat to international peace and security.

Finally, as the President said in his remarks this morning, freedom and democracy are under attack. The American people need to know that we are facing a different

DID YOU KNOW?

Casualties of September 11

When two hijacked airplanes struck the North and South Towers of the World Trade Center, approximately 150,000 people were in the two buildings. Emergency responders, immediately realizing the possibility of a building collapse, supervised an emergency evacuation which undoubtedly saved tens of thousands of lives and mitigated the total casualties. In the process, the Fire Department of New York lost 343 firefighters; 74 members of the Port Authority of New York and New Jersey and 37 members of the New York Police Department also died in the attacks. At least 2,185 civilians died in the towers, along with 246 passengers and crew aboard the hijacked airplanes. Another 125 people died in the Pentagon when it was struck by another aircraft. The victims came from at least 62 nations. Given the chaos of the situation and the aftermath, and the challenge of identifying the human remains found at each site, an exact tally of the dead may never be certain. The official death toll for the attacks currently stands at 2,996.

enemy than we have ever faced. Those are the President's words. In this case, we have specific and credible information that the White House and Air Force One were also intended targets of these attacks.

As the President also said in his remarks, this battle will take time and resolve; and, make no mistake, we will prevail.

. . .

Q: And then on the subject of rallying this international coalition, does that indicate that the President would wait, or try to get the support—either operational support or political support of other nations before responding to these attacks?

MR. FLEISCHER: Well, I'm not going to indicate anything about—speculate about any type of response. You've heard what the President said and his words speak for themselves about America's resolve.

However, as I indicated in my opening statement, the President is very heartened as a result of the world reaction and the solidarity that the world is showing at all levels in so many nations toward what has happened. And the President is going to continue to talk to leaders around the world as he builds this coalition.

Q: Did the President secure the support of President Jiang and President Putin in those phone calls?

MR. FLEISCHER: Let me try to give you a little more specific information on each of those phone calls. The President, as I indicated, spoke twice with President Putin—once for five minutes, the second time for seven minutes. He thanked—the President thanked President Putin for his call and for the message of condolence that President Putin sent yesterday.

President Putin informed President Bush that he had signed a decree that there be a moment of silence at Russia, and throughout Russia, at noon tomorrow, with flags at half-mast, to express the outrage and solidarity of the Russian people with the American people.

The two Presidents agreed that they will work closely together in the coming weeks to fight those responsible for yesterday's acts of terrorism.

The President's phone call with President Jiang of China lasted for approximately 10 minutes. President Bush thanked President Jiang for his condolences and concern for the American people, as well. And the two agreed to work together also to combat terrorism, which is another indication, as I mentioned, of the coalition the President is seeking to form as the world unites in the fight against terrorism.

Q: Given the scale and the level of killing in these attacks yesterday, can the President assure the American people that the response will be commensurate with that?

MR. FLEISCHER: Terry, I'm just not going to speculate about the response. You have what the President said about how the United States will prevail. But I'm not going to go beyond that; I'm not going to speculate. And I leave it at that.

Q: Can you say how close the U.S. is to knowing who is responsible for the attacks?

MR. FLEISCHER: The United States is in the process of gathering all the facts about this matter. The full resources of the federal government at all levels have been dedicated to this. And we will continue to gather those facts and ascertain all the information available.

Q: What is the practical effect of invoking Article 5 of NATO, that it's an attack against the entire alliance?

MR. FLEISCHER: It is a message of solidarity with NATO. And I'm not going to go beyond that, in terms of anything else that has a practical effect. It is highly unusual, if not unprecedented, for NATO to have taken this step.

Q: Ari, is the White House going to make an open-ended request to Congress for funding, or is there going to be a figure given to Congress?

MR. FLEISCHER: No, Keith, the President thinks it's important that this not become an open-ended request. The President—and by the way, the meeting with the congressional leaders today, the bipartisan congressional leaders, was a very important and stirring meeting of patriotism. The outpouring of support, shoulder to shoulder, regardless of anybody's political party, was wonderful, it was impressive, and it should make every American proud.

The President will continue to work with Congress, but he does not think it should be an open-ended commitment.

Q: Ari, all the fingers are being pointed at Osama bin Laden and Afghanistan; he is being helped by, supported by Taliban and bases in Pakistan. So are we talking about now going against Afghanistan or Pakistan? And if it happened, then it is all in the name of Islam. So is it time now for the United States not to wait anymore, more innocent people will be killed in the name of terrorism?

MR. FLEISCHER: I was asked earlier about who we believe is the source of this. And I indicated that the United States continues to gather the facts about that information. So your question presupposes the answer, and I'm not prepared to do that.

Q: Surely, investigators have uncovered reams of credible information that you've chosen not to release. Why did you decide to release this information to us today and just this information?

MR. FLEISCHER: Because just as the President said in his remarks this morning—and I'm quoting from the President—"The American people need to know that we are facing a different enemy than we have ever faced." And the President, having said that, thought it was appropriate to let the American people know the lengths to which those who perpetrated these terrorist acts were prepared to go in an attack on our nation.

Q: Is the President satisfied, and should the American people be satisfied, with the performance of the intelligence community in this country, given what happened yesterday?

MR. FLEISCHER: The President believes that the intelligence community and the nation's military are the best in the world. And, clearly, something yesterday took place in New York that was not foreseen, that we had no specific information about. But the President's focus right now is on helping those who have lost their—the families of those who have lost their lives and those who are suffering in this tragedy; and then on taking whatever the appropriate next steps should be.

Q: Ari, in terms of the President's statement this morning that this was an act of war, was it the realization that both the White House and Air Force One were targeted that elevated his language to talk about an act of war? Was it a threat against the head of this country that elevated it to that level?

MR. FLEISCHER: John, I think that the actions against the soil of the United States are what led the President to say that this was an act of war against the United States.

Q: But why not use the word "war" last night in his televised address to the nation? What changed overnight to ratchet up that rhetoric?

MR. FLEISCHER: I think that you are just going to continue to hear the President speak out on a regular basis, and the President will share his thoughts with you as his thoughts develop as a result of the conversations he has with the security team, and as he thinks this matter through in his mind, and shares information with the public.

Q: And how much money are you talking about in this spending request? You know, are we correct to assume it's in the billions of dollars?

MR. FLEISCHER: That's a correct assumption. And, again, once we have specific information, more specific than that, I will get it to you. But the President made it clear that this should not be an open-ended commitment.

Q: Ari, given the President's language today, is there any discussion here of asking Congress for a declaration of war?

MR. FLEISCHER: You know, again, as the President said, there were acts of war that were carried out against our country. And the President will continue to work with Congress on any appropriate measures at the appropriate time.

But, you know, this is also a different situation from situations our nation has faced in the past, and the President is cognizant of that. As the President indicated, in this case, as we ascertain information, we are dealing, at least at this point, with nameless, faceless people. And it is a different type of war than it was, say, when you knew the capitol of the country that attacked you.

So we will continue to work with the Congress on appropriate language on the appropriate time.

Q: Ari, as to the meeting with the leaders of Congress today, does the President come out of that thinking he has carte blanche in a response, et cetera?

MR. FLEISCHER: No, the President does not think that. The President is going to want to continue to consult. The President is going to continue to lead. But the President understands that at all times, it's important to work with Congress. But it's particularly important now to consult with the Congress.

One of the greatest strengths of our country is that we are a constitution-based democracy. Our Constitution and our nation have survived acts of terror and attacks on our nation before. And the President knows that the strength of our nation comes from that Constitution, which gives an important role to Congress. And he will continue to consult closely with Congress and its leaders.

Q: Let me ask you about the idea of willingness to attack those who host terrorism. Is this a change in the U.S. policy for how we treat these countries who may not have participated in the act, but may have known that these terrorists were in-country? Is this a change in U.S. policy? And, if so, where does it come from?

MR. FLEISCHER: Well, you know, I'm not—I don't know if this is a change or not. Of course, given the fact that President Bush has been in office, now, for nine months, this is, I think, an example of how President Bush is going to address this in a resolute manner. The President's words speak for themselves about what he said and why he said it, and everyone should be clear about what the President said.

Q: Ari, as a result of the extensive briefings that the President has now had since the attacks of yesterday morning, does he have any reason to believe that there are any further attacks that may be planned?

MR. FLEISCHER: As the President indicated today in his remarks, it is not business as usual. And there are heightened security and tightened security measures in place. He has also said that our nation is going to move forward. So at all times, the United States government will continue to be vigilant and protective of its citizens. We do live in an open and free society. But obviously the attacks that were planned yesterday were executed yesterday.

Q: Ari, can I ask again, by saying that these are acts of war, what exactly does that mean practically, when the President says that? Where does that take him?

MR. FLEISCHER: That the United States was attacked. American soil was attacked. And the President will describe this, as he always has and he always does, in a frank and forthright fashion.

Q: On the phrase "act of war," are you saying that is just a phrase describing what happened? Or does it carry any legal, or political, or constitutional significance?

MR. FLEISCHER: I think the American people know that when the United States is attacked in the manner it was attacked, this is an act of war. And I think there is no other way to describe it. And I think that's what the American people expect from their President, is a President who will talk with them straight and direct about it.

Source: Office of the Press Secretary, September 12, 2001. National Archives. Available online at http://georgewbush-whitehouse.archives.gov/news/releases/2001/09/20010912-8.html.

ANALYSIS

Barely 24 hours after the attacks of September 11, 2001, the president of the United States had already spoken to several of the most powerful world leaders, and called for support from the United Nations and the North Atlantic Treaty Organization, both of which responded with alacrity. White House spokesperson Ari Fleischer refused to answer a number of questions that pried for specific planned military and intelligence community responses. He did indicate a dedication on the part of the administration to work directly with Congress, and not to pursue an open-ended financial commitment. This soon after the attacks, while there were indications of the likely perpetrators, Fleischer was unwilling to offer any definitive evidence of whom to blame for the attacks.

- **Document 26: EPA Initiates Emergency Response Activities**
- **When:** September 13, 2001
- **Where:** Washington, D.C.
- **Significance:** In the immediate aftermath of the September 11 attacks, the U.S. Environmental Protection Agency (EPA) quickly realized that enormous contamination of the Manhattan region would result from the destruction of the World Trade Center, and might present a significant health hazard to survivors in the area. This press release sought to reassure New York citizens, and the American public as a whole, that the EPA was taking major steps to assess the damage and mitigate its effects.

DOCUMENT

United States Environmental Protection Agency
Environmental News
EPA Initiates Emergency Response Activities,
Reassures Public About Environmental Hazards

U.S. Environmental Protection Agency Administrator Christie Whitman today announced that EPA is taking steps to ensure the safety of rescue workers and the public at the World Trade Center and the Pentagon disaster sites, and to protect the environment. EPA is working with state, federal, and local agencies to monitor and respond to potential environmental hazards and minimize any environmental effects of the disasters and their aftermath.

At the request of the New York City Department of Health, EPA and the U.S. Department of Labor's Occupational Safety and Health Administration (OSHA) have been on the scene at the World Trade Center monitoring exposure to potentially contaminated dust and debris. Monitoring and sampling conducted on Tuesday and Wednesday have been very reassuring about potential exposure of rescue crews and the public to environmental contaminants.

EPA's primary concern is to ensure that rescue workers and the public are not exposed to elevated levels of asbestos, acidic gases or other contaminants from the debris. Sampling of ambient air quality found either no asbestos or very low levels of asbestos. Sampling of bulk materials and dust found generally low levels of asbestos.

The levels of lead, asbestos and volatile organic compounds in air samples taken on Tuesday in Brooklyn, downwind from the World Trade Center site, were not detectable or not of concern.

Additional sampling of both ambient air quality and dust particles was conducted Wednesday night in lower Manhattan and Brooklyn, and results were uniformly acceptable.

"EPA is greatly relieved to have learned that there appears to be no significant levels of asbestos dust in the air in New York City," said Administrator Whitman. "We are working closely with rescue crews to ensure that all appropriate precautions are taken. We will continue to monitor closely."

Public health concerns about asbestos contamination are primarily related to long-term exposure. Short-term, low-level exposure of the type that might have been produced by the collapse of the World Trade Center buildings is unlikely to cause significant health effects. EPA and OSHA will work closely with rescue and cleanup crews to minimize their potential exposure, but the general public should be very reassured by initial sampling.

EPA and OSHA will continue to monitor and sample for asbestos, and will work with the appropriate officials to ensure that rescue workers, cleanup crews and the general public are properly informed about appropriate steps that should be taken to ensure proper handling, transportation and disposal of potentially contaminated debris or materials.

EPA is taking steps to ensure that response units implement appropriate engineering controls to minimize environmental hazards, such as water sprays and rinsing to prevent or minimize potential exposure and limit releases of potential contaminants beyond the debris site.

EPA is also conducting downwind sampling for potential chemical and asbestos releases from the World Trade Center debris site. In addition, EPA has deployed federal On-Scene Coordinators to the Washington, D.C. Emergency Operations Center, Fort Meade, and FEMA's [Federal Emergency Management Agency] alternate Regional Operations Center in Pennsylvania, and has deployed an On-Scene Coordinator to the Virginia Emergency Operations Center.

Under its response authority, EPA will use all available resources and staff experts to facilitate a safe emergency response and cleanup.

EPA will work with other involved agencies as needed to:

- procure and distribute respiratory and eye protection equipment in co-operation with the Dept. of Health and Human Services;
- provide health and safety training upon request;
- design and implement a site monitoring plan;
- provide technical assistance for site control and decontamination; and provide some 3000 asbestos respirators, 60 self-contained breathing apparatuses and 10,000 protective clothing suits to the two disaster sites.

New York Governor George E. Pataki has promised to provide emergency electric generators to New York City in efforts to restore lost power caused by Tuesday's tragedy, and EPA will work with State authorities to expedite any necessary permits for those generators.

OSHA is also working with Consolidated Edison regarding safety standards for employees who are digging trenches because of leaking gas lines underground.

OSHA has advised Con Edison to provide its employees with appropriate respirators so they can proceed with emergency work, shutting off gas leaks in the city.

Source: Environmental Protection Agency, "EPA Initiates Emergency Response Activities, Reassures Public about Environmental Hazards," September 13, 2001. Available online at http://yosemite.epa.gov/opa/admpress.nsf/b1ab9f485b0989 72852562e7004dc686/d7ada9cf2d39c0a185256acc007c097f?OpenDocument.

ANALYSIS

Although the EPA responded quickly to assess the potential environmental hazards created in the aftermath of the September 11 attacks, and their testing demonstrated low levels of toxic chemicals, first responders at the September 11 sites, as well as cleanup crews who worked the area for the following months and years, have reported far higher than normal levels of contamination-related illnesses. Unfortunately, although the initial testing reported contamination levels lower than expected, and within tolerable exposure limits, many of the first reactors and cleanup crew developed long-term illnesses, likely due to inhaling toxic chemicals. In particular, respiratory ailments and certain types of cancer associated with exposure to contaminants have been reported within those populations. In recognition of the dangers braved by the individuals who responded to the crisis, the U.S. government created a September 11 assistance fund to offset the costs of medical care associated with operations at the site.

- **Document 27: Authorization for the Use of Military Force**
- **When:** September 18, 2001
- **Where:** Washington, D.C.
- **Significance:** This act, passed by the Senate and House of Representatives and signed into law, authorized the president of the United States to utilize military force to end the threat of terror attacks upon the United States. Such force could be applied wherever necessary, and against any nation, organization, or individual who, in the president's determination, was involved in the attacks or harbored anyone who participated or planned them, or who represents a future threat of further attacks.

DOCUMENT

107th Congress
Joint Resolution
    To authorize the use of United States Armed Forces against those responsible for the recent attacks launched against the United States.

Whereas, on September 11, 2001, acts of treacherous violence were committed against the United States and its citizens; and

Whereas, such acts render it both necessary and appropriate that the United States exercise its rights to self-defense and to protect United States citizens both at home and abroad; and

Whereas, in light of the threat to the national security and foreign policy of the United States posed by these grave acts of violence; and

Whereas, such acts continue to pose an unusual and extraordinary threat to the national security and foreign policy of the United States; and

Whereas, the President has authority under the Constitution to take action to deter and prevent acts of international terrorism against the United States: Now, therefore, be it

> **DID YOU KNOW?**
>
> **War Powers Act**
>
> In October 1973, The U.S. Congress passed the War Powers Resolution over President Richard M. Nixon's veto. It severely curtailed the president's ability to use military force without an explicit authorization from Congress to do so. In a national emergency, the War Powers Resolution allows the U.S. president to deploy military forces to foreign locales, but Congress must be informed of the deployment within 48 hours. If Congress does not consent to the deployment, the president cannot leave the troops abroad for more than 60 days, and must complete their full withdrawal within 90 days.

Resolved by the Senate and House of Representatives of the United States of America in Congress assembled,

SECTION 1. SHORT TITLE.

This joint resolution may be cited as the "Authorization for Use of Military Force."

SEC. 2. AUTHORIZATION FOR USE OF UNITED STATES ARMED FORCES.

(a) IN GENERAL.—That the President is authorized to use all necessary and appropriate force against those nations, organizations, or persons he determines planned, authorized, committed, or harbored such organizations or persons, in order to prevent any future acts of international terrorism against the United States by such nations, organizations or persons.

(b) WAR POWERS RESOLUTION REQUIREMENTS.—

(1) SPECIFIC STATUTORY AUTHORIZATION.—Consistent with section 8 (a)(1) of the War Powers Resolution, the Congress declares that this section is intended to constitute specific statutory authorization within the meaning of section 5(b) of the War Powers Resolution.

(2) APPLICABILITY OF OTHER REQUIREMENTS.—Nothing in this resolution supersedes any requirement of the War Powers Resolution.

Approved September 18, 2001

Source: Public Law 107-40; 115 Stat. 225.

ANALYSIS

The Authorization to Use Military Force (AUMF) was the formal mechanism by which the legislature granted approval to President George W. Bush, and his successors in the office, to utilize military force against the perpetrators of the September 11 attacks and any person, organization, or nation allied with them or offering them safe haven. It was initially interpreted by the public as a license to attack Afghanistan and, if necessary, to launch a ground invasion with the purpose of destroying Al Qaeda and capturing or killing its leader, Osama bin Laden. However, because the AUMF was passed only a week after the attacks, and the investigation had not made a final determination regarding who was definitely responsible for them, it was a decidedly vague document. Al Qaeda had already established "franchises" in the Arabian Peninsula, and was on verge of forming alliances with other terror organizations in Africa and the Middle East. Thus, the AUMF authorized the deployment of American troops to a wide variety of locations around the globe, eventually leading to activities ranging from Western Africa to the Philippine Islands. Because the AUMF did not specify Al Qaeda as the primary target, and because it left open the possibility of attacking nations or organizations allied with the September 11 attackers, it has been used to justify the invasion of Iraq in 2003, intervention in Libya in 2011, aerial attacks in Yemen and Somalia against Al Qaeda affiliates, and the deployment of troops to Iraq and Syria to confront the forces of the Islamic State.

- **Document 28: President George W. Bush, Address to Congress**
- **When:** September 20, 2001
- **Where:** Washington, D.C.
- **Significance:** Nine days after the deadliest terror attacks in world history, President George W. Bush chose to address a joint session of Congress, an action most commonly associated with the annual State of the Union address. In his speech, the president sought to reassure a nervous public that the homeland was safe from further attack, and to project an air of confident defiance toward Al Qaeda.

DOCUMENT

Address Before a Joint Session of the Congress on the United States Response to the Terrorist Attacks of September 11
September 20, 2001

Mr. Speaker, Mr. President Pro Tempore, Members of Congress, and fellow Americans: In the normal course of events, Presidents come to this Chamber to report on the state of the Union. Tonight, no such report is needed. It has already been delivered by the American people.

We have seen it in the courage of passengers, who rushed terrorists to save others on the ground, passengers like an exceptional man named Todd Beamer. And would you please help me to welcome his wife, Lisa Beamer, here tonight.

We have seen the State of our Union in the endurance of rescuers, working past exhaustion. We have seen the unfurling of flags, the lighting of candles, the giving of blood, the saying of prayers in English, Hebrew, and Arabic. We have seen the decency of a loving and giving people who have made the grief of strangers their own.

My fellow citizens, for the last 9 days, the entire world has seen for itself the state of our Union, and it is strong.

Tonight we are a country awakened to danger and called to defend freedom. Our grief has turned to anger and anger to resolution. Whether we bring our enemies to justice or bring justice to our enemies, justice will be done.

I thank the Congress for its leadership at such an important time. All of America was touched, on the evening of the tragedy, to see Republicans and Democrats joined together on the steps of this Capitol, singing "God Bless America." And you did more than sing, you acted, by delivering $40 billion to rebuild our communities and meet the needs of our military.

Speaker Hastert, Minority Leader Gephardt, Majority Leader Daschle, and Senator Lott, I thank you for your friendship, for your leadership, and for your service to our country.

And on behalf of the American people, I thank the world for its outpouring of support. America will never forget the sounds of our national anthem playing at Buckingham Palace, on the streets of Paris, and at Berlin's Brandenburg Gate. We will not forget South Korean children gathering to pray outside our Embassy in Seoul, or the prayers of sympathy offered at a mosque in Cairo. We will not forget moments of silence and days of mourning in Australia and Africa and Latin America.

Nor will we forget the citizens of 80 other nations who died with our own: dozens of Pakistanis; more than 130 Israelis; more than 250 citizens of India; men and women from El Salvador, Iran, Mexico, and Japan; and hundreds of British citizens. America has no truer friend than Great Britain. Once again, we are joined together in a great cause—so honored the British Prime Minister has crossed an ocean to show his unity with America. Thank you for coming, friend.

On September 11th, enemies of freedom committed an act of war against our country. Americans have known wars, but for the past 136 years, they have been wars on foreign soil, except for one Sunday in 1941. Americans have known the casualties of war, but not at the center of a great city on a peaceful morning. Americans have known surprise attacks but never before on thousands of civilians. All of this was brought upon us in a single day, and night fell on a different world, a world where freedom itself is under attack.

DID YOU KNOW?

George W. Bush

George W. Bush was elected president in 2000, after one of the closest and most contentious elections in modern history. The results of the election did not become final until December 2000, when the U.S. Supreme Court ruled on the legality of recount efforts in Florida. During the first eight months of his presidency, Bush faced significant opposition from a large segment of the public, and counterterrorism was a relatively low priority. On September 11, 2001, he was visiting an elementary school when the first airplane struck the World Trade Center. Bush was initially informed of the strike, but not realizing it was a deliberate attack, he chose to remain at the elementary school until the second aircraft struck. At that point, President Bush flew to Offut Air Force Base near Omaha, but chose to return to Washington, D.C., by the end of the day. Bush quickly shifted from a source of controversy to a powerful wartime leader, and his resolve galvanized the nation for a long and bloody war with Al Qaeda. In the aftermath of the attacks, his nationwide approval ratings hovered around 90 percent. Much of this goodwill was squandered with the invasion of Iraq, which many citizens viewed as an unnecessary distraction from the fight against Al Qaeda in Afghanistan, and by the end of his presidency, his approval ratings were well below 50 percent.

Americans have many questions tonight. Americans are asking, who attacked our country? The evidence we have gathered all points to a collection of loosely affiliated terrorist organizations known as Al Qaida. They are some of the murderers indicted for bombing American Embassies in Tanzania and Kenya, and responsible for bombing the U.S.S. *Cole*. Al Qaida is to terror what the Mafia is to crime. But its goal is not making money. Its goal is remaking the world and imposing its radical beliefs on people everywhere.

The terrorists practice a fringe form of Islamic extremism that has been rejected by Muslim scholars and the vast majority of Muslim clerics, a fringe movement that perverts the peaceful teachings of Islam. The terrorists' directive commands them to kill Christians and Jews, to kill all Americans, and make no distinctions among military and civilians, including women and children.

This group and its leader, a person named Usama bin Laden, are linked to many other organizations in different countries, including the Egyptian Islamic Jihad and the Islamic Movement of Uzbekistan. There are thousands of these terrorists in more than 60 countries. They are recruited from their own nations and neighborhoods and brought to camps in places like Afghanistan, where they are trained in the tactics of terror. They are sent back to their homes or sent to hide in countries around the world to plot evil and destruction.

The leadership of Al Qaida has great influence in Afghanistan and supports the Taliban regime in controlling most of that country. In Afghanistan, we see Al Qaida's vision for the world. Afghanistan's people have been brutalized. Many are starving, and many have fled. Women are not allowed to attend school. You can be jailed for owning a television. Religion can be practiced only as their leaders dictate. A man can be jailed in Afghanistan if his beard is not long enough.

The United States respects the people of Afghanistan—after all, we are currently its largest source of humanitarian aid—but we condemn the Taliban regime. It is not only repressing its own people; it is threatening people everywhere by sponsoring and sheltering and supplying terrorists. By aiding and abetting murder, the Taliban regime is committing murder.

And tonight, the United States of America makes the following demands on the Taliban: Deliver to United States authorities all the leaders of Al Qaida who hide in your land. Release all foreign nationals, including American citizens, you have unjustly imprisoned. Protect foreign journalists, diplomats, and aid workers in your country. Close immediately and permanently every terrorist training camp in Afghanistan, and hand over every terrorist and every person in their support structure to appropriate authorities. Give the United States full access to terrorist training camps, so we can make sure they are no longer operating. These demands are not open to negotiation or discussion. The Taliban must act and act immediately. They will hand over the terrorists, or they will share in their fate.

I also want to speak tonight directly to Muslims throughout the world. We respect your faith. It's practiced freely by many millions of Americans and by millions more in countries that America counts as friends. Its teachings are good and peaceful, and those who commit evil in the name of Allah blaspheme the name of Allah. The terrorists are traitors to their own faith, trying, in effect, to hijack Islam itself. The enemy of America is not our many Muslim friends; it is not our many Arab friends. Our enemy is a radical network of terrorists and every government that supports them.

Our war on terror begins with Al Qaida, but it does not end there. It will not end until every terrorist group of global reach has been found, stopped, and defeated.

Americans are asking, why do they hate us? They hate what we see right here in this Chamber, a democratically elected government. Their leaders are self-appointed. They hate our freedoms—our freedom of religion, our freedom of speech, our freedom to vote and assemble and disagree with each other.

They want to overthrow existing governments in many Muslim countries, such as Egypt, Saudi Arabia, and Jordan. They want to drive Israel out of the Middle East. They want to drive Christians and Jews out of vast regions of Asia and Africa.

These terrorists kill not merely to end lives but to disrupt and end a way of life. With every atrocity, they hope that America grows fearful, retreating from the world and forsaking our friends. They stand against us, because we stand in their way.

We are not deceived by their pretenses to piety. We have seen their kind before. They are the heirs of all the murderous ideologies of the 20th century. By sacrificing human life to serve their radical visions, by abandoning every value except the will to power, they follow in the path of fascism and Nazism and totalitarianism. And they will follow that path all the way, to where it ends, in history's unmarked grave of discarded lies.

Americans are asking, how will we fight and win this war? We will direct every resource at our command, every means of diplomacy, every tool of intelligence, every instrument of law enforcement, every financial influence, and every necessary weapon of war, to the disruption and to the defeat of the global terror network.

This war will not be like the war against Iraq a decade ago, with a decisive liberation of territory and a swift conclusion. It will not look like the air war above Kosovo 2 years ago, where no ground troops were used and not a single American was lost in combat.

Our response involves far more than instant retaliation and isolated strikes. Americans should not expect one battle but a lengthy campaign, unlike any other we have ever seen. It may include dramatic strikes, visible on TV, and covert operations, secret even in success. We will starve terrorists of funding, turn them one against another, drive them from place to place, until there is no refuge or no rest. And we will pursue nations that provide aid or safe haven to terrorism. Every nation, in every region, now has a decision to make. Either you are with us, or you are with the terrorists. From this day forward, any nation that continues to harbor or support terrorism will be regarded by the United States as a hostile regime.

Our Nation has been put on notice: We are not immune from attack. We will take defensive measures against terrorism to protect Americans. Today dozens of Federal departments and agencies, as well as State and local governments, have responsibilities affecting homeland security. These efforts must be coordinated at the highest level. So tonight I announce the creation of a Cabinet-level position reporting directly to me, the Office of Homeland Security. And tonight I also announce a distinguished American to lead this effort to strengthen American security, a military veteran, an effective Governor, a true patriot, a trusted friend, Pennsylvania's Tom Ridge. He will lead, oversee, and coordinate a comprehensive national strategy to safeguard our country against terrorism and respond to any attacks that may come.

These measures are essential. But the only way to defeat terrorism as a threat to our way of life is to stop it, eliminate it, and destroy it where it grows. Many will be involved in this effort, from FBI agents to intelligence operatives to the reservists we have called to active duty. All deserve our thanks, and all have our prayers. And tonight, a few miles from the damaged Pentagon, I have a message for our military: Be ready. I've called the Armed Forces to alert, and there is a reason. The hour is coming when America will act, and you will make us proud.

This is not, however, just America's fight, and what is at stake is not just America's freedom. This is the world's fight. This is civilization's fight. This is the fight of all who believe in progress and pluralism, tolerance and freedom.

We ask every nation to join us. We will ask, and we will need, the help of police forces, intelligence services, and banking systems around the world. The United States is grateful that many nations and many international organizations have already responded, with sympathy and with support, nations from Latin America, to Asia, to Africa, to Europe, to the Islamic world. Perhaps the NATO Charter reflects best the attitude of the world: An attack on one is an attack on all.

The civilized world is rallying to America's side. They understand that if this terror goes unpunished, their own cities, their own citizens may be next. Terror, unanswered, can not only bring down buildings, it can threaten the stability of legitimate governments. And you know what? We're not going to allow it.

Americans are asking, what is expected of us? I ask you to live your lives and hug your children. I know many citizens have fears tonight, and I ask you to be calm and resolute, even in the face of a continuing threat.

I ask you to uphold the values of America and remember why so many have come here. We are in a fight for our principles, and our first responsibility is to live by them. No one should be singled out for unfair treatment or unkind words because of their ethnic background or religious faith.

I ask you to continue to support the victims of this tragedy with your contributions. Those who want to give can go to a central source of information, libertyunites.org, to find the names of groups providing direct help in New York, Pennsylvania, and Virginia.

The thousands of FBI agents who are now at work in this investigation may need your cooperation, and I ask you to give it.

I ask for your patience with the delays and inconveniences that may accompany tighter security and for your patience in what will be a long struggle.

I ask your continued participation and confidence in the American economy. Terrorists attacked a symbol of American prosperity. They did not touch its source. America is successful because of the hard work and creativity and enterprise of our people. These were the true strengths of our economy before September 11th, and they are our strengths today.

And finally, please continue praying for the victims of terror and their families, for those in uniform, and for our great country. Prayer has comforted us in sorrow and will help strengthen us for the journey ahead.

Tonight I thank my fellow Americans for what you have already done and for what you will do. And ladies and gentlemen of the Congress, I thank you, their representatives, for what you have already done and for what we will do together.

Tonight we face new and sudden national challenges. We will come together to improve air safety, to dramatically expand the number of air marshals on domestic flights, and take new measures to prevent hijacking. We will come together to promote stability and keep our airlines flying, with direct assistance during this emergency.

We will come together to give law enforcement the additional tools it needs to track down terror here at home. We will come together to strengthen our intelligence capabilities, to know the plans of terrorists before they act and find them before they strike. We will come together to take active steps that strengthen America's economy and put our people back to work.

Tonight we welcome two leaders who embody the extraordinary spirit of all New Yorkers, Governor George Pataki and Mayor Rudolph Giuliani. As a symbol of America's resolve, my administration will work with Congress and these two leaders to show the world that we will rebuild New York City.

After all that has just passed, all the lives taken and all the possibilities and hopes that died with them, it is natural to wonder if America's future is one of fear. Some speak of an age of terror. I know there are struggles ahead and dangers to face. But this country will define our times, not be defined by them. As long as the United States of America is determined and strong, this will not be an age of terror; this will be an age of liberty, here and across the world.

Great harm has been done to us. We have suffered great loss. And in our grief and anger, we have found our mission and our moment. Freedom and fear are at war. The advance of human freedom, the great achievement of our time and the great hope of every time, now depends on us. Our Nation—this generation—will lift a dark threat of violence from our people and our future. We will rally the world to this cause by our efforts, by our courage. We will not tire; we will not falter; and we will not fail.

It is my hope that in the months and years ahead, life will return almost to normal. We'll go back to our lives and routines, and that is good. Even grief recedes with time and grace. But our resolve must not pass. Each of us will remember what happened that day and to whom it happened. We'll remember the moment the news came, where we were, and what we were doing. Some will remember an image of a fire or a story of rescue. Some will carry memories of a face and a voice gone forever.

And I will carry this: It is the police shield of a man named George Howard, who died at the World Trade Center trying to save others. It was given to me by his mom, Arlene, as a proud memorial to her son. It is my reminder of lives that ended and a task that does not end. I will not forget this wound to our country and those who inflicted it. I will not yield; I will not rest; I will not relent in waging this struggle for freedom and security for the American people.

The course of this conflict is not known, yet its outcome is certain. Freedom and fear, justice and cruelty have always been at war, and we know that God is not neutral between them.

Fellow citizens, we'll meet violence with patient justice, assured of the rightness of our cause and confident of the victories to come. In all that lies before us, may God grant us wisdom, and may He watch over the United States of America.

Thank you.

Source: Public Papers of the Presidents of the United States: George W. Bush (2001, Book 2). Washington, D.C.: Government Printing Office, 1140–1144.

ANALYSIS

In this presidential address, George W. Bush spoke before a joint session of Congress, in the same fashion used for the annual State of the Union address. He expanded upon his remarks from the night of September 11, 2001 (see Document 24), reflecting the information discovered by preliminary investigations into the terror attacks. After two weeks, the president was able to lay responsibility for the attacks with Al Qaeda, and to promise to wage war upon it and upon Osama bin Laden until the threat, and quite probably the terror organization, was destroyed. Bush cautioned the American public that the war would not be quick, cheap, or easy, and that the nation would undoubtedly face setbacks in the struggle. He promised not to lose resolve in the face of reverses, and to lead the American military in the fight to come. This speech is also noteworthy because, in it, the president put forth a warning to all of the nations of the world, specifically, that those who abet terrorism, or harbor its proponents, would be considered enemies of the United States, and could expect to be attacked without further warning if they continued their support of Al Qaeda and its affiliates. To most American citizens, this was a natural outgrowth of the rage building from the September 11 attacks. To some world leaders, though, this signified a new phase of American imperialism, as the United States would apparently make all determinations of the guilt or innocence of nations, and would use force to impose its decrees upon the world. Nations soon began to align themselves with or against the American crusade to annihilate Al Qaeda, setting the stage for a global struggle between the world's foremost military power and the most dangerous international terrorist organization.

- **Document 29: Executive Order 13224**
- **When:** September 23, 2001
- **Where:** Washington, D.C.
- **Significance:** President George W. Bush formally issued an executive order designed to shut down the primary funding mechanism for terrorist organizations. In this order, he expanded and strengthened the actions taken earlier by the United Nations and previous administrations (see Documents 12, 15, and 17).

DOCUMENT

Executive Order 13224—Blocking Property and Prohibiting Transactions with Persons Who Commit, Threaten to Commit, or Support Terrorism
September 23, 2001

I, George W. Bush, President of the United States of America, find that grave acts of terrorism and threats of terrorism committed by foreign terrorists, including the terrorist attacks in New York, Pennsylvania, and the Pentagon committed on September 11, 2001, acts recognized and condemned in UNSCR [United Nations Security Council Resolution] 1368 of September 12, 2001, and UNSCR 1269 of October 19, 1999, and the continuing and immediate threat of further attacks on United States nationals or the United States constitute an unusual and extraordinary threat to the national security, foreign policy, and economy of the United States, and in furtherance of my proclamation of September 14, 2001, Declaration of National Emergency by Reason of Certain Terrorist Attacks, hereby declare a national emergency to deal with that threat. I also find that because of the pervasiveness and expansiveness of the financial foundation of foreign terrorists, financial sanctions may be appropriate for those foreign persons that support or otherwise associate with these foreign terrorists. I also find that a need exists for further consultation and cooperation with, and sharing of information by, United States and foreign financial institutions as an additional tool to enable the United States to combat the financing of terrorism.

I hereby order:

Section 1. Except to the extent required by section 203(b) of IEEPA [International Emergency Economic Powers Act] (50 U.S.C. 1702(b)), or provided in regulations, orders, directives, or licenses that may be issued pursuant to this order, and notwithstanding any contract entered into or any license or permit granted prior to the effective date of this order, all property and interests in property of the following persons that are in the United States or that hereafter come within the United States, or that hereafter come within the possession or control of United States persons are blocked:

(a) foreign persons listed in the Annex to this order;

(b) foreign persons determined by the Secretary of State, in consultation with the Secretary of the Treasury and the Attorney General, to have committed, or to pose a significant risk of committing, acts of terrorism that threaten the security of U.S. nationals or the national security, foreign policy, or economy of the United States;

(c) persons determined by the Secretary of the Treasury, in consultation with the Secretary of State and the Attorney General, to be owned or controlled by, or to act for or on behalf of those persons listed in the Annex to this order or those persons determined to be subject to subsection 1(b), 1(c), or 1(d)(i) of this order;

(d) except as provided in section 5 of this order and after such consultation, if any, with foreign authorities as the Secretary of State, in consultation with the Secretary of the Treasury and the Attorney General, deems appropriate in the exercise of his discretion, persons determined by the Secretary of the Treasury, in consultation with the Secretary of State and the Attorney General;

(i) to assist in, sponsor, or provide financial, material, or technological support for, or financial or other services to or in support of, such acts of terrorism or those persons listed in the Annex to this order or determined to be subject to this order; or

(ii) to be otherwise associated with those persons listed in the Annex to this order or those persons determined to be subject to subsection 1(b), 1(c), or 1(d)(i) of this order.

Sec. 2. Except to the extent required by section 203(b) of IEEPA (50 U.S.C. 1702 (b)), or provided in regulations, orders, directives, or licenses that may be issued pursuant to this order, and notwithstanding any contract entered into or any license or permit granted prior to the effective date:

(a) any transaction or dealing by United States persons or within the United States in property or interests in property blocked pursuant to this order is prohibited, including but not limited to the making or receiving of any contribution of funds, goods, or services to or for the benefit of those persons listed in the Annex to this order or determined to be subject to this order;

(b) any transaction by any United States person or within the United States that evades or avoids, or has the purpose of evading or avoiding, or attempts to violate, any of the prohibitions set forth in this order is prohibited; and

(c) any conspiracy formed to violate any of the prohibitions set forth in this order is prohibited.

Sec. 3. For purposes of this order:

(a) the term "person" means an individual or entity;

(b) the term "entity" means a partnership, association, corporation, or other organization, group, or subgroup;

(c) the term "United States person" means any United States citizen, permanent resident alien, entity organized under the laws of the United States (including foreign branches), or any person in the United States; and

(d) the term "terrorism" means an activity that—

(i) involves a violent act or an act dangerous to human life, property, or infrastructure; and

(ii) appears to be intended—

(A) to intimidate or coerce a civilian population;

(B) to influence the policy of a government by intimidation or coercion; or

(C) to affect the conduct of a government by mass destruction, assassination, kidnapping, or hostage-taking.

Sec. 4. I hereby determine that the making of donations of the type specified in section 203(b)(2) of IEEPA (50 U.S.C. 1702(b)(2)) by United States persons to persons determined to be subject to this order would seriously impair my ability to deal with the national emergency declared in this order, and would endanger Armed Forces of the United States that are in a situation where imminent involvement in hostilities is clearly indicated by the circumstances, and hereby prohibit such donations as provided by section 1 of this order. Furthermore, I hereby determine that the

Trade Sanctions Reform and Export Enhancement Act of 2000 (title IX, Public Law 106–387) shall not affect the imposition or the continuation of the imposition of any unilateral agricultural sanction or unilateral medical sanction on any person determined to be subject to this order because imminent involvement of the Armed Forces of the United States in hostilities is clearly indicated by the circumstances.

Sec. 5. With respect to those persons designated pursuant to subsection 1(d) of this order, the Secretary of the Treasury, in the exercise of his discretion and in consultation with the Secretary of State and the Attorney General, may take such other actions than the complete blocking of property or interests in property as the President is authorized to take under IEEPA and UNPA [United Nations Participation Act of 1945] if the Secretary of the Treasury, in consultation with the Secretary of State and the Attorney General, deems such other actions to be consistent with the national interests of the United States, considering such factors as he deems appropriate.

Sec. 6. The Secretary of State, the Secretary of the Treasury, and other appropriate agencies shall make all relevant efforts to cooperate and coordinate with other countries, including through technical assistance, as well as bilateral and multilateral agreements and arrangements, to achieve the objectives of this order, including the prevention and suppression of acts of terrorism, the denial of financing and financial services to terrorists and terrorist organizations, and the sharing of intelligence about funding activities in support of terrorism.

Sec. 7. The Secretary of the Treasury, in consultation with the Secretary of State and the Attorney General, is hereby authorized to take such actions, including the promulgation of rules and regulations, and to employ all powers granted to the President by IEEPA and UNPA as may be necessary to carry out the purposes of this order. The Secretary of the Treasury may redelegate any of these functions to other officers and agencies of the United States Government. All agencies of the United States Government are hereby directed to take all appropriate measures within their authority to carry out the provisions of this order.

Sec. 8. Nothing in this order is intended to affect the continued effectiveness of any rules, regulations, orders, licenses, or other forms of administrative action issued, taken, or continued in effect heretofore or hereafter under 31 C.F.R. chapter V, except as expressly terminated, modified, or suspended by or pursuant to this order.

Sec. 9. Nothing contained in this order is intended to create, nor does it create, any right, benefit, or privilege, substantive or procedural, enforceable at law by a party against the United States, its agencies, officers, employees or any other person.

Sec. 10. For those persons listed in the Annex to this order or determined to be subject to this order who might have a constitutional presence in the United States, I find that because of the ability to transfer funds or assets instantaneously, prior notice to such persons of measures to be taken pursuant to this order would render these measures ineffectual. I therefore determine that for these measures to be effective in addressing the national emergency declared in this order, there need be no prior notice of a listing or determination made pursuant to this order.

Sec. 11. (a) This order is effective at 12:01 a.m. eastern daylight time on September 24, 2001.

(b) This order shall be transmitted to the Congress and published in the *Federal Register*.

George W. Bush
The White House,
September 23, 2001

Source: 66 Federal Register 49079.

ANALYSIS

This executive order was one of the first direct actions taken by the Bush administration to undermine and ultimately defeat Al Qaeda. It was designed to not only cut off any financial support to the terrorist organization and its allies, but also criminalize any attempt to donate to false-front charities that had long served as a revenue stream for Al Qaeda. This order is significant not just for halting the flow of material aid to Osama bin Laden and his followers, but also for demonstrating that the U.S. government would use all of the powers at its disposal, to include diplomacy, legal initiatives, and economic means, to supplement the forthcoming military response to the September 11 attacks.

- **Document 30: The President's Constitutional Authority to Conduct Military Operations against Terrorists and Nations Supporting Them**
- **When:** September 25, 2001
- **Where:** Washington, D.C.
- **Significance:** This extensive memorandum, written by Deputy Assistant Attorney General John Yoo, laid out an extremely broad argument regarding presidential power in the effort to combat terror. Yoo believed there were few limits on presidential activity in pursuit of national security, a position that soon dominated the George W. Bush administration's relationship with Congress.

DOCUMENT

The President's Constitutional Authority to Conduct Military Operations against Terrorists and Nations Supporting Them

The President has broad constitutional power to take military action in response to the terrorist attacks on the United States on September 11, 2001. Congress has acknowledged this inherent executive power in both the War Powers Resolution and the Joint Resolution passed by Congress on September 14, 2001.

The President has constitutional power not only to retaliate against any person, organization, or state suspected of involvement in terrorist attacks on the United States, but also against foreign states suspected of harboring or supporting such organizations.

The President may deploy military force preemptively against terrorist organizations or the states that harbor or support them, whether or not they can be linked to the specific terrorist incidents of September 11.
September 25, 2001
MEMORANDUM OPINION FOR THE DEPUTY COUNSEL TO THE PRESIDENT

You have asked for our opinion as to the scope of the President's authority to take military action in response to the terrorist attacks on the United States on September 11, 2001. We conclude that the President has broad constitutional power to use military force. Congress has acknowledged this inherent executive power in both the War Powers Resolution, Pub. L. No. 93-148, 87 Stat. 555 (1973), *codified at* 50 U.S.C. §§ 1541–1548 (the "WPR"), and in the Joint Resolution passed by Congress on September 14, 2001, Pub. L. No. 107-40, 115 Stat. 224 (2001). Further, the President has the constitutional power not only to retaliate against any person, organization, or state suspected of involvement in terrorist attacks on the United States, but also against foreign states suspected of harboring or supporting such organizations. Finally, the President may deploy military force preemptively against terrorist organizations or the states that harbor or support them, whether or not they can be linked to the specific terrorist incidents of September 11.

Constitutional Structure. Our reading of the text is reinforced by analysis of the constitutional structure. First, it is clear that the Constitution secures all federal executive power in the President to ensure a unity in purpose and energy in action. "Decision, activity, secrecy, and dispatch will generally characterize the proceedings of one man in a much more eminent degree than the proceedings of any greater number." *The Federalist* No. 70, at 424 (Alexander Hamilton) (Clinton Rossiter ed., 1961). The centralization of authority in the President alone is particularly crucial in matters of national defense, war, and foreign policy, where a unitary executive can evaluate threats, consider policy choices, and mobilize national resources with a speed and energy that is far superior to any other branch. As Hamilton noted, "Energy in the executive is a leading character in the definition of good government. It is essential to the protection of the community against foreign attacks." *Id.* at 423. This is no less true in war. "Of all the cares or concerns of government, the direction of war most peculiarly demands those qualities which distinguish the exercise of power by a single hand." *Id.* No. 74, at 447 (Alexander Hamilton).

Second, the Constitution makes clear that the process used for conducting military hostilities is different from other government decision-making. In the area of

---

DID YOU KNOW?

Sunni

The Sunni are one of the two major sects of Islam, and include more than 80 percent of the global Muslim population. The Sunni branch of Islam, which split from the Shi'a in the seventh century after the death of the Prophet Mohammed, adheres to the idea that the leadership of the Muslim community should pass to leaders chosen from the community at large, rather than on a hereditary basis. Sunnis comprise the majority in virtually every country with a large Muslim population, with the exceptions of Azerbaijan, Bahrain, Iran, and Iraq. Despite their minority status in Iraq, Sunnis governed that nation until the parliamentary elections held in 2005. Al Qaeda, the Islamic State, and Hamas are all extremely radical organizations that profess adherence to the Sunni faith.

domestic legislation, the Constitution creates a detailed, finely wrought procedure in which Congress plays the central role. In foreign affairs, however, the Constitution does not establish a mandatory, detailed, Congress-driven procedure for taking action. Rather, the Constitution vests the two branches with different powers—the President as Commander in Chief, Congress with control over funding and declaring war—without requiring that they follow a specific process in making war. By establishing this framework, the Framers expected that the process for war-making would be far more flexible, and capable of quicker, more decisive action, than the legislative process. Thus, the President may use his Commander-in-Chief and executive powers to use military force to protect the Nation, subject to congressional appropriations and control over domestic legislation.

Third, the constitutional structure requires that any ambiguities in the allocation of a power that is executive in nature—such as the power to conduct military hostilities—must be resolved in favor of the Executive Branch. Article II, Section 1 provides that "[t]he executive Power shall be vested in a President of the United States." U.S. Const. art. II, § 1. By contrast, Article I's Vesting Clause gives Congress only the powers "herein granted." *Id.* art. I, § 1. This difference in language indicates that Congress's legislative powers are limited to the list enumerated in Article I, Section 8, while the President's powers include inherent executive powers that are unenumerated in the Constitution. To be sure, Article II lists specifically enumerated powers in addition to the Vesting Clause, and some have argued that this limits the "executive Power" granted in the Vesting Clause to the powers on that list. But the purpose of the enumeration of executive powers in Article II was not to define and cabin the grant in the Vesting Clause. Rather, the Framers unbundled some plenary powers that had traditionally been regarded as "executive," assigning elements of those powers to Congress in Article I, while expressly reserving other elements as enumerated executive powers in Article II. So, for example, the King's traditional power to declare war was given to Congress under Article I, while the Commander-in-Chief authority was expressly reserved to the President in Article II. Further, the Framers altered other plenary powers of the King, such as treaties and appointments, assigning the Senate a share in them in Article II itself. Thus, the enumeration in Article II marks the points at which several traditional executive powers were diluted or reallocated. Any other unenumerated executive powers, however, were conveyed to the President by the Vesting Clause.

There can be little doubt that the decision to deploy military force is "executive" in nature, and was traditionally so regarded. It calls for action and energy in execution, rather than the deliberate formulation of rules to govern the conduct of private individuals. Moreover, the Framers understood it to be an attribute of the executive. "The direction of war implies the direction of the common strength," wrote Alexander Hamilton, "and the power of directing and employing the common strength forms a usual and essential part in the definition of the executive authority." *The Federalist* No. 74, at 447 (Alexander Hamilton) (Clinton Rossiter ed., 1961). As a result, to the extent that the constitutional text does not explicitly allocate the power to initiate military hostilities to a particular branch, the Vesting Clause provides that it remain among the President's unenumerated powers.

Fourth, depriving the President of the power to decide when to use military force would disrupt the basic constitutional framework of foreign relations. From the very beginnings of the Republic, the vesting of the executive, Commander-in-Chief, and treaty powers in the Executive Branch has been understood to grant the President plenary control over the conduct of foreign relations. As Secretary of State Thomas Jefferson observed during the first Washington Administration, "[t]he constitution has divided the powers of government into three branches [and] has declared that the executive powers shall be vested in the president, submitting only special articles of it to a negative by the senate." Thomas Jefferson, Opinion on the Powers of the Senate (1790), *reprinted in* 5 *The Writings of Thomas Jefferson* at 161 (Paul L. Ford ed., 1895). Due to this structure, Jefferson continued, "[t]he transaction of business with foreign nations is executive altogether; it belongs, then, to the head of that department, except as to such portions of it as are specially submitted to the senate. Exceptions are to be construed strictly." *Id.* In defending President Washington's authority to issue the Neutrality Proclamation, Alexander Hamilton came to the same interpretation of the President's foreign affairs powers. According to Hamilton, Article II "ought . . . to be considered as intended . . . to specify and regulate the principal articles implied in the definition of Executive Power; leaving the rest to flow from the general grant of that power." Alexander Hamilton, Pacificus No. 1 (1793), *reprinted in* 15 *The Papers of Alexander Hamilton* at 33, 39 (Harold C. Syrett et al. eds., 1969). As future Chief Justice John Marshall famously declared a few years later, "The President is the sole organ of the nation in its external relations, and its sole representative with foreign nations. . . . The [executive] department . . . is entrusted with the whole foreign intercourse of the nation. . . ." 10 Annals of Cong. 613-14 (1800). Given the agreement of Jefferson, Hamilton, and Marshall, it has not been difficult for the Executive Branch consistently to assert the President's plenary authority in foreign affairs ever since.

Conducting military hostilities is a central tool for the exercise of the President's plenary control over the conduct of foreign policy. There can be no doubt that the use of force protects the Nation's security and helps it achieve its foreign policy goals. Construing the Constitution to grant such power to another branch could prevent the President from exercising his core constitutional responsibilities in foreign affairs. Even in the cases in which the Supreme Court has limited executive authority, it has also emphasized that we should not construe legislative prerogatives to prevent the Executive Branch "from accomplishing its constitutionally assigned functions." *Nixon v. Adm'r of Gen. Servs.*, 433 U.S. 425, 443 (1977).

Source: Memorandum, John Yoo to David Kris, September 25, 2001, available at http://www.justice.gov/olc/opinion/president%E2%80%99s-constitutional-authority-conduct-military-operations-against-terrorists-and.

ANALYSIS

With this memorandum, John Yoo laid out a very broad understanding of presidential power during national emergencies, and argued that the president has the sole authority to determine how and when the U.S. military should be used to ensure national security. While Yoo believed that the congressional "power of the purse" provided a check upon executive authority, he also suggested that the president need not abide by the provisions of the War Powers Act. Further, he noted that while Congress passed an Authorization to Use Military Force, it should be considered more of an act of solidarity than a true authorization, as he believed the president did not need congressional permission or support to engage in military operations against terrorist organizations. Yoo's theory, if it held up, greatly enhanced the effective power of the presidency, as it enabled the president to deploy U.S. military forces anywhere in the world under the aegis of fighting against terrorism. Both President George W. Bush and President Barack Obama have effectively followed Yoo's logic, as each has made unilateral decisions to deploy military forces to engage in hostilities against terrorist organizations.

- **Document 31: Speech of Sayyed Hassan Nasrallah**
- **When:** September 28, 2001
- **Where:** Beirut, Lebanon
- **Significance:** Nasrallah is the leader of Hezbollah, a Lebanese militant group listed by the U.S. State Department as a foreign terrorist organization. He sought to frame the September 11 attacks, and the likely aftermath, as an Israeli plot to provoke warfare between Christians and Muslims for their own ends.

DOCUMENT

We meet again in this place that has witnessed many occasions marking dates of resistance and martyrdom. However, the marking of this anniversary is one of the means that shows our support and solidarity with the Palestinian people and its steadfastness and determination to regain its dignity and hold shrines. . .

Recent events in the U.S. have temporarily pushed away the Palestinian Intifada from the center stage of international and Arab attention. I believe that these events have a deep link regarding the likely reasons or the expected results with the current conflict in the region.

Since September 11, the Israeli enemy rushed to accuse the Islamic movements in Lebanon and Palestine and concentrated on some names like, Hizbollah, Hamas and Islamic Jihad. This happened at a time when all of America was in confusion. If the Israelis had such information why they have waited until now to reveal it, why they didn't give it to the U.S. in advance?

On the other hand America rushed to accuse the Arabs and Muslims as being those behind the attacks, placing them in a circle of blame, increasing the wave of hatred against Arabs and Muslims all over the U.S., Canada and Australia. Shortly afterwards, the American administration declared a war on terrorism and spoke of forming an international coalition against terrorism. In light of recent developments I would like to mention the following:

- The Arabs, Muslims and their governments, parties and clerics denounce the killing of innocent people anywhere in the world whether it is Hiroshima, Nagasaki, Deir Yassin, Sabra and Shatila, Qana or New York.

- It is distressing to see that the entire world is expected to take part in the denouncing hysteria only because the events occurred in America and those killed are American.

- When Arabs or Muslims are killed as happened in Sabra, Shatila and Qana then this is an entirely different issue. The American administration didn't denounce those or other massacres. In addition, it prevented the international community from denouncing such actions and used its veto in the U.N. Security Council to do so...

> ### DID YOU KNOW?
>
> #### Shi'a
>
> The Shi'a are one of the two largest sects within Islam, and include nearly 20 percent of the global Muslim population, as well as the majority in Azerbaijan, Bahrain, Iran, and Iraq. Members of the Shi'a faith, which split from the Sunni faction in the seventh century after the death of the Prophet Mohammed, argue that the Islamic community should be led by the direct descendants of the Prophet. Clerics exercise greater power within the Shi'a community, with the highest ranking, the ayatollahs, often holding temporal political power in addition to their religious authority. Hezbollah is the most well-known terrorist organization within the Shi'a faith.

I want to emphasize that America is not honest in fighting terrorism and the proof is its support to Israel. It also is not qualified to lead an international coalition for the reasons I mentioned earlier. America will continue its support of some terrorist groups in the world while at the same time creating an image of a generic Muslim enemy.

After the collapse of the Soviet Union they said Islam is the new enemy but when they found that more than one billion would be their enemies and that that would work counter to U.S. interests, they fell back and divided Islam into two groups, moderates and extremists. American arrogance and superiority implies that it should create an enemy and now it is terrorism. Bush has declared his war against terrorism and declared the coalition of good and Justice in the face of terrorism and Osama Bin Ladin. But what is next?

The U.S. has set up its goals and it is not serious. It is only a pretext to increase its domination in the world and a pretext to have military presence in Afghanistan and mid Asia very close to the Qezzween Sea [Caspian Sea]. America wants its bases to spread anywhere in the world and it is prohibited to any to oppose but whoever opposes becomes accused of harboring terrorism. It must be very clear to every Arab and Muslim and any honored man in this world that [it] is prohibited to offer any sort of support to America in its aggression against the people of Afghanistan.

We reject the arrogant rhetoric of Bush in the U.S. Congress and we consider it an enormous insult to all governments and peoples of the world. We consider any aggression against Afghanistan to be an aggression against innocent and oppressed people and it will face denunciation from our side.

We call on all to set aside fear and not to be subject to American dictation. What brings hope is that many countries in the world did not answer the American call. Many countries have spoken out, some calling for reason and wisdom, others saying we have to define terrorism and some want the United Nations to lead and the Security Council to lead the campaign against terrorism. I respect those who have raised their concerns. Bush imagined that the world would obediently prostrate itself before him, surrendering to his leadership.

I thank the leaders of Lebanon, Syria and Iran and all governments of Arab and Islamic world who refused to label Lebanese and Palestinian resistance as terrorist groups.

I want to advise some Arab and Muslim leaderships, specifically some enthusiastic Islamic movements, not to be dragged into what the U.S. has called a crusade war. If this was the intent of Bush and Barliskonee [Italian prime minister Silvio Berlusconi] we shouldn't be dragged into that. No Muslim should consider that this is a war of Christianity against Islam. It is a tragedy if we think that way.

The Zionist desire is to see a world war between Christians and Muslims. The majority of Muslims and Christians reject terrorism and have honored positions in fighting Israel and Zionism. Some have sacrificed themselves for the legitimate cause of Lebanon, Palestine and Syria and the Arab and Islamic world. No one should be dragged into a war of this kind.

Anyone in this world who destroys a church in retaliation for setting a mosque on fire is acting in the Zionists' interest. The declared war against Arabs and Muslims has only something to do with the materialistic, capitalist and arrogant mentality and has nothing to do with Jesus Christ or with Christianity or with Christians. We have to be wise enough, I am deeply concerned that some extremist Arabs and Islamists who are closed-minded may infiltrate our body and we may be dragged into reaction. We don't need to be enticed to any state of reactionary anger or to fall for this trap. At this time we need the highest degree of wisdom and reason.

We are determined to pursue the line of Resistance until our land is liberated and detainees in Israeli prisons are freed. We will continue our support of the Palestinian people in their Intifada with money, weapons, media coverage and public presence. I want to reiterate and say to our Palestinian people that if we wanted to swap the Lebanese detainees for the four Israeli soldiers that we have we were able to [do] that. However, we insist in all negotiation rounds with the German mediators that the Palestinian detainees must be part of the swap operation. We continue to discuss with the mediators the number of the detainees in a way that preserves the dignity of the struggling people of Palestine.

We will continue our support of the Palestinian Resistance and we are ready for direct military interference from Lebanese territory when we feel that the Palestinian Resistance is in urgent need for that support. Our position after the events of September 11th remains unchanged from the position we held prior to September 11th. What goals were pursued before that date will continue to be pursued after that date. September 11th may have changed America or the world but does not change our position and will not affect our right to liberate our land and to free our detainees.

All of us must be armed with faith in God and self-confidence to face future dangerous periods as we have in the past.

Source: Hezbollah English-language website, http://www.hizbollah.org/english/frames/index_eg.htm.

ANALYSIS

By framing the September 11 attacks as an outgrowth of Israeli plotting and Zionism, Nasrallah sought to distance his own organization, a radical Shi'a group, from Al Qaeda, a Sunni faction of radical Islam. At the same time, Nasrallah sought to return the Arab-Israeli conflict to the forefront of discussions in the Muslim world, and portray the September 11 attacks as a distraction from the larger and more important issue of Palestinian statehood and Lebanese sovereignty. Nasrallah neither supported nor condemned the attacks, a position which he noted might put him at odds with President George W. Bush, who had framed the struggle with Al Qaeda as one between good and evil, in which the people of the world were categorically aligned with or against the United States, with no possibility for neutral positions. Nasrallah sought to equate the September 11 attacks with other violent incidents, to include the atomic bombings of Hiroshima and Nagasaki, as a means to suggest that the United States had no grounds to engage in morality arguments that might condemn some or all of the Muslim or Arab world. Although Hezbollah attacked U.S. forces in a Beirut barracks in 1983, the organization has not openly attacked American citizens for more than two decades, suggesting that it has chosen to focus primarily upon its regional interests rather than provoking American retaliation. Also, Hezbollah has engaged in significant efforts to transition to a legitimate political party in Lebanon, complete with efforts at governance of certain regions, and possibly cannot afford to draw the attention of the United States at a critical period in its own development.

- **Document 32: United Nations Security Council Resolution 1373**
- **When:** September 28, 2001
- **Where:** United Nations, New York City
- **Significance:** This resolution, passed in the immediate aftermath of the September 11 attacks, called upon all UN member states to freeze the assets of terror organizations, prohibit any material support to them, and stand in solidarity with one another in the struggle against global terrorism.

DOCUMENT

The Security Council,
Reaffirming its resolutions 1269 (1999) of 19 October 1999 and 1368 (2001) of 12 September 2001,

DID YOU KNOW?

Al Qaeda Plays the Stock Market?

In the aftermath of the September 11 attacks, major airlines' stock prices plummeted in a predictable reaction to the tragedy. Market analysts detected that a substantial amount of airline stock had been "short sold," a technique of stock trading that allows the seller to profit if he or she can correctly anticipate a significant decline in prices. Investigators from the Federal Bureau of Investigation and the Securities and Exchange Commission tested the hypothesis that front companies for Al Qaeda might have used their insider knowledge of the impending attacks to reap enormous financial windfalls on behalf of the very organization that carried out the attacks. Although the investigation concluded that no such manipulation of the stock market had occurred, the possibility of a fiscally savvy terror group making such a move in the future led to a change in the stock market monitoring systems to prevent such an act, and to potentially provide warning of an impending attack.

Reaffirming also its unequivocal condemnation of the terrorist attacks which took place in New York, Washington, D.C. and Pennsylvania on 11 September 2001, and expressing its determination to prevent all such acts,

Reaffirming further that such acts, like any act of international terrorism, constitute a threat to international peace and security,

Reaffirming the inherent right of individual or collective self-defence as recognized by the Charter of the United Nations as reiterated in resolution 1368 (2001),

Reaffirming the need to combat by all means, in accordance with the Charter of the United Nations, threats to international peace and security caused by terrorist acts,

Deeply concerned by the increase, in various regions of the world, of acts of terrorism motivated by intolerance or extremism,

Calling on States to work together urgently to prevent and suppress terrorist acts, including through increased cooperation and full implementation of the relevant international conventions relating to terrorism,

Recognizing the need for States to complement international cooperation by taking additional measures to prevent and suppress, in their territories through all lawful means, the financing and preparation of any acts of terrorism,

Reaffirming the principle established by the General Assembly in its declaration of October 1970 (resolution 2625 (XXV)) and reiterated by the Security Council in its resolution 1189 (1998) of 13 August 1998, namely that every State has the duty to refrain from organizing, instigating, assisting or participating in terrorist acts in another State or acquiescing in organized activities within its territory directed towards the commission of such acts,

Acting under Chapter VII of the Charter of the United Nations,

1. *Decides* that all States shall:

(a) Prevent and suppress the financing of terrorist acts;

(b) Criminalize the willful provision or collection, by any means, directly or indirectly, of funds by their nationals or in their territories with the intention that the funds should be used, or in the knowledge that they are to be used, in order to carry out terrorist acts;

(c) Freeze without delay funds and other financial assets or economic resources of persons who commit, or attempt to commit, terrorist acts or participate in or facilitate the commission of terrorist acts; of entities owned or controlled directly or indirectly by such persons; and of persons and entities acting on behalf of, or at the direction of such persons and entities, including funds derived or generated from property owned or controlled directly or indirectly by such persons and associated persons and entities;

(d) Prohibit their nationals or any persons and entities within their territories from making any funds, financial assets or economic resources or financial or other related services available, directly or indirectly, for the benefit of persons who commit or attempt to commit or facilitate or participate in the commission of terrorist acts, of entities owned or controlled, directly or indirectly, by such persons and of persons and entities acting on behalf of or at the direction of such persons;

2. *Decides also* that all States shall:

(a) Refrain from providing any form of support, active or passive, to entities or persons involved in terrorist acts, including by suppressing recruitment of members of terrorist groups and eliminating the supply of weapons to terrorists;

(b) Take the necessary steps to prevent the commission of terrorist acts, including by provision of early warning to other States by exchange of information;

(c) Deny safe haven to those who finance, plan, support, or commit terrorist acts, or provide safe havens;

(d) Prevent those who finance, plan, facilitate or commit terrorist acts from using their respective territories for those purposes against other States or their citizens;

(e) Ensure that any person who participates in the financing, planning, preparation or perpetration of terrorist acts or in supporting terrorist acts is brought to justice and ensure that, in addition to any other measures against them, such terrorist acts are established as serious criminal offences in domestic laws and regulations and that the punishment duly reflects the seriousness of such terrorist acts;

(f) Afford one another the greatest measure of assistance in connection with criminal investigations or criminal proceedings relating to the financing or support of terrorist acts, including assistance in obtaining evidence in their possession necessary for the proceedings;

(g) Prevent the movement of terrorists or terrorist groups by effective border controls and controls on issuance of identity papers and travel documents, and through measures for preventing counterfeiting, forgery or fraudulent use of identity papers and travel documents;

3. *Calls* upon all States to:

(a) Find ways of intensifying and accelerating the exchange of operational information, especially regarding actions or movements of terrorist persons or networks; forged or falsified travel documents; traffic in arms, explosives or sensitive materials; use of communications technologies by terrorist groups; and the threat posed by the possession of weapons of mass destruction by terrorist groups;

(b) Exchange information in accordance with international and domestic law and cooperate on administrative and judicial matters to prevent the commission of terrorist acts;

(c) Cooperate, particularly through bilateral and multilateral arrangements and agreements, to prevent and suppress terrorist attacks and take action against perpetrators of such acts;

4. *Notes* with concern the close connection between international terrorism and transnational organized crime, illicit drugs, money-laundering, illegal arms-trafficking, and illegal movement of nuclear, chemical, biological and other potentially deadly materials, and in this regard *emphasizes* the need to enhance coordination of efforts on national, subregional, regional and international levels in

order to strengthen a global response to this serious challenge and threat to international security;

5. *Declares* that acts, methods, and practices of terrorism are contrary to the purposes and principles of the United Nations and that knowingly financing, planning and inciting terrorist acts are also contrary to the purposes and principles of the United Nations.

Source: Security Council Resolution 1373. S/Res/1373 (2001). United Nations. Available at: https://www.unodc.org/tldb/pdf/Res_1373_2001.pdf. Used by permission of the United Nations.

ANALYSIS

The excerpts of this resolution demonstrate that the 2001 membership of the UN Security Council had a firm grasp of the mechanisms utilized by international terror organizations. In particular, this resolution called upon all states to freeze financial assets in the hopes of paralyzing, or at least significantly slowing, the activities of terror groups. It also called upon states to exercise better control over borders, noting that international terror organizations were able to thrive in large part due to their inherent mobility. The resolution recognized that groups accused of terrorism by one state are often considered political movements in other regions, and urged all nations to consider terrorism to be the common enemy of humanity. It also illustrated the connections between terror organizations and international crime syndicates, which constitute a key source of financial and logistical support for many terror groups.

- **Document 33: State Department Report on Foreign Terrorist Organizations**
- **When:** October 5, 2001
- **Where:** Washington, D.C.
- **Significance:** This report demonstrated the U.S. State Department's understanding of hostile groups in the world that should be formally considered terrorist organizations in the immediate aftermath of the September 11 attacks. The designation was key to determining which groups could be targeted by military and intelligence organizations.

DOCUMENT

Background

The Secretary of State designates **Foreign Terrorist Organizations** (FTOs), in consultation with the Attorney General and the Secretary of the Treasury. These designations are undertaken pursuant to the Immigration and Nationality Act, as amended by the Antiterrorism and Effective Death Penalty Act of 1996. FTO designations are valid for two years, after which they must be redesignated or they automatically expire. Redesignation after two years is a positive act and represents a determination by the Secretary of State that the organization has continued to engage in terrorist activity and still meets the criteria specified in law.

- In October 1997, former Secretary of State Madeleine K. Albright approved the designation of the first 30 groups as Foreign Terrorist Organizations.
- In October 1999, Secretary Albright re-certified 27 of these groups' designations but allowed three organizations to drop from the list because their involvement in terrorist activity had ended and they no longer met the criteria for designation.
- Secretary Albright designated one new FTO in 1999 (al Qa'ida) and another in 2000 (Islamic Movement of Uzbekistan).
- Secretary of State Colin L. Powell has designated two new FTOs (Real IRA and AUC) in 2001.
- In October 2001, Secretary Powell re-certified the designation of 26 of the 28 FTOs whose designation was due to expire, and combined two previously designated groups (Kahane Chai and Kach) into one.

Current List of Designated Foreign Terrorist Organizations (as of October 5, 2001)

1. Abu Nidal Organization (ANO)	17. Palestinian Islamic Jihad (PIJ)
2. Abu Sayyaf Group	18. Palestine Liberation Front (PLF)
3. Armed Islamic Group (GIA)	19. Popular Front for the Liberation of Palestine (PFLP)
4. Aum Shinrikyo	
5. Basque Fatherland and Liberty (ETA)	20. PFLP-General Command (PFLP-GC)
6. Gama'a al-Islamiyya (Islamic Group)	21. al-Qa'ida
7. HAMAS (Islamic Resistance Movement)	22. Real IRA
8. Harakat ul-Mujahidin (HUM)	23. Revolutionary Armed Forces of Colombia (FARC)
9. Hizballah (Party of God)	
10. Islamic Movement of Uzbekistan (IMU)	24. Revolutionary Nuclei (formerly ELA)
11. al-Jihad (Egyptian Islamic Jihad)	25. Revolutionary Organization 17 November
12. Kahane Chai (Kach)	26. Revolutionary People's Liberation Army/Front (DHKP/C)
13. Kurdistan Workers' Party (PKK)	
14. Liberation Tigers of Tamil Eelam (LTTE)	27. Shining Path (Sendero Luminoso, SL)
15. Mujahedin-e Khalq Organization (MEK)	28. United Self-Defense Forces of Colombia (AUC)
16. National Liberation Army (ELN)	

Legal Criteria for Designation

1. The organization must be *foreign*.
2. The organization must engage in terrorist activity as defined in Section 212 (a)(3)(B) of the Immigration and Nationality Act.
3. The organization's activities must threaten the security of U.S. nationals *or* the national security (national defense, foreign relations, *or* the economic interests) of the United States.

DID YOU KNOW?

State Sponsors of Terrorism

In addition to maintaining a list of designated foreign terrorist organizations, the U.S. Department of State also maintains a list of state sponsors of terrorism. As of 2016, there are three states on the list: Iran, designated on January 19, 1984; Sudan, designated on August 12, 1993; and Syria, designated on December 29, 1979. The original list, generated on December 29, 1979, included Iraq, Libya, South Yemen, and Syria. Cuba was added in 1982, Iran in 1984, North Korea in 1988, and Sudan in 1993. South Yemen was dropped from the list in 1990 when it merged with Yemen; Iraq in 2004 after a U.S.-led coalition deposed Saddam Hussein; Libya in 2006 after it renounced its pursuit of weapons of mass destruction and its support of terror groups; North Korea in 2008 as part of a nuclear limitations negotiation; and Cuba in 2015 as part of the normalization of relations between the United States and its island neighbor. Inclusion on the list carries significant economic and diplomatic penalties that make trade and even discussions with the United States exceedingly difficult.

Effects of Designation

Legal

1. It is unlawful for a person in the United States or subject to the jurisdiction of the United States to provide funds or other material support to a designated FTO.
2. Representatives and certain members of a designated FTO, if they are aliens, can be denied visas or excluded from the United States.
3. U.S. financial institutions must block funds of designated FTOs and their agents and report the blockage to the Office of Foreign Assets Control, U.S. Department of the Treasury.

Other Effects

1. Deters donations or contributions to named organizations
2. Heightens public awareness and knowledge of terrorist organizations
3. Signals to other governments our concern about named organizations
4. Stigmatizes and isolates designated terrorist organizations internationally

The Process

The Secretary of State makes decisions concerning the designation and redesignation of FTOs following an exhaustive interagency review process in which all evidence of a group's activity, from both classified and open sources, is scrutinized. The State Department, working closely with the Justice and Treasury Departments and the intelligence community, prepares a detailed "administrative record" which documents the terrorist activity of the designated FTO. Seven days before publishing an FTO designation in the Federal Register, the Department of State provides classified notification to Congress.

Under the statute, designations are subject to judicial review. In the event of a challenge to a group's FTO designation in federal court, the U.S. government relies upon the administrative record to defend the Secretary's decision. These administrative records contain intelligence information and are therefore classified.

FTO designations expire in two years unless renewed. The law allows groups to be added at any time following a decision by the Secretary, in consultation with the Attorney General and the Secretary of the Treasury. The Secretary may also revoke designations after determining that there are grounds for doing so and notifying Congress.

Source: U.S. Department of State Archive, http://2001-2009.state.gov/s/ct/rls/rpt/fto/2001/5258.htm.

ANALYSIS

In 1996, the State Department, Treasury Department, and Department of Justice began cooperating to determine official designations of terror organizations. The resulting lists were required by the Antiterrorism and Effective Death Penalty Act of 1996, and the first list was created in 1997. Al Qaeda has appeared continuously on the list since its creation, and several of its regional franchises and affiliates are on the most recent list. Placement upon this list certifies that the U.S. government prohibits American citizens from supporting the organization in question, and that all statutes applying to the prevention of terrorism are in effect regarding the organization. While it is possible to be removed from the list if an organization renounces terror and takes significant steps toward disarmament, the general trend has been for an increase in the number and ferocity of organizations upon the list. Radical Islamic groups have constituted approximately half of the total number of groups on the terrorist organization list for most of its existence.

- **Document 34: President George W. Bush, Address to the Nation Announcing Strikes against Al Qaeda Training Camps and Taliban Military Installations in Afghanistan**
- **When:** October 7, 2001
- **Where:** Washington, D.C.
- **Significance:** In this prime-time address to the nation, the president announced that U.S. military forces had commenced airstrikes in Afghanistan, aiming to topple the Taliban government and destroy Al Qaeda. These strikes were the first publicly acknowledged retaliation for the September 11 attacks.

DOCUMENT

Good afternoon. On my orders, the United States military has begun strikes against Al Qaida terrorist training camps and military installations of the Taliban regime in Afghanistan. These carefully targeted actions are designed to disrupt the use of Afghanistan as a terrorist base of operations and to attack the military capability of the Taliban regime.

We are joined in this operation by our staunch friend, Great Britain. Other close friends, including Canada, Australia, Germany, and France, have pledged forces as the operation unfolds. More than 40 countries in the Middle East, Africa, Europe,

DID YOU KNOW?

The United States and Declarations of War

The United States last formally declared war during World War II, yet it has fought a series of wars in Korea, Vietnam, and the Middle East in the subsequent decades. A formal declaration of war gives the president almost unlimited powers, making it a major foreign policy decision. Under the UN Charter, states are only allowed to declare war upon one another under extremely limited circumstances. This has not stopped the U.S. government from declaring wars in symbolic fashion, such as the War on Poverty, the War on Drugs, and, most recently, the War on Terror.

and across Asia have granted air transit or landing rights. Many more have shared intelligence. We are supported by the collective will of the world.

More than 2 weeks ago, I gave Taliban leaders a series of clear and specific demands: Close terrorist training camps; hand over leaders of the Al Qaida network; and return all foreign nationals, including American citizens, unjustly detained in your country. None of these demands were met. And now the Taliban will pay a price. By destroying camps and disrupting communications, we will make it more difficult for the terror network to train new recruits and coordinate their evil plans.

Initially, the terrorists may burrow deeper into caves and other entrenched hiding places. Our military action is also designed to clear the way for sustained, comprehensive, and relentless operations to drive them out and bring them to justice.

At the same time, the oppressed people of Afghanistan will know the generosity of America and our allies. As we strike military targets, we'll also drop food, medicine, and supplies to the starving and suffering men and women and children of Afghanistan.

The United States of America is a friend to the Afghan people, and we are the friends of almost a billion worldwide who practice the Islamic faith. The United States of America is an enemy of those who aid terrorists and of the barbaric criminals who profane a great religion by committing murder in its name.

This military action is a part of our campaign against terrorism, another front in a war that has already been joined through diplomacy, intelligence, the freezing of financial assets, and the arrests of known terrorists by law enforcement agents in 38 countries. Given the nature and reach of our enemies, we will win this conflict by the patient accumulation of successes, by meeting a series of challenges with determination and will and purpose.

Today we focus on Afghanistan, but the battle is broader. Every nation has a choice to make. In this conflict, there is no neutral ground. If any government sponsors the outlaws and killers of innocents, they have become outlaws and murderers, themselves. And they will take that lonely path at their own peril.

I'm speaking to you today from the Treaty Room of the White House, a place where American Presidents have worked for peace. We're a peaceful nation. Yet, as we have learned so suddenly and so tragically, there can be no peace in a world of sudden terror. In the face of today's new threat, the only way to pursue peace is to pursue those who threaten it.

We did not ask for this mission, but we will fulfill it. The name of today's military operation is Enduring Freedom. We defend not only our precious freedoms but also the freedom of people everywhere to live and raise their children free from fear.

I know many Americans feel fear today. And our Government is taking strong precautions. All law enforcement and intelligence agencies are working aggressively around America, around the world, and around the clock. At my request, many Governors have activated the National Guard to strengthen airport security. We have called up Reserves to reinforce our military capability and strengthen the protection of our homeland.

In the months ahead, our patience will be one of our strengths: patience with the long waits that will result from tighter security; patience and understanding that it will take time to achieve our goals; patience in all the sacrifices that may come.

Today those sacrifices are being made by members of our Armed Forces who now defend us so far from home, and by their proud and worried families. A Commander in Chief sends America's sons and daughters into a battle in a foreign land only after the greatest care and a lot of prayer. We ask a lot of those who wear our uniform. We ask them to leave their loved ones, to travel great distances, to risk injury, even to be prepared to make the ultimate sacrifice of their lives. They are dedicated; they are honorable; they represent the best of our country. And we are grateful.

To all the men and women in our military, every sailor, every soldier, every air-man, every coastguardsman, every marine, I say this: Your mission is defined; your objectives are clear; your goal is just; you have my full confidence; and you will have every tool you need to carry out your duty.

I recently received a touching letter that says a lot about the state of America in these difficult times, a letter from a fourth-grade girl with a father in the military: "As much as I don't want my dad to fight," she wrote, "I'm willing to give him to you."

This is a precious gift, the greatest she could give. This young girl knows what America is all about. Since September 11, an entire generation of young Americans has gained new understanding of the value of freedom and its cost in duty and in sacrifice.

The battle is now joined on many fronts. We will not waver; we will not tire; we will not falter; and we will not fail. Peace and freedom will prevail.

Thank you. May God continue to bless America.

Source: Public Papers of the Presidents of the United States: George W. Bush (2001, Book 2). Washington, D.C.: Government Printing Office, 1201–1202.

ANALYSIS

In this address, President George W. Bush informed the American public that he had ordered a series of airstrikes in Afghanistan, with the goal of destroying Al Qaeda and toppling the Taliban government. In this regard, Bush demonstrated that his threat to consider those who harbor terror organizations was not an idle one. The airstrikes represented the first phase in a war that extended more than a decade and cost the lives of more than 2,000 U.S. military personnel. Traditionally, presidents have not informed the public of the specifics of impending military action, for fear of alerting the enemy, but have offered public speeches announcing the commencement of hostilities once the initial phases of conflict have commenced. In this regard, President Bush's address differed somewhat from recent similar events, in that it was conducted simultaneously with some of the attacks. However, because the Taliban possessed no significant modern air defenses, Bush's remarks did nothing to increase the jeopardy of American service personnel, and preempted media coverage of the same events. The speech is noteworthy in that it not only explained the ongoing military activity, but also continued to expand the narrative of a just war with the United States and its allies fighting an evil enemy to the death, with no room for compromise and no goal but the complete destruction of Al Qaeda and any nation or group that sought to aid it.

- **Document 35: USA PATRIOT Act of 2001 (Public Law 107-56)**
- **When:** October 26, 2001
- **Where:** Washington, D.C.
- **Significance:** The USA PATRIOT Act, passed in the immediate aftermath of the September 11 attacks, provided significant information-gathering powers to U.S. government agencies, but was perceived by many to substantially impede upon privacy rights guaranteed to all American citizens.

DOCUMENT

SUMMARY AS OF:

10/24/2001—Passed House without amendment.

Uniting and Strengthening America by Providing Appropriate Tools Required to Intercept and Obstruct Terrorism (USA PATRIOT ACT) Act of 2001

Title I: Enhancing Domestic Security Against Terrorism—Establishes in the Treasury the Counterterrorism Fund.

(Sec. 102) Expresses the sense of Congress that: (1) the civil rights and liberties of all Americans, including Arab Americans, must be protected, and that every effort must be taken to preserve their safety; (2) any acts of violence or discrimination against any Americans be condemned; and (3) the Nation is called upon to recognize the patriotism of fellow citizens from all ethnic, racial, and religious backgrounds.

(Sec. 103) Authorizes appropriations for the Federal Bureau of Investigation's (FBI) Technical Support Center.

(Sec. 104) Authorizes the Attorney General to request the Secretary of Defense to provide assistance in support of Department of Justice (DOJ) activities relating to the enforcement of Federal criminal code (code) provisions regarding the use of weapons of mass destruction during an emergency situation involving a weapon (currently, chemical weapon) of mass destruction.

(Sec. 105) Requires the Director of the U.S. Secret Service to take actions to develop a national network of electronic crime task forces throughout the United

States to prevent, detect, and investigate various forms of electronic crimes, including potential terrorist attacks against critical infrastructure and financial payment systems.

(Sec. 106) Modifies provisions relating to presidential authority under the International Emergency Powers Act to: (1) authorize the President, when the United States is engaged in armed hostilities or has been attacked by a foreign country or foreign nationals, to confiscate any property subject to U.S. jurisdiction of a foreign person, organization, or country that he determines has planned, authorized, aided, or engaged in such hostilities or attacks (the rights to which shall vest in such agency or person as the President may designate); and (2) provide that, in any judicial review of a determination made under such provisions, if the determination was based on classified information such information may be submitted to the reviewing court ex parte and in camera.

Title II: Enhanced Surveillance Procedures—

Amends the Federal criminal code to authorize the interception of wire, oral, and electronic communications for the production of evidence of: (1) specified chemical weapons or terrorism offenses; and (2) computer fraud and abuse.

(Sec. 203) Amends rule 6 of the Federal Rules of Criminal Procedure (FRCrP) to permit the sharing of grand jury information that involves foreign intelligence or counterintelligence with Federal law enforcement, intelligence, protective, immigration, national defense, or national security officials (such officials), subject to specified requirements.

Authorizes an investigative or law enforcement officer, or an attorney for the Government, who, by authorized means, has obtained knowledge of the contents of any wire, oral, or electronic communication or evidence derived therefrom to disclose such contents to such officials to the extent that such contents include foreign intelligence or counterintelligence.

Directs the Attorney General to establish procedures for the disclosure of information (pursuant to the code and the FRCrP) that identifies a United States person, as defined in the Foreign Intelligence Surveillance Act of 1978 (FISA).

Authorizes the disclosure of foreign intelligence or counterintelligence obtained as part of a criminal investigation to such officials.

(Sec. 204) Clarifies that nothing in code provisions regarding pen registers shall be deemed to affect the acquisition by the Government of specified foreign intelligence information, and that procedures under FISA shall be the exclusive means by which

---

DID YOU KNOW?

Anthrax Attacks of 2001

One week after the September 11 attacks, envelopes laced with anthrax spores were mailed to several media outlets. The spores can cause serious and possibly fatal infections if inhaled or if they come into prolonged contact with human skin. Due to their microscopic size, the spores can also spread quickly through a building's climate control system. The spores are also extremely hardy and difficult to eradicate from a contaminated location. After the initial attacks, two more letters containing anthrax spores were mailed to Senators Tom Daschle and Patrick Leahy in October 2001. The anthrax letters triggered a nationwide panic after it was demonstrated that they could spread to other pieces of mail in the sorting facilities used by the U.S. Postal Service. Five U.S. citizens were killed by the anthrax infections, with 17 more severely wounded. Thousands of U.S. personnel were forced to take anti-infection medicines, and members of the U.S. military were ordered to undergo an anthrax immunization program. The attacks caused the temporary closure of several buildings for decontamination, and major changes in the handling of postal mail. Theories soon proliferated that Al Qaeda was behind the attacks, although no evidence of such links has ever been made public. An immense federal investigation determined the letters were sent by Bruce Ivins, a scientist at the military biowarfare laboratories housed at Fort Detrick, Maryland. Ivins committed suicide in 2008, and the FBI closed its investigation in 2010.

electronic surveillance and the interception of domestic wire and oral (current law) and electronic communications may be conducted.

(Sec. 205) Authorizes the Director of the FBI to expedite the employment of personnel as translators to support counter-terrorism investigations and operations without regard to applicable Federal personnel requirements. Requires: (1) the Director to establish such security requirements as necessary for such personnel; and (2) the Attorney General to report to the House and Senate Judiciary Committees regarding translators.

(Sec. 206) Grants roving surveillance authority under FISA after requiring a court order approving an electronic surveillance to direct any person to furnish necessary information, facilities, or technical assistance in circumstances where the Court finds that the actions of the surveillance target may have the effect of thwarting the identification of a specified person.

(Sec. 207) Increases the duration of FISA surveillance permitted for non-U.S. persons who are agents of a foreign power.

(Sec. 208) Increases (from seven to 11) the number of district court judges designated to hear applications for and grant orders approving electronic surveillance. Requires that no fewer than three reside within 20 miles of the District of Columbia.

(Sec. 209) Permits the seizure of voice-mail messages under a warrant.

(Sec. 210) Expands the scope of subpoenas for records of electronic communications to include the length and types of service utilized, temporarily assigned network addresses, and the means and source of payment (including any credit card or bank account number).

(Sec. 211) Amends the Communications Act of 1934 to permit specified disclosures to Government entities, except for records revealing cable subscriber selection of video programming from a cable operator.

(Sec. 212) Permits electronic communication and remote computing service providers to make emergency disclosures to a governmental entity of customer electronic communications to protect life and limb.

(Sec. 213) Authorizes Federal district courts to allow a delay of required notices of the execution of a warrant if immediate notice may have an adverse result and under other specified circumstances.

(Sec. 214) Prohibits use of a pen register or trap and trace devices in any investigation to protect against international terrorism or clandestine intelligence activities that is conducted solely on the basis of activities protected by the first amendment to the U.S. Constitution.

(Sec. 215) Authorizes the Director of the FBI (or designee) to apply for a court order requiring production of certain business records for foreign intelligence and international terrorism investigations. Requires the Attorney General to report to the House and Senate Intelligence and Judiciary Committees semi-annually.

(Sec. 216) Amends the code to: (1) require a trap and trace device to restrict recoding or decoding so as not to include the contents of a wire or electronic communication; (2) apply a court order for a pen register or trap and trace devices to any person or entity providing wire or electronic communication service in the United States whose assistance may facilitate execution of the order; (3) require specified records kept on any pen register or trap and trace device on a packet-switched data network of a provider of electronic communication service to the public; and (4) allow a trap and trace device to identify the source (but not the contents) of a wire or electronic communication.

(Sec. 217) Makes it lawful to intercept the wire or electronic communication of a computer trespasser in certain circumstances.

(Sec. 218) Amends FISA to require an application for an electronic surveillance order or search warrant to certify that a significant purpose (currently, the sole or main purpose) of the surveillance is to obtain foreign intelligence information.

(Sec. 219) Amends rule 41 of the FRCrP to permit Federal magistrate judges in any district in which terrorism-related activities may have occurred to issue search warrants for searches within or outside the district.

(Sec. 220) Provides for nationwide service of search warrants for electronic evidence.

(Sec. 221) Amends the Trade Sanctions Reform and Export Enhancement Act of 2000 to extend trade sanctions to the territory of Afghanistan controlled by the Taliban.

Title IV: Protecting the Border
Subtitle B: Enhanced Immigration Provisions—Amends the Immigration and Nationality Act to broaden the scope of aliens ineligible for admission or deportable due to terrorist activities to include an alien who: (1) is a representative of a political, social, or similar group whose political endorsement of terrorist acts undermines U.S. antiterrorist efforts; (2) has used a position of prominence to endorse terrorist activity, or to persuade others to support such activity in a way that undermines U.S. antiterrorist efforts (or the child or spouse of such an alien under specified circumstances); or (3) has been associated with a terrorist organization and intends to engage in threatening activities while in the United States.

(Sec. 411) Includes within the definition of "terrorist activity" the use of any weapon or dangerous device.
    Redefines "engage in terrorist activity" to mean, in an individual capacity or as a member of an organization, to: (1) commit or to incite to commit, under circumstances indicating an intention to cause death or serious bodily injury, a terrorist activity; (2) prepare or plan a terrorist activity; (3) gather information on potential targets for terrorist activity; (4) solicit funds or other things of value for a terrorist activity or a terrorist organization (with an exception for lack of knowledge); (5) solicit any individual to engage in prohibited conduct or for terrorist organization membership (with an exception for lack of knowledge); or (6) commit an act

that the actor knows, or reasonably should know, affords material support, including a safe house, transportation, communications, funds, transfer of funds or other material financial benefit, false documentation or identification, weapons (including chemical, biological, or radiological weapons), explosives, or training for the commission of a terrorist activity; to any individual who the actor knows or reasonably should know has committed or plans to commit a terrorist activity; or to a terrorist organization (with an exception for lack of knowledge).

Defines "terrorist organization" as a group: (1) designated under the Immigration and Nationality Act or by the Secretary of State; or (2) a group of two or more individuals, whether related or not, which engages in terrorist-related activities.

Provides for the retroactive application of amendments under this Act. Stipulates that an alien shall not be considered inadmissible or deportable because of a relationship to an organization that was not designated as a terrorist organization prior to enactment of this Act. States that the amendments under this section shall apply to all aliens in exclusion or deportation proceedings on or after the date of enactment of this Act.

Directs the Secretary of State to notify specified congressional leaders seven days prior to designating an organization as a terrorist organization. Provides for organization redesignation or revocation.

(Sec. 412) Provides for mandatory detention until removal from the United States (regardless of any relief from removal) of an alien certified by the Attorney General as a suspected terrorist or threat to national security. Requires release of such alien after seven days if removal proceedings have not commenced, or the alien has not been charged with a criminal offense. Authorizes detention for additional periods of up to six months of an alien not likely to be deported in the reasonably foreseeable future only if release will threaten U.S. national security or the safety of the community or any person. Limits judicial review to habeas corpus proceedings in the U.S. Supreme Court, the U.S. Court of Appeals for the District of Columbia, or any district court with jurisdiction to entertain a habeas corpus petition. Restricts to the U.S. Court of Appeals for the District of Columbia the right of appeal of any final order by a circuit or district judge.

(Sec. 413) Authorizes the Secretary of State, on a reciprocal basis, to share criminal- and terrorist-related visa lookout information with foreign governments.

(Sec. 414) Declares the sense of Congress that the Attorney General should: (1) fully implement the integrated entry and exit data system for airports, seaports, and land border ports of entry with all deliberate speed; and (2) begin immediately establishing the Integrated Entry and Exit Data System Task Force. Authorizes appropriations.

Requires the Attorney General and the Secretary of State, in developing the integrated entry and exit data system, to focus on the use of biometric technology and the development of tamper-resistant documents readable at ports of entry.

(Sec. 415) Amends the Immigration and Naturalization Service Data Management Improvement Act of 2000 to include the Office of Homeland Security in the Integrated Entry and Exit Data System Task Force.

(Sec. 416) Directs the Attorney General to implement fully and expand the foreign student monitoring program to include other approved educational institutions like air flight, language training, or vocational schools.

(Sec. 417) Requires audits and reports on implementation of the mandate for machine readable passports.

(Sec. 418) Directs the Secretary of State to: (1) review how consular officers issue visas to determine if consular shopping is a problem; and (2) if it is a problem, take steps to address it, and report on them to Congress.

Title V: Removing Obstacles to Investigating Terrorism—Authorizes the Attorney General to pay rewards from available funds pursuant to public advertisements for assistance to DOJ to combat terrorism and defend the Nation against terrorist acts, in accordance with procedures and regulations established or issued by the Attorney General, subject to specified conditions, including a prohibition against any such reward of $250,000 or more from being made or offered without the personal approval of either the Attorney General or the President.

(Sec. 502) Amends the State Department Basic Authorities Act of 1956 to modify the Department of State rewards program to authorize rewards for information leading to: (1) the dismantling of a terrorist organization in whole or significant part; and (2) the identification or location of an individual who holds a key leadership position in a terrorist organization. Raises the limit on rewards if the Secretary State determines that a larger sum is necessary to combat terrorism or defend the Nation against terrorist acts.

(Sec. 503) Amends the DNA Analysis Backlog Elimination Act of 2000 to qualify a Federal terrorism offense for collection of DNA for identification.

(Sec. 504) Amends FISA to authorize consultation among Federal law enforcement officers regarding information acquired from an electronic surveillance or physical search in terrorism and related investigations or protective measures.

(Sec. 505) Allows the FBI to request telephone toll and transactional records, financial records, and consumer reports in any investigation to protect against international terrorism or clandestine intelligence activities only if the investigation is not conducted solely on the basis of activities protected by the first amendment to the U.S. Constitution.

(Sec. 506) Revises U.S. Secret Service jurisdiction with respect to fraud and related activity in connection with computers. Grants the FBI primary authority to investigate specified fraud and computer related activity for cases involving espionage, foreign counter-intelligence, information protected against unauthorized disclosure for reasons of national defense or foreign relations, or restricted data, except for offenses affecting Secret Service duties.

(Sec. 507) Amends the General Education Provisions Act and the National Education Statistics Act of 1994 to provide for disclosure of educational records to the Attorney General in a terrorism investigation or prosecution.

Title VIII: Strengthening the Criminal Laws Against Terrorism—Amends the Federal criminal code to prohibit specific terrorist acts or otherwise destructive, disruptive, or violent acts against mass transportation vehicles, ferries, providers, employees, passengers, or operating systems.

(Sec. 802) Amends the Federal criminal code to: (1) revise the definition of "international terrorism" to include activities that appear to be intended to affect the conduct of government by mass destruction; and (2) define "domestic terrorism" as activities that occur primarily within U.S. jurisdiction, that involve criminal acts dangerous to human life, and that appear to be intended to intimidate or coerce a civilian population, to influence government policy by intimidation or coercion, or to affect government conduct by mass destruction, assassination, or kidnapping.

(Sec. 803) Prohibits harboring any person knowing or having reasonable grounds to believe that such person has committed or to be about to commit a terrorism offense.

(Sec. 804) Establishes Federal jurisdiction over crimes committed at U.S. facilities abroad.

(Sec. 805) Applies the prohibitions against providing material support for terrorism to offenses outside of the United States.

(Sec. 806) Subjects to civil forfeiture all assets, foreign or domestic, of terrorist organizations.

(Sec. 808) Expands: (1) the offenses over which the Attorney General shall have primary investigative jurisdiction under provisions governing acts of terrorism transcending national boundaries; and (2) the offenses included within the definition of the Federal crime of terrorism.

(Sec. 809) Provides that there shall be no statute of limitations for certain terrorism offenses if the commission of such an offense resulted in, or created a foreseeable risk of, death or serious bodily injury to another person.

(Sec. 810) Provides for alternative maximum penalties for specified terrorism crimes.

(Sec. 811) Makes: (1) the penalties for attempts and conspiracies the same as those for terrorism offenses; (2) the supervised release terms for offenses with terrorism predicates any term of years or life; and (3) specified terrorism crimes Racketeer Influenced and Corrupt Organizations statute predicates.

(Sec. 814) Revises prohibitions and penalties regarding fraud and related activity in connection with computers to include specified cyber-terrorism offenses.

(Sec. 816) Directs the Attorney General to establish regional computer forensic laboratories, and to support existing laboratories, to develop specified cyber-security capabilities.

(Sec. 817) Prescribes penalties for knowing possession in certain circumstances of biological agents, toxins, or delivery systems, especially by certain restricted persons.

Title IX: Improved Intelligence—Amends the National Security Act of 1947 to require the Director of Central Intelligence (DCI) to establish requirements and priorities for foreign intelligence collected under the Foreign Intelligence Surveillance Act of 1978 and to provide assistance to the Attorney General (AG) to ensure that information derived from electronic surveillance or physical searches is disseminated for efficient and effective foreign intelligence purposes. Requires the inclusion of international terrorist activities within the scope of foreign intelligence under such Act.

(Sec. 903) Expresses the sense of Congress that officers and employees of the intelligence community should establish and maintain intelligence relationships to acquire information on terrorists and terrorist organizations.

(Sec. 904) Authorizes deferral of the submission to Congress of certain reports on intelligence and intelligence-related matters until: (1) February 1, 2002; or (2) a date after February 1, 2002, if the official involved certifies that preparation and submission on February 1, 2002, will impede the work of officers or employees engaged in counterterrorism activities. Requires congressional notification of any such deferral.

(Sec. 905) Requires the AG or the head of any other Federal department or agency with law enforcement responsibilities to expeditiously disclose to the DCI any foreign intelligence acquired in the course of a criminal investigation.

(Sec. 906) Requires the AG, DCI, and Secretary of the Treasury to jointly report to Congress on the feasibility and desirability of reconfiguring the Foreign Asset Tracking Center and the Office of Foreign Assets Control to provide for the analysis and dissemination of foreign intelligence relating to the financial capabilities and resources of international terrorist organizations.

(Sec. 907) Requires the DCI to report to the appropriate congressional committees on the establishment and maintenance of the National Virtual Translation Center for timely and accurate translation of foreign intelligence for elements of the intelligence community.

(Sec. 908) Requires the AG to provide a program of training to Government officials regarding the identification and use of foreign intelligence.

Source: The preceding summary of the USA PATRIOT Act of 2001 is courtesy of the Congressional Research Service and can be found at the Library of Congress website, http://thomas.loc.gov/cgi-bin/bdquery/z?d107:HR03162:@@@D&summ2 =m&. The full text of the USA PATRIOT Act of 2001 is available at http://www .gpo.gov/fdsys/pkg/PLAW-107publ56/pdf/PLAW-107publ56.pdf.

ANALYSIS

More than anything, the USA PATRIOT Act was designed to remove barriers to counterterrorism activities that had arisen through bureaucratic inefficiencies, poor cooperation between intelligence and law enforcement agencies, and time-consuming or expensive methods of intercepting communications of terrorist suspects. However, there were critics who claimed that the act gave the federal government unprecedented powers for surveillance without sufficient judicial oversight. One of the most effective aspects of the act was that it significantly tightened controls upon the international transfer of cash and financial instruments, and it had a major effect upon money-laundering practices. In the years following its passage, a number of civil rights groups brought lawsuits against provisions of the act, although the majority of the provisions remained intact. In March 2006, Congress made most of the intelligence collection aspects of the USA PATRIOT Act permanent, eliminating the sunset provision that accompanied the original legislation. This renewal made clear that congressional leaders believed the act had proven effective in the War on Terror, and also that the war was likely to continue for the foreseeable future.

- **Document 36: President George W. Bush, Remarks to the United Nations General Assembly**
- **When:** November 10, 2001
- **Where:** United Nations, New York City
- **Significance:** After commencing combat operations in Afghanistan against the Taliban and Al Qaeda, President Bush sought to rally international support not just to fight against Al Qaeda, but also to end the scourge of terrorism through global cooperation.

DOCUMENT

Thank you, Mr. Secretary-General, Mr. President, distinguished delegates, and ladies and gentlemen. We meet in a hall devoted to peace, in a city scarred by violence, in a Nation awakened to danger, in a world uniting for a long struggle. Every civilized nation here today is resolved to keep the most basic commitment of civilization: We will defend ourselves and our future against terror and lawless violence.

The United Nations was founded in this cause. In a Second World War, we learned there is no isolation from evil. We affirmed that some crimes are so terrible they offend humanity, itself. And we resolved that the aggressions and ambitions of the wicked must be opposed early, decisively, and collectively, before they threaten us all. That evil has returned, and that cause is renewed.

A few miles from here, many thousands still lie in a tomb of rubble. Tomorrow the Secretary-General, the President of the General Assembly, and I will visit that site, where the names of every nation and region that lost citizens will be read aloud. If we were to read the names of every person who died, it would take more than 3 hours.

Those names include a citizen of Gambia whose wife spent their fourth wedding anniversary, September the 12th, searching in vain for her husband. Those names include a man who supported his wife in Mexico, sending home money every week. Those names include a young Pakistani who prayed toward Mecca five times a day and died that day trying to save others.

The suffering of September the 11th was inflicted on people of many faiths and many nations. All of the victims, including Muslims, were killed with equal indifference and equal satisfaction by the terrorist leaders. The terrorists are violating the tenets of every religion, including the one they invoke.

Last week the Sheikh of Al-Azhar University, the world's oldest Islamic institution of higher learning, declared that terrorism is a disease and that Islam prohibits killing innocent civilians. The terrorists call their cause holy, yet they fund it with drug dealing. They encourage murder and suicide in the name of a great faith that forbids both. They dare to ask God's

> **DID YOU KNOW?**
>
> **The Economic Costs of September 11**
>
> The September 11 attacks cost Al Qaeda approximately $500,000. In exchange for this relatively modest sum, the attacks cost U.S. corporations and government entities over $100 billion. In addition, the subsequent wars in Afghanistan and Iraq have cost at least $2 trillion in immediate costs, with some estimates much higher. Increased personnel and veterans' care from the wars will likely at least double the final tab for the two wars. A conservative estimate places the Al Qaeda rate of return at roughly $10 million in damages for every dollar spent by the terror organization. In human costs, the 19 hijackers killed nearly 3,000 victims in the attacks and subsequent building collapses, a ratio of more than 1:150.

blessing as they set out to kill innocent men, women, and children. But the God of Isaac and Ishmael would never answer such a prayer. And a murderer is not a martyr; he is just a murderer.

Time is passing. Yet, for the United States of America, there will be no forgetting September the 11th. We will remember every rescuer who died in honor. We will remember every family that lives in grief. We will remember the fire and ash, the last phone calls, the funerals of the children.

And the people of my country will remember those who have plotted against us. We are learning their names. We are coming to know their faces. There is no corner of the Earth distant or dark enough to protect them. However long it takes, their hour of justice will come.

Every nation has a stake in this cause. As we meet, the terrorists are planning more murder—perhaps in my country, or perhaps in yours. They kill because they aspire to dominate. They seek to overthrow governments and destabilize entire regions. Last week, anticipating this meeting of the General Assembly, they denounced the United Nations. They called our Secretary-General a criminal and condemned all Arab nations here as traitors to Islam.

Few countries meet their exacting standards of brutality and oppression. Every other country is a potential target. And all the world faces the most horrifying prospect of all: These same terrorists are searching for weapons of mass destruction, the tools to turn their hatred into holocaust. They can be expected to use chemical, biological, and nuclear weapons the moment they are capable of doing so. No hint of conscience would prevent it.

This threat cannot be ignored. This threat cannot be appeased. Civilization, itself, the civilization we share, is threatened. History will record our response and judge or justify every nation in this hall.

The civilized world is now responding. We act to defend ourselves and deliver our children from a future of fear. We choose the dignity of life over a culture of death.

We choose lawful change and civil disagreement over coercion, subversion, and chaos. These commitments—hope and order, law and life—unite people across cultures and continents. Upon these commitments depend all peace and progress. For these commitments, we are determined to fight.

The United Nations has risen to this responsibility. On the 12th of September, these buildings opened for emergency meetings of the General Assembly and the Security Council. Before the Sun had set, these attacks on the world stood condemned by the world. And I want to thank you for this strong and principled stand.

I also thank the Arab and Islamic countries that have condemned terrorist murder. Many of you have seen the destruction of terror in your own lands. The terrorists are increasingly isolated by their own hatred and extremism. They cannot hide behind Islam. The authors of mass murder and their allies have no place in any culture and no home in any faith.

The conspiracies of terror are being answered by an expanding global coalition. Not every nation will be a part of every action against the enemy. But every nation in our coalition has duties. These duties can be demanding, as we in America are learning. We have already made adjustments in our laws and in our daily lives. We're taking new measures to investigate terror and to protect against threats.

The leaders of all nations must now carefully consider their responsibilities and their future. Terrorist groups like Al Qaida depend upon the aid or indifference of governments. They need the support of a financial infrastructure and safe havens to train and plan and hide.

Some nations want to play their part in the fight against terror, but tell us they lack the means to enforce their laws and control their borders. We stand ready to help. Some governments still turn a blind eye to the terrorists, hoping the threat will pass them by. They are mistaken. And some governments, while pledging to uphold the principles of the U.N., have cast their lot with the terrorists. They support them and harbor them, and they will find that their welcomed guests are parasites that will weaken them and eventually consume them. For every regime that sponsors terror, there is a price to be paid. And it will be paid. The allies of terror are equally guilty of murder and equally accountable to justice.

The Taliban are now learning this lesson. That regime and the terrorists who support it are now virtually indistinguishable. Together, they promote terror abroad and impose a reign of terror on the Afghan people. Women are executed in Kabul's soccer stadium. They can be beaten for wearing socks that are too thin. Men are jailed for missing prayer meetings.

The United States, supported by many nations, is bringing justice to the terrorists in Afghanistan. We're making progress against military targets, and that is our objective. Unlike the enemy, we seek to minimize, not maximize, the loss of innocent life.

I'm proud of the honorable conduct of the American military. And my country grieves for all the suffering the Taliban have brought upon Afghanistan, including the terrible burden of war. The Afghan people do not deserve their present rulers. Years of Taliban misrule have brought nothing but misery and starvation. Even before this current crisis, 4 million Afghans depended on food from the United

States and other nations, and millions of Afghans were refugees from Taliban oppression.

I make this promise to all the victims of that regime: The Taliban's days of harboring terrorists and dealing in heroin and brutalizing women are drawing to a close. And when that regime is gone, the people of Afghanistan will say with the rest of the world, "Good riddance."

I can promise, too, that America will join the world in helping the people of Afghanistan rebuild their country. Many nations, including mine, are sending food and medicine to help Afghans through the winter. America has airdropped over 1.3 million packages of rations into Afghanistan. Just this week, we airlifted 20,000 blankets and over 200 tons of provisions into the region. We continue to provide humanitarian aid, even while the Taliban try to steal the food we send.

More help eventually will be needed. The United States will work closely with the United Nations and development banks to reconstruct Afghanistan after hostilities there have ceased and the Taliban are no longer in control. And the United States will work with the U.N. to support a post-Taliban Government that represents all of the Afghan people.

In this war of terror, each of us must answer for what we have done or what we have left undone. After tragedy, there is a time for sympathy and condolence. And my country has been very grateful for both. The memorials and vigils around the world will not be forgotten. But the time for sympathy has now passed; the time for action has now arrived.

The most basic obligations in this new conflict have already been defined by the United Nations. On September the 28th, the Security Council adopted Resolution 1373. Its requirements are clear: Every United Nations member has a responsibility to crack down on terrorist financing. We must pass all necessary laws in our own countries to allow the confiscation of terrorist assets. We must apply those laws to every financial institution in every nation.

We have a responsibility to share intelligence and coordinate the efforts of law enforcement. If you know something, tell us. If we know something, we'll tell you. And when we find the terrorists, we must work together to bring them to justice. We have a responsibility to deny any sanctuary, safe haven, or transit to terrorists. Every known terrorist camp must be shut down, its operators apprehended, and evidence of their arrest presented to the United Nations. We have a responsibility to deny weapons to terrorists and to actively prevent private citizens from providing them.

These obligations are urgent, and they are binding on every nation with a place in this chamber. Many governments are taking these obligations seriously, and my country appreciates it. Yet, even beyond Resolution 1373, more is required, and more is expected of our coalition against terror.

We're asking for a comprehensive commitment to this fight. We must unite in opposing all terrorists, not just some of them. In this world, there are good causes and bad causes, and we may disagree on where that line is drawn. Yet, there is no such thing as a good terrorist. No national aspiration, no remembered wrong can ever justify the deliberate murder of the innocent. Any government that rejects this principle, trying to pick and choose its terrorist friends, will know the consequences.

We must speak the truth about terror. Let us never tolerate outrageous conspiracy theories concerning the attacks of September the 11th, malicious lies that attempt to shift the blame away from the terrorists, themselves, away from the guilty. To inflame ethnic hatred is to advance the cause of terror.

The war against terror must not serve as an excuse to persecute ethnic and religious minorities in any country. Innocent people must be allowed to live their own lives, by their own customs, under their own religion. And every nation must have avenues for the peaceful expression of opinion and dissent. When these avenues are closed, the temptation to speak through violence grows.

We must press on with our agenda for peace and prosperity in every land. My country is pledged to encouraging development and expanding trade. My country is pledged to investing in education and combating AIDS and other infectious diseases around the world. Following September 11th, these pledges are even more important. In our struggle against hateful groups that exploit poverty and despair, we must offer an alternative of opportunity and hope.

The American Government also stands by its commitment to a just peace in the Middle East. We are working toward a day when two states, Israel and Palestine, live peacefully together within secure and recognized borders as called for by the Security Council resolutions. We will do all in our power to bring both parties back into negotiations. But peace will only come when all have sworn off forever incitement, violence, and terror.

And finally, this struggle is a defining moment for the United Nations, itself. And the world needs its principled leadership. It undermines the credibility of this great institution, for example, when the Commission on Human Rights offers seats to the world's most persistent violators of human rights. The United Nations depends, above all, on its moral authority, and that authority must be preserved.

The steps I described will not be easy. For all nations, they will require effort. For some nations, they will require great courage. Yet, the cost of inaction is far greater. The only alternative to victory is a nightmare world where every city is a potential killing field.

As I've told the American people, freedom and fear are at war. We face enemies that hate not our policies but our existence, the tolerance of openness and creative culture that defines us. But the outcome of this conflict is certain: There is a current in history, and it runs toward freedom. Our enemies resent it and dismiss it. But the dreams of mankind are defined by liberty: the natural right to create and build and worship and live in dignity. When men and women are released from oppression and isolation, they find fulfillment and hope, and they leave poverty by the millions.

These aspirations are lifting up the peoples of Europe, Asia, Africa, and the Americas, and they can lift up all of the Islamic world.

We stand for the permanent hopes of humanity, and those hopes will not be denied. We're confident, too, that history has an author who fills time and eternity with His purpose. We know that evil is real, but good will prevail against it. This is the teaching of many faiths, and in that assurance we gain strength for a long journey.

It is our task, the task of this generation, to provide the response to aggression and terror. We have no other choice, because there is no other peace.

We did not ask for this mission, yet there is honor in history's call. We have a chance to write the story of our times, a story of courage defeating cruelty and light overcoming darkness. This calling is worthy of any life and worthy of every nation. So let us go forward, confident, determined, and unafraid.

Thank you very much.

Source: Public Papers of the Presidents of the United States: George W. Bush (2001, Book 2), Washington, D.C.: Government Printing Office, 1375–1379.

ANALYSIS

As President George W. Bush had previously established in addresses to the American public, he viewed the struggle between the United States and terrorism as a fight between freedom and fear, good and evil, the civilized world and barbarity. In his speech to the United Nations, he called upon the states of the world to unite with America in working to eliminate terror organizations and end the practice of terrorism. His rhetorical flourishes included a reminder that the victims of the September 11 attacks were not solely Americans, a list of all the ways the United States had recently worked to help the citizens of the world, and a thinly veiled threat that nations found to be cooperating with Al Qaeda, or even tolerating its presence within their borders, faced the same military destruction that had been hitting the Taliban in Afghanistan for the previous five weeks. His address galvanized some nations, particularly the Western democracies, but it also served a very polarizing function, starkly demonstrating that the United States would tolerate no middle ground in the fight against terrorism.

- **Document 37: Detention, Treatment, and Trial of Certain Noncitizens in the War against Terrorism**
- **When:** November 13, 2001
- **Where:** Washington, D.C.
- **Significance:** This military order issued by President George W. Bush set the parameters upon how Al Qaeda members, and members of affiliated terror organizations, were to be captured and detained by U.S. military forces. It established that for the burgeoning conflict with Al Qaeda, any disposition of prisoners would be through military rather than law enforcement channels.

DOCUMENT

By the authority vested in me as President and as Commander in Chief of the Armed Forces of the United States by the Constitution and the laws of the United States of America, including the Authorization for Use of Military Force Joint

DID YOU KNOW?

Ward Churchill and Academic Freedom

In 2001, Professor Ward Churchill chaired the Department of Ethnic Studies at the University of Colorado. In the weeks after the September 11 attacks, he penned an extremely controversial essay, "Some People Push Back: On the Justice of Roosting Chickens." When he distributed it on the Internet, it triggered a firestorm of criticism and calls for his termination by the university, even though he claimed protection under the tenure system. In the essay, Churchill argued that the September 11 attacks were a logical, acceptable, and entirely foreseeable consequence of U.S. military and economic activities in the Middle East. He referred to the Pentagon victims as legitimate targets due to their participation in the military-industrial complex. The World Trade Center victims, whom he dubbed "little Eichmanns," deserved their fate, in his view, because of American financial preeminence in the world and their role in forcing other nations to live under U.S. domination. Churchill was eventually terminated from the university after an investigation determined that he was guilty of academic dishonesty in other published works. He sued for wrongful termination and eventually won the lawsuit, but the judge refused to order the university to reinstate him to his position, and awarded Churchill damages of $1. The American Civil Liberties Union and the American Association of University Professors decried the termination as an attack upon academic freedom, further reinforcing the perception among many U.S. citizens that university faculty are too far divorced from the mainstream and should not be guaranteed lifetime employment through the tenure process.

Resolution (Public Law 107-40, 115 Stat. 224) and sections 821 and 836 of title 10, United States Code, it is hereby ordered as follows:

Section 1. Findings.

(a) International terrorists, including members of al Qaida, have carried out attacks on United States diplomatic and military personnel and facilities abroad and on citizens and property within the United States on a scale that has created a state of armed conflict that requires the use of the United States Armed Forces.

(b) In light of grave acts of terrorism and threats of terrorism, including the terrorist attacks on September 11, 2001, on the headquarters of the United States Department of Defense in the national capital region, on the World Trade Center in New York, and on civilian aircraft such as in Pennsylvania, I proclaimed a national emergency on September 14, 2001 (Proc. 7463, Declaration of National Emergency by Reason of Certain Terrorist Attacks).

(c) Individuals acting alone and in concert involved in international terrorism possess both the capability and the intention to undertake further terrorist attacks against the United States that, if not detected and prevented, will cause mass deaths, mass injuries, and massive destruction of property, and may place at risk the continuity of the operations of the United States Government.

(d) The ability of the United States to protect the United States and its citizens, and to help its allies and other cooperating nations protect their nations and their citizens, from such further terrorist attacks depends in significant part upon using the United States Armed Forces to identify terrorists and those who support them, to disrupt their activities, and to eliminate their ability to conduct or support such attacks.

(e) To protect the United States and its citizens, and for the effective conduct of military operations and prevention of terrorist attacks, it is necessary for individuals subject to this order pursuant to section 2 hereof to be detained, and, when tried, to be tried for violations of the laws of war and other applicable laws by military tribunals.

(f) Given the danger to the safety of the United States and the nature of international terrorism, and to the extent provided by and under this order, I find consistent with section 836 of title 10, United States Code, that it is not practicable to apply in military commissions under this order the principles of law and the rules of evidence generally recognized in the trial of criminal cases in the United States district courts.

(g) Having fully considered the magnitude of the potential deaths, injuries, and property destruction that would result from potential acts of terrorism against the United States, and the probability that such acts will occur, I have determined that an extraordinary emergency exists for national defense purposes, that this emergency constitutes an urgent and compelling government interest, and that issuance of this order is necessary to meet the emergency.

Sec. 2. *Definition and Policy.*

(a) The term "individual subject to this order" shall mean any individual who is not a United States citizen with respect to whom I determine from time to time in writing that: (1) there is reason to believe that such individual, at the relevant times,

(i) is or was a member of the organization known as al Qaida;

(ii) has engaged in, aided or abetted, or conspired to commit, acts of international terrorism, or acts in preparation therefor, that have caused, threaten to cause, or have as their aim to cause, injury to or adverse effects on the United States, its citizens, national security, foreign policy, or economy; or

(iii) has knowingly harbored one or more individuals described in subparagraphs (i) or (ii) of subsection 2(a)(1) of this order; and

(2) it is in the interest of the United States that such individual be subject to this order.

(b) It is the policy of the United States that the Secretary of Defense shall take all necessary measures to ensure that any individual subject to this order is detained in accordance with section 3, and, if the individual is to be tried, that such individual is tried only in accordance with section 4.

(c) It is further the policy of the United States that any individual subject to this order who is not already under the control of the Secretary of Defense but who is under the control of any other officer or agent of the United States or any State shall, upon delivery of a copy of such written determination to such officer or agent, forthwith be placed under the control of the Secretary of Defense.

Sec. 3. *Detention Authority of the Secretary of Defense.* Any individual subject to this order shall be—

(a) detained at an appropriate location designated by the Secretary of Defense outside or within the United States;

(b) treated humanely, without any adverse distinction based on race, color, religion, gender, birth, wealth, or any similar criteria;

(c) afforded adequate food, drinking water, shelter, clothing, and medical treatment;

(d) allowed the free exercise of religion consistent with the requirements of such detention; and

(e) detained in accordance with such other conditions as the Secretary of Defense may prescribe.

Sec. 4. *Authority of the Secretary of Defense Regarding Trials of Individuals Subject to this Order.*

(a) Any individual subject to this order shall, when tried, be tried by military commission for any and all offenses triable by military commission that such individual is alleged to have committed, and may be punished in accordance with the penalties provided under applicable law, including life imprisonment or death.

(b) As a military function and in light of the findings in section 1, including subsection (f) thereof, the Secretary of Defense shall issue such orders and regulations, including orders for the appointment of one or more military commissions, as may be necessary to carry out subsection (a) of this section.

(c) Orders and regulations issued under subsection (b) of this section shall include, but not be limited to, rules for the conduct of the proceedings of military commissions, including pretrial, trial, and post-trial procedures, modes of proof, issuance of process, and qualifications of attorneys, which shall at a minimum provide for—

(1) military commissions to sit at any time and any place, consistent with such guidance regarding time and place as the Secretary of Defense may provide;

(2) a full and fair trial, with the military commission sitting as the triers of both fact and law;

(3) admission of such evidence as would, in the opinion of the presiding officer of the military commission (or instead, if any other member of the commission so requests at the time the presiding officer renders that opinion, the opinion of the commission rendered at that time by a majority of the commission), have probative value to a reasonable person;

(4) in a manner consistent with the protection of information classified or classifiable under Executive Order 12958 of April 17, 1995, as amended, or any successor Executive Order, protected by statute or rule from unauthorized disclosure, or otherwise protected by law, (A) the handling of, admission into evidence of, and access to materials and information, and (B) the conduct, closure of, and access to proceedings;

(5) conduct of the prosecution by one or more attorneys designated by the Secretary of Defense and conduct of the defense by attorneys for the individual subject to this order;

(6) conviction only upon the concurrence of two-thirds of the members of the commission present at the time of the vote, a majority being present;

(7) sentencing only upon the concurrence of two-thirds of the members of the commission present at the time of the vote, a majority being present; and

(8) submission of the record of the trial, including any conviction or sentence, for review and final decision by me or by the Secretary of Defense if so designated by me for that purpose.

Sec. 5. *Obligation of Other Agencies to Assist the Secretary of Defense.*

Departments, agencies, entities, and officers of the United States shall, to the maximum extent permitted by law, provide to the Secretary of Defense such assistance as he may request to implement this order.

Sec. 6. *Additional Authorities of the Secretary of Defense.*

(a) As a military function and in light of the findings in section 1, the Secretary of Defense shall issue such orders and regulations as may be necessary to carry out any of the provisions of this order.

(b) The Secretary of Defense may perform any of his functions or duties, and may exercise any of the powers provided to him under this order (other than under section 4(c)(8) hereof) in accordance with section 113(d) of title 10, United States Code.

Sec. 7. *Relationship to Other Law and Forums.*

(a) Nothing in this order shall be construed to—

(1) authorize the disclosure of state secrets to any person not otherwise authorized to have access to them;

(2) limit the authority of the President as Commander in Chief of the Armed Forces or the power of the President to grant reprieves and pardons; or

(3) limit the lawful authority of the Secretary of Defense, any military commander, or any other officer or agent of the United States or of any State to detain or try any person who is not an individual subject to this order.

(b) With respect to any individual subject to this order—

(1) military tribunals shall have exclusive jurisdiction with respect to offenses by the individual; and

(2) the individual shall not be privileged to seek any remedy or maintain any proceeding, directly or indirectly, or to have any such remedy or proceeding sought on the individual's behalf, in (i) any court of the United States, or any State thereof, (ii) any court of any foreign nation, or (iii) any international tribunal.

(c) This order is not intended to and does not create any right, benefit, or privilege, substantive or procedural, enforceable at law or equity by any party, against the United States, its departments, agencies, or other entities, its officers or employees, or any other person.

(d) For purposes of this order, the term "State" includes any State, district, territory, or possession of the United States.

(e) I reserve the authority to direct the Secretary of Defense, at any time hereafter, to transfer to a governmental authority control of any individual subject to this order. Nothing in this order shall be construed to limit the authority of any such governmental authority to prosecute any individual for whom control is transferred.

George W. Bush
The White House,
November 13, 2001

Source: Weekly Compilation of Presidential Documents, Vol. 37, Issue 46 (November 19, 2001), 1665–1668. Available at http://www.gpo.gov/fdsys/pkg/WCPD -2001-11-19/content-detail.html.

ANALYSIS

During wartime, presidents have almost always sought to expand the power of their office, often for the sake of expediency in prosecuting a conflict. In this regard, President George W. Bush was no different from the likes of Abraham Lincoln and Franklin Delano Roosevelt. This military order firmly established that the Department of Defense would take the lead in combating terrorism, and other federal agencies would be required to cooperate with military initiatives. In addition to providing the combat power necessary to destroy Al Qaeda, the Department of

Defense also became the primary detaining authority for enemies captured during the conflict. Those captives would not be considered civil prisoners; hence, they could expect no right to have legal representation or to launch lawsuits or other legal actions challenging their detention. Although held by the military, they would not be considered prisoners of war, and thus the Geneva Conventions Relative to the Treatment of Prisoners of War (1949) did not apply to these individuals. Although the military order calls for humane treatment, and nondiscrimination regarding race, religion, or country of origin, it makes no provision for the release of a prisoner captured in error. Instead, it essentially created a legal limbo for anyone captured by the military forces of the United States, who could theoretically be held indefinitely, or at least as long as the conflict with Al Qaeda continued. The U.S. government would have no obligation to prove any form of legal case against the individuals being held, and this order essentially announced that no American or international court would have jurisdiction over the prisoners, wherever they were to be housed. When coupled with the decision to place enemy captives at the naval base in Guantanamo, Cuba, the prisoners had very little recourse but to hope that the U.S. government might eventually decide to release them from confinement.

- **Document 38: Joint Inquiry Staff Statement, Part I, Statement of Eleanor Hill, Staff Director**
- **When:** September 18, 2002
- **Where:** Washington, D.C.
- **Significance:** Eleanor Hill, staff director for the joint inquiry staff of a joint congressional inquiry into intelligence agencies activities surrounding the time of the September 11 attacks, offered a statement summarizing the general knowledge levels of the intelligence community regarding the intentions and capabilities of Al Qaeda operatives.

DOCUMENT

Intelligence Information on Possible Terrorist Use of Airplanes as Weapons

Central to the September 11 attacks was the terrorists' use of airplanes as weapons. In the aftermath of the terrorist attacks, there was much discussion about the extent to which our Government was, or could have been, aware of the threat of terrorist attacks of this type and the extent to which adequate precautions were taken to address that threat. We therefore asked the question: Did the Intelligence Community have any information in its possession prior to September 11, 2001 indicating that terrorists were contemplating using airplanes as weapons?

Based on our review to date of the requested information, we believe that the Intelligence Community was aware of the potential for this type of terrorist attack, but did not produce any specific assessments of the likelihood that terrorists would use airplanes as weapons.

Our review has uncovered several examples of intelligence reporting on the possible use of airplanes as weapons in terrorist operations. As with the intelligence reports indicating Bin Ladin's intentions to strike inside the United States, the credibility of the sources is sometimes questionable, and the information is often sketchy. Nevertheless, we did find reporting on this kind of potential threat including the following:

- In December 1994, Algerian Armed Islamic Group terrorists hijacked an Air France flight in Algiers and threatened to crash it into the Eiffel Tower. French authorities deceived the terrorists into thinking the plane did not have enough fuel to reach Paris and diverted it to Marseilles. A French anti-terrorist force stormed the plane and killed all four terrorists;

- In January 1995, a Philippine National Police raid turned up materials in a Manila apartment indicating that three individuals—Ramzi Yousef, Abdul Murad and Khalid Shaykh Mohammad—planned, among other things, to crash an airplane into CIA headquarters. The Philippine National Police said that the same group was responsible for the bombing of a Philippine airliner on December 12, 1994. Information on the threat was passed to the FAA, which briefed U.S. and major foreign carriers;

- In January 1996, the Intelligence Community obtained information concerning a planned suicide attack by individuals associated with Shaykh Omar Adb al-Rahman and a key al-Qa'ida operative. The plan was to fly to the United States from Afghanistan and attack the White House;

- In October 1996, the Intelligence Community obtained information regarding an Iranian plot to hijack a Japanese plane over Israel and crash it into Tel Aviv. An individual would board the plane in the Far Fast. During the flight, he would commandeer the aircraft, order it to fly over Tel Aviv, and then crash the plane into the city;

- In 1997, one of the units at FBI headquarters became concerned about the possibility of a terrorist group using an unmanned aerial vehicle (UAV) for terrorist attacks. The FBI and CIA became aware of reporting that this group had purchased a UAV. At the time, the agencies' view was that the only reason that this group would need a UAV would be for either reconnaissance or attack. There was more concern about the possibility of an attack outside the United States, for example, by flying a UAV into a U.S. Embassy or a visiting U.S. delegation;

- In August 1998, the Intelligence Community obtained information that a group of unidentified Arabs planned to fly an explosive-laden plane from a foreign country into the World Trade Center. The information was passed to the FBI and the FAA. The FAA found the plot highly unlikely given the state of that foreign country's aviation program. Moreover, they believed that a flight originating outside the United States would be detected before it reached its intended target inside the United States. The FBI's New York office took no action on the information, filing the communication in the office's bomb repository file. The Intelligence Community has acquired additional information since then indicating there may be links between this group and other terrorist groups, including al-Qa'ida;

- In September 1998, the Intelligence Community obtained information that Usama Bin Ladin's next operation could possibly involve flying an aircraft loaded with explosives into a U.S. airport and detonating it; this information was provided to senior U.S. Government officials in late 1998;

- In November 1998, the Intelligence Community obtained information that the Turkish Kaplancilar, an Islamic extremist group, had planned a suicide attack to coincide with celebrations marking the death of Ataturk. The conspirators, who were arrested, planned to crash an airplane packed with explosives into Ataturk's tomb during a government ceremony. The Turkish press said the group had cooperated with Usama Bin Ladin. The FBI's New York office included this incident in one of its Usama Bin Ladin databases;

- In February 1999, the Intelligence Community obtained information that Iraq had formed a suicide pilot unit it planned to use against British and U.S. forces in the Persian Gulf. The CIA commented that this was highly unlikely and probably disinformation;

- In March 1999, the Intelligence Community obtained information regarding plans by an al-Qa'ida member, who was a U.S. citizen, to fly a hang glider into the Egyptian Presidential Palace and then detonate the explosives he was carrying. The individual, who received hang glider training in the United States, brought a hang glider back to Afghanistan. However, various problems arose during the testing of the glider. He was subsequently arrested and is in custody abroad;

- In April 2000, the Intelligence Community obtained information regarding an alleged Bin Ladin plot to hijack a 747. The source, who was a "walk-in" to the FBI's Newark office, claimed that he had been to a training camp in Pakistan where he learned hijacking techniques and received arms training. He also stated that he was supposed to meet five to six other individuals in the United States who would also participate in the plot. They were instructed to use all necessary force to take over the plane because there would be pilots among the hijacking team. The plan was to fly the plane to Afghanistan, and if they would not make it there, that they were to blow up the plane. Although the individual passed an FBI polygraph, the FBI was never able to verify any aspect of his story or identify his contacts in the United States; and

- In August 2001, the Intelligence Community obtained information regarding a plot to either bomb the U.S. Embassy in Nairobi from an airplane or crash an airplane into it. The Intelligence Community learned that two people who were reportedly acting on instructions from Usama Bin Ladin met in October 2000 to discuss this plot.

The CIA disseminated several of these reports to the FBI and to agencies that would be responsible for taking preventive actions, including the FAA. The FAA has staff assigned to the DCI's CTC [Director of Central Intelligence's Counterterrorism Center], the FBI's Counterterrorism Division, and to the State Department's Diplomatic Security Service to gather relevant intelligence for domestic use. The FAA is responsible for issuing information circulars, security directives and emergency amendments to the directives alerting domestic and international airports and airlines of threats identified by the Intelligence Community.

Despite these reports, the Intelligence Community did not produce any specific assessments of the likelihood that terrorists would use airplanes as weapons. Again, this may have been driven in part by resource issues in the area of intelligence analysis. Prior to September 11, 2001, the CTC had forty analysts to analyze terrorism issues worldwide, with only one of the five branches focused on terrorist tactics. As a result, prior to September 11, 2001, the only terrorist tactic on which the CTC performed strategic analysis was the possible use of chemical, biological, radiological and nuclear weapons (CBRN) because there was more obvious potential for mass casualties.

At the FBI, our review found that, prior to September 11, 2001, support for ongoing investigations and

> ## DID YOU KNOW?
>
> ### Conspiracy Theories
>
> As tends to be the case for virtually every catastrophic event in human history, a host of conspiracy theories regarding the causes of the September 11 attacks have emerged in the aftermath. Some of the earliest theories argued that the U.S. government tried to cover up its own failure to detect and prevent the attack. Others took the argument further, suggesting that the government knew about the attack before it occurred, but allowed it to happen as it would supply political gain. Some of the most extreme theories directly blame the attacks upon the government, which could use the outrage of the American public as an excuse to launch military operations in the Middle East for economic gain. Agencies other than Al Qaeda have also been blamed for the attacks, including suggestions that the Israeli government might be behind the attacks. The conspiracy theories continue to circulate, despite Osama bin Laden's public pronouncement of responsibility for the attacks, and the detailed confession supplied by Khalid Sheikh Mohammed regarding the planning and execution of the attacks.

operations was favored, in terms of allocating resources, over long-term, strategic analysis. We were told, during the course of our FBI interviews, that prevention occurs in the operational units, not through strategic analysis, and that, prior to September 11, the FBI had insufficient resources to do both. We were also told that the FBI's al-Qa'ida-related analytic expertise had been "gutted" by transfers to operational units and that, as a result, the FBI's analytic unit had only one individual working on al-Qa'ida at the time of the September 11 attacks.

While focused strategic analysis was lacking, the subject of aviation-related terrorism was included in some broader terrorist threat assessments, such as the National Intelligence Estimates (NIE) on terrorism. For example, the 1995 NIE on terrorism mentioned the plot to down 12 U.S.-owned airliners. The NIE also cited the consideration the Bojinka conspirators gave to attacking CIA headquarters using an aircraft loaded with explosives. The FAA worked with the Intelligence Community on this analysis and actually drafted the section of the NIE addressing the threat to civil aviation. That section contained the following language:

> Our review of the evidence . . . suggests the conspirators were guided in their selection of the method and venue of attack by carefully studying security procedures in place in the region. If terrorists operating in this country [the United States] are similarly methodical, they will identify serious vulnerabilities in the security system for domestic flights.

The 1997 update to the 1995 NIE on terrorism included the following language:

> Civil aviation remains a particularly attractive target in light of the fear and publicity the downing of an airliner would evoke and the revelations last summer of the US air transport sectors' vulnerabilities.

As a result of the increasing threats to aviation, Congress passed Section 310 of the Federal Aviation Reauthorization Act of 1996, requiring the FAA and the FBI to conduct joint threat and vulnerability assessments of security at select "high risk" U.S. airports and to provide Congress with an annual report. In the December 2000 report, the FBI and FAA published a classified assessment that suggested less concern about the threat to domestic aviation:

> FBI investigations confirm domestic and international terrorist groups operating within the U.S. but do not suggest evidence of plans to target domestic civil aviation. Terrorist activity within the U.S. has focused primarily on fundraising, recruiting new members, and disseminating propaganda. While international terrorists have conducted attacks on U.S. soil, these acts represent anomalies in their traditional targeting which focuses on U.S. interests overseas.

In short, less than a year prior to the September 11 attacks and notwithstanding historical intelligence information to the contrary, the FBI and FAA had assessed the prospects of a terrorist incident targeting domestic civil aviation in the United States as relatively low.

After September 11, 2001, the CIA belatedly acknowledged some of the information that was available regarding the use of airplanes as weapons. A draft analysis dated November 19, 2001, "The 11 September Attacks: A Preliminary Assessment," states:

> We do not know the process by which Bin Ladin and his lieutenants decided to hijack planes with the idea of flying them into buildings in the United States, but the idea of hijacking planes for suicide attacks had long been current in jihadist circles. For example, GIA terrorists from Algeria had planned to crash a Air France jet into the Eiffel Tower in December 1994, and Ramzi Yousef—a participant in the 1993 World Trade Center bombing—planned to explode 12 US jetliners in mid-air over the Pacific in the mid-1990s. Likewise the World Trade Center had long been a target of terrorist bombers.

Despite the intelligence available in recent years, our review to date has found no indications that, prior to September 11, analysts in the Intelligence Community were:

- Cataloguing information regarding the use of airplanes as weapons as a terrorist tactic;
- Sending requirements to collectors to look for additional information on this threat; or

- Considering the likelihood that Usama Bin Ladin, al-Qa'ida, or any other terrorist group, would attack the United States or U.S. interests in this way.

Source: House Permanent Select Committee on Intelligence and Senate Select Committee on Intelligence, *Joint Inquiry into Intelligence Community Activities before and after the Terrorist Attacks of September 11, 2001,* Senate Report 107-351 (December 2002), available at https://fas.org/irp/congress/2002_hr/091802hill.html.

ANALYSIS

Eleanor Hill served as the staff director for a joint inquiry into the activities of the intelligence community in the months leading up to the September 11 attacks, as well as in the aftermath of the event. In this testimony before the joint inquiry, she offers a summary of the staff's findings. While it is clear that the intelligence community had developed some sources indicating a desire by Al Qaeda operatives to hijack aircraft, it is also clear that the committee did not feel the success of the September 11 attacks was a direct result of any intelligence failures, per se. Rather, the staff concluded that the likelihood of connecting disparate information collected from a wide variety of sources was nearly impossible. However, they also found that the intelligence community budgets and personnel had been sharply reduced in the aftermath of the Cold War, in the mistaken belief that the world had become a safer place and that the United States faced no significant external threats.

- **Document 39: Richard Clarke, Testimony before the 9/11 Commission**
- **When:** March 24, 2004
- **Where:** Washington, D.C.
- **Significance:** Clarke served as the top counterterrorism official in the administration of President William Clinton. He attempted to warn his successor, Condoleezza Rice, of the dangers presented by Al Qaeda (see Document 19). In his testimony, Clarke offers explanations for the government's failure to detect and stop the September 11 attacks, and takes responsibility for those failures.

DOCUMENT

Testimony of Richard A. Clarke before the National Commission on Terrorist Attacks upon the United States

I am appreciative of the opportunity the Commission is offering for me to provide my observations about what went wrong in the struggle against al Qida, both before and after 9-11. I want the families of the victims to know that we tried to stop those attacks, that some people tried very hard. I want them to know why we failed and what I think we need to do to insure that nothing like that ever happens again.

I have testified for twenty hours before the House-Senate Joint Inquiry committee and before this Commission in closed hearings. Therefore, I will limit my prepared testimony to a chronological review of key facts and then provide some conclusions and summary observations, which may form the basis for further questions. My observations and answers to any questions are limited by my memory, because I do not have access to government files or classified information for purposes of preparing for this hearing.

I was assigned to the National Security Council staff in 1992 and had terrorism as part of my portfolio until late 2001. Terrorism became the predominant part of my duties during the mid-1990s and I was appointed National Coordinator for Counter-terrorism in 1998.

1. *Terrorism without US Retaliation in the 1980s*: In the 1980s, Hizballah killed 278 United States Marines in Lebanon and twice destroyed the US embassy. They kidnapped and killed other Americans, including the CIA Station chief. There was no direct US military retaliation. In 1989, 259 people were killed on Pan Am 103. There was no direct US military retaliation. The George H.W. Bush administration did not have a formal counter-terrorism policy articulated in an NSC Presidential decision document.

2. *Terrorism Early in the Clinton Administration*: Within the first few weeks of the Clinton administration, there was terrorism in the US: the attack on the CIA gatehouse and the attack on the World Trade Center. CIA and FBI concluded at the time that there was no organization behind those attacks. Similarly, they did not report at the time that al Qida was involved in the planned attack on Americans in Yemen in 1992 or the Somali attacks on US and other peacekeepers in 1993. Indeed, CIA and FBI did not report the existence of an organization named al Qida until the mid-1990s, seven years after it was apparently created. Nonetheless, the 1993 attacks and then the terrorism in the Tokyo subway and the Oklahoma City bombing caused the Clinton Administration to increase its focus on terrorism and to expand funding for counter-terrorism programs.

As a result of intelligence and law enforcement operations, most of those involved in the World Trade Center attack of 1993, the planned attacks on the UN and New York tunnels, the CIA gatehouse shootings, the Oklahoma City bombing, and the attempted assassination of former President Bush were successfully apprehended.

The Clinton Administration responded to Iraqi terrorism against the US in 1993 with a military retaliation and against Iranian terrorism against the US in 1996 at Khobar Towers with a covert action. Both US responses were accompanied by warning that further anti-US terrorism would result in greater retaliation. Neither Iraq nor Iran engaged in anti-US terrorism subsequently. (Iraqis did, of course, later engage in anti-US terrorism in 2003–4.)

3. *Identifying the al Qida Threat*: The White House urged CIA in 1994 to place greater focus on what the Agency called "the terrorist financier, Usama bin Ladin." After the creation of a "virtual station" to examine bin Ladin, CIA identified a

multi-national network of cells and of affiliated terrorist organizations. That network was attempting to wage "jihad" in Bosnia and planned to have a significant role in a new Bosnian government. US and Allied actions halted the war in Bosnia and caused most of the al Qida related jihadists to leave. The White House asked CIA and DOD to develop plans for operating against al Qida in Sudan, the country of its headquarters. Neither department was able successfully to develop a plan to do so. Immediately following Usama bin Ladin's move to Afghanistan, the White House requested that plans be developed to operate against al Qida there. CIA developed ties to a group which reported on al Qida activity, but which was unable to mount successful operations against al Qida in Afghanistan. CIA opposed using its own personnel to do so.

4. *Sudan*: While bin Ladin was in Sudan, he was hosted by its leader, Hasan Turabi. Under Turabi, Sudan had become a safe haven for many terrorist groups, but bin Ladin had special status. He funded many development programs such as roads and dined often with Turabi and his family. Turabi and bin Ladin were ideological brethren. Following the assassination attempt on Egyptian President Mubarek, the US and Egypt successfully proposed UN sanctions on Sudan because of its support of terrorism. Because of the growing economic damage to Sudan due to its support of terrorism, bin Ladin offered to move to Afghanistan. Sudan at no time detained him, nor was there ever a credible offer by Sudan to arrest and render him. This is in contrast to Sudan's arrest of the terrorist known as Carlos the Jackal, who the Sudanese then handed over in chains to French authorities.

5. *1998 Turning Point*: In 1996, CIA had been directed to develop its capability to operate against al Qida in Afghanistan and elsewhere. CIA operations identified and disrupted al Qida cells in several countries. In 1997, a federal grand jury began reviewing evidence against al Qida and in 1998 indicted Usama bin Ladin. Several terrorists, including bin Ladin, issued a fatwa against the United States.

In August, al Qida attacked two US embassies in East Africa. Following the attacks, the United States responded militarily with cruise missile attacks on al Qida facilities. President Clinton was widely criticized for doing so. A US Marine deployment, combined with CIA activity, disrupted a third attack planned in Tirana, Albania.

President Clinton requested the Chairman of the Joint Chiefs to develop follow-on military strike plans, including the use of US Special Forces. The Chairman recommended against using US forces on the ground in Afghanistan, but placed submarines with cruise missiles off shore awaiting timely intelligence of the location of Usama bin Ladin.

The President also requested CIA to develop follow-on covert action plans. He authorized lethal activity in a series of directives which progressively expanded the authority of CIA to act against al Qida in Afghanistan.

Diplomatic activity also increased, including UN sanctions against the Taliban regime in Afghanistan and pressure on Pakistan to cooperate further in attempts to end the Taliban support for al Qida.

6. *National Coordinator*: In 1998, I was appointed by the President to a newly created position of National Coordinator for Security, Infrastructure Protection and Counter-terrorism. Although the Coordinator was appointed to the Cabinet level

NSC Principals Committee, the position was limited at the request of the departments and agencies. The Coordinator had no budget, only a dozen staff, and no ability to direct actions by the departments or agencies. The President authorized ten security and counter-terrorism programs and assigned leadership on each program (e.g. Transportation Security) to an agency lead.

7. *1999:* The Clinton Administration continued to pursue intelligence, including covert action, military, law enforcement, and diplomatic activity to disrupt al Qida.

CIA was unable to develop timely intelligence to support the planned follow-on military strikes. On three occasions, CIA reported it knew where Usama bin Ladin was, but all three times the Director of Central Intelligence recommended against military action because of the poor quality of the intelligence. Eventually, the US submarines on station for the military operation returned to normal duties. CIA's assets in Afghanistan were unable to utilize the lethal covert action authorities and CIA recommended against placing its own personnel in Afghanistan to carry out the operations. Captures of al Qida personnel outside of Afghanistan continued.

In December, 1999 intelligence and law enforcement information indicated that al Qida was planning attacks against the US. The President ordered the Principals Committee to meet regularly to prevent the attacks. That Cabinet level committee met throughout December, 1999 to review intelligence and develop counter-measures. The planned al Qida attacks were averted.

Despite our inability to locate Usama bin Ladin in one place long enough to launch an attack, I urged that we engage in a bombing campaign of al Qida facilities in Afghanistan. That option was deferred by the Principals Committee.

8. *Terrorists in the US*: FBI had the responsibility for finding al Qida related activities or terrorists in the US. In the 1996–1999 timeframe, they regularly responded to me and to the National Security Advisor that there were no known al Qida operatives or activities in the US. On my trips to FBI field offices, I found that al Qida was not a priority (except in the New York office). Following the Millennium Alert, FBI Executive Assistant Director Dale Watson attempted to have the field offices act more aggressively to find al Qida related activities. The Bureau was, however, less than proactive in identifying al Qida related fund raising, recruitment, or other activities in the United States. Several programs to increase our ability to respond to terrorism in the US were initiated both in the FBI and in other departments, including programs to train and equip first responders.

9. *2000:* The President, displeased with the inability of CIA to eliminate the al Qida leadership, asked for additional options. The NSC staff proposed that the Predator, unmanned aerial vehicle, be used to find the leadership. CIA objected. The National Security Advisor, however, eventually obtained Agency agreement to fly the Predator on a "proof of concept" mission without any link to military or CIA forces standing by. CIA wanted to experiment with the concept before developing a command and control system that incorporated Predator information with attack capabilities. The flights ended when the high winds of winter precluded the operation of the aircraft. The experiment had proved successful in locating the al Qida leadership.

In October 2000, the USS Cole was attacked in Yemen. Following the attack, the Principals considered military retaliation. CIA and FBI were, however, unwilling to state that those who had conducted the attack were al Qida or related to the facilities and personnel in Afghanistan. The Principals directed that the Politico-Military Plan against al Qida be updated with additional options. Among those options were aiding Afghan factions to fight the Taliban and al Qida and creating an armed version of the Predator unmanned aircraft to use against the al Qida leadership. Military strike options, including cruise missiles, bombing, and use of US Special Forces were also included.

As the Clinton Administration came to an end, three attacks on the US had been definitively tied to al Qida, (the World Trade Center 1993, the Embassies in 1998 and the Cole in 2000), in which a total of 35 Americans had been killed over eight years.

To counter al Qida's growing threat, a global effort had been initiated involving intelligence activities, covert action, diplomacy, law enforcement, financial action, and military capability. Nonetheless, the organization continued to enjoy a safe haven in Afghanistan.

10. *2001*: On January 24, 2001 I requested in writing an urgent meeting of the NSC Principals committee to address the al Qida threat. That meeting took place on September 4, 2001. It was preceded by a number of Deputies Committee meetings, beginning in April. Those meetings considered proposals to step up activity against al Qida, including military assistance to anti-Taliban Afghan factions.

In June and July, intelligence indicated an increased likelihood of a major al Qida attack against US targets, probably in Saudi Arabia or Israel. In response, the interagency Counter-terrorism Security Group agreed upon a series of steps including a series of warning notices that an attack could take place in the US. Notices were sent to federal agencies (Immigration, Customs, Coast Guard, FAA, FBI, DOD, and State), state and local police, airlines, and airports.

In retrospect, we know that there was information available to some in the FBI and CIA that al Qida operatives had entered the United States. That information was not shared with the senior FBI counter-terrorism official (Dale Watson) or with me, despite the heightened state of concern in the Counter-terrorism Security Group.

Observations and Conclusions

Although there were people in the FBI, CIA, Defense Department, State Department, and White House who worked very hard to destroy al Qida before it did catastrophic damage to the US, there were many others who found the prospect of significant al Qida attacks remote. In both CIA and the military there was reluctance at senior career levels to fully utilize all of the capabilities available. There was risk aversion. FBI was, throughout much of this period, organized, staffed, and equipped in such a way that it was ineffective in dealing with the domestic terrorist threat from al Qida.

At the senior policy levels in the Clinton Administration, there was an acute understanding of the terrorist threat, particularly al Qida. That understanding resulted in a vigorous program to counter al Qida including lethal covert action, but it did not include a willingness to resume bombing of Afghanistan. Events in the Balkans, Iraq, the Peace Process, and domestic politics occurring at the same time as the anti-terrorism effort played a role.

The Bush Administration saw terrorism policy as important but not urgent, prior to 9-11. The difficulty in obtaining the first Cabinet level (Principals) policy meeting on terrorism and the limited Principals' involvement sent unfortunate signals to the bureaucracy about the Administration's attitude toward the al Qida threat.

The US response to al Qida following 9-11 has been partially effective. Unfortunately, the US did not act sufficiently quickly to insert US forces to capture or kill the al Qida leadership in Afghanistan. Nor did we employ sufficient US and Allied forces to stabilize that country. In the ensuing 30 months, al Qida has morphed into a decentralized network, with its national and regional affiliates operating effectively and independently. There have been more major al Qida related attacks globally in the 30 months since 9-11 than there were in the 30 months preceding it. Hostility toward the US in the Islamic world has increased since 9-11, largely as a result of the invasion and occupation of Iraq. Thus, new terrorist cells are likely being created, unknown to US intelligence.

To address the continuing threat from radical Islamic terrorism, the US and its allies must become increasingly focused and effective in countering the ideology that motivates that terrorism.

Source: National Commission on Terrorist Attacks upon the United States, available at www.9-11commission.gov/hearings/hearing8/clarke_statement.pdf.

ANALYSIS

Richard Clarke's testimony offered broad explanations of the state of U.S. counterterrorism policy prior to the September 11 attacks. In his opinion, the United States did not take the threat of terror attacks seriously, and thus left itself dangerously vulnerable to a large-scale attack. He argues that the three presidents prior to the attacks had all struggled to grasp the full nature of the problem, and that the administrations of Ronald Reagan and George H. W. Bush had both failed to respond to terror attacks with a vigorous military reaction, emboldening terror organizations to increase the scope and frequency of their attacks.

One of the more controversial aspects of Clarke's testimony came from his decision to announce to the victims' families that their government had failed to take the necessary measures to defend the nation, and that while some government officials had tried hard, their efforts were irrelevant due to that failure. Clarke's decision to openly critique the George W. Bush administration for its failure to take the Al Qaeda threat seriously angered many of the administration's defenders, but it is hard not to agree that the Bush administration placed a much greater emphasis upon countering any Iraqi activity than it did upon deterring and defeating Al Qaeda. While Clarke remains a polarizing figure within the national defense community, his testimony before the commission is a stark reminder that hard work is far less important in the War on Terror than achieving positive results.

- **Document 40: Final Report of the National Commission on Terrorist Attacks upon the United States**
- **When:** July 22, 2004
- **Where:** Washington, D.C.
- **Significance:** The final report of the National Commission on Terrorist Attacks upon the United States represents the official government account regarding the September 11 attacks. Not only did the commission seek to identify the failures in security measures that allowed the attack to succeed, but it was also charged with making broad and specific recommendations for the federal government to counter future attacks and more effectively prosecute the War on Terror.

DOCUMENT

Excerpts from the Executive Summary, Final Report of the National Commission on Terrorist Attacks upon the United States

A Shock, Not a Surprise

The 9/11 attacks were a shock, but they should not have come as a surprise. Islamist extremists had given plenty of warning that they meant to kill Americans indiscriminately and in large numbers. Although Usama Bin Ladin himself would not emerge as a signal threat until the 1990s, the threat of Islamist terrorism grew over the decade.

In February 1993, a group led by Ramzi Yousef tried to bring down the World Trade Center with a truck bomb. They killed six and wounded a thousand. Plans by Omar Abdel Rahman and others to blow up the Holland and Lincoln tunnels and other New York City landmarks were frustrated when the plotters were arrested. In October 1993, Somali tribesmen shot down U.S. helicopters, killing 18 and wounding 73 that came to be known as "Black Hawk down." Years later it would be learned that those Somali tribesmen had received help from al Qaeda.

In early 1995, police in Manila uncovered a plot by Ramzi Yousef to blow up a dozen U.S. airliners while they were flying over the Pacific. In November 1995, a car bomb exploded outside the office of the U.S. program manager for the Saudi National Guard in Riyadh, killing five Americans and two others. In June 1996, a truck bomb demolished the Khobar Towers apartment complex in Dharan, Saudi Arabia, killing 19 U.S. servicemen and wounding hundreds. The Attack was carried out primarily by Saudi Hezbollah, an organization that had received help from the government of Iran.

Until 1997, the U.S. intelligence community viewed Bin Ladin as a financier of terrorism, not as a terrorist leader. In February 1998, Usama Bin Ladin and four

Victims' Compensation Fund

In the aftermath of the September 11 attacks, the U.S. Congress established a fund to compensate victims of the attacks and their survivors. Although controversial in nature, the families of most of the victims eventually accepted the government offer, which totaled over $7 billion. Some survivors argued that the compensation was inadequate to meet their needs, a public position that triggered a small but significant backlash within the American public due to the perception that they were attempting to profit from the deaths of their family members. The average settlement to the families of those killed was over $2 million, and was based upon the age and income of the victim. The average compensation given to the nearly 3,000 injured victims was approximately $400,000. Eventually, only 80 families opted to launch private lawsuits rather than accept the government offer, most of them related to victims on board the doomed aircraft who chose to sue the airline companies for failing to maintain adequate security. A total of 13 families of victims did not respond in any fashion to the government offer, choosing to ignore it entirely for unknown or undisclosed reasons.

others issued a self-styled fatwa, publicly declaring that it was God's decree that every Muslim should try his utmost to kill any American, military or civilian, anywhere in the world, because of American "occupation" of Islam's holy places and aggression against Muslims.

In August 1998, Bin Ladin's group, al Qaeda, carried out near-simultaneous truck bomb attacks on the U.S. embassies in Nairobi, Kenya, and Dar es Salaam, Tanzania. The attacks killed 224 people, including 12 Americans, and wounded thousands more.

In December 1999, Jordanian police foiled a plot to bomb hotels and other sites frequented by American tourists, and a U.S. Customs agent arrested Ahmed Ressam at the U.S. Canadian border as he was smuggling in explosives intended for an attack on Los Angeles International Airport.

In October 2000, an al Qaeda team in Aden, Yemen, used a motorboat filled with explosives to blow a hole in the side of a destroyer, the USS *Cole*, almost sinking the vessel and killing 17 American sailors.

The 9/11 attacks on the World Trade Center and the Pentagon were far more elaborate, precise, and destructive than any of these earlier assaults. But by September 2001, the executive branch of the U.S. government, the Congress, the news media, and the American public had received clear warning that Islamic terrorists meant to kill Americans in high numbers.

September 11, 2001

The day began with the 19 hijackers getting through a security checkpoint system that they had evidently analyzed and knew how to defeat. Their success rate in penetrating the system was 19 for 19. They took over the four flights, taking advantage of air crews and cockpits that were not prepared for the contingency of a suicide hijacking.

On 9/11, the defense of U.S. air space depended on close interaction between two federal agencies: the Federal Aviation Administration (FAA) and North American Aerospace Defense Command (NORAD). Existing protocols on 9/11 were unsuited in every respect for an attack in which hijacked planes were used as weapons.

What ensued was a hurried attempt to improvise a defense by civilians who had never handled a hijacked aircraft that attempted to disappear, and by a military unprepared for the transformation of commercial aircraft into weapons of mass destruction.

A shootdown authorization was not communicated to the NORAD air defense sector until 28 minutes after United 93 had crashed in Pennsylvania. Planes were scrambled, but ineffectively, as they did not know where to go or what targets they were to intercept. And once the shootdown order was given, it was not communicated to the pilots. In short, while leaders in Washington believed that the fighters circling above them had been instructed to "take out" hostile aircraft, the only orders actually conveyed to the pilots were to "ID type and tail."

Like the national defense, the emergency response on 9/11 was necessarily improvised.

In New York City, the Fire Department of New York, the New York Police Department, the Port Authority of New York and New Jersey, the building employees, and the occupants of the buildings did their best to cope with the effects of almost unimaginable events—unfolding furiously over 102 minutes. Casualties were nearly 100 percent at and above the impact zones and were very high among first responders who stayed in danger as they tried to save lives. Despite weaknesses in preparations for disaster, failure to achieve unified incident command, and inadequate communications among responding agencies, all but approximately one hundred of the thousands of civilians who worked below the impact zone escaped, often with help from the emergency responders.

At the Pentagon, while there were also problems of command and control, the emergency response was generally effective. The Incident Command System, a formalized management structure for emergency response in place in the National Capital Region, overcame the inherent complications of a response across local, state, and federal jurisdictions.

Operational Opportunities

We write with the benefit and handicap of hindsight. We are mindful of the danger of being unjust to men and women who made choices in conditions of uncertainty and in circumstances over which they often had little control.

Nonetheless, there were specific points of vulnerability in the plot and opportunities to disrupt it. Operational failures—opportunities that were not or could not be exploited by the organizations and systems of that time—included

- not watchlisting future hijackers Hazmi and Mihdhar, not trailing them after they traveled to Bangkok, and not informing the FBI about one future hijacker's U.S. visa or his companion's travel to the United States;
- not sharing information linking individuals in the *Cole* attack to Mihdhar;
- not taking adequate steps in time to find Mihdhar or Hazmi in the United States;
- not linking the arrest of Zacarias Moussaoui, described as interested in flight training for the purpose of using an airplane in a terrorist act, to the heightened indications of attack;
- not discovering false statements on visa applications;
- not recognizing passports manipulated in a fraudulent manner;
- not expanding no-fly lists to include names from terrorist watchlists;
- not searching airline passengers identified by the computer-based CAPPS screening system; and
- not hardening aircraft cockpit doors or taking other measures to prepare for the possibility of suicide hijackings.

General Findings

Since the plotters were flexible and resourceful, we cannot know whether any single step or series of steps would have defeated them. What we can say with confidence is that none of the measures adopted by the U.S. government from 1998 to 2001 disturbed or even delayed the progress of the al Qaeda plot. Across the government, there were failures of imagination, policy, capabilities, and management.

Imagination

The most important failure was one of imagination. We do not believe leaders understood the gravity of the threat. The terrorist danger from Bin Ladin and al Qaeda was not a major topic for policy debate among the public, the media, or in the Congress. Indeed, it barely came up during the 2000 presidential campaign.

Al Qaeda's new brand of terrorism presented challenges to U.S. governmental institutions that they were not well-designed to meet. Though top officials all told us that they understood the danger, we believe there was uncertainty among them as to whether this was just a new and especially venomous version of the ordinary terrorist threat the United States had lived with for decades, or it was indeed radically new, posing a threat beyond any yet experienced.

As late as September 4, 2001, Richard Clarke, the White House staffer long responsible for counterterrorism policy coordination, asserted that the government had not yet made up its mind how to answer the question: "Is al Qida a big deal?"

A week later came the answer.

Policy

Terrorism was not the overriding national security concern for the U.S. government under either the Clinton or the pre-9/11 Bush administration.

The policy challenges were linked to this failure of imagination. Officials in both the Clinton and Bush administrations regarded a full U.S. invasion of Afghanistan as practically inconceivable before 9/11.

Capabilities

Before 9/11, the United States tried to solve the al Qaeda problem with the capabilities it had used in the last stages of the Cold War and its immediate aftermath. These capabilities were insufficient. Little was done to expand or reform them.

The CIA had minimal capacity to conduct paramilitary operations with its own personnel, and it did not seek a large-scale expansion of these capabilities before 9/11. The CIA also needed to improve its capability to conduct intelligence from human agents.

At no point before 9/11 was the Department of Defense fully engaged in the mission of countering al Qaeda, even though this was perhaps the most dangerous foreign enemy threatening the United States.

America's homeland defenders faced outward. NORAD itself was barely able to retain any alert bases at all. Its planning scenarios occasionally considered the danger of hijacked aircraft being guided to American targets, but only aircraft that were coming from overseas.

The most serious weaknesses in agency capabilities were in the domestic arena. The FBI did not have the capability to link the collective knowledge of agents in the field to national priorities. Other domestic agencies deferred to the FBI.

FAA capabilities were weak. Any serious examination of the possibility of a sui-cide hijacking could have suggested changes to fix glaring vulnerabilities—expand-ing no-fly lists, searching passengers identified by the CAPPS screening system, deploying federal air marshals domestically, hardening cockpit doors, alerting air crews to a different kind of hijacking possibility than they had been trained to expect. Yet the FAA did not adjust either its own training or training with NORAD to take account of threats other than those experienced in the past.

Management

The missed opportunities to thwart the 9/11 plot were also symptoms of a broader inability to adapt the way government manages problems to the new challenges of the twenty-first century. Action officers should have been able to draw on all avail-able knowledge about al Qaeda in the government. Management should have ensured that information was shared and duties were clearly assigned across agen-cies, and across the foreign-domestic divide.

There were also broader management issues with respect to how top leaders set priorities and allocated resources. For instance, on December 4, 1998, DCI Tenet issued a directive to several CIA officials and the DDCI for Community Manage-ment, stating: "We are at war. I want no resources or people spared in this effort, either inside CIA or the Community." The memorandum had little overall effect on mobilizing the CIA or the intelligence community. This episode indicates the limitations of the DCI's authority over the direction of the intelligence community, including agencies within the Department of Defense.

The U.S. government did not find a way of pooling intelligence and using it to guide the planning and assignment of responsibilities for joint operations involving entities as disparate as the CIA, the FBI, the State Department, the military, and the agencies involved in homeland security.

What to Do? A Global Strategy

The enemy is not just "terrorism." It is the threat posed specifically by Islamist ter-rorism, by Bin Ladin and others who draw on a long tradition of extreme intolerance within a minority strain of Islam that does not distinguish politics from religion, and distorts both.

The enemy is not Islam, the great world faith, but a perversion of Islam. The enemy goes beyond al Qaeda to include the radical ideological movement, inspired in part by al Qaeda, that has spawned other terrorist groups and violence. Thus our strategy must match our means to two ends: dismantling the al Qaeda net-work and, in the long term, prevailing over the ideology that contributes to Islamist terrorism.

The first phase of our post-9/11 efforts rightly included military action to topple the Taliban and pursue al Qaeda. This work continues. But long-term success demands the use of all elements of national power: diplomacy, intelligence, covert action, law enforcement, economic policy, foreign aid, public diplomacy, and homeland defense. If we favor one tool while neglecting others, we leave ourselves vulnerable and weaken our national effort.

What should Americans expect from their government? The goal seems unlimited: Defeat terrorism anywhere in the world. But Americans have also been told to expect the worst: An attack is probably coming; it may be more devastating still.

Vague goals match an amorphous picture of the enemy. Al Qaeda and other groups are popularly described as being all over the world, adaptable, resilient, needing little higher-level organization, and capable of anything. It is an image of an omnipotent hydra of destruction. That image lowers expectations of government effectiveness.

It lowers them too far. Our report shows a determined and capable group of plotters. Yet the group was fragile and occasionally left vulnerable by the marginal, unstable people often attracted to such causes. The enemy made mistakes. The U.S. government was not able to capitalize on them.

No president can promise that a catastrophic attack like that of 9/11 will not happen again. But the American people are entitled to expect that officials will have realistic objectives, clear guidance, and effective organization. They are entitled to see standards for performance so they can judge, with the help of their elected representatives, whether the objectives are being met.

We propose a strategy with three dimensions: (1) attack terrorists and their organizations, (2) prevent the continued growth of Islamic terrorism, and (3) protect against and prepare for terrorist attacks.

How to Do It? A Different Way of Organizing Government

The strategy we have recommended is elaborate, even as presented here very briefly. To implement it will require a government better organized than the one that exists today, with its national security institutions designed half a century ago to win the Cold War. Americans should not settle for incremental, ad hoc adjustments to a system created a generation ago for a world that no longer exists.

Our detailed recommendations are designed to fit together. Their purpose is clear: to build unity of effort across the U.S. government. As one official now serving on the front lines overseas put it to us: "One fight, one team."

We call for unity of effort in five areas, beginning with unity of effort on the challenge of counterterrorism itself:

- unifying strategic intelligence and operational planning against Islamist terrorists across the foreign-domestic divide with a National Counterterrorism Center;
- unifying the intelligence community with a new National Intelligence Director;

- unifying the many participants in the counterterrorism effort and their knowledge in a network-based information sharing system that transcends traditional governmental boundaries
- unifying and strengthening congressional oversight to improve quality and accountability; and
- strengthening the FBI and homeland defenders.

* * *

We call on the American people to remember how we all felt on 9/11, to remember not only the unspeakable horror but how we came together as a nation—one nation. Unity of purpose and unity of effort are the way we will defeat this enemy and make America safer for our children and grandchildren.

We look forward to a national debate on the merits of what we have recommended, and we will participate vigorously in that debate.

Source: National Commission on Terrorist Attacks upon the United States, *Executive Summary of the Final Report of the National Commission on Terrorist Attacks upon the United States*. The executive summary, and the full report plus all supporting documents, is available at http://govinfo.library.unt.edu/911/report/index.htm.

ANALYSIS

The 9/11 Commission brought together dozens of elective officials, government experts, respected scholars, and other community leaders to investigate the September 11 attacks and make policy and structural recommendations for future efforts to defend against terrorist attacks. It was created at the behest of both houses of Congress and President George W. Bush. Formed in late 2002, the commission held 12 public hearings sessions, beginning on March 31, 2003, and ending on June 17, 2004. In those hearings, hundreds of individuals offered testimony, evidence, and counsel to the commission, which ultimately consolidated its findings in the final report. The commission found that there were ample opportunities for the U.S. government to disrupt the September 11 attacks, but that failures to understand the nature of the threat, the inability of agencies to efficiently cooperate with one another, and a certain degree of overconfidence about the effectiveness of existing security measures all conspired to render the U.S. civilian air traffic system vulnerable to attack and exploitation. Once the attack commenced, while individuals and organizations did their best to respond quickly and properly, there was simply no mechanism for a coordinated response, and hence, the only factor that served to spoil the ambitions of the hijackers was the initiative of the passengers aboard one of the attacked aircraft.

The final report of the commission proved very even-handed in determining blame for the failures on September 11, but its primary objective was to offer recommendations for future initiatives that might prevent further catastrophic attacks upon the homeland. The commission went so far as to recommend a radical reorganization of the nation's military, intelligence, and law enforcement agencies, recognizing that the existing structure had been created more than a generation earlier, and no longer fit the needs of the nation in the modern security environment. Although not all of the commission's recommendations were put into action, the final report served as a catalyst for a renewed discussion of the proper security apparatus of the United States, and allowed for a reasoned solution rather than a knee-jerk reaction in the immediate aftermath of the September 11 attacks.

3

DOCUMENTS FROM
THE PRESIDENCY OF
GEORGE W. BUSH, 2002–2008

- Document 41: Memorandum, John Yoo and Robert J. Delahunty to William J. Haynes II
- **When:** January 9, 2002
- **Where:** Washington, D.C.
- **Significance:** In this memorandum, Deputy Assistant Attorney General John Yoo laid out the legal argument that members of the Taliban and Al Qaeda should not be entitled to lawful combatant status, and hence should not be protected by the Geneva Convention Relative to the Treatment of Prisoners of War.

DOCUMENT

MEMORANDUM FOR WILLIAM J. HAYNES II
GENERAL COUNSEL, DEPARTMENT OF DEFENSE

FROM: John Yoo
Deputy Assistant Attorney General
Robert J. Delahunty
Special Counsel

RE: *Application of Treaties and Laws to al Qaeda and Taliban Detainees*

You have asked for our Office's views concerning the effect of international treaties and federal laws on the treatment of individuals detained by the U.S. Armed Forces during the conflict in Afghanistan. In particular, you have asked whether the laws of armed conflict apply to the conditions of detention and the procedures for trial of members of al Qaeda and the Taliban militia. We conclude that these treaties do not protect members of the al Qaeda organization, which as a non-State actor cannot be a party to the international agreements governing war. We further conclude that these treaties do not apply to the Taliban militia. This memorandum expresses no view as to whether the President should decide, as a matter of policy, that the U.S. Armed Forces should adhere to the standards of conduct in those treaties with respect to the treatment of prisoners.

We believe it most useful to structure the analysis of these questions by focusing on the War Crimes Act, 18 U.S.C. §2441 (Supp. III 1997) ("WCA"). The WCA directly incorporates several provisions of international treaties governing the laws of war into the federal criminal code. Part I of this memorandum describes the WCA and the most relevant treaties that it incorporates: the four 1949 Geneva Conventions, which generally regulate the treatment of non-combatants, such as prisoners of war ("POWs"), the injured and sick, and civilians.

Part II examines whether al Qaeda detainees can claim the protections of these agreements. Al Qaeda is merely a violent political movement or organization and not a nation-state. As a result, it is ineligible to be a signatory to any treaty. Because of the novel nature of this conflict, moreover, we do not believe that al Qaeda would be included in non-international forms of armed conflict to which some provisions of the Geneva Conventions might apply. Therefore, neither the Geneva Conventions nor the WCA regulate the detention of al Qaeda prisoners captured during the Afghanistan conflict.

Part III discusses whether the same treaty provisions, as incorporated through the WCA, apply to the treatment of captured members of the Taliban militia. We believe that the Geneva Conventions do not apply for several reasons. First, the Taliban was not a government and Afghanistan was not—even prior to the beginning of the present conflict—a functioning State during the period in which they engaged in hostilities against the United States and its allies. Afghanistan's status as a failed state is ground alone to find that members of the Taliban militia are not entitled to enemy POW status under the Geneva Conventions. Further, it is clear that the President has the constitutional authority to suspend our treaties with Afghanistan pending the restoration of a legitimate government capable of performing Afghanistan's treaty obligations. Second, it appears from the public evidence that the Taliban militia may have been so intertwined with al Qaeda as to be functionally indistinguishable from it. To the extent that the Taliban militia was more akin to a non-governmental organization that used military force to pursue its religious and political ideology than a functioning government, its members would be on the same legal footing as al Qaeda.

In Part IV, we address the question whether any customary international law of armed conflict might apply to the al Qaeda or Taliban militia members detained during the course of the Afghanistan conflict. We conclude that customary international law, whatever its source and content, does not bind the President, or restrict the actions of the United States military, because it does not constitute federal law recognized under the Supremacy Clause of the Constitution. The President, however, has the constitutional authority as Commander in Chief to interpret and apply the customary or common laws of war in such a way that they would extend to the conduct of members of both al Qaeda and the Taliban, and also to the conduct of the U.S. Armed Forces towards members of those groups taken as prisoners in Afghanistan.

Source: Department of Justice, Memorandum for William J. Haynes II, Application of Treaties and Laws to Al Qaeda and Taliban Detainees. January 9, 2002. Available online at http://nsarchive.gwu.edu/torturingdemocracy/documents/20020109.pdf.

ANALYSIS

This memorandum contains a much longer explanation of each of the topics summarized in the excerpt above. Yoo and Delahunty pushed the bounds of the argument regarding the legal status of captives to the logical limit. In particular, equating the Taliban fighters and Al Qaeda seems far-fetched, as does declaring the Taliban a nongovernment entity in a failed state. In an earlier communication, the United States had demanded that the Taliban capture and turn over Osama bin Laden. In the space of only a few months, the perception of the Taliban changed from that of a government with sufficient control over its territory to guarantee the capture of the world's most notorious terror leader into a mere faction in a fractured and chaotic region. The direct intervention of the U.S. military, which helped to destroy the Taliban's hold on power, is ignored as a factor in the Taliban's inability to control Afghanistan. There is little doubt that the Geneva Conventions did not apply to Al Qaeda captives, but the Taliban militia, despite being less professional than the norms for Western government representatives, still constituted the primary military wing of the Taliban, and should have been considered a legal fighting force. The attempt to delegitimize the Taliban appears to be a justification for its replacement with a government more to the liking of U.S. authorities.

- **Document 42: Donald Rumsfeld to Chairman, Joint Chiefs of Staff**
- **When:** January 19, 2002
- **Where:** Washington, D.C.
- **Significance:** This memorandum officially informed the nation's top military commander that detainees held at Guantanamo Bay would be formally denied prisoner-of-war status as defined by the Geneva Convention of 1949.

DOCUMENT

MEMORANDUM FOR CHAIRMAN OF THE JOINT CHIEFS OF STAFF
SUBJECT: Status of Taliban and Al Qaida
Transmit the following to the Combatant Commanders:

The United States has determined that Al Qaida and Taliban individuals under the control of the Department of Defense are not entitled to prisoner of war status for purposes of the Geneva Conventions of 1949.

The Combatant Commander shall, in detaining Al Qaida and Taliban individuals under the control of the Department of Defense, treat them humanely and, to the extent appropriate and consistent with military necessity, in a manner consistent with the principles of the Geneva Conventions of 1949.

The Combatant Commanders shall transmit this order to subordinate commanders, including Commander, Joint Task Force 160, for implementation.

Keep me appropriately informed of the implementation of this order.

Source: Department of Defense, Memorandum for Chairman of the Joint Chiefs of Staff, Status of Taliban and Al Qaida, January 19, 2002. Available online at http://nsarchive.gwu.edu/torturingdemocracy/documents/20020119.pdf.

ANALYSIS

Through this brief memorandum, Secretary of Defense Donald Rumsfeld made the key determination that individuals fighting on behalf of Al Qaeda and the Taliban would not be considered lawful combatants, and as such, the Geneva Convention Relative to Prisoners of War (1949) would not apply to their capture and detention. While the memorandum essentially called for detainees to be afforded the treatment demanded by the Geneva Convention, by labeling them unlawful combatants, the U.S. government placed them beyond the international protections guaranteed to the uniformed members of military services. This designation made perfect sense for members of Al Qaeda, who failed on all four counts required by the convention for a combatant to claim legal status. Those four elements are that the individual bear arms openly, wear a uniform or recognizable device, and belong to a hierarchical organization with commanders responsible for the behavior of subordinates, and that those organizations follow the laws of war. The Taliban's military personnel, in many but not all cases, did fulfill the spirit of the Geneva requirements, if not always the letter, particularly in the first months of the U.S. invasion. Many nations and human rights groups protested the U.S. determination that all captives fighting on behalf of Al Qaeda or the Taliban should be condemned as illegal combatants. However, in the environment of the United States, where a follow-on attack to the September 11 actions was considered entirely likely, this determination might have been inevitable.

DID YOU KNOW?

International Laws of War and Terrorists

The internal law that governs the acceptable practices of belligerents in warfare is collectively called the laws of armed conflict. Detailed laws protect legal combatants on the battlefield from unnecessary violence and suffering, and guarantee a combatant's right to surrender to the enemy. To qualify for such protections, a combatant must fulfill four conditions:

1. Bear arms openly.
2. Wear a uniform or other device recognizable from a distance.
3. Function in a hierarchy in which superiors are responsible for the behavior of subordinates.
4. Obey the laws of war, including those governing surrenders.

In general, terror organizations tend to fail on all four conditions, and no terror organization has ever consistently followed the requirements. In order to survive, terrorists typically have to conceal their ability and intentions to engage in violence, their identification with a terror group, and their relationship with leaders of the organization. Also, by most definitions, terrorism violates the laws of war because it entails attacks upon noncombatant populations. Thus, terrorists cannot claim protection under the laws of war.

- **Document 43: George W. Bush, State of the Union Address**
- **When:** January 29, 2002
- **Where:** Washington, D.C.
- **Significance:** In his first State of the Union address, President George W. Bush announced progress in Afghanistan and a renewed determination to destroy Al Qaeda.

DOCUMENT

Address before a Joint Session of the Congress on the State of the Union

Thank you very much. Mr. Speaker, Vice President Cheney, Members of Congress, distinguished guests, fellow citizens: As we gather tonight, our Nation is at war; our economy is in recession; and the civilized world faces unprecedented dangers. Yet, the state of our Union has never been stronger.

We last met in an hour of shock and suffering. In 4 short months, our Nation has comforted the victims, begun to rebuild New York and the Pentagon, rallied a great coalition, captured, arrested, and rid the world of thousands of terrorists, destroyed Afghanistan's terrorist training camps, saved a people from starvation, and freed a country from brutal oppression.

The American flag flies again over our Embassy in Kabul. Terrorists who once occupied Afghanistan now occupy cells at Guantanamo Bay. And terrorist leaders who urged followers to sacrifice their lives are running for their own.

Our cause is just, and it continues. Our discoveries in Afghanistan confirmed our worst fears and showed us the true scope of the task ahead. We have seen the depth of our enemies' hatred in videos where they laugh about the loss of innocent life. And the depth of their hatred is equaled by the madness of the destruction they design. We have found diagrams of American nuclear powerplants and public water facilities, detailed instructions for making chemical weapons, surveillance maps of American cities, and thorough descriptions of landmarks in America and throughout the world.

Our Nation will continue to be steadfast and patient and persistent in the pursuit of two great objectives. First, we will shut down terrorist camps, disrupt terrorist plans, and bring terrorists to justice. And second, we must prevent the terrorists and regimes who seek chemical, biological, or nuclear weapons from threatening the United States and the world.

Our military has put the terror training camps of Afghanistan out of business, yet camps still exist in at least a dozen countries. A terrorist underworld, including groups like Hamas, Hizballah, Islamic Jihad, Jaish-e-Mohammed, operates in remote jungles and deserts and hides in the centers of large cities.

While the most visible military action is in Afghanistan, America is acting elsewhere. We now have troops in the Philippines, helping to train that country's armed forces to go after terrorist cells that have executed an American and still hold hostages. Our soldiers, working with the Bosnian Government, seized terrorists who were plotting to bomb our Embassy. Our Navy is patrolling the coast of Africa to block the shipment of weapons and the establishment of terrorist camps in Somalia.

My hope is that all nations will heed our call and eliminate the terrorist parasites who threaten their countries and our own. Many nations are acting forcefully. Pakistan is now cracking down on terror, and I admire the strong leadership of President Musharraf. But some governments will be timid in the face of terror. And make no mistake about it: If they do not act, America will.

Our second goal is to prevent regimes that sponsor terror from threatening America or our friends and allies with weapons of mass destruction. Some of these regimes have been pretty quiet since September the 11th, but we know their true nature.

North Korea is a regime arming with missiles and weapons of mass destruction, while starving its citizens.

Iran aggressively pursues these weapons and exports terror, while an unelected few repress the Iranian people's hope for freedom.

Iraq continues to flaunt its hostility toward America and to support terror. The Iraqi regime has plotted to develop anthrax and nerve gas and nuclear weapons for over a decade. This is a regime that has already used poison gas to murder thousands of its own citizens, leaving the bodies of mothers huddled over their dead children. This is a regime that agreed to international inspections, then kicked out the inspectors. This is a regime that has something to hide from the civilized world.

States like these and their terrorist allies constitute an axis of evil, arming to threaten the peace of the world. By seeking weapons of mass destruction, these regimes pose a grave and growing danger. They could provide these arms to terrorists, giving them the means to match their hatred. They could attack our allies or attempt to blackmail the United States. In any of these cases, the price of indifference would be catastrophic.

We will work closely with our coalition to deny terrorists and their state sponsors the materials, technology, and expertise to make and deliver weapons of mass destruction. We will develop and deploy effective missile defenses to protect America and our allies from sudden attack. And all nations should know: America will do what is necessary to ensure our Nation's security.

We'll be deliberate; yet, time is not on our side. I will not wait on events while dangers gather. I will not stand by as peril draws closer and closer. The United States of America will not permit the world's most dangerous regimes to threaten us with the world's most destructive weapons.

Our war on terror is well begun, but it is only begun. This campaign may not be finished on our watch; yet, it must be and it will be waged on our watch. We can't stop short. If we stop now, leaving terror camps intact and terrorist states unchecked, our sense of security would be false and temporary. History has called America and our allies to action, and it is both our responsibility and our privilege to fight freedom's fight.

Our first priority must always be the security of our Nation, and that will be reflected in the budget I send to Congress. My budget supports three great goals for America: We will win this war; we will protect our homeland; and we will revive our economy.

The next priority of my budget is to do everything possible to protect our citizens and strengthen our Nation against the ongoing threat of another attack. Time and distance from the events of September the 11th will not make us safer unless we act on its lessons. America is no longer protected by vast oceans. We are protected from attack only by vigorous action abroad and increased vigilance at home.

During these last few months, I've been humbled and privileged to see the true character of this country in a time of testing. Our enemies believed America was weak and materialistic, that we would splinter in fear and selfishness. They were as wrong as they are evil.

The American people have responded magnificently, with courage and compassion, strength and resolve. As I have met the heroes, hugged the families, and looked into the tired faces of rescuers, I have stood in awe of the American people.

None of us would ever wish the evil that was done on September the 11th. Yet, after America was attacked, it was as if our entire country looked into a mirror and saw our better selves. We were reminded that we are citizens with obligations to each other, to our country, and to history. We began to think less of the goods we can accumulate and more about the good we can do.

For too long our culture has said, "If it feels good, do it." Now America is embracing a new ethic and a new creed, "Let's roll."

The last time I spoke here, I expressed the hope that life would return to normal. In some ways, it has. In others, it never will. Those of us who have lived through these challenging times have been changed by them. We've come to know truths that we will never question: Evil is real, and it must be opposed. Beyond all differences of race or creed, we are one country, mourning together and facing danger together. Deep in the American character, there is honor, and it is stronger than cynicism. And many have discovered again that even in tragedy—especially in tragedy—God is near.

In a single instant, we realized that this will be a decisive decade in the history of liberty, that we've been called to a unique role in human events. Rarely has the world faced a choice more clear or consequential.

Our enemies send other people's children on missions of suicide and murder. They embrace tyranny and death as a cause and a creed. We stand for a different choice, made long ago on the day of our founding. We affirm it again today. We choose freedom and the dignity of every life.

Steadfast in our purpose, we now press on. We have known freedom's price. We have shown freedom's power. And in this great conflict, my fellow Americans, we will see freedom's victory.

Thank you all. May God bless.

Source: Public Papers of the Presidents of the United States: George W. Bush (2002, Book 1). Washington D.C.: Government Printing Office, 129–136.

ANALYSIS

The president offers a State of the Union address to the nation once per year, traditionally by a joint address to both houses of Congress. In the 2002 address, President George W. Bush offered, among other things, a progress report in the War on Terror. He also made the infamous charge that North Korea, Iran, and Iraq constituted an "axis of evil," a collection of state sponsors of terrorism that constituted a threat to the civilized world. In particular, he singled out Iraq as a nation determined to obtain weapons of mass destruction, led by a dictator who had shown no hesitation to use chemical weapons against his own citizens. President Bush noted that the War on Terror would not be a short conflict, and might not be concluded during his administration, but vowed to take any steps necessary, and to pay any price, to destroy Al Qaeda and any group that supported it.

- **Document 44: White House Memorandum on Humane Treatment of Enemy Captives**
- **When:** February 7, 2002
- **Where:** Washington, D.C.
- **Significance:** President George W. Bush sent this memorandum to key officials declaring that Al Qaeda and Taliban prisoners would not be entitled to the protections of the Geneva Convention Relative to Prisoners of War, but would be treated in a humane fashion.

DOCUMENT

SUBJECT: Humane Treatment of Taliban and al Qaeda Detainees

1. Our recent extensive discussions regarding the status of al Qaeda and Taliban detainees confirm that the application of Geneva Convention Relative to the Treatment of Prisoners of War of August 12, 1949, (Geneva) to the conflict with al Qaeda and the Taliban involves complex legal questions. By its terms, Geneva applies to conflicts involving "High Contracting Parties," which can only be states. Moreover, it assumes the existence of "regular" armed forces fighting on behalf of states. However, the war against terrorism ushers in a new paradigm, one in which groups with broad, international reach commit horrific acts against innocent civilians, sometimes with the direct support of states. Our nation recognizes that this new paradigm—ushered in not by us, but by terrorists—requires new thinking in the law of war, but thinking that should nevertheless be consistent with the principles of Geneva.

2. Pursuant to my authority as commander in chief and chief executive of the United States, and relying on the opinion of the Department of Justice dated January 22, 2002, and on the legal opinion rendered by the attorney general in his letter of February 1, 2002, I hereby determine as follows:

a. I accept the legal conclusion of the Department of Justice and determine that none of the provisions of Geneva apply to our conflict with al Qaeda in Afghanistan or elsewhere throughout the world because, among other reasons, al Qaeda is not a High Contracting Party to Geneva.

b. I accept the legal conclusion of the attorney general and the Department of Justice that I have the authority under the Constitution to suspend Geneva as between the United States and Afghanistan, but I decline to exercise that authority at this time. Accordingly, I determine that the provisions of Geneva will apply to our present conflict with the Taliban. I reserve the right to exercise the authority in this or future conflicts.

c. I also accept the legal conclusion of the Department of Justice and determine that common Article 3 of Geneva does not apply to either al Qaeda or Taliban

DID YOU KNOW?

The Selection of Guantanamo Bay as a Prison Site

As the pace of U.S. operations against Al Qaeda increased in late 2001 and early 2002, the number of captured enemy fighters concurrently grew. These enemy combatants presented a problem, as they clearly did not qualify for prisoner-of-war status, under the Geneva Conventions, but also did not represent civil prisoners who could be easily tried in a criminal court. A series of escapes from temporary holding compounds in Afghanistan demonstrated the need for a more secure location, but bringing them to American soil might trigger constitutional protections that would make interrogations difficult or impossible. The Bush administration's solution was to place the captives at the U.S. naval base located at Guantanamo Bay, Cuba. While not ideal, the location was firmly under control and faced no external security threats, all but guaranteeing there would be no escapes.

detainees, because, among other reasons, the relevant conflicts are international in scope and common Article 3 applies only to "armed conflict not of an international character."

d. Based on the facts supplied by the Department of Defense and the recommendation of the Department of Justice, I determine that the Taliban detainees are unlawful combatants and, therefore, do not qualify as prisoners of war under Article 4 of Geneva. I note that, because Geneva does not apply to our conflict with al Qaeda, al Qaeda detainees also do not qualify as prisoners of war.

3. Of course, our values as a nation, values that we share with many nations in the world, call for us to treat detainees humanely, including those who are not legally entitled to such treatment. Our nation has been and will continue to be a strong supporter of Geneva and its principles. As a matter of policy, the United States Armed Forces shall continue to treat detainees humanely and, to the extent appropriate and consistent with military necessity, in a manner consistent with the principles of Geneva.

4. The United States will hold states, organizations, and individuals who gain control of United States personnel responsible for treating such personnel humanely and consistent with applicable law.

5. I hereby reaffirm the order previously issued by the secretary of defense to the United States Armed Forces requiring that the detainees be treated humanely and, to the extent appropriate and consistent with military necessity, in a manner consistent with the principles of Geneva.

6. I hereby direct the secretary of state to communicate my determinations in an appropriate manner to our allies, and other countries and international organizations cooperating in the war against terrorism of global reach.

Source: George W. Bush. "Humane Treatment of Al Qaeda and Taliban Detainees," Memorandum for the Vice President, the Secretary of State, the Secretary of Defense, the Attorney General, Chief of Staff to the President, Director of Central Intelligence, Assistant to the President for National Security Affairs, and Chairman of the Joint Chiefs of Staff, February 7, 2002. The memorandum was released after a Freedom of Information Act request, and can be found in full at http://nsarchive.gwu.edu/NSAEBB/NSAEBB127/02.02.07.pdf.

ANALYSIS

President Bush refers to a series of Department of Justice determinations that the conflict with Al Qaeda in Afghanistan and elsewhere, while international in nature, did not require adherence to the Geneva Convention Relative to Prisoners of War

(1949). It is noteworthy that the memorandum cites the fact that Al Qaeda is not a party to the treaty as a key determining factor, given that the Geneva Convention requires all signatories to adhere to its provisions even when facing enemies that have neither signed nor promised to follow its provisions. However, the behavior of Al Qaeda members in general made them ineligible for the protections of Geneva, which requires lawful combatants to wear a uniform or recognizable device, bear arms openly, follow a hierarchical rank structure, and follow the laws of war themselves. In contrast, representatives of the Taliban would be accorded prisoner-of-war status, at least for the time being, although the president noted that the Department of Justice argued he had the right to suspend Geneva in the conflict at any time. Although the memorandum called for the humane treatment of enemy combatants, it did not define the term "humane," and thus left open the possibility of harsh interrogation techniques, particularly waterboarding, that many considered to be inhumane.

- **Document 45: Military Commission Order No. 1**
- **When:** March 21, 2002
- **Where:** Washington, D.C.
- **Significance:** As the American-led invasion of Afghanistan progressed, the coalition members began to capture enemy personnel. These captives represented a significant problem, in that they were not deemed lawful combatants under the Geneva Convention, and hence could not claim prisoner-of-war status. By default, they became classified simply as enemy detainees, but their disposition created a thorny problem, namely, could they be put on trial for engaging in acts of terrorism or illegal military activities? With this order, Secretary of Defense Donald Rumsfeld established a military tribunal system tasked with trying and sentencing enemy captives for their activities.

DOCUMENT

Department of Defense
Military Commission Order No. 1
March 21, 2002
SUBJECT: Procedures for Trials by Military Commissions of Certain Non-United States Citizens in the War Against Terrorism

1. PURPOSE
This Order implements policy, assigns responsibilities, and prescribes procedures under references (a) and (b) for trials before military commissions of individuals subject to the President's Military Order. These procedures shall be implemented and construed so as to ensure that any such individual receives a full and fair trial before a military commission, as required by the President's Military Order.

DID YOU KNOW?

Uighurs and Asylum

Guantanamo Bay has held captives from dozens of nations, most of them Muslim states in the Middle East or Southwest Asia. One group of prisoners captured while fighting for Al Qaeda came from a surprising source: 22 ethnic Uighurs from Western China were captured in Afghanistan, but found to have little intelligence value or status within Al Qaeda. There was little desire to retain them at the prison, but sending them to Chinese custody would almost certainly result in their execution, as the Chinese government has struggled to suppress a Uighur insurgency for decades. Thus, they presented a quandary, until several nations, including Albania, Bermuda, El Salvador, Palau, and Slovakia, offered them asylum once they were determined to present no further threat to the United States. The men were quietly transferred and allowed to join the civil society of their new homes. Many reportedly struggled to adapt to their new lives and, because they are not classified as prisoners, have chosen to leave their asylum nations and return to Asia.

Unless otherwise directed by the Secretary of Defense, and except for supplemental procedures established pursuant to the President's Military Order or this Order, the procedures prescribed herein and no others shall govern such trials.

2. ESTABLISHMENT OF MILITARY COMMISSIONS

In accordance with the President's Military Order, the Secretary of Defense or a designee ("Appointing Authority") may issue orders from time to time appointing one or more military commissions to try individuals subject to the President's Military Order and appointing any other personnel necessary to facilitate such trials.

3. JURISDICTION

A. Over Persons

A military commission appointed under this Order ("Commission") shall have jurisdiction over only an individual or individuals ("the Accused") (1) subject to the President's Military Order and (2) alleged to have committed an offense in a charge that has been referred to the Commission by the Appointing Authority.

B. Over Offenses

Commissions established hereunder shall have jurisdiction over violations of the laws of war and all other offenses triable by military commission.

C. Maintaining Integrity of Commission Proceedings

The Commission may exercise jurisdiction over participants in its proceedings as necessary to preserve the integrity and order of the proceedings.

4. COMMISSION PERSONNEL

A. Members

(1) Appointment

The Appointing Authority shall appoint the members and the alternate member or members of each Commission. The alternate member or members shall attend all sessions of the Commission, but the absence of an alternate member shall not preclude the Commission from conducting proceedings. In case of incapacity, resignation, or removal of any member, an alternate member shall take the place of that member. Any vacancy among the members or alternate members occurring after a trial has begun may be filled by the Appointing Authority, but the substance of all prior proceedings and evidence taken in that case shall be made known to that new member or alternate member before the trial proceeds.

(2) Number of Members

Each Commission shall consist of at least three but no more than seven members, the number being determined by the Appointing Authority. For each such Commission, there shall also be one or two alternate members, the number being determined by the Appointing Authority.

(3) Qualifications

Each member and alternate member shall be a commissioned officer of the United States armed forces ("Military Officer"), including without limitation reserve personnel on active duty, National Guard personnel on active duty in Federal service, and retired personnel recalled to active duty. The Appointing Authority shall appoint members and alternate members determined to be competent to perform the duties involved. The Appointing Authority may remove members and alternate members for good cause.

(4) Presiding Officer

From among the members of each Commission, the Appointing Authority shall designate a Presiding Officer to preside over the proceedings of that Commission. The Presiding Officer shall be a Military Officer who is a judge advocate of any United States armed force.

B. Prosecution

(1) Office of the Chief Prosecutor

The Chief Prosecutor shall be a judge advocate of any United States armed force, shall supervise the overall prosecution efforts under the President's Military Order, and shall ensure proper management of personnel and resources.

(2) Prosecutors and Assistant Prosecutors

Consistent with any supplementary regulations or instructions issued under Section 7(A), the Chief Prosecutor shall detail a Prosecutor and, as appropriate, one or more Assistant Prosecutors to prepare charges and conduct the prosecution for each case before a Commission ("Prosecution"). Prosecutors and Assistant Prosecutors shall be (a) Military Officers who are judge advocates of any United States armed force, or (b) special trial counsel of the Department of Justice who may be made available by the Attorney General of the United States.

C. Defense

(1) Office of the Chief Defense Counsel

The Chief Defense Counsel shall be a judge advocate of any United States armed force, shall supervise the overall defense efforts under the President's Military Order, shall ensure proper management of personnel and resources, shall preclude conflicts of interest, and shall facilitate proper representation of all Accused.

(2) Detailed Defense Counsel.

Consistent with any supplementary regulations or instructions, the Chief Defense Counsel shall detail one or more Military Officers who are judge advocates of any United States armed force to conduct the defense for each case before a Commission ("Detailed Defense Counsel").

(3) Choice of Counsel

(a) The Accused may select a Military Officer who is a judge advocate of any United States armed force to replace the Accused's Detailed Defense Counsel, provided that Military Officer has been determined to be available in accordance with any applicable supplementary regulations or instructions. After such selection of a new Detailed Defense Counsel, the original Detailed Defense Counsel will be relieved of all duties with respect to that case. If requested by the Accused, however, the Appointing Authority may allow the original Detailed Defense Counsel to continue to assist in representation of the Accused as another Detailed Defense Counsel.

(b) The Accused may also retain the services of a civilian attorney of the Accused's own choosing and at no expense to the United States Government ("Civilian Defense Counsel"), provided that attorney: (i) is a United States citizen; (ii) is admitted to the practice of law in a State, district, territory, or possession of the United States, or before a Federal court; (iii) has not been the subject of any sanction or disciplinary action by any court, bar, or other competent governmental authority for relevant misconduct; (iv) has been determined to be eligible for access to information classified at the level SECRET or higher under the authority of and in accordance with the procedures prescribed in reference (c); and (v) has signed a written agreement to comply with all applicable regulations or instructions for counsel, including any rules of court for conduct during the course of proceedings. Civilian attorneys may be pre-qualified as members of the pool of available attorneys if, at the time of application, they meet the relevant criteria, or they may be qualified on an *ad hoc* basis after being requested by an Accused. Representation by Civilian Defense Counsel will not relieve Detailed Defense Counsel of the duties specified in Section 4(C)(2). The qualification of a Civilian Defense Counsel does not guarantee that person's presence at closed Commission proceedings or that person's access to any information protected under Section 6(D)(5).

5. PROCEDURES ACCORDED THE ACCUSED

The following procedures shall apply with respect to the Accused:

A. The Prosecution shall furnish to the Accused, sufficiently in advance of trial to prepare a defense, a copy of the charges in English and, if appropriate, in another language that the Accused understands.

B. The Accused shall be presumed innocent until proven guilty.

C. A Commission member shall vote for a finding of Guilty as to an offense if and only if that member is convinced beyond a reasonable doubt, based on the evidence admitted at trial, that the Accused is guilty of the offense.

D. At least one Detailed Defense Counsel shall be made available to the Accused sufficiently in advance of trial to prepare a defense and until any findings and sentence become final.

E. The Prosecution shall provide the Defense with access to evidence the Prosecution intends to introduce at trial and with access to evidence known to the Prosecution that tends to exculpate the Accused.

F. The Accused shall not be required to testify during trial. A Commission shall draw no adverse inference from an Accused's decision not to testify. This subsection shall not preclude admission of evidence of prior statements or conduct of the Accused.

G. If the Accused so elects, the Accused may testify at trial on the Accused's own behalf and shall then be subject to cross-examination.

H. The Accused may obtain witnesses and documents for the Accused's defense, to the extent necessary and reasonably available as determined by the Presiding Officer. The Appointing Authority shall order that such investigative or other resources be made available to the Defense as the Appointing Authority deems necessary for a full and fair trial.

I. The Accused may have Defense Counsel present evidence at trial in the Accused's defense and cross-examine each witness presented by the Prosecution who appears before the Commission.

J. The Prosecution shall ensure that the substance of the charges, the proceedings, and any documentary evidence are provided in English and, if appropriate, in another language that the Accused understands. The Appointing Authority may appoint one or more interpreters to assist the Defense, as necessary.

K. The Accused may be present at every stage of the trial before the Commission, unless the Accused engages in disruptive conduct that justifies exclusion by the Presiding Officer. Detailed Defense Counsel may not be excluded from any trial proceeding or portion thereof.

L. Except by order of the Commission for good cause shown, the Prosecution shall provide the Defense with access before sentencing proceedings to evidence the Prosecution intends to present in such proceedings.

M. The Accused may make a statement during sentencing proceedings.

N. The Accused may have Defense Counsel submit evidence to the Commission during sentencing proceedings.

O. The Accused shall be afforded a trial open to the public (except proceedings closed by the Presiding Officer).

P. The Accused shall not again be tried by any Commission for a charge once a Commission's finding on that charge becomes final.

6. CONDUCT OF THE TRIAL

The Commission shall:

(1) Provide a full and fair trial.

(2) Proceed impartially and expeditiously, strictly confining the proceedings to a full and fair trial of the charges, excluding irrelevant evidence, and preventing any unnecessary interference or delay.

(3) Hold open proceedings except where otherwise decided by the Appointing Authority or the Presiding Officer in accordance with the President's Military Order and this Order. Grounds for closure include the protection of information classified or classifiable under reference (d); information protected by law or rule from unauthorized disclosure; the physical safety of participants in Commission proceedings, including prospective witnesses; intelligence and law enforcement sources, methods, or activities; and other national security interests. The Presiding Officer may decide to close all or part of a proceeding on the Presiding Officer's own initiative or based upon a presentation, including an *ex parte in camera* presentation by either the Prosecution or the Defense. A decision to close a proceeding or portion thereof may include a decision to exclude the Accused, Civilian Defense Counsel, or any other person, but Detailed Defense Counsel may not be excluded from any trial proceeding or portion thereof. Except with the prior authorization of the Presiding Officer and subject to Section 9, Defense Counsel may not disclose any information presented during a closed session to individuals excluded from such proceeding or part thereof. Open proceedings may include, at the discretion of the Appointing Authority, attendance by the public and accredited press, and public release of transcripts at the appropriate time. Proceedings should be open to the maximum extent practicable. Photography, video, or audio broadcasting, or recording of or at Commission

proceedings shall be prohibited, except photography, video, and audio recording by the Commission pursuant to the direction of the Presiding Officer as necessary for preservation of the record of trial.

C. Oaths

(1) Members of a Commission, all Prosecutors, all Defense Counsel, all court reporters, all security personnel, and all interpreters shall take an oath to perform their duties faithfully.

(2) Each witness appearing before a Commission shall be examined under oath, as provided in Section 6(D)(2)(b).

(3) An oath includes an affirmation. Any formulation that appeals to the conscience of the person to whom the oath is administered and that binds that person to speak the truth, or, in the case of one other than a witness, properly to perform certain duties, is sufficient.

D. Evidence

(1) Admissibility

Evidence shall be admitted if, in the opinion of the Presiding Officer (or instead, if any other member of the Commission so requests at the time the Presiding Officer renders that opinion, the opinion of the Commission rendered at that time by a majority of the Commission), the evidence would have probative value to a reasonable person.

(2) Witnesses

(a) Production of Witnesses

The Prosecution or the Defense may request that the Commission hear the testimony of any person, and such testimony shall be received if found to be admissible and not cumulative. The Commission may also summon and hear witnesses on its own initiative. The Commission may permit the testimony of witnesses by telephone, audiovisual means, or other means; however, the Commission shall consider the ability to test the veracity of that testimony in evaluating the weight to be given to the testimony of the witness.

(b) Testimony

Testimony of witnesses shall be given under oath or affirmation. The Commission may still hear a witness who refuses to swear an oath or make a solemn undertaking; however, the Commission shall consider the refusal to swear an oath or give an affirmation in evaluating the weight to be given to the testimony of the witness.

(c) Examination of Witnesses

A witness who testifies before the Commission is subject to both direct examination and cross-examination. The Presiding Officer shall maintain order in the proceedings and shall not permit badgering of witnesses or questions that are not material to the issues before the Commission. Members of the Commission may question witnesses at any time.

(d) Protection of Witnesses

The Presiding Officer shall consider the safety of witnesses and others, as well as the safeguarding of Protected Information as defined in Section 6(D)(5)(a), in determining the appropriate methods of receiving testimony and evidence. The Presiding Officer may hear any presentation by the Prosecution or the Defense, including an *ex parte*, *in camera* presentation, regarding the safety of potential witnesses before determining the ways in which witnesses and evidence will be protected. The Presiding Officer may authorize any methods appropriate for the protection of witnesses and evidence. Such methods may include, but are not limited to: testimony by telephone, audiovisual means, or other electronic means; closure of the proceedings; introduction of prepared declassified summaries of evidence; and the use of pseudonyms.

(3) Other Evidence

Subject to the requirements of Section 6(D)(1) concerning admissibility, the Commission may consider any other evidence including, but not limited to, testimony from prior trials and proceedings, sworn or unsworn written statements, physical evidence, or scientific or other reports.

F. Voting

Members of the Commission shall deliberate and vote in closed conference. A Commission member shall vote for a finding of Guilty as to an offense if and only if that member is convinced beyond a reasonable doubt, based on the evidence admitted at trial, that the Accused is guilty of the offense. An affirmative vote of two-thirds of the members is required for a finding of Guilty. When appropriate, the Commission may adjust a charged offense by exceptions and substitutions of language that do not substantially change the nature of the offense or increase its seriousness, or it may vote to convict of a lesser-included offense. An affirmative vote of two-thirds of the members is required to determine a sentence, except that a sentence of death requires a unanimous, affirmative vote of all of the members. Votes on findings and sentences shall be taken by secret, written ballot.

G. Sentence

Upon conviction of an Accused, the Commission shall impose a sentence that is appropriate to the offense or offenses for which there was a finding of Guilty, which sentence may include death, imprisonment for life or for any lesser term, payment of a fine or restitution, or such other lawful punishment or condition of punishment as the Commission shall determine to be proper. Only a Commission of seven members may sentence an Accused to death. A Commission may (subject to rights of third parties) order confiscation of any property of a convicted Accused, deprive that Accused of any stolen property, or order the delivery of such property to the United States for disposition.

Source: Department of Defense, Office of Military Commissions. Available online at http://www.mc.mil/Portals/0/milcomord1.pdf.

ANALYSIS

In theory, Secretary Rumsfeld's order conformed with previous practices by establishing war crimes tribunals convened by a military authority. Special attention is paid to the challenges presented by the War on Terror, to include the potential necessity to hold closed sessions, to prohibit the accused from hearing the source of some of the accusations, and to limit the accused's opportunity to confront witnesses. This order allowed the tribunal very broad leeway regarding the types of testimony and evidence that it would consider, and did not prohibit the inclusion of unsworn testimony, information obtained through coercive methods, or written evidence whose author was not available for questioning. In 2006, the Supreme Court ruled in *Hamdan v. Rumsfeld* that these types of commissions would not fulfill the requirements for trials under the Uniform Code of Military Justice or the standards of international law (see Document 65).

- **Document 46: National Strategy for Homeland Security**
- **When:** July 2002
- **Where:** Washington, D.C.
- **Significance:** This was the first attempt by the newly created Department of Homeland Security to offer a comprehensive strategy for the defense of the nation from external nonstate threats.

DOCUMENT

Executive Summary

This document is the first *National Strategy for Homeland Security*. The purpose of the *Strategy* is to mobilize and organize our Nation to secure the U.S. homeland from terrorist attacks. This is an exceedingly complex mission that requires coordinated and focused effort from our entire society—the federal government, state and local governments, the private sector, and the American people.

People and organizations all across the United States have taken many steps to improve our security since the September 11 attacks, but a great deal of work remains. The *National Strategy for Homeland Security* will help to prepare our Nation for the work ahead in several ways. It provides direction to the federal government departments and agencies that have a role in homeland security. It suggests steps that state and local governments, private companies and organizations, and individual Americans can take to improve our security and offers incentives for them to do so. It recommends certain actions to the Congress. In this way, the *Strategy* provides a framework for the contributions that we all can make to secure our homeland.

The *National Strategy for Homeland Security* is the beginning of what will be a long struggle to protect our Nation from terrorism. It establishes a foundation upon which to organize our efforts and provides initial guidance to prioritize the work ahead. The *Strategy* will be adjusted and amended over time. We must be prepared to adapt as our enemies in the war on terrorism alter their means of attack.

Strategic Objectives

The strategic objectives of homeland security in order of priority are to:

- Prevent terrorist attacks within the United States;
- Reduce America's vulnerability to terrorism; and
- Minimize the damage and recover from attacks that do occur.

Threat and Vulnerability

Unless we act to prevent it, a new wave of terrorism, potentially involving the world's most destructive weapons, looms in America's future. It is a challenge as formidable as any ever faced by our Nation. But we are not daunted. We possess the determination and the resources to defeat our enemies and secure our homeland against the threats they pose.

One fact dominates all homeland security threat assessments: terrorists are strategic actors. They choose their targets deliberately based on the weaknesses they observe in our defenses and our preparedness. We must defend ourselves against a wide range of means and methods of attack. Our enemies are working to obtain chemical, biological, radiological, and nuclear weapons for the purpose of wreaking unprecedented damage on America. Terrorists continue to employ conventional means of attack, while at the same time gaining expertise in less traditional means, such as cyber attacks. Our society presents an almost infinite array of potential targets that can be attacked through a variety of methods.

Our enemies seek to remain invisible, lurking in the shadows. We are actively engaged in uncovering them. Al-Qaeda remains America's most immediate and serious threat despite our success in disrupting its network in Afghanistan and elsewhere. Other international terrorist organizations, as well as domestic terrorist groups, possess the will and capability to attack the United States.

Critical Mission Areas

The *National Strategy for Homeland Security* aligns and focuses homeland security functions into six critical mission areas: intelligence and warning, border and transportation security, domestic counterterrorism, protecting critical infrastructure, defending against catastrophic terrorism, and emergency preparedness and response. The first three mission areas focus primarily on preventing terrorist attacks; the next two on reducing our Nation's vulnerabilities; and the final one on minimizing the damage and recovering from attacks that do occur. The *Strategy* provides a framework to align the resources of the federal budget directly to the task of securing the homeland.

Intelligence and Warning. Terrorism depends on surprise. With it, a terrorist attack has the potential to do massive damage to an unwitting and unprepared target. Without it, the terrorists stand a good chance of being preempted by authorities, and even if they are not, the damage that results from their attacks is likely to be less severe. The United States will take every necessary action to avoid being surprised by another terrorist attack. We must have an intelligence and warning system that can detect terrorist activity before it manifests itself in an attack so that proper preemptive, preventative, and protective action can be taken.

The *National Strategy for Homeland Security* identifies five major initiatives in this area:

- Enhance the analytic capabilities of the FBI;
- Build new capabilities through the Information Analysis and Infrastructure Protection Division of the proposed Department of Homeland Security;

- Implement the Homeland Security Advisory System;
- Utilize dual-use analysis to prevent attacks; and
- Employ "red team" techniques.

Border and Transportation Security. America historically has relied heavily on two vast oceans and two friendly neighbors for border security, and on the private sector for most forms of domestic transportation security. The increasing mobility and destructive potential of modern terrorism has required the United States to rethink and renovate fundamentally its systems for border and transportation security. Indeed, we must now begin to conceive of border security and transportation security as fully integrated requirements because our domestic transportation systems are inextricably intertwined with the global transport infrastructure. Virtually every community in America is connected to the global transportation network by the seaports, airports, highways, pipelines, railroads, and waterways that move people and goods into, within, and out of the Nation. We must therefore promote the efficient and reliable flow of people, goods, and services across borders, while preventing terrorists from using transportation conveyances or systems to deliver implements of destruction.

The *National Strategy for Homeland Security* identifies six major initiatives in this area:

- Ensure accountability in border and transportation security;
- Create "smart borders";
- Increase the security of international shipping containers;
- Implement the Aviation and Transportation Security Act of 2001;
- Recapitalize the U.S. Coast Guard; and
- Reform immigration services.

The President proposed to Congress that the principal border and transportation security agencies—the Immigration and Naturalization Service, the U.S. Customs Service, the U.S. Coast Guard, the Animal and Plant Health Inspection Service, and the Transportation Security Agency—be transferred to the new Department of Homeland Security. This organizational reform will greatly assist in the implementation of all the above initiatives.

Domestic Counterterrorism. The attacks of September 11 and the catastrophic loss of life and property that resulted have redefined the mission of federal, state, and local law enforcement authorities. While law enforcement agencies will continue to investigate and prosecute criminal activity, they should now assign priority to preventing and interdicting terrorist activity within the United States. The Nation's state and local law enforcement officers will be critical in this effort. Our Nation will use all legal means—both traditional and nontraditional—to identify, halt, and, where appropriate, prosecute terrorists in the United States. We will pursue not only the individuals directly involved in terrorist activity but also their sources of support: the people and organizations that knowingly fund the terrorists and those that provide them with logistical assistance.

Effectively reorienting law enforcement organizations to focus on counterterrorism objectives requires decisive action in a number of areas. The *National Strategy for Homeland Security* identifies six major initiatives in this area:

- Improve intergovernmental law enforcement coordination;
- Facilitate apprehension of potential terrorists;
- Continue ongoing investigations and prosecutions;
- Complete FBI restructuring to emphasize prevention of terrorist attacks;
- Target and attack terrorist financing; and
- Track foreign terrorists and bring them to justice.

Protecting Critical Infrastructure and Key Assets. Our society and modern way of life are dependent on networks of infrastructure—both physical networks such as our energy and transportation systems and virtual networks such as the Internet. If terrorists attack one or more pieces of our critical infrastructure, they may disrupt entire systems and cause significant damage to the Nation. We must therefore improve protection of the individual pieces and interconnecting systems that make up our critical infrastructure. Protecting America's critical infrastructure and key assets will not only make us more secure from terrorist attack, but will also reduce our vulnerability to natural disasters, organized crime, and computer hackers.

America's critical infrastructure encompasses a large number of sectors. The U.S. government will seek to deny terrorists the opportunity to inflict lasting harm to our Nation by protecting the assets, systems, and functions vital to our national security, governance, public health and safety, economy, and national morale.

The *National Strategy for Homeland Security* identifies eight major initiatives in this area:

- Unify America's infrastructure protection effort in the Department of Homeland Security;
- Build and maintain a complete and accurate assessment of America's critical infrastructure and key assets;
- Enable effective partnership with state and local governments and the private sector;
- Develop a national infrastructure protection plan;
- Secure cyberspace;
- Harness the best analytic and modeling tools to develop effective protective solutions;
- Guard America's critical infrastructure and key assets against "inside" threats; and
- Partner with the international community to protect our transnational infrastructure.

Defending against Catastrophic Threats. The expertise, technology, and material needed to build the most deadly weapons known to mankind—including chemical biological, radiological, and nuclear weapons—are spreading inexorably. If our enemies acquire these weapons, they are likely to try to use them. The consequences of such an attack could be far more devastating than those we suffered on September 11—a chemical, biological, radiological, or nuclear terrorist attack in the United States could cause large numbers of casualties, mass psychological disruption, contamination and significant economic damage, and could overwhelm local medical capabilities.

Currently, chemical, biological, radiological, and nuclear detection capabilities are modest and response capabilities are dispersed throughout the country at every level of government. While current arrangements have proven adequate for a variety of natural disasters and even the September 11 attacks, the threat of terrorist attacks using chemical biological, radiological, and nuclear weapons requires new approaches, a focused strategy, and a new organization.

The *National Strategy for Homeland Security* identifies six major initiatives in this area:

- Prevent terrorist use of nuclear weapons through better sensors and procedures;
- Detect chemical and biological materials and attacks;
- Improve chemical sensors and decontamination techniques;
- Develop broad spectrum vaccines, antimicrobials, and antidotes;
- Harness the scientific knowledge and tools to counter terrorism; and
- Implement the Select Agent Program.

Emergency Preparedness and Response. We must prepare to minimize the damage and recover from any future terrorist attacks that may occur despite our best efforts at prevention. An effective response to a major terrorist incident—as well as a natural disaster—depends on being prepared. Therefore, we need a comprehensive national system to bring together and coordinate all necessary response assets quickly and effectively. We must plan, equip, train, and exercise many different response units to mobilize without warning for any emergency.

Many pieces of this national emergency response system are already in place. America's first line of defense in the aftermath of any terrorist attack is its first responder community—police officers, firefighters, emergency medical providers, public works personnel, and emergency management officials. Nearly three million state and local first responders regularly put their lives on the line to save the lives of others and make our country safer.

Yet multiple plans currently govern the federal government's support of first responders during an incident of national significance. These plans and the government's overarching policy for counterterrorism are based on an artificial and unnecessary distinction between "crisis management" and "consequence management." Under the President's proposal, the Department of Homeland Security will consolidate federal response plans and build a national system for incident management in cooperation with state and local government. Our federal, state, and local governments would ensure that all response personnel and organizations are properly equipped, trained, and exercised to respond to all terrorist threats and attacks in the United States. Our emergency preparedness and response efforts would also engage the private sector and the American people.

The *National Strategy for Homeland Security* identifies twelve major initiatives in this area:

- Integrate separate federal response plans into a single all-discipline incident management plan;
- Create a national incident management system;
- Improve tactical counterterrorist capabilities;

- Enable seamless communication among all responders;
- Prepare health care providers for catastrophic terrorism;
- Augment America's pharmaceutical and vaccine stockpiles;
- Prepare for chemical, biological, radiological, and nuclear decontamination;
- Plan for military support to civil authorities;
- Build the Citizen Corps;
- Implement the First Responder Initiative of the Fiscal Year 2003 Budget;
- Build a national training and evaluation system; and
- Enhance the victim support system.

Conclusion: Priorities for the Future

The *National Strategy for Homeland Security* sets a broad and complex agenda for the United States. The *Strategy* has defined many different goals that need to be met, programs that need to be implemented, and responsibilities that need to be fulfilled. But creating a strategy is, in many respects, about setting priorities—about recognizing that some actions are more critical or more urgent than others.

The President's Fiscal Year 2003 Budget proposal, released in February 2002, identified four priority areas for additional resources and attention in the upcoming year:

- Support first responders;
- Defend against bioterrorism;
- Secure America's borders; and
- Use 21st-century technology to secure the homeland.

Work has already begun on the President's Fiscal Year 2004 Budget. Assuming the Congress passes legislation to implement the President's proposal to create the Department of Homeland Security, the Fiscal Year 2004 Budget will fully reflect the reformed organization of the executive branch for homeland security. That budget will have an integrated and simplified structure based on the six critical mission areas defined by the *Strategy*. Furthermore, at the time the *National Strategy for Homeland Security* was published, it was expected that the Fiscal Year 2004 Budget would attach priority to the following specific items for substantial support:

- Enhance the analytic capabilities of the FBI;
- Build new capabilities through the Information Analysis and Infrastructure Protection Division of the proposed Department of Homeland Security;
- Create "smart borders";
- Improve the security of international shipping containers;
- Recapitalize the U.S. Coast Guard;
- Prevent terrorist use of nuclear weapons through better sensors and procedures;
- Develop broad spectrum vaccines, antimicrobials, and antidotes; and
- Integrate information sharing across the federal government.

In the intervening months, the executive branch will prepare detailed implementation plans for these and many other initiatives contained within the *National*

Strategy for Homeland Security. These plans will ensure that the taxpayers' money is spent only in a manner that achieves specific objectives with clear performance-based measures of effectiveness.

Source: Department of Homeland Security, http://www.dhs.gov/publication/first-national-strategy-homeland-security.

ANALYSIS

Strategic documents are designed to give broad guidance to the agencies tasked with carrying them out. Like most, the "National Strategy for Homeland Security" offers a large number of overarching principles and goals, with very little concrete explanation for how to achieve any of the objectives. The document is more about framing and shaping the problem than about presenting any solutions. This strategy is significant for a number of reasons. First, it consolidates most of the major federal agencies tasked with homeland security functions into a single, theoretically more efficient, hierarchical structure. Second, it identifies terrorism in general, and Al Qaeda in particular, as the greatest threat to U.S. national security in 2002. Third, it correctly identifies the potential catastrophic failures in national security, specifically the possibility of Al Qaeda using chemical, biological, or nuclear weapons against U.S. targets. And finally, it clarifies the role to be played by organizations not controlled by the newly formed Department of Homeland Security, such as the military, federal intelligence agencies, and local law enforcement.

- **Document 47: National Security Strategy for the United States**
- **When:** September 17, 2002
- **Where:** Washington, D.C.
- **Significance:** Every four years, the presidential administration releases a national security strategy. This public document establishes the broad guidance for various federal agencies tasked with carrying out national security and defense.

DOCUMENT

The United States of America is fighting a war against terrorists of global reach. The enemy is not a single political regime or person or religion or ideology. The enemy is terrorism—premeditated, politically motivated violence perpetrated against innocents.

In many regions, legitimate grievances prevent the emergence of a lasting peace. Such grievances deserve to be, and must be, addressed within a political process.

But no cause justifies terror. The United States will make no concessions to terrorist demands and strike no deals with them. We make no distinction between terrorists and those who knowingly harbor or provide aid to them.

The struggle against global terrorism is different from any other war in our history. It will be fought on many fronts against a particularly elusive enemy over an extended period of time. Progress will come through the persistent accumulation of successes— some seen, some unseen.

Today our enemies have seen the results of what civilized nations can, and will, do against regimes that harbor, support, and use terrorism to achieve their political goals. Afghanistan has been liberated; coalition forces continue to hunt down the Taliban and al-Qaida. But it is not only this battlefield on which we will engage terrorists. Thousands of trained terrorists remain at large with cells in North America, South America, Europe, Africa, the Middle East, and across Asia.

> ## DID YOU KNOW?
>
> ### Anniversary Attacks
>
> Anniversaries of the September 11 attacks have typically been accompanied by heightened security around the world. Nevertheless, Al Qaeda and affiliated groups have managed to carry out major attacks in spite of the increased awareness. On March 11, 2004, exactly 30 months after the September 11 attacks, 10 bombs were detonated by Al Qaeda operatives on the Madrid commuter train system. The explosions, timed to hit during the morning rush hour, killed 190 commuters and wounded nearly 2,000 more. On September 11, 2012, the U.S. consulate in Benghazi, Libya, was attacked by dozens of Al Qaeda fighters. The attacks killed four Americans, including Ambassador J. Christopher Stevens, the first U.S. ambassador killed in the line of duty since 1988 and the sixth U.S. ambassador to be killed by a terrorist attack.

Our priority will be first to disrupt and destroy terrorist organizations of global reach and attack their leadership; command, control, and communications; material support; and finances. This will have a disabling effect upon the terrorists' ability to plan and operate.

We will continue to encourage our regional partners to take up a coordinated effort that isolates the terrorists. Once the regional campaign localizes the threat to a particular state, we will help ensure the state has the military, law enforcement, political, and financial tools necessary to finish the task.

The United States will continue to work with our allies to disrupt the financing of terrorism. We will identify and block the sources of funding for terrorism, freeze the assets of terrorists and those who support them, deny terrorists access to the international financial system, protect legitimate charities from being abused by terrorists, and prevent the movement of terrorists' assets through alternative financial networks.

However, this campaign need not be sequential to be effective, the cumulative effect across all regions will help achieve the results we seek.

We will disrupt and destroy terrorist organizations by:

- direct and continuous action using all the elements of national and international power. Our immediate focus will be those terrorist organizations of global reach and any terrorist or state sponsor of terrorism which attempts to gain or use weapons of mass destruction (WMD) or their precursors;
- defending the United States, the American people, and our interests at home and abroad by identifying and destroying the threat before it reaches our

borders. While the United States will constantly strive to enlist the support of the international community, we will not hesitate to act alone, if necessary, to exercise our right of self-defense by acting preemptively against such terrorists, to prevent them from doing harm against our people and our country; and

• denying further sponsorship, support, and sanctuary to terrorists by convincing or compelling states to accept their sovereign responsibilities.

We will also wage a war of ideas to win the battle against international terrorism. This includes:

• using the full influence of the United States, and working closely with allies and friends, to make clear that all acts of terrorism are illegitimate so that terrorism will be viewed in the same light as slavery, piracy, or genocide: behavior that no respectable government can condone or support and all must oppose;

• supporting moderate and modern government, especially in the Muslim world, to ensure that the conditions and ideologies that promote terrorism do not find fertile ground in any nation;

• diminishing the underlying conditions that spawn terrorism by enlisting the international community to focus its efforts and resources on areas most at risk; and

• using effective public diplomacy to promote the free flow of information and ideas to kindle the hopes and aspirations of freedom of those in societies ruled by the sponsors of global terrorism.

While we recognize that our best defense is a good offense, we are also strengthening America's homeland security to protect against and deter attack.

This Administration has proposed the largest government reorganization since the Truman Administration created the National Security Council and the Department of Defense. Centered on a new Department of Homeland Security and including a new unified military command and a fundamental reordering of the FBI, our comprehensive plan to secure the homeland encompasses every level of government and the cooperation of the public and the private sector.

This strategy will turn adversity into opportunity. For example, emergency management systems will be better able to cope not just with terrorism but with all hazards. Our medical system will be strengthened to manage not just bioterror, but all infectious diseases and mass-casualty dangers.

Our border controls will not just stop terrorists, but improve the efficient movement of legitimate traffic.

While our focus is protecting America, we know that to defeat terrorism in today's globalized world we need support from our allies and friends. Wherever possible, the United States will rely on regional organizations and state powers to meet their obligations to fight terrorism. Where governments find the fight against terrorism beyond their capacities, we will match their willpower and their resources with whatever help we and our allies can provide. As we pursue the terrorists in

Afghanistan, we will continue to work with international organizations such as the United Nations, as well as non-governmental organizations, and other countries to provide the humanitarian, political, economic, and security assistance necessary to rebuild Afghanistan so that it will never again abuse its people, threaten its neighbors, and provide a haven for terrorists.

In the war against global terrorism, we will never forget that we are ultimately fighting for our democratic values and way of life. Freedom and fear are at war, and there will be no quick or easy end to this conflict. In leading the campaign against terrorism, we are forging new, productive international relationships and redefining existing ones in ways that meet the challenges of the twenty-first century.

Source: National Security Strategy of the United States, 2002, 5–7. Available at www.state.gov/documents/organization/63562.pdf.

ANALYSIS

The "National Security Strategy of the United States" is a quadrennial document that allows the president to offer broad guidance to the elements of the executive branch associated with national defense. Even in the 2002 edition, the first released after the September 11 attacks, terrorism is enumerated as only one of several major threats to the national security of the United States. This is a significant departure from the first "National Strategy for Homeland Security," released just two months prior (see Document 46). The segment of the National Security Strategy dedicated to the terrorism threat notes that the struggle against terrorism is not simply one to eliminate a violent organization motivated by extreme views of religion. It is a titanic struggle between two competing worldviews that might not be capable of coexistence—and it reminds us that the United States cannot forego its national character and freedom in order to defeat an enemy that would seek to destroy both, lest we complete the work of groups like Al Qaeda from within. This edition of the "National Security Strategy" offered broad guidance for the military engagement with Al Qaeda and for winning the war of information and ideology, a distinction that previous strategies had not attempted to make.

- **Document 48: Al Qaeda Training Manual**
- **When:** October 2002
- **Where:** Manchester, England
- **Significance:** This manual was discovered during a raid on a home used by Al Qaeda militants. It was translated into English and introduced into evidence in a New York court during the trial of suspects associated with the 1998 embassy bombings in Dar es Salaam and Nairobi.

DOCUMENT

FIRST LESSON
GENERAL INTRODUCTION
Principles of Military Organization:
Military Organization has three main principles without which it cannot be established:

1. Military Organization commander and advisory council
2. The soldiers (individual members)
3. A clearly defined strategy

Military Organization Requirements:
The Military Organization dictates a number of requirements to assist it in confrontation and endurance. These are:

1. Forged documents and counterfeit currency
2. Apartments and hiding places
3. Communication means
4. Transportation means
5. Information
6. Arms and ammunition
7. Transport

Missions Required of the Military Organization:
The main mission for which the Military Organization is responsible is:
The overthrow of the godless regimes and their replacement with an Islamic regime.
Other missions consist of the following:

1. Gathering information about the enemy, the land, the installations, and the neighbors.
2. Kidnapping enemy personnel, documents, secrets, and arms.
3. Assassinating enemy personnel as well as foreign tourists.
4. Freeing the brothers who are captured by the enemy.
5. Spreading rumors and writing statements that instigate people against the enemy..
6. Blasting and destroying the places of amusement, immorality, and sin; not a vital target.

DID YOU KNOW?

Al Qaeda's Lone Wolves

Frustrated in its attempts to carry out follow-on attacks against the United States with trained operatives, Al Qaeda turned its attention toward inspiring attacks by American citizens against their countrymen. Most of the recruitment of these attackers was carried out over the Internet, and the subjects were expected to choose their own targets and use their own resources. On November 5, 2009, Major Nidal Hasan, a psychologist in the U.S. Army, opened fire on fellow service personnel at Fort Hood, Texas. Before being subdued by law enforcement, Hasan managed to kill 13 and wound 32 more. On May 1, 2010, Pakistani-American Faisal Shahzad unsuccessfully tried to detonate a car bomb in Times Square, New York. If successful, his attack might have killed hundreds in the crowded tourist locale. On November 26, 2010, Somali-born Mohamed Osman Mohamud attempted to detonate a car bomb at the Portland Christmas tree–lighting ceremony. In each case, investigators found links to Al Qaeda recruiters and propagandists operating through the Internet. In particular, American-born Anwar al-Awlaki had proven exceptionally effective at convincing these so-called lone wolves to attempt attacks with the intent of causing mass casualties.

7. Blasting and destroying the embassies and attacking vital economic centers.

8. Blasting and destroying bridges leading into and out of the cities.

Importance of the Military Organization:

1. Removal of those personalities that block the call's path. All types of military and civilian intellectuals and thinkers for the state.

2. Proper utilization of the individuals' unused capabilities.

3. Precision in performing tasks, and using collective views on completing a job from all aspects, not just one.

4. Controlling the work and not fragmenting it or .deviating from it.

5. Achieving long-term goals such as the establishment of an Islamic state and short-term goals such as operations against enemy individuals and sectors.

6. Establishing the conditions for possible confrontation with the regressive regimes and their persistence.

7. Achieving discipline in secrecy and through tasks.

SECOND LESSON
NECESSARY QUALIFICATIONS AND CHARACTERISTICS FOR THE
ORGANIZATION'S MEMBERS
1. Islam:

The member of the Organization must be Moslem. How can an unbeliever, someone from a revealed religion [Christian, Jew], a secular person, a communist, etc. protect Islam and Moslems and defend their goals and secrets when he does not believe in that religion [Islam]? The Israeli Army requires that a fighter be of the Jewish religion. Likewise, the command leadership in the Afghan and Russian armies requires anyone with an officer's position to be a member of the communist party.

2. Commitment to the Organization's Ideology:

This commitment frees the Organization's members from conceptual problems.

3. Maturity:

The requirements of military work are numerous, and a minor cannot perform them. The nature of hard and continuous work in dangerous conditions requires a great deal of psychological, mental, and intellectual fitness, which are not usually found in a minor.

4. Sacrifice:

He [the member] has to be willing to do the work and undergo martyrdom for the purpose of achieving the goal and establishing the religion of majestic Allah on earth.

5. Listening and Obedience:

In the military, this is known today as discipline. It is expressed by how the member obeys the orders given to him. That is what our religion urges.

6. Keeping Secrets and Concealing Information

[This secrecy should be used] even with the closest people, for deceiving the enemies is not easy.

7. Free of Illness

The Military Organization's member must fulfill this important requirement.

8. Patience

[The member] should have plenty of patience for [enduring] afflictions if he is overcome by the enemies. He should not abandon this great path and sell himself and his religion to the enemies for his freedom. He should be patient in performing the work, even if it lasts a long time.

9. Tranquility and "Unflappability"

[The member] should have a calm personality that, allows him to endure psychological traumas such as those· involving bloodshed, murder, arrest, imprisonment, and reverse psychological traumas such as killing one or all of his Organization's comrades. [He should be able] to carry out the work.

10. Intelligence and Insight

When the prophet—Allah bless and keep him—sent Hazifa Ben Al-Yaman to spy on the polytheist and [Hafiza] sat among them, Abou Soufian said, "Let each one of you look at his companion." Hazifa said to his companion, "Who are you?" The companion replied, "So-and-so son of so-and-so."

11. Caution and Prudence

In his battle against the king of Tomedia, the Roman general Speer sent an emissary to discuss with that king the matter of truce between the two armies. In reality, he had sent him to learn about the Tomedians' ability to fight. The general picked Lilius, one of his top commanders, for that task and sent with him some of his officers, disguised as slaves. During that mission, one of the king's officers, Sifax, pointed to one of the [disguised] slaves and yelled, "That slave is a Roman officer I had met in a neighboring city. He was wearing a Roman uniform." At that point, Lilius used a clever trick and managed to divert the attention of the Tomedians from that by turning to the disguised officer and quickly slapping him on the face a number of times. He reprimanded him for wearing a Roman officer's· uniform when he was a slave and for claiming a status that he did not deserve. The officer accepted the slaps quietly.. He bowed his head in humility and shame, as slaves do. Thus, Sifax men thought that officer was really a slave because they could not imagine that a Roman officer would accept these hits without defending himself.

12. Truthfulness and Counsel

The Commander of the faithful Omar Ibn Al-Khattab—may Allah be pleased with him—asserted that this characteristic was vital in those who gather information and work as spies against the Moslems' enemies. He [Omar] sent a letter to Saad Ibn Abou Wakkas—may Allah be pleased with him—saying, "If you step foot on your enemies' land, get spies on them. Choose those whom you count on for their truthfulness and advice, whether Arabs or inhabitants of that land. Liars' accounts would not benefit you, even if some of them were true; the deceiver is a spy against you and not for you."

13. Ability to Observe and Analyze

The Israeli Mossad received news that some Palestinians were going to attack an Israeli El Al airplane. That plane was going to Rome with Golda Meir—Allah's curse upon her—the Prime Minister at the time, on board. The Palestinians had managed to use a clever trick that allowed them to wait for the arrival of the plane without being questioned by anyone. They had beaten a man who sold potatoes, kidnapped him, and hidden him. They made two holes in the top of that peddler's cart and placed two tubes next to the chimney through which two Russian-made "Strella" missiles could be launched. The Mossad officers traveled the airport back and forth looking for [anything] that [could] lead them to the Palestinians. One officer passed the potato cart twice without noticing anything. On his third time, he noticed three chimneys, but only one of them was working with smoke coming out of it. He quickly steered toward the cart and hit it hard. The cart overturned, and the Palestinians were captured.

14. Ability to Act, Change Positions, and Conceal Oneself

THIRD LESSON
COUNTERFEIT CURRENCY AND FORGED DOCUMENTS
Financial Security Precautions:

1. Dividing operational funds into two parts: One part is to be invested in projects that offer financial return, and the other is to be saved and not spent except during operations.
2. Not placing operational funds [all] in one place.
3. Not telling the Organization members about the location of the funds.
4. Having proper protection while carrying large amounts of money.
5. Leaving the money with non-members and spending it as needed.

Forged Documents (Identity Cards, Records Books, Passports). The following security precautions should be taken:

1. Keeping the passport in a safe place so it would not be seized by the security apparatus, and the brother it belongs to would have to negotiate its return. (I'll give you your passport if you give me information).
2. All documents of the undercover brother, such as identity cards and passport, should be falsified.
3. When the undercover brother is traveling with a certain identity card or passport, he should know all pertinent [information] such as the name, profession, and place of residence.
4. The brother who has special work status (commander, communication link) should have more than one identity card and passport. He should learn the contents of each, the nature of the [indicated] profession, and the dialect of the residence area listed in the document.
5. The photograph of the brother in these documents should be without a beard. It is preferable that the brother's public photograph [on these documents] be also without a beard. If he already has one [document] showing a photograph with a beard, he should replace it.
6. When using an identity document in different names, no more than one such document should be carried at one time.
7. The validity of the falsified travel documents should always be confirmed.

8. All falsification matters should be carried out through .the command and not haphazardly.

9. Married brothers should not add their wives to their passports.

10. When a brother is carrying the forged passport of a certain country, he should not travel to that country.. It is easy to detect forgery at the airport, and the dialect of the brother is different from that of the people from that country.

Security Precautions Related to the Organizations' Given Names:

1. The name given by the Organization [to the brother] should not be odd in comparison with other names used around him.

2. A brother should not have more than one name in the area where he lives.

FOURTH LESSON
ORGANIZATION
MILITARY BASES "APARTMENTS AND HIDING PLACES"
Definition of Bases:

These are apartments, hiding places, command centers, etc., in which secret operations are executed against the enemy.

These bases may be in cities, and are [then] called homes or apartments. They may be in mountainous, harsh terrain far from the enemy, and are [then] called hiding places or bases.

During the initial stages, the Military Organization usually uses apartments in cities as places for launching assigned missions, such as collecting information, observing members of the ruling regime, etc.

Hiding places and bases in mountains and harsh terrain are used at later stages, from which Jihad [holy war] groups are dispatched to execute assassination operations of enemy individuals, bomb their centers, and capture their weapons. In some Arab countries such as Egypt, where there are no mountains or harsh terrain, all stages of Jihad work would take place in cities. The opposite was true in Afghanistan, where initially Jihad work was in the cities, then the warriors shifted to mountains and harsh terrain. There, they started battling the Communists.

Security Precautions Related to Apartments:

1. Choosing the apartment carefully as far as the location, the size for the work necessary (meetings, storage, arms, fugitives, work preparation).

2. It is preferable to rent apartments on the ground floor to facilitate escape and digging of trenches.

3. Preparing secret locations in the apartment for securing documents, records, arms, and other important items.

4. Preparing ways of vacating the apartment in case of a surprise attack (stands, wooden ladders).

5. Under no circumstances should anyone know about the apartment except those who use it.

6. Providing the necessary cover for the people who frequent the apartment (students, workers, employees, etc.).

7. Avoiding seclusion and isolation from the population and refraining from going to the apartment at suspicious times.

8. It is preferable to rent these apartments using false names, appropriate cover, and non-Moslem appearance.

9. A single brother should not rent more than one apartment in the same area, from the same agent, or using the same rental office.

10. Care should be exercised not to rent apartments that are known to the security apparatus [such as] those used for immoral or prior Jihad activities.

11. Avoiding police stations and government buildings. Apartments should not be rented near those places.

12. When renting these apartments, one should avoid isolated or deserted locations so the enemy would not be able to catch those living there easily.

13. It is preferable to rent apartments in newly developed areas where people do not know one another. Usually, in older quarters people know one another and strangers are easily identified, especially since these quarters have many informers.

14. Ensuring that there has been no surveillance prior to the members entering the apartment.

15. Agreement among those living in the apartment on special ways of knocking on the door and special signs prior to entry into the building's main gate to indicate to those who wish to enter that the place is safe and not being monitored. Such signs include hanging out a towel, opening a curtain, placing a cushion in a special way, etc.

16. If there is a telephone in the apartment, calls should be answered in an agreed-upon manner among those who use the apartment. That would prevent mistakes that would, otherwise, lead to revealing the names and nature of the occupants.

17. For apartments, replacing the locks and keys with new ones. As for the other entities (camps, shops, mosques), appropriate security precautions should be taken depending on the entity's importance and role in the work.

18. Apartments used for undercover work should not be visible from higher apartments in order not to expose the nature of the work.

19. In a newer apartment, avoid talking loud because prefabricated ceilings and walls [used in the apartments] do not have the same thickness as those in old ones.

20. It is necessary to have at hand documents supporting the undercover [member]. In the case of a physician, there should be an actual medical diploma, membership in the [medical] union, the government permit, and the rest of the routine procedures known in that country.

21. The cover should blend well [with the environment]. For example, selecting a doctor's clinic in an area where there are clinics, or in a location suitable for it.

22. The cover of those who frequent the location should match the cover of that location. For example, a common laborer should not enter a fancy hotel because that would be suspicious and draw attention.

Source: Department of Justice. Available online at www.justice.gov/sites/default/files/ag/legacy/2002/10/08/manualpart1_1.pdf.

ANALYSIS

This training manual covers the basics of undercover tradecraft. It incorporates elements of Carlos Marighella's *Minimanual of the Urban Guerrilla* as well as Mao Zedong's theory of insurrections. While it is not the only such training manual discovered in materials held by Al Qaeda operatives, this manual offered very practical advice regarding the most common Western detection methods for potential terrorist attacks. Its discovery was a chilling reminder that Al Qaeda and other terror organizations continually seek to refine their methods of infiltration and attack, and disseminate the best practices to their members. The original manual had a substantial number of religious references to inspire the reader and justify their activities, in addition to the operational guidance.

- **Document 49: Osama bin Laden's Letter to the American People**
- **When:** November 2002
- **Where:** Unknown
- **Significance:** In this letter, bin Laden offered his justifications for Al Qaeda's attacks against the United States and other Western nations. The letter was written in Arabic and translated into English for publication in the *Observer*. It includes a list of grievances to allow unlimited violence against Western citizens, and demands that must be met for the violence to stop.

DOCUMENT

In the Name of Allah, the Most Gracious, the Most Merciful,

Permission to fight (against disbelievers) is given to those (believers) who are fought against, because they have been wronged and surely, Allah is Able to give them (believers) victory. [Quran 22:39]

Those who believe, fight in the Cause of Allah, and those who disbelieve, fight in the cause of Taghut (anything worshipped other than Allah e.g. Satan). So fight you against the friends of Satan; ever feeble is indeed the plot of Satan. [Quran 4:76]

Some American writers have published articles under the title "On what basis are we fighting?" These articles have generated a number of responses, some of which adhered to the truth and were based on Islamic Law, and others which have not. Here we wanted to outline the truth—as an explanation and warning—hoping for Allah's reward, seeking success and support from Him.

While seeking Allah's help, we form our reply based on two questions directed at the Americans:

(Q1) Why are we fighting and opposing you?

(Q2) What are we calling you to, and what do we want from you?

As for the first question: Why are we fighting and opposing you? The answer is very simple:

(1) Because you attacked us and continue to attack us.

(a) You attacked us in Palestine:

(i) Palestine, which has sunk under military occupation for more than 80 years. The British handed over Palestine, with your help and your support, to the Jews, who have occupied it for more than 50 years; years overflowing with oppression, tyranny, crimes, killing, expulsion, destruction and devastation. The creation and continuation of Israel is one of the greatest crimes, and you are the leaders of its criminals. And of course there is no need to explain and prove the degree of American support for Israel. The creation of Israel is a crime which must be erased. Each and every person whose hands have become polluted in the contribution towards this crime must pay its price, and pay for it heavily.

(ii) It brings us both laughter and tears to see that you have not yet tired of repeating your fabricated lies that the Jews have a historical right to Palestine, as it was promised to them in the Torah. Anyone who disputes with them on this alleged fact is accused of anti-semitism. This is one of the most fallacious, widely-circulated fabrications in history. The people of Palestine are pure Arabs and original Semites. It is the Muslims who are the inheritors of Moses (peace be upon him) and the inheritors of the real Torah that has not been changed. Muslims believe in all of the Prophets, including Abraham, Moses, Jesus and Muhammad, peace and blessings of Allah be upon them all. If the followers of Moses have been promised a right to Palestine in the Torah, then the Muslims are the most worthy nation of this.

When the Muslims conquered Palestine and drove out the Romans, Palestine and Jerusalem returned to Islam, the religion of all the Prophets peace be upon them. Therefore, the call to a historical right to Palestine cannot be raised against the Islamic Ummah that believes in all the Prophets of Allah (peace and blessings be upon them)—and we make no distinction between them.

DID YOU KNOW?

Osama bin Laden

Osama bin Laden, the founder of Al Qaeda, was born to the family of a billionaire construction magnate in Saudi Arabia. He abandoned university studies to travel to Pakistan, where he joined the mujahideen resistance to the Soviet occupation of Afghanistan. His family finances, experience with heavy construction equipment, and personal contacts all proved extremely useful to the mujahideen. In 1988, bin Laden and a small group formed Al Qaeda, which quickly grew to several thousand members. In 1990, bin Laden offered his group as a defensive force to prevent any Iraqi aggression toward Saudi Arabia, but his offer was rejected in favor of inviting a U.S.-led coalition to establish defenses inside the kingdom. In 1992, the Saudi government banished bin Laden for speaking out against the regime, and he moved his operations to Sudan until 1996, when he shifted to Afghanistan. Bin Laden gradually came to believe the United States was the source of evil in the Middle East, and embarked upon radical plans to attack American citizens and drive American influence from the region. He spent the 10 years after the September 11 attacks in hiding before intelligence agencies tracked him to a compound in Abbottabad, Pakistan. On May 2, 2011, U.S. Navy SEALs attacked the compound and killed bin Laden, ending the most intense manhunt in history.

(iii) The blood pouring out of Palestine must be equally revenged. You must know that the Palestinians do not cry alone; their women are not widowed alone; their sons are not orphaned alone.

(b) You attacked us in Somalia; you supported the Russian atrocities against us in Chechnya, the Indian oppression against us in Kashmir, and the Jewish aggression against us in Lebanon.

(c) Under your supervision, consent and orders, the governments of our countries which act as your agents, attack us on a daily basis;

(i) These governments prevent our people from establishing the Islamic Shariah, using violence and lies to do so.

(ii) These governments give us a taste of humiliation, and place us in a large prison of fear and subdual.

(iii) These governments steal our Ummah's wealth and sell them to you at a paltry price.

(iv) These governments have surrendered to the Jews, and handed them most of Palestine, acknowledging the existence of their state over the dismembered limbs of their own people.

(v) The removal of these governments is an obligation upon us, and a necessary step to free the Ummah, to make the Shariah the supreme law and to regain Palestine. And our fight against these governments is not separate from our fight against you.

(d) You steal our wealth and oil at paltry prices because of your international influence and military threats. This theft is indeed the biggest theft ever witnessed by mankind in the history of the world.

(e) Your forces occupy our countries; you spread your military bases throughout them; you corrupt our lands, and you besiege our sanctities, to protect the security of the Jews and to ensure the continuity of your pillage of our treasures.

(f) You have starved the Muslims of Iraq, where children die every day. It is a wonder that more than 1.5 million Iraqi children have died as a result of your sanctions, and you did not show concern. Yet when 3000 of your people died, the entire world rises and has not yet sat down.

(g) You have supported the Jews in their idea that Jerusalem is their eternal capital, and agreed to move your embassy there. With your help and under your protection, the Israelis are planning to destroy the Al-Aqsa mosque. Under the protection of your weapons, Sharon entered the Al-Aqsa mosque, to pollute it as a preparation to capture and destroy it.

(2) These tragedies and calamities are only a few examples of your oppression and aggression against us. It is commanded by our religion and intellect that the oppressed have a right to return the aggression. Do not await anything from us but Jihad, resistance and revenge. Is it in any way rational to expect that after America has attacked us for more than half a century, that we will then leave her to live in security and peace?!!

(3) You may then dispute that all the above does not justify aggression against civilians, for crimes they did not commit and offenses in which they did not partake:

(a) This argument contradicts your continuous repetition that America is the land of freedom, and its leaders in this world. Therefore, the American people are the ones who choose their government by way of their own free will; a choice which stems from their agreement to its policies. Thus the American people have chosen, consented to, and affirmed their support for the Israeli oppression of the Palestinians, the occupation and usurpation of their land, and its continuous killing, torture, punishment and expulsion of the Palestinians. The American people have the ability and choice to refuse the policies of their Government and even to change it if they want.

(b) The American people are the ones who pay the taxes which fund the planes that bomb us in Afghanistan, the tanks that strike and destroy our homes in Palestine, the armies which occupy our lands in the Arabian Gulf, and the fleets which ensure the blockade of Iraq. These tax dollars are given to Israel for it to continue to attack us and penetrate our lands. So the American people are the ones who fund the attacks against us, and they are the ones who oversee the expenditure of these monies in the way they wish, through their elected candidates.

(c) Also the American army is part of the American people. It is this very same people who are shamelessly helping the Jews fight against us.

(d) The American people are the ones who employ both their men and their women in the American Forces which attack us.

(e) This is why the American people cannot be not innocent of all the crimes committed by the Americans and Jews against us.

(f) Allah, the Almighty, legislated the permission and the option to take revenge. Thus, if we are attacked, then we have the right to attack back. Whoever has destroyed our villages and towns, then we have the right to destroy their villages and towns. Whoever has stolen our wealth, then we have the right to destroy their economy. And whoever has killed our civilians, then we have the right to kill theirs.

The American Government and press still refuses to answer the question:

Why did they attack us in New York and Washington?

If Sharon is a man of peace in the eyes of Bush, then we are also men of peace!!! America does not understand the language of manners and principles, so we are addressing it using the language it understands.

(Q2) As for the second question that we want to answer: What are we calling you to, and what do we want from you?

(1) The first thing that we are calling you to is Islam.

(a) The religion of the Unification of God; of freedom from associating partners with Him, and rejection of this; of complete love of Him, the Exalted; of complete submission to His Laws; and of the discarding of all the opinions, orders, theories and religions which contradict with the religion He sent down to His Prophet Muhammad (peace be upon him). Islam is the religion of all the prophets, and makes no distinction between them—peace be upon them all.

It is to this religion that we call you; the seal of all the previous religions. It is the religion of Unification of God, sincerity, the best of manners, righteousness, mercy, honour, purity, and piety. It is the religion of showing kindness to others, establishing justice between them, granting them their rights, and defending the oppressed and the persecuted. It is the religion of enjoining the good and forbidding the evil with the hand, tongue and heart. It is the religion of Jihad in the way of Allah so that Allah's Word and religion reign Supreme. And it is the religion of unity and agreement on the obedience to Allah, and total equality between all people, without regarding their colour, sex, or language.

(b) It is the religion whose book—the Quran—will remained preserved and unchanged, after the other Divine books and messages have been changed. The Quran is the miracle until the Day of Judgment. Allah has challenged anyone to bring a book like the Quran or even ten verses like it.

(2) The second thing we call you to, is to stop your oppression, lies, immorality and debauchery that has spread among you.

(a) We call you to be a people of manners, principles, honour, and purity; to reject the immoral acts of fornication, homosexuality, intoxicants, gambling's, and trading with interest.

We call you to all of this that you may be freed from that which you have become caught up in; that you may be freed from the deceptive lies that you are a great nation, that your leaders spread amongst you to conceal from you the despicable state to which you have reached.

(b) It is saddening to tell you that you are the worst civilization witnessed by the history of mankind:

(i) You are the nation who, rather than ruling by the Shariah of Allah in its Constitution and Laws, choose to invent your own laws as you will and desire. You separate religion from your policies, contradicting the pure nature which affirms Absolute Authority to the Lord and your Creator. You flee from the embarrassing question posed to you: How is it possible for Allah the Almighty to create His creation, grant them power over all the creatures and land, grant them all the amenities of life, and then deny them that which they are most in need of: knowledge of the laws which govern their lives?

(ii) You are the nation that permits Usury, which has been forbidden by all the religions. Yet you build your economy and investments on Usury. As a result of this, in all its different forms and guises, the Jews have taken control of your economy, through which they have then taken control of your media, and now control all aspects of your life making you their servants and achieving their aims at your expense; precisely what Benjamin Franklin warned you against.

(iii) You are a nation that permits the production, trading and usage of intoxicants. You also permit drugs, and only forbid the trade of them, even though your nation is the largest consumer of them.

(iv) You are a nation that permits acts of immorality, and you consider them to be pillars of personal freedom. You have continued to sink down this abyss from level to level until incest has spread amongst you, in the face of which neither your sense of honour nor your laws object.

Who can forget your President Clinton's immoral acts committed in the official Oval office? After that you did not even bring him to account, other than that he "made a mistake," after which everything passed with no punishment. Is there a worse kind of event for which your name will go down in history and remembered by nations?

(v) You are a nation that permits gambling in its all forms. The companies practice this as well, resulting in the investments becoming active and the criminals becoming rich.

(vi) You are a nation that exploits women like consumer products or advertising tools calling upon customers to purchase them. You use women to serve passengers, visitors, and strangers to increase your profit margins. You then rant that you support the liberation of women.

(vii) You are a nation that practices the trade of sex in all its forms, directly and indirectly. Giant corporations and establishments are established on this, under the name of art, entertainment, tourism and freedom, and other deceptive names you attribute to it.

(viii) And because of all this, you have been described in history as a nation that spreads diseases that were unknown to man in the past. Go ahead and boast to the nations of man, that you brought them AIDS as a Satanic American Invention.

(xi) You have destroyed nature with your industrial waste and gases more than any other nation in history. Despite this, you refuse to sign the Kyoto agreement so that you can secure the profit of your greedy companies and industries.

(x) Your law is the law of the rich and wealthy people, who hold sway in their political parties, and fund their election campaigns with their gifts. Behind them stand the Jews, who control your policies, media and economy.

(xi) That which you are singled out for in the history of mankind, is that you have used your force to destroy mankind more than any other nation in history; not to defend principles and values, but to hasten to secure your interests and profits. You who dropped a nuclear bomb on Japan, even though Japan was ready to negotiate an end to the war. How many acts of oppression, tyranny and injustice have you carried out, O callers to freedom?

(xii) Let us not forget one of your major characteristics: your duality in both manners and values; your hypocrisy in manners and principles. All manners, principles and values have two scales: one for you and one for the others.

(a) The freedom and democracy that you call to is for yourselves and for white race only; as for the rest of the world, you impose upon them your monstrous, destructive policies and Governments, which you call the "American friends." Yet you prevent them from establishing democracies. When the Islamic party in Algeria wanted to practice democracy and they won the election, you unleashed your agents in the Algerian army onto them, and to attack them with tanks and guns, to imprison them and torture them—a new lesson from the "American book of democracy"!!!

(b) Your policy on prohibiting and forcibly removing weapons of mass destruction to ensure world peace: it only applies to those countries which you do not permit to possess such weapons. As for the countries you consent to, such as Israel, then they are allowed to keep and use such weapons to defend their security. Anyone else who you suspect might be manufacturing or keeping these kinds of weapons, you call them criminals and you take military action against them.

(c) You are the last ones to respect the resolutions and policies of International Law, yet you claim to want to selectively punish anyone else who does the same. Israel has for more than 50 years been pushing UN resolutions and rules against the wall with the full support of America.

(d) As for the war criminals which you censure and form criminal courts for—you shamelessly ask that your own are granted immunity!! However, history will not forget the war crimes that you committed against the Muslims and the rest of the world;

those you have killed in Japan, Afghanistan, Somalia, Lebanon and Iraq will remain a shame that you will never be able to escape. It will suffice to remind you of your latest war crimes in Afghanistan, in which densely populated innocent civilian villages were destroyed, bombs were dropped on mosques causing the roof of the mosque to come crashing down on the heads of the Muslims praying inside. You are the ones who broke the agreement with the Mujahideen when they left Qunduz, bombing them in Jangi fort, and killing more than 1,000 of your prisoners through suffocation and thirst. Allah alone knows how many people have died by torture at the hands of you and your agents. Your planes remain in the Afghan skies, looking for anyone remotely suspicious.

(e) You have claimed to be the vanguards of Human Rights, and your Ministry of Foreign affairs issues annual reports containing statistics of those countries that violate any Human Rights. However, all these things vanished when the Mujahideen hit you, and you then implemented the methods of the same documented governments that you used to curse. In America, you captured thousands the Muslims and Arabs, took them into custody with neither reason, court trial, nor even disclosing their names. You issued newer, harsher laws.

What happens in Guatanamo is a historical embarrassment to America and its values, and it screams into your faces—you hypocrites, "What is the value of your signature on any agreement or treaty?"

(3) What we call you to thirdly is to take an honest stance with yourselves—and I doubt you will do so—to discover that you are a nation without principles or manners, and that the values and principles to you are something which you merely demand from others, not that which you yourself must adhere to.

(4) We also advise you to stop supporting Israel, and to end your support of the Indians in Kashmir, the Russians against the Chechens and to also cease supporting the Manila Government against the Muslims in Southern Philippines.

(5) We also advise you to pack your luggage and get out of our lands. We desire for your goodness, guidance, and righteousness, so do not force us to send you back as cargo in coffins.

(6) Sixthly, we call upon you to end your support of the corrupt leaders in our countries. Do not interfere in our politics and method of education. Leave us alone, or else expect us in New York and Washington.

(7) We also call you to deal with us and interact with us on the basis of mutual interests and benefits, rather than the policies of subdual, theft and occupation, and not to continue your policy of supporting the Jews because this will result in more disasters for you.

If you fail to respond to all these conditions, then prepare for fight with the Islamic Nation. The Nation of Monotheism, that puts complete trust on Allah and fears none other than Him. The Nation which is addressed by its Quran with the words: "Do you fear them? Allah has more right that you should fear Him if you are believers. Fight against them so that Allah will punish them by your hands and disgrace them and give you victory over them and heal the breasts of believing people. And remove the anger of their (believers') hearts. Allah accepts the repentance of whom He wills. Allah is All-Knowing, All-Wise." [Quran 9:13-1]

The Nation of honour and respect:

But honour, power and glory belong to Allah, and to His Messenger (Muhammad—peace be upon him) and to the believers. [Quran 63:8]

So do not become weak (against your enemy), nor be sad, and you will be superior (in victory) if you are indeed (true) believers. [Quran 3:139]

The Nation of Martyrdom; the Nation that desires death more than you desire life:

Think not of those who are killed in the way of Allah as dead. Nay, they are alive with their Lord, and they are being provided for. They rejoice in what Allah has bestowed upon them from His bounty and rejoice for the sake of those who have not yet joined them, but are left behind (not yet martyred) that on them no fear shall come, nor shall they grieve. They rejoice in a grace and a bounty from Allah, and that Allah will not waste the reward of the believers. [Quran 3:169–171]

The Nation of victory and success that Allah has promised:

It is He Who has sent His Messenger (Muhammad peace be upon him) with guidance and the religion of truth (Islam), to make it victorious over all other religions even though the Polytheists hate it. [Quran 61:9]

Allah has decreed that 'Verily it is I and My Messengers who shall be victorious.' Verily Allah is All-Powerful, All-Mighty. [Quran 58:21]

The Islamic Nation that was able to dismiss and destroy the previous evil Empires like yourself; the Nation that rejects your attacks, wishes to remove your evils, and is prepared to fight you. You are well aware that the Islamic Nation, from the very core of its soul, despises your haughtiness and arrogance.

If the Americans refuse to listen to our advice and the goodness, guidance and righteousness that we call them to, then be aware that you will lose this Crusade Bush began, just like the other previous Crusades in which you were humiliated by the hands of the Mujahideen, fleeing to your home in great silence and disgrace. If the Americans do not respond, then their fate will be that of the Soviets who fled from Afghanistan to deal with their military defeat, political breakup, ideological downfall, and economic bankruptcy.

This is our message to the Americans, as an answer to theirs. Do they now know why we fight them and over which form of ignorance, by the permission of Allah, we shall be victorious?

Source: "Bin Laden's 'Letter to America,' Sunday November 24, 2002." *Guardian Observer Worldview Extra.* Available at http://www.theguardian.com/world/2002/nov/24/theobserver.

ANALYSIS

Through this and other communications, bin Laden sought to lay the blame for the September 11 attacks, and all subsequent terror activities, at the feet of Western governments, particularly the United States. At the same time, he sought to influence uncommitted third parties by portraying the conflict as one of a religious rather than political character. The implication for observers is that any attempt to influence events in the Middle East, and in particular Saudi Arabia or the Israel-Palestine conflict, might trigger attacks by Al Qaeda. At the same time, bin Laden offers a theological underpinning for the Al Qaeda attacks, suggesting that they are entirely justified as the only means at hand for defending the faith against Western infidels and crusaders.

- **Document 50: Homeland Security Act of 2002, Title XIV**
- **When:** November 25, 2002
- **Where:** Washington, D.C.
- **Significance:** The Homeland Security Act created a new cabinet-level agency charged with providing a coordinated effort to protect against and respond to terrorism and natural disasters within the United States. Title XIV of the act established a program to arm pilots of commercial airlines as a means of defense against a repetition of the September 11 hijackings.

DOCUMENT

TITLE XIV—ARMING PILOTS AGAINST TERRORISM
SEC. 1401. SHORT TITLE.
This title may be cited as the "Arming Pilots Against Terrorism Act."
SEC. 1402. FEDERAL FLIGHT DECK OFFICER PROGRAM.
(a) IN GENERAL.—Subchapter I of chapter 449 of title 49, United States Code, is amended by adding at the end the following:
§ 44921. Federal flight deck officer program
(a) ESTABLISHMENT.—The Under Secretary of Transportation for security shall establish a program to deputize volunteer pilots of air carriers providing passenger air transportation or intrastate passenger air transportation as federal law enforcement officers to defend the flight decks of aircraft of such air carriers against acts of criminal violence or air piracy. Such officers shall be known as "Federal flight deck officers."
(b) PROCEDURAL REQUIREMENTS.—
(1) IN GENERAL.—Not later than 3 months after the date of enactment of this section, the Under Secretary shall establish procedural requirements to carry out the program under this section.

(2) COMMENCEMENT OF PROGRAM.— Beginning 3 months after the date of enactment of this section, the Under Secretary shall begin the process of training and deputizing pilots who are qualified to be Federal flight deck officers as Federal flight deck officers under the program.

(3) ISSUES TO BE ADDRESSED.—The procedural requirements established under paragraph (1) shall address the following issues:

(A) The type of firearm to be used by a Federal flight deck officer.

(B) The type of ammunition to be used by a Federal flight deck officer.

(C) The standards and training needed to qualify and requalify as a Federal flight deck officer.

(D) The placement of the firearm of a Federal flight deck officer on board the aircraft to ensure both its security and its ease of retrieval in an emergency.

(E) An analysis of the risk of catastrophic failure of an aircraft as a result of the discharge (including an accidental discharge) of a firearm to be used in the program into the avionics, electrical systems, or other sensitive areas of the aircraft.

(F) The division of responsibility between pilots in the event of an act of criminal violence or air piracy if only 1 pilot is a Federal flight deck officer and if both pilots are Federal flight deck officers.

(G) Procedures for ensuring that the firearm of a Federal flight deck officer does not leave the cockpit if there is a disturbance in the passenger cabin of the aircraft or if the pilot leaves the cockpit for personal reasons.

(H) Interaction between a Federal flight deck officer and a Federal air marshal on board the aircraft.

(I) The process for selection of pilots to participate in the program based on their fitness to participate in the program, including whether an additional background check should be required beyond that required by section 44936(a)(1).

(J) Storage and transportation of firearms between flights, including international flights, to ensure the security of the firearms, focusing particularly on whether such security would be enhanced by requiring storage of the firearm at the airport when the pilot leaves the airport to remain overnight away from the pilot's base airport.

(K) Methods for ensuring that security personnel will be able to identify whether a pilot is authorized to carry a firearm under the program.

(L) Methods for ensuring that pilots (including Federal flight deck officers) will be able to identify whether a passenger is a law enforcement officer who is authorized to carry a firearm aboard the aircraft.

(M) Any other issues that the Under Secretary considers necessary.

(N) The Under Secretary's decisions regarding the methods for implementing each of the foregoing procedural requirements shall be subject to review only for abuse of discretion.

DID YOU KNOW?

Follow-on Airplane Attacks

Despite heightened security procedures for airlines, Al Qaeda operatives have not abandoned attempts to destroy airliners full of passengers. On December 22, 2001, British citizen and Muslim-convert Richard Colvin Reid smuggled explosives onto an international flight in his shoes. During the flight, he attempted to detonate the explosives but was stopped and subdued by fellow passengers and the flight crew. On December 25, 2009, Umar Farouk Abdulmutallab smuggled an improvised explosive device onto an aircraft inside his underwear. Like Reid, his attempts to detonate the bomb failed, in large part due to the perception and quick reactions of others on the flight. Each incident has led to changes in airline security screening procedures.

(4) PREFERENCE.—In selecting pilots to participate in the program, the Under Secretary shall give preference to pilots who are former military or law enforcement personnel.

(c) TRAINING, SUPERVISION, AND EQUIPMENT.—

(1) IN GENERAL.—The Under Secretary shall only be obligated to provide the training, supervision, and equipment necessary for a pilot to be a Federal flight deck officer under this section at no expense to the pilot or the air carrier employing the pilot.

(2) TRAINING.—

(A) IN GENERAL.—The Under Secretary shall base the requirements for the training of Federal flight deck officers under subsection (b) on the training standards applicable to Federal air marshals; except that the Under Secretary shall take into account the differing roles and responsibilities of Federal flight deck officers and Federal air marshals.

(B) ELEMENTS.—The training of a Federal flight deck officer shall include, at a minimum, the following elements:

(i) Training to ensure that the officer achieves the level of proficiency with a firearm required under subparagraph (C)(i).

(ii) Training to ensure that the officer maintains exclusive control over the officer's firearm at all times, including training in defensive maneuvers.

(iii) Training to assist the officer in determining when it is appropriate to use the officer's firearm and when it is appropriate to use less than lethal force.

(C) TRAINING IN USE OF FIREARMS.—

(i) STANDARD.—In order to be deputized as a Federal flight deck officer, a pilot must achieve a level of proficiency with a firearm that is required by the Under Secretary. Such level shall be comparable to the level of proficiency required of Federal air marshals.

(ii) CONDUCT OF TRAINING.—The training of a Federal flight deck officer in the use of a firearm may be conducted by the Under Secretary or by a firearms training facility approved by the Under Secretary.

(iii) REQUALIFICATION.—The Under Secretary shall require a Federal flight deck officer to requalify to carry a firearm under the program. Such requalification shall occur at an interval required by the Under Secretary.

(d) DEPUTIZATION.—

(1) IN GENERAL.—The Under Secretary may deputize, as a Federal flight deck officer under this section, a pilot who submits to the Under Secretary a request to be such an officer and whom the Under Secretary determines is qualified to be such an officer.

(2) QUALIFICATION.—A pilot is qualified to be a Federal flight deck officer under this section if—

(A) the pilot is employed by an air carrier;

(B) the Under Secretary determines (in the Under Secretary's discretion) that the pilot meets the standards established by the Under Secretary for being such an officer; and

(C) the Under Secretary determines that the pilot has completed the training required by the Under Secretary.

(3) DEPUTIZATION BY OTHER FEDERAL AGENCIES.—The Under Secretary may request another Federal agency to deputize, as Federal flight deck officers under this section, those pilots that the Under Secretary determines are qualified to be such officers.

(4) REVOCATION.—The Under Secretary may, (in the Under Secretary's discretion) revoke the deputization of a pilot as a Federal flight deck officer if the Under Secretary finds that the pilot is no longer qualified to be such an officer.

(e) COMPENSATION.—Pilots participating in the program under this section shall not be eligible for compensation from the Federal Government for services provided as a Federal flight deck officer. The Federal Government and air carriers shall not be obligated to compensate a pilot for participating in the program or for the pilot's training or qualification and requalification to carry firearms under the program.

(f) AUTHORITY TO CARRY FIREARMS.—

(1) IN GENERAL.—The Under Secretary shall authorize a Federal flight deck officer to carry a firearm while engaged in providing air transportation or intrastate air transportation. Notwithstanding subsection (c)(1), the officer may purchase a firearm and carry that firearm aboard an aircraft of which the officer is the pilot in accordance with this section if the firearm is of a type that may be used under the program.

(2) PREEMPTION.—Notwithstanding any other provision of Federal or State law, a Federal flight deck officer, whenever necessary to participate in the program, may carry a firearm in any State and from 1 State to another State.

(3) CARRYING FIREARMS OUTSIDE UNITED STATES.—In consultation with the Secretary of State, the Under Secretary may take such action as may be necessary to ensure that a Federal flight deck officer may carry a firearm in a foreign country whenever necessary to participate in the program.

(g) AUTHORITY TO USE FORCE.—Notwithstanding section 44903(d), the Under Secretary shall prescribe the standards and circumstances under which a Federal flight deck officer may use, while the program under this section is in effect, force (including lethal force) against an individual in the defense of the flight deck of an aircraft in air transportation or intrastate air transportation.

(h) LIMITATION ON LIABILITY.—

(1) LIABILITY OF AIR CARRIERS.—An air carrier shall not be liable for damages in any action brought in a Federal or State court arising out of a Federal flight deck officer's use of or failure to use a firearm.

(2) LIABILITY OF FEDERAL FLIGHT DECK OFFICERS.—A Federal flight deck officer shall not be liable for damages in any action brought in a Federal or State court arising out of the acts or omissions of the officer in defending the flight deck of an aircraft against acts of criminal violence or air piracy unless the officer is guilty of gross negligence or willful misconduct.

(3) LIABILITY OF FEDERAL GOVERNMENT.—For purposes of an action against the United States with respect to an act or omission of a Federal flight deck officer in defending the flight deck of an aircraft, the officer shall be treated as an employee of the Federal Government under chapter 171 of title 28, relating to tort claims procedure.

(i) PROCEDURES FOLLOWING ACCIDENTAL DISCHARGES.—If an accidental discharge of a firearm under the pilot program results in the injury or death of a passenger or crew member on an aircraft, the Under Secretary—

(1) shall revoke the deputization of the Federal flight deck officer responsible for that firearm if the Under Secretary determines that the discharge was attributable to the negligence of the officer; and

(2) if the Under Secretary determines that a shortcoming in standards, training, or procedures was responsible for the accidental discharge, the Under Secretary may temporarily suspend the program until the shortcoming is corrected.

(j) LIMITATION ON AUTHORITY OF AIR CARRIERS.—No air carrier shall prohibit or threaten any retaliatory action against a pilot employed by the air carrier from becoming a Federal flight deck officer under this section. No air carrier shall—

(1) prohibit a Federal flight deck officer from piloting an aircraft operated by the air carrier; or

(2) terminate the employment of a Federal flight deck officer, solely on the basis of his or her volunteering for or participating in the program under this section.

(2) PILOT DEFINED.—The term "pilot" means an individual who has final authority and responsibility for the operation and safety of the flight or, if more than 1 pilot is required for the operation of the aircraft or by the regulations under which the flight is being conducted, the individual designated as second in command.

SEC. 1403. CREW TRAINING.

(2) ADDITIONAL REQUIREMENTS.—In updating the training guidance, the Under Secretary, in consultation with the Administrator, shall issue a rule to—

(A) require both classroom and effective hands-on situational training in the following elements of self defense:

(i) recognizing suspicious activities and determining the seriousness of an occurrence;

(ii) deterring a passenger who might present a problem;

(iii) crew communication and coordination;

(iv) the proper commands to give to passengers and attackers;

(v) methods to subdue and restrain an attacker;

(vi) use of available items aboard the aircraft for self-defense;

(vii) appropriate and effective responses to defend oneself, including the use of force against an attacker;

(viii) use of protective devices assigned to crew members (to the extent such devices are approved by the Administrator or Under Secretary);

(ix) the psychology of terrorists to cope with their behavior and passenger responses to that behavior; and

(x) how to respond to aircraft maneuvers that may be authorized to defend against an act of criminal violence or air piracy;

(B) require training in the proper conduct of a cabin search, including the duty time required to conduct the search; (C) establish the required number of hours of training and the qualifications for the training instructors;

(D) establish the intervals, number of hours, and elements of recurrent training;

(E) ensure that air carriers provide the initial training required by this paragraph within 24 months of the date of enactment of this subparagraph; and

(F) ensure that no person is required to participate in any hands-on training activity that that person believes will have an adverse impact on his or her health or safety.

Source: Department of Homeland Security, http://www.dhs.gov/homeland -security-act-2002.

ANALYSIS

Although a federal sky marshals program existed prior to the September 11 attacks, it had far too few members to actually place an armed agent on every commercial flight in the United States. This aspect of the Homeland Security Act sought both to enhance the security of domestic flights and to introduce a degree of uncertainty to would-be hijackers who might try to seize control of airliners in-flight. Coupled with enhanced cockpit security procedures, this act made it far less likely that a terrorist attack could seize control of an aircraft and convert it into a flying bomb. While this may have deterred a repetition of the September 11 attacks, it did not remove airliners as a target. For example, on December 25, 2009, Umar Farouk Abdulmutallab attempted to detonate an explosive device concealed within his underwear during a flight from Amsterdam to Detroit. Other bombings have brought down airliners in the post-9/11 era, including the October 31, 2015, bombing of a Russian airliner departing Sharm el-Sheikh, Egypt.

- **Document 51: American Library Association Resolution on the USA PATRIOT Act**
- **When:** January 29, 2003
- **Where:** Chicago, IL
- **Significance:** The American Library Association (ALA) publicly opposed the implementation of certain elements of the USA PATRIOT Act, particularly the possibility that the federal government would monitor the Internet activities of patrons at public libraries.

DOCUMENT

Resolution on the USA Patriot Act and Related Measures That Infringe on the Rights of Library Users

WHEREAS, The American Library Association affirms the responsibility of the leaders of the United States to protect and preserve the freedoms that are the foundation of our democracy; and

WHEREAS, Libraries are a critical force for promoting the free flow and unimpeded distribution of knowledge and information for individuals, institutions, and communities; and

WHEREAS, The American Library Association holds that suppression of ideas undermines a democratic society; and

WHEREAS, Privacy is essential to the exercise of free speech, free thought, and free association; and, in a library, the subject of users' interests should not be examined or scrutinized by others; and

WHEREAS, Certain provisions of the USA PATRIOT Act, the revised Attorney General Guidelines to the Federal Bureau of Investigation, and other related measures expand the authority of the federal government to investigate citizens and non-citizens, to engage in surveillance, and to threaten civil rights and liberties guaranteed under the United States Constitution and Bill of Rights; and

WHEREAS, The USA PATRIOT Act and other recently enacted laws, regulations, and guidelines increase the likelihood that the activities of library users, including their use of computers to browse the Web or access e-mail, may be under government surveillance without their knowledge or consent; now, therefore, be it

RESOLVED, That the American Library Association opposes any use of governmental power to suppress the free and open exchange of knowledge and information or to intimidate individuals exercising free inquiry; and, be it further

RESOLVED, That the American Library Association encourages all librarians, library administrators, library governing bodies, and library advocates to educate their users, staff, and communities about the process for compliance with the USA PATRIOT Act and other related measures and about the dangers to individual privacy and the confidentiality of library records resulting from those measures; and, be it further

RESOLVED, That the American Library Association urges librarians everywhere to defend and support user privacy and free and open access to knowledge and information; and, be it further

RESOLVED, That the American Library Association will work with other organizations, as appropriate, to protect the rights of inquiry and free expression; and, be it further

RESOLVED, That the American Library Association will take actions as appropriate to obtain and publicize information about the surveillance of libraries and library users by law enforcement agencies and to assess the impact on library users and their communities; and, be it further

RESOLVED, That the American Library Association urges all libraries to adopt and implement patron privacy and record retention policies that affirm that "the collection of personally identifiable information should only be a matter of routine or policy when necessary for the fulfillment of the mission of the library" (ALA *Privacy: An Interpretation of the Library Bill of Rights*); and, be it further

RESOLVED, That the American Library Association considers sections of the USA PATRIOT Act are a present danger to the constitutional rights and privacy rights of library users and urges the United States Congress to:

1. provide active oversight of the implementation of the USA PATRIOT Act and other related measures, and the revised Attorney General Guidelines to the Federal Bureau of Investigation;
2. hold hearings to determine the extent of the surveillance on library users and their communities; and
3. amend or change the sections of these laws and the guidelines that threaten or abridge the rights of inquiry and free expression; and, be it further

RESOLVED, That this resolution be forwarded to the President of the United States, to the Attorney General of the United States, to Members of both Houses of Congress, to the library community, and to others as appropriate.

Source: ALA Council, "Resolution on the USA PATRIOT Act and Related Measures That Infringe on the Rights of Library Users," January 29, 2003. Used by permission of the American Library Association.

ANALYSIS

Public libraries are a key source of Internet access for many U.S. citizens, particularly those living in impoverished communities. Further, citizens without Internet access are at a significant disadvantage in many aspects of modern life. To the ALA, any attempt by the federal government to monitor the Internet activities of private citizens in a public location represented an infringement upon the free exchange of ideas and information and, as such, an attack upon the First Amendment rights of all Americans. Librarians further resented the implication that they might be forced to turn over the individual records of patrons, essentially coopting librarians into a monitoring arm of law enforcement. The ALA urged the president and legislature to modify the offending aspects of the PATRIOT Act, and at least implied support for the passive disobedience of library officials throughout the nation should they be ordered to monitor and report upon the Internet usage of patrons.

- **Document 52: National Strategy for Combating Terrorism**
- **When:** February 2003
- **Where:** Washington, D.C.
- **Significance:** The "National Strategy for Combating Terrorism" is a subservient document to the National Security Strategy, and enhances the federal government's broad approach to counterterrorism activities. The 2003 edition established the executive branch's concept of the recent history of terrorism, the motivations behind it, and the best ways to combat terror organizations.

DOCUMENT

The Nature of the Terrorist Threat Today

The Structure of Terror

Despite their diversity in motive, sophistication, and strength, terrorist organizations share a basic structure.

At the base, underlying conditions such as poverty, corruption, religious conflict and ethnic strife create opportunities for terrorists to exploit. Some of these conditions are real and some manufactured. Terrorists use these conditions to justify their actions and expand their support. The belief that terror is a legitimate means to address such conditions and effect political change is a fundamental problem enabling terrorism to develop and grow.

The international environment defines the boundaries within which terrorists' strategies take shape. As a result of freer, more open borders this environment unwittingly provides access to havens, capabilities, and other support to terrorists. But access alone is not enough.

Terrorists must have a physical base from which to operate. Whether through ignorance, inability, or intent, states around the world still offer havens—both physical (e.g., safe houses, training grounds) and virtual (e.g., reliable communication and financial networks)—that terrorists need to plan, organize, train, and conduct their operations. Once entrenched in a safe operating environment, the organization can begin to solidify and expand. The terrorist organization's structure, membership, resources, and security determine its capabilities and reach.

At the top of the structure, the terrorist leadership provides the overall direction and strategy that links all these factors and thereby breathes life into a terror campaign. The leadership becomes the catalyst for terrorist action. The loss of the leadership can cause many organizations to collapse. Some groups, however, are more resilient and can promote new leadership should the original fall or fail.

Still others have adopted a more decentralized organization with largely autonomous cells, making our challenge even greater.

The Changing Nature of Terrorism

While retaining this basic structure, the terrorist challenge has changed considerably over the past decade and likely will continue to evolve. Ironically, the particular nature of the terrorist threat we face today springs in large part from some of our past successes.

In the 1970s and 1980s, the United States and its allies combated generally secular and nationalist

---

DID YOU KNOW?

Weapons of Mass Destruction

The term "weapon of mass destruction" (WMD) refers to a biological, chemical, nuclear, or radiological weapon capable of inflicting mass casualties or extensive devastation. Typically, WMDs are the province of national research programs with large budgets and advanced scientific expertise. However, knowledge regarding WMDs has proliferated in the information age, making lower-budget, less-effective WMDs potentially accessible to terrorist organizations. In 1996, the Japanese group Aum Shinrikyo used Sarin gas for an attack on the Tokyo subway system that killed 12 and incapacitated more than 5,000 victims. Al Qaeda in Iraq has used chlorine bombs to enhance the effectiveness of its attacks on civilian targets. The Islamic State and Al Qaeda have both attempted to purchase nuclear weapons on the black market, thus far without success.

terrorist groups, many of which depended upon active state sponsors. While problems of state sponsorship of terrorism continue, years of sustained counterterrorism efforts, including diplomatic and economic isolation, have convinced some governments to curtail or even abandon support for terrorism as a tool of statecraft. The collapse of the Soviet Union—which provided critical backing to terrorist groups and certain state sponsors—accelerated the decline in state sponsorship. Many terrorist organizations were effectively destroyed or neutralized, including the Red Army Faction, Direct Action, and Communist Combatant Cells in Europe, and the Japanese Red Army in Asia. Such past successes provide valuable lessons for the future.

With the end of the Cold War, we also saw dramatic improvements in the ease of transnational communication, commerce, and travel. Unfortunately, the terrorists adapted to this new international environment and turned the advances of the 20th century into the destructive enablers of the 21st century.

A New Global Environment

Al-Qaida exemplifies how terrorist networks have twisted the benefits and conveniences of our increasingly open, integrated, and modernized world to serve their destructive agenda. The al-Qaida network is a multinational enterprise with operations in more than 60 countries. Its camps in Afghanistan provided sanctuary and its bank accounts served as a trust fund for terrorism. Its global activities are coordinated through the use of personal couriers and communication technologies emblematic of our era—cellular and satellite phones, encrypted e-mail, internet chat rooms, videotape, and CD-roms. Like a skilled publicist, Usama bin Laden and al-Qaida have exploited the international media to project his image and message worldwide.

Members of al-Qaida have traveled from continent to continent with the ease of a vacationer or business traveler. Despite our coalition's successes in Afghanistan and around the world, some al-Qaida operatives have escaped to plan additional terrorist attacks. In an age marked by unprecedented mobility and migration, they readily blend into communities wherever they move.

They pay their way with funds raised through front businesses, drug trafficking, credit card fraud, extortion, and money from covert supporters. They use ostensibly charitable organizations and non-governmental organizations (NGOs) for funding and recruitment. Money for their operations is transferred surreptitiously through numerous banks, money exchanges, and alternate remittance systems (often known as "hawalas")—some legitimate and unwitting, others not.

These terrorists are also transnational in another, more fundamental way—their victims. The September 11 attacks murdered citizens from Australia, Brazil, China, Egypt, El Salvador, France, Germany, India, Israel, Jordan, Japan, Pakistan, Russia, South Africa, Switzerland, Turkey, the United Kingdom and scores of other countries.

As the al-Qaida network demonstrates, the terrorist threat today is mutating into something quite different from its predecessors. Terrorists can now use the advantage of technology to disperse leadership, training, and logistics not just regionally but globally. Establishing and moving cells in virtually any country is relatively easy in a world where more than 140 million people live outside of their country of origin and millions of people cross international borders every day.

Furthermore, terrorist groups have become increasingly self-sufficient by exploiting the global environment to support their operations. Whether it is the FARC's involvement in the cocaine trade in Colombia, al-Qaida's profiting from the poppy fields in Afghanistan, or Abu Sayyaf's kidnapping for profit in the Philippines, terrorists are increasingly using criminal activities to support and fund their terror. In addition to finding sanctuary within the boundaries of a state sponsor, terrorists often seek out states where they can operate with impunity because the central government is unable to stop them. Such areas are found in the Americas, Europe, the Middle East, Africa, and Asia. More audaciously, foreign terrorists also establish cells in the very open, liberal, and tolerant societies that they plan to attack.

Availability of Weapons of Mass Destruction (WMD)

Weapons of mass destruction pose a direct and serious threat to the United States and the entire international community. The probability of a terrorist organization using a chemical, biological, radiological, or nuclear weapon, or high-yield explosives, has increased significantly during the past decade. The availability of critical technologies, the willingness of some scientists and others to cooperate with terrorists, and the ease of intercontinental transportation enable terrorist organizations to more easily acquire, manufacture, deploy, and initiate a WMD attack either on U.S. soil or abroad.

While new instruments of terror such as cyber attacks are on the rise, and other conventional instruments of terror have not diminished, the availability and potential use of a WMD is in a category by itself.

We know that some terrorist organizations have sought to develop the capability to use WMD to attack the United States and our friends and allies. Motivated by extreme, even apocalyptic ideologies, some terrorists' ambitions to inflict mayhem seem unlimited. The Aum Shinrikyo's unsuccessful efforts to deploy biological weapons and its lethal 1995 sarin gas attack in the Tokyo subway provided an early warning of such willingness to acquire and use WMD. In 1998, Usama bin Laden proclaimed the acquisition of WMD a "religious duty," and evidence collected in Afghanistan proves al-Qaida sought to fulfill this "duty." The threat of terrorists acquiring and using WMD is a clear and present danger. A central goal must be to prevent terrorists from acquiring or manufacturing the WMD that would enable them to act on their worst ambitions.

Summary

While terrorism is not new, today's terrorist threat is different from that of the past. Modern technology has enabled terrorists to plan and operate worldwide as never before. With advanced telecommunications they can coordinate their actions among dispersed cells while remaining in the shadows. Today's terrorists increasingly enjoy a force-multiplier effect by establishing links with other like-minded organizations around the globe. Now, with a WMD capability, they have the potential to magnify the effects of their actions many fold. The new global environment, with its resultant terrorist interconnectivity, and WMD are changing the nature of terrorism. Our strategy's effectiveness ultimately depends upon how well we address these key facets of the terrorist threat.

Strategic Intent

The intent of our national strategy is to stop terrorist attacks against the United States, its citizens, its interests, and our friends and allies around the world and ultimately, to create an international environment inhospitable to terrorists and all those who support them. To accomplish these tasks we will simultaneously act on four fronts.

The United States and its partners will *defeat* terrorist organizations of global reach by attacking their sanctuaries; leadership; command, control, and communications; material support; and finances. This approach will have a cascading effect across the larger terrorist landscape, disrupting the terrorists' ability to plan and operate. As a result, it will force these organizations to disperse and then attempt to reconsolidate along regional lines to improve their communications and cooperation.

As this dispersion and organizational degradation occurs, we will work with regional partners to implement a coordinated effort to squeeze, tighten, and isolate the terrorists. Once the regional campaign has localized the threat, we will help states develop the military, law enforcement, political, and financial tools necessary to finish the task. However, this campaign need not be sequential to be effective; the cumulative effect across all geographic regions will help achieve the results we seek.

We will *deny* further sponsorship, support, and sanctuary to terrorists by ensuring other states accept their responsibilities to take action against these international threats within their sovereign territory. UNSCR 1373 and the 12 UN counterterrorism conventions and protocols establish high standards that we and our international partners expect others to meet in deed as well as word.

Where states are willing and able, we will reinvigorate old partnerships and forge new ones to combat terrorism and coordinate our actions to ensure that they are mutually reinforcing and cumulative.

Where states are weak but willing, we will support them vigorously in their efforts to build the institutions and capabilities needed to exercise authority over all their territory and fight terrorism where it exists.

Where states are reluctant, we will work with our partners to convince them to change course and meet their international obligations.

Where states are unwilling, we will act decisively to counter the threat they pose and, ultimately, to compel them to cease supporting terrorism.

We will *diminish* the underlying conditions that terrorists seek to exploit by enlisting the international community to focus its efforts and resources on the areas most at risk. We will maintain the momentum generated in response to the September 11 attacks by working with our partners abroad and various international forums to keep combating terrorism at the forefront of the international agenda.

Most importantly, we will *defend* the United States, our citizens, and our interests at home and abroad by both proactively protecting our homeland and extending our defenses to ensure we identify and neutralize the threat as early as possible.

Victory in the War Against Terror

Victory against terrorism will not occur as a single, defining moment. It will not be marked by the likes of the surrender ceremony on the deck of the USS Missouri that ended World War II. However, through the sustained effort to compress the scope and capability of terrorist organizations, isolate them regionally, and destroy them within state borders, the United States and its friends and allies will secure a world in which our children can live free from fear and where the threat of terrorist attacks does not define our daily lives.

Victory, therefore, will be secured only as long as the United States and the international community maintain their vigilance and work tirelessly to prevent terrorists from inflicting horrors like those of September 11, 2001.

Source: National Strategy for Combating Terrorism, 2003, 5–12. Full text available at www.state.gov/documents/organization/60172.pdf.

ANALYSIS

The "National Strategy for Combating Terrorism," like other strategic documents, tends to be about establishing the parameters a problem, to include defining the key elements and setting priorities for different aspects of the issue. It is noteworthy that the 2003 iteration of this periodically issued document contained a discussion of WMD and the fear that a terror organization might seek to obtain and use such devices. Although Al Qaeda had thus far failed to utilize WMD, other terrorists had developed and deployed them, and the Bush administration largely believed it was only a matter of time before Al Qaeda obtained a chemical, biological, or nuclear weapon that it would immediately use against a Western target. Not coincidentally, the search for WMD was a major element of the justification to invade Iraq in 2003, a move that provoked a major confrontation between U.S. military forces and Al Qaeda affiliates. The strategy did note that the United States had extensive experience with terror organizations prior to the September 11 attacks, and that such experience supplied useful lessons for the ongoing counterterrorism efforts of the 21st century, but it also suggested that those lessons might be of limited utility because the nature of terrorism and the enemy being faced had fundamentally altered from the nationalist groups of the 1970s and 1980s. This excerpt concludes on a rather grim reminder that not only will the War on Terror not end in a clear fashion akin to the surrender that ended World War II, but also it might effectively continue forever, so long as the conditions that lead to terrorist activities remain a part of the global environment.

- Document 53: Donald Rumsfeld to USSOUTHCOM Commander
- **When:** April 16, 2003
- **Where:** Washington, D.C.
- **Significance:** This memorandum authorized 24 interrogation techniques for use at Guantanamo Bay in the interrogation of enemy combatants held at the facility. Waterboarding was not on the list, but other forms of coercion were present.

DOCUMENT

MEMORANDUM FOR THE COMMANDER, US SOUTHERN COMMAND
SUBJECT: Counter-Resistance Techniques in the War on Terrorism

I have considered the report of the Working Group that I directed be established on January 15, 2003.

I approve the use of specified counter-resistance techniques, subject to the following:

a. The techniques I authorize are those lettered A–X, set out at Tab A.

b. These techniques must be used with all the safeguards described at Tab B.

c. Use of these techniques is limited to interrogations of unlawful combatants held at Guantanamo Bay, Cuba.

I reiterate that US Armed Forces shall continue to treat detainees humanely and, to the extent appropriate and consistent with military necessity, in a manner consistent with the principles of the Geneva Conventions. In addition, if you intend to use techniques B, I, O, or X, you must specifically determine that military necessity requires its use and notify me in advance.

If, in your view, you require additional interrogation techniques for a particular detainee, you should provide me, via the Chairman of the Joint Chiefs of Staff, a written request describing the proposed technique, recommended safeguards, and the rationale for applying it with an identified detainee.

Nothing in this memorandum in any way restricts your existing authority to maintain good order and discipline among detainees.

Tab A: Interrogation Techniques

The use of techniques A–X is subject to the general safeguards as provided below as well as specific implementation guidelines to be provided by the appropriate authority. Specific implementation guidance with respect to techniques A–Q is provided in Army Field Manual 34–52. Further implementation guidance with respect to techniques R–X will need to be developed by the appropriate authority.

Of the techniques set forth below, the policy aspects of certain techniques should be considered to the extent those policy aspects reflect the views of other major U.S. partner nations. Where applicable, the description of the technique is annotated to include a summary of the policy issues that should be considered before application of the technique.

A. Direct: Asking straightforward questions.

B. Incentive/Removal of Incentive: Providing a reward or removing a privilege, above and beyond those that are required by the Geneva Convention, from detainees. [Caution: Other nations that believe that detainees are entitled to POW protections may consider that provision and retention of religious items (e.g. the Koran) are protected under international law (see, Geneva III, Article 34). Although the provisions of the Geneva Convention are not applicable to the interrogation of unlawful combatants, consideration should be given to these views prior to application of the technique.]

C. Emotional Love: Playing on the love a detainee has for an individual or group.

D. Emotional Hate: Playing on the hatred a detainee has for an individual or group.

E. Fear Up Harsh: Significantly increasing the fear level in a detainee.

F. Fear Up Mild: Moderately increasing the fear level in a detainee.

G. Reduced Fear: Reducing the fear level in a detainee.

H. Pride and Ego Up: Boosting the ego of a detainee.

I. Pride and Ego Down: Attacking or insulting the ego of a detainee, not beyond the limits that would apply to a POW. [Caution: Article 17 of Geneva III provides, "Prisoners of war who refuse to answer may not be threatened, insulted, or exposed to any unpleasant or disadvantageous treatment of any kind."] Other nations that believe that detainees are entitled to POW protections may consider this technique inconsistent with the provisions of Geneva. Although the provisions of Geneva are not applicable to the interrogation of unlawful combatants, consideration should be given to these views prior to application of the technique.

J. Futility: Invoking the feeling of futility in a detainee.

K. We Know All: Convincing the detainee that the interrogator knows the answer to questions he asks the detainee.

L. Establish Your Identity: Convincing the detainee that the interrogator has mistaken the detainee for someone else.

M. Repetition Approach: Continuously repeating the same question to the detainee within interrogation periods of normal duration.

N. File and Dossier: Convincing detainee that the interrogator has a damning and inaccurate file, which must be fixed.

O. Mutt and Jeff: A team consisting of a friendly and harsh interrogator. The harsh interrogator might employ the Pride and Ego Down technique. [Caution: Other nations that believe that POW protections apply to detainees may view this technique as inconsistent with Geneva III, Article 13 which provides that POWs must be protected against acts of intimidation. Although the provisions of Geneva are not applicable to the interrogation of unlawful combatants, consideration should be given to these views prior to application of the technique.]

P. Rapid Fire: Questioning in rapid succession without allowing detainee to answer.

Q. Silence: Staring at the detainee to encourage discomfort.

R. Change of Scenery Up: Removing the detainee from the standard interrogation setting (generally to a location more pleasant, but no worse).

S. Change of Scenery Down: Removing the detainee from the standard interrogation setting and placing him in a setting that may be less comfortable; would not constitute a substantial change in environmental quality.

T. Dietary Manipulation: Changing the diet of a detainee; no intended deprivation of food or water; no adverse medical or cultural effect and without intent to deprive subject of food or water, e.g., hot rations to MREs [meals ready to eat].

U. Environmental Manipulation: Altering the environment to create moderate discomfort (e.g. adjusting temperature or introducing an unpleasant smell). Conditions would not be such that they would injure the detainee. Detainee would be accompanied by interrogator at all times. [Caution: Based on court cases in other countries, some nations may view application of this technique in certain circumstances to be inhumane. Consideration of these views should be given prior to use of this technique.]

V. Sleep Adjustment: Adjusting the sleeping times of the detainee (e.g. reversing sleep cycles from night to day.) This technique is NOT sleep deprivation.

W. False Flag: Convincing the detainee that individuals from a country other than the United States are interrogating him.

X. Isolation: Isolating the detainee from other detainees while still complying with the basic standards of treatment. [Caution: The use of isolation as an interrogation technique requires detailed implementation instructions, including specific guidelines regarding the length of isolation, medical and psychological review, and approval for extensions of the length of isolation by the appropriate level in the chain of command. This technique is not known to have been generally used for interrogation purposes for longer than 30 days. Those nations that believe detainees are subject to POW protections may view use of this technique as inconsistent with the requirements of Geneva III, Article 13 which provides that POWs must be protected against acts of intimidation; Article 14 which provides that POWs are entitled to respect for their person; Article 34 which prohibits coercion and Article 126 which ensures access and basic standards of treatment. Although the provisions of Geneva are not applicable to the interrogation of unlawful combatants, consideration should be given to these views prior to application of the technique.]

Tab B: General Safeguards

Application of these interrogation techniques is subject to the following general safeguards: (i) limited to use only at strategic interrogation facilities; (ii) there is a good basis to believe that the detainee possesses critical intelligence;

(iii) the detainee is medically and operationally evaluated as suitable (considering all techniques to be used in combination); (iv) interrogators are specifically trained for the technique(s); (v) a specific interrogation plan (including reasonable safeguards, limits on duration, intervals between applications, termination criteria and the presence or availability of qualified medical personnel) has been developed; (vi) there is appropriate supervision; and, (vii) there is appropriate specified senior approval for use with any specific detainee (after considering the foregoing and receiving legal advice).

The purpose of all interviews and interrogations is to get the most information from a detainee with the least intrusive method, always applied in a humane and lawful manner with sufficient oversight by trained investigators or interrogators. Operating instructions must be developed based on command policies to insure uniform, careful, and safe application of any interrogations of detainees.

Interrogations must always be planned, deliberate actions that take into account numerous, often interlocking factors such as a detainee's current and past performance in both detention and interrogation, a detainee's emotional and physical strengths and weaknesses, an assessment of possible approaches that may work on a certain detainee in an effort to gain the trust of the detainee, strengths and weaknesses of interrogators, and augmentation by other personnel for a certain detainee based on other factors.

Interrogation approaches are designed to manipulate the detainee's emotions and weaknesses to gain his willing cooperation. Interrogation operations are never conducted in a vacuum: they are conducted in close cooperation with the units detailing the individuals. The policies established by the detaining units that pertain to searching, silencing, and segregating also play a role in the interrogation of a detainee. Detainee interrogation involves developing a plan tailored to an individual and approved by senior interrogators. Strict adherence to policies/standard operating procedures governing the administration of interrogation techniques and oversight is essential.

It is important that interrogators be provided reasonable latitude to vary techniques depending on the detainee's culture, strengths, weaknesses, environment, extent of training in resistance techniques as well as the urgency of obtaining information that the detainee is known to have.

While techniques are considered individually within this analysis, it must be understood that in practice, techniques are usually used in combination; the cumulative effect of all techniques to be employed must be considered before any decisions are made regarding approval for particular situations. The title of a particular technique is not always fully descriptive of a particular technique. With respect to the employment of any techniques involving physical contact, stress or that could produce physical pain or harm, a detailed explanation of that technique must be provided to the decision authority prior to any decision.

Source: Department of Defense, Memorandum for the Commander, US Southern Command, April 16, 2003. Available online at https://www.thetorturedatabase.org/files/foia_subsite/pdfs/DOJOLC000023.pdf.

ANALYSIS

This memorandum not only established the acceptable techniques to be utilized in interrogation of prisoners at Guantanamo Bay, but also left no room for doubt that anything resembling torture would not be a tolerable practice. Although the memorandum repeatedly noted that the Geneva Convention Relative to POWs did not apply to the unlawful combatants within the detainee population, it also reminded interrogators that some nations disagreed with the U.S. determination not to apply the convention to the detainees. None of the techniques could be construed to cause physical, mental, or emotional damage to a detainee. Given the assumption that those detainees possessing significant, actionable intelligence had also likely received training in resistance techniques to thwart questioning, interrogators at Guantanamo Bay were unlikely to have major successes in developing significant intelligence through the approved techniques.

- **Document 54: Condoleezza Rice's Remarks at the 104th National Convention of the Veterans of Foreign Wars**
- **When:** August 25, 2003
- **Where:** Crawford, TX
- **Significance:** Condoleezza Rice first served as the National Security Advisor in the Bush administration, before being named Secretary of State. Her remarks offered an update of the progress of the War on Terror, and also a cautionary note that the conflict would continue for the foreseeable future. They also signaled a pivot within the administration to focus more upon Iraq and less upon Afghanistan as the key to victory and long-term regional stability.

DOCUMENT

Thank you for this opportunity to speak...

For more than a century, you have been doing the important work of helping to ensure that our veterans and our active-duty soldiers receive the respect and the benefits they deserve. In all of your activities, you honor the dead by helping the living, and it is a privilege to be with you.

It has been almost two years since the September 11 attacks, and it is worth taking a moment to reflect and report on the strategy that America has pursued in responding to that awful day.

No less than December 7, 1941, September 11, 2001 forever changed the lives of every American and the strategic perspective of the United States. That day produced an acute sense of our vulnerability to attacks hatched in distant lands, that come without warning, bringing tragedy to our shores.

DID YOU KNOW?

West Point and the World Trade Center

Cadets of the U.S. Military Academy (USMA) at West Point take great pride in their service to the nation as well as their loyalty to their alma mater. Since the September 11 attacks, every West Point class has volunteered to attend the academy in a time of war, and graduated from it expecting to face grave danger in combating terror organizations. Each cadet has the opportunity to design a personalized class ring that signifies his or her alumni status. Members of the USMA class of 2016 have rings made of alloys containing recovered steel from the World Trade Center.

We have marked real progress since September 11, but we get regular reminders that the world continues to be an unsafe place. Last week, terrorists struck in Baghdad and Jerusalem, killing more than three dozen innocent people. These bombings confirm that our enemies are engaged in a war on freedom, and they will target all people living in freedom—including women, children, or relief workers. The ultimate goal of the terrorists is to impose a system based on tyranny and oppression, and they terrorize free people to break our spirit and our resolve. But we cannot and will not shrink from this fight. The freedoms and the way of life we hold sacred are at stake.

From the very beginning of this war on terror, President Bush has delivered a clear and consistent message to the terrorists. In a speech just nine days after the September 11 attacks, he said, "Our war on terror begins with al Qaida, but it does not end there. It will not end until every terrorist group of global reach has been found, stopped, and defeated."

And following last week's bombing in Baghdad, he said, "Our will cannot be shaken. We will persevere through every hardship. We will continue this war on terror until the killers are brought to justice. And we will prevail."

The President has backed up these words with action. We have taken the fight to the terrorists themselves—using all instruments of our national power to root out terror networks and hold accountable states that harbor terrorists.

The war on terror must be fought on the offense—defense of the homeland is a vital mission—but the President has been clear, we will take the fight to the terrorists.

As a result, nearly two-thirds of al Qaida's senior leaders, operational managers, and key facilitators have been captured or killed, and the rest are on the run—permanently.

That's a tribute to the skill of our troops and our intelligence officials, many of whom have operated under extreme weather conditions on extended missions far from home.

Rooting the Taliban out of Afghanistan was the first battle because they had provided the home base and primary sanctuary for al Qaida. Today, across the globe, unparalleled law enforcement and intelligence cooperation efforts are underway, successfully breaking up and disrupting terrorist networks.

And the United States and many other nations are helping Afghans rebuild their country and form a representative government, with democratic institutions, so that Afghanistan is never again a haven for terrorism.

Confronting Saddam Hussein was also essential. His regime posed a threat to the security of the United States and the world. This was a regime that pursued, had used, and possessed weapons of mass destruction.

He had links to terror; had twice invaded other nations; defied the international community and seventeen UN resolutions for twelve years; and gave every indication that he would never disarm and never comply with the just demands of the world. That threat could not be allowed to remain—and to grow.

Now that Saddam's regime is gone, the people of Iraq are more free and seeing real progress. Step by step, normal life in Iraq is being reborn as basic services are restored—in some cases beyond pre-war levels—transportation networks are rebuilt and the economy is revived.

Let me be very clear, the terrorists know that a free Iraq can change the face of the Middle East. That is why they, together with the remnants of the old regime, are fighting as if this is a life and death struggle. It is—and the terrorists will lose. Already there are new opportunities for a different kind of Middle East.

Transformation in the Middle East will require a commitment of many years. I do not mean that we will need to maintain a military presence in Iraq, as was the case in Europe. I do mean that America and our friends and allies must engage broadly throughout the region, across many fronts, including diplomatic, economic, and cultural. And—as in Europe—our efforts must work in full partnership with the peoples of the region who share our commitment to human freedom.

The transformation of the Middle East is the only guarantee that it will no longer produce ideologies of hatred that lead men to fly airplanes into buildings in New York or Washington.

We must remain patient. When Americans begin a noble cause, we finish it. We are 117 days from the end of major combat operations in Iraq. That is not very long.

There is an understandable tendency to look back on America's experience in post-War Germany and see only the successes. But as some of you here today surely remember, the road we traveled was very difficult. 1945 through 1947 was an especially challenging period. Germany was not immediately stable or prosperous. SS officers—called "werewolves"—engaged in sabotage and attacked both coalition forces and those locals cooperating with them—much like today's Baathist and Fedayeen remnants.

It is also true that democracy is not easy. Its institutions are not the natural embodiment of human nature. And our own history should remind us that the union of democratic principle and practice is always a work in progress. When the Founding Fathers said "We the People," they did not mean me. My ancestors were considered three-fifths of a person.

I am confident we will meet this challenge, because the central players will include America's men and women in uniform. Just as America's soldiers of yesteryear made priceless contributions to the security of Europe following World War II, and then to the security and prosperity of Asia in the next decade, the professionalism and commitment of our soldiers will help countries like Afghanistan and Iraq recover from years of tyranny and steadily move toward democracy and prosperity. In both nations, our troops face difficult conditions, and America appreciates their sacrifice.

Every one of America's soldiers, like every one of you, took an oath to defend this nation. There is no higher calling, and America and the world are a better place thanks to your labors. All of you are also part of a rich military tradition that reaches back more than two centuries, and which is being carried forward today by our men and women in uniform. There is a common bond of duty and honor among those who have served, and a respect for those who have marched down the same path.

And on behalf of President Bush, I thank you, for all that you have done to advance human freedom in the United States and throughout the world.

Source: White House Archives, http://georgewbush-whitehouse.archives.gov/news/releases/2003/08/text/20030825-1.html.

ANALYSIS

Condoleezza Rice's speech to the Veterans of Foreign Wars served several purposes. First, it enlisted the support of military veterans from previous conflicts, and helped to link them to the ongoing operations in Afghanistan and Iraq. Second, it demonstrated that to the Bush administration, the invasion of Iraq was another conflict zone in the much larger War on Terror, rather than an entirely separate conflict. Rice reminded her listeners that previous American occupations had not been without problems, and that whitewashing the past ignored the valuable lessons it offered to modern challenges. While there was very little controversial in her speech, it was a harbinger of where most of the military resources and personnel would be directed for the remainder of the War on Terror, and demonstrated a very optimistic outlook on the potential of a democratic society in Iraq.

- **Document 55: Donald Rumsfeld, Memorandum to Department of Defense Key Leaders**
- **When:** October 16, 2003
- **Where:** Washington, D.C.
- **Significance:** Secretary of Defense Donald Rumsfeld held a conference in October with top commanders to discuss ongoing military operations in Afghanistan and Iraq. Afterward, he sent this memorandum to key defense leaders, asking them to consider broad questions regarding the War on Terror.

DOCUMENT

FROM: Donald Rumsfeld
SUBJECT: Global War on Terrorism

The questions I posed to combatant commanders this week were: Are we winning or losing the Global War on Terror? Is DoD changing fast enough to deal with the new 21st century security environment? Can a big institution change fast enough? Is the USG changing fast enough?

DoD has been organized, trained and equipped to fight big armies, navies and air forces. It is not possible to change DoD fast enough to successfully fight the global war on terror; an alternative might be to try to fashion a new institution, either within DoD or elsewhere—one that seamlessly focuses the capabilities of several departments and agencies on this key problem.

With respect to global terrorism, the record since September 11th seems to be:

We are having mixed results with Al Qaida, although we have put considerable pressure on them—nonetheless, a great many remain at large.

USG has made reasonable progress in capturing or killing the top 55 Iraqis.

USG has made somewhat slower progress tracking down the Taliban—Omar, Hekmatyar, etc.

With respect to the Ansar Al-Islam, we are just getting started.

Have we fashioned the right mix of rewards, amnesty, protection and confidence in the US?

Does DoD need to think through new ways to organize, train, equip and focus to deal with the global war on terror?

Are the changes we have and are making too modest and incremental? My impression is that we have not yet made truly bold moves, although we have made many sensible, logical moves in the right direction, but are they enough?

Today, we lack metrics to know if we are winning or losing the global war on terror. Are we capturing, killing or deterring and dissuading more terrorists every day than the madrassas and the radical clerics are recruiting, training and deploying against us?

Does the US need to fashion a broad, integrated plan to stop the next generation of terrorists? The US is putting relatively little effort into a long-range plan, but we are putting a great deal of effort into trying to stop terrorists. The cost-benefit ratio is against us! Our cost is billions against the terrorists' costs of millions.

Do we need a new organization?

How do we stop those who are financing the radical madrassa schools?

Is our current situation such that "the harder we work, the behinder we get"?

It is pretty clear that the coalition can win in Afghanistan and Iraq in one way or another, but it will be a long, hard slog.

Does CIA need a new finding?

Should we create a private foundation to entice radical madrassas to a more moderate course?

What else should we be considering?

Please be prepared to discuss this at our meeting on Saturday or Monday.

Thanks.

Source: Donald Rumsfeld to Richard Myers, Paul Wolfowitz, Peter Pace, and Douglas Feith, October 16, 2003. Available online at http://www.sourcewatch.org/index.php/Rumsfeld_Memo_16_October_2003.

ANALYSIS

This memo, initially sent to General Richard Myers, the chairman of the joint chiefs of staff; Paul Wolfowitz, the deputy secretary of defense; General Peter Pace, commandant of the U.S. Marine Corps, and Douglas Feith, undersecretary of defense for policy, caused immediate consternation in the press when it was leaked by an unknown source. Rumsfeld's musings suggested to many that the top official at the Department of Defense did not have a firm grasp upon the current state of the War on Terror, and lacked even a metric to determine progress. It also demonstrated that Rumsfeld tended to treat the Iraq and Afghanistan conflicts as one collective war, rather than two radically different struggles against markedly different opponents. The fact that the memorandum was leaked was a strong indicator that at least some elements of the military were beginning to lose faith in Rumsfeld's ability to lead the Pentagon in the War on Terror.

- **Document 56: U.S. Army, Information Paper, "Allegations of Detainee Abuse in Iraq and Afghanistan"**
- **When:** April 2, 2004
- **Where:** Washington, D.C.
- **Significance:** This memorandum, prepared by an officer in the U.S. Army Judge Advocate General's Corps, detailed the current status of 62 separate cases of alleged detainee abuse in Afghanistan and Iraq. Twenty-six of the cases resulted in deaths. The most illuminating cases are included in this excerpt.

DOCUMENT

INFORMATION PAPER

DAJA-ZA

SUBJECT: Allegations of Detainee Abuse in Iraq and Afghanistan

1. Purpose. To provide information on investigations into allegations of detainee abuse and/or death in Iraq and Afghanistan.

2. Background.

a. A total of sixty-two (62) cases of detainee abuse and/or death have been or are being investigated; forty-six (46) are being investigated by CID and sixteen (16) others are being investigated at the unit level.

b. As noted in paragraph 3, of the forty-six (46) cases investigated by CID, twenty-six (26) cases involve detainee deaths and twenty (20) cases involve other allegations of detainee abuse (e.g., assault). Command dispositions in these cases are included, where known. Of the twenty-six (26) cases involving detainee deaths, twelve (12) investigations have been closed in cases where the death was determined to be due to natural causes or the cause of death was undetermined (i.e., no apparent evidence of abuse).

3. Discussion of CID Investigations.

a. Death Investigations:

(10) On 11 Sep 03, at the Forward Operating Base Packhorse detention facility, an Iraqi detainee died while in US custody. An enlisted Soldier, while on guard duty, failed to follow the ROE and shot the detainee who was throwing rocks. Case closed and referred to the command for appropriate action. The Soldier was reduced to E-1 and administratively discharged in lieu of trial by court-martial.

(13) On 6 Nov 03, an Afghani detainee was found dead in his cell at FOB Gereshk, AF. He had bruising about his hips, groin, and buttocks. An autopsy could not establish a cause of death. The manner of death is currently classified as undetermined. Investigation continues.

(14) On 24 Nov 03, four Iraqi detainees were shot and killed while trying to escape Abu Ghraib Prison. Investigation determined the shootings were justified.

(17) On 3 Jan 04, an Iraqi national was drowned after he was allegedly pushed off a bridge by Soldiers in Samarra. Further, the Soldiers are alleged to have conspired to cover up the incident. Investigation continues.

(19) On 9 Jan 04, CID was notified of the suspicious death of an Iraqi detainee. The detainee, a former Iraqi Army LTC, was taken into custody on 4 Jan 04 and was subsequently placed in an isolation cell and questioned at least two times in ensuing days. An examination of the detainee remains disclosed that there was extensive bruising on his upper body. On 11 Jan 04, an autopsy was conducted by an Armed Forces Medical Examiner. His preliminary report indicates the cause of death as blunt force injuries and asphyxia, with the manner of death listed as homicide. Investigation continues.

(24) On 28 Feb 2004, a SGT attempted to detain an Iraqi; the Iraqi resisted when the SGt attempted to place flexi-cuffs on him. A PFC raised his weapon to protect the SGT. The SGT was able to complete the cuffing process and was leading the detainee away when the PFC believed that the Iraqi was lunging at the SGT. The PFC fired one round from his weapon which struck the detainee in the head and killed him. CID is still investigating.

b. Other Abuse Allegations.

(5) On 13 Jun 03, a SGT punched, kicked and slapped a detainee. SGT pled guilty at a BCD Special Court-Martial and sentenced to reduction to E-1 and 60 days confinement.

(7) On 20 Jun 03, a 1LT detained several individuals suspected of looting and placed them in the back of a truck. He later took one detainee, a young boy, from the truck, pointed his pistol at the boy's head, and fired a round away from the boy in an effort to scare him. Case referred to a General Court-Martial; 1LT's request to resign in lieu of court-martial was approved by HQDA with OTH discharge.

(10) On 20 Aug 03, at Forward Operating Base Gunner, Iraq, an Iraqi being detained in US custody was physically assaulted and threatened by a battalion commander (LTC [REDACTED]), three enlisted Soldiers and an interpreter after the detainee refused to provide information. Case closed and referred to the command for appropriate action. The enlisted Soldiers received Article 15 punishment; LTC [REDACTED] was relieved of his command and, after an Article 32 hearing, received nonjudicial punishment. He also submitted a request to retire from active duty.

(14) On 7 Oct 03, at the Abu Ghraib detention facility, three active duty male enlisted Soldiers assigned to Co. A, 519th MI Bn, Ft Bragg, NC allegedly sexually assaulted and threatened a female Iraqi detainee. Investigation continues.

Source: U.S. Army Criminal Investigation Command, "Allegations of Detainee Abuse in Iraq and Afghanistan" report, April 2, 2004. Available online at https://www.thetorturedatabase.org/files/foia_subsite/pdfs/DOD054957.pdf.

ANALYSIS

When the United States led a coalition that invaded Iraq in 2003, much of the focus was taken away from ongoing operations in Afghanistan. Little planning had been conducted for how to deal with thousands of Iraqi captives, and as a result, much of the treatment of prisoners of war was carried out on a poorly improvised basis. These specific cases are interesting for a number of reasons. First, there were relatively few instances of alleged abuse in the first year of the Iraq War, which suggests that U.S. forces behaved remarkably well toward Iraqi prisoners. Second, when allegations were made and found to be credible, they were thoroughly investigated by the Criminal Investigations Division of the U.S. Army. Third, when U.S. soldiers were found to be guilty of infractions, they faced severe punishments, to include imprisonment, the end of military careers, major reductions in rank, and forfeiture of pay. Finally, despite the relatively low number of alleged instances of detainee abuse in the initial year of the conflict, in subsequent years, as the war became one of counterinsurgency rather than conventional operations, the number of allegations sharply rose, and became a global scandal when abuses at Abu Ghraib prison became public knowledge.

- **Document 57: Memorandum for the Record, "Detainees Basic Tenant Rights"**
- **When:** June 15, 2004
- **Where:** Multinational Force—Iraq Headquarters, Baghdad, Iraq
- **Significance:** This memorandum discusses the acceptable forms of restraints and punishments that could be visited upon detainees, to include periods of confinement in very small concrete cells or being chained to the floor of a detention facility. These options were not limited to combatant detainees; they could also be applied to civilians captured in the war zone.

DOCUMENT

HEADQUARTERS
MULTINATIONAL FORCE—IRAQ
OFFICE OF THE DEPUTY COMMANDING GENERAL, DETAINEE OPERATIONS
BAGHDAD, IRAQ
MNFI-D
MEMORANDUM FOR RECORD
SUBJECT: Detainees Basic Tenant Rights IAW Geneva Convention and Army Regulations

1. AR 1908, Enemy Prisoners of War, Detained Personnel, Civilian Internees, and Other Detainees, outlines the minimum standard of living for detainees in permanent internment facilities, but does not address temporary holding facilities of a capturing unit.

2. FM 3-19.40, Internment/Resettlement Operations, identifies the basic safeguards that are mandated for all types of detainees.

a. Provide first aid and medical treatment for all detainees that are equal to the treatment that would be given to US casualties.

b. Provide food and water. These supplies must be commensurate to those for US and allied forces.

c. Provide firm, humane treatment.

d. Allow captives to use protective equipment in case of hostile fire or NBC [nuclear, biological, or chemical] threat.

e. Do not locate captives near obvious targets. (e.g. ammunition sites, fuel points, etc.)

3. The Geneva Convention Relative to the Protection of Civilian Persons in Time of War, 12 August 1949, deals with the status and treatment of civilian internees, in that it must be humane in nature. The capturing unit is responsible for proper and humane treatment of detainees from the moment of capture or other apprehension.

4. FM 3-19.40 does not articulate the minimum standard a capturing [unit] must provide in the form of shelter or manner of detention, thus the standard must be relative to that of a forward collection point. A forward collection point as a minimum has a guard force based on METT-TC [mission, enemy, terrain and weather, troops and support, time, and civil considerations], food and water, latrine facility, trench or overhead cover, and concertina wire establishing a perimeter. It is understood that all these requirements are based on METT-TC and security for both the detainees and capturing unit must be a planning consideration. The guard force is necessary to monitor the detainees, especially in the event of a medical emergency (e.g. heart attack, seizure, or stroke) that could result in permanent injury or death if not treated immediately by medical personnel. These tenants fall under the preamble of humane treatment in the Geneva Convention.

5. FM 3-19.40 provides suggestions of a detention facility but does not limit the ground commander on other types of detention methods or means to secure the detainees, as long as the method or means does not violate the Geneva Convention and meets the basic safeguards outlined in FM 3-19.40. AR 190-8 specifically prohibits any measure of such character to cause physical suffering or extermination of the Civilian Internee.

a. Use of chains bolted to the floor as a means of securing detainees for a short period of time that allow the detainee the ability to stand, sit, or lay down is acceptable as long as the minimum requirements/safeguards listed in paragraphs two and four are adhered to. (A short period of time is defined as not to exceed 14 days, as outlined in [REDACTED] for the amount of time a detainee can be held prior to evacuation to a Coalition Holding Facility, Baghdad Central collection Facility.)

b. Securing detainees in a cement cell with dimensions of 4 feet long, 3.1 feet high, and 1.5 feet wide secured by a sliding metal door is acceptable for a short duration not to exceed 24 hours. The cell does not provide for good ventilation, lighting, or observation by guard force. In addition, long periods of detention in this type of facility would cause physical suffering to the detainee violating AR 190-8 and the provisions of the Geneva Convention. In addition, the minimum requirements/safeguards listed in paragraphs two and four apply here also.

6. Point of contact for this memorandum is the undersigned [REDACTED].

Source: Office of the Deputy Commanding General, Baghdad, Iraq. Memorandum for Record: Detainees Basic Tenant Rights IAW Geneva Convention and Army Regulations, June 15, 2004. Available online at https://www.thetorturedatabase .org/files/foia_subsite/pdfs/DOD056704.pdf.

ANALYSIS

The American Civil Liberties Union (ACLU) obtained this document through a Freedom of Information Act request, and placed it into a database of documents related to the wars in Afghanistan and Iraq. The ACLU argued that this type of document demonstrated that the United States was actively engaged in mistreating its captives and that commanders had essentially received permission to engage in torturous practices. This memorandum, circulated throughout U.S. forces operating in Iraq, offers a glimpse into some of the developing allegations of inhumane treatment of enemy captives. Being confined in a concrete cell too small for the occupant to stand or lay down, for 24 hours straight, violates the spirit and the letter of the Geneva Convention Relative to the Treatment of Prisoners of War, and can only be considered a punitive and coercive measure. Further, there is no explanation of how often a detainee could be placed in such a location—only that it cannot be for more than 24 hours at a stretch. Unfortunately, this could indicate that the detainee would be placed in the cell for 24 hours, removed for a brief interrogation period, and then returned to the cell for another 24-hour period.

- **Document 58: Justice John Paul Kennedy's Concurrence, *Rasul v. Bush***
- **When:** June 28, 2004
- **Where:** Washington, D.C.
- **Significance:** The Supreme Court case of *Rasul v. Bush* revolved around the question of whether detainees at Guantanamo Bay (and by extension, in other locations) had the right to petition U.S. courts for a writ of habeas corpus, which would essentially allow them to challenge the reasoning behind their detention. Prior to the case, the detainees could be held indefinitely, and had no right to legal counsel or even contact with outsiders. When the case granted victory to Rasul, it opened the door to further legal challenges against detention.

DOCUMENT

Kennedy, J., concurring in judgment
SUPREME COURT OF THE UNITED STATES
Nos. 03—334 and 03—343
ON WRITS OF CERTIORARI TO THE UNITED STATES COURT OF
APPEALS FOR THE DISTRICT OF COLUMBIA CIRCUIT
Justice Kennedy, concurring in the judgment.

The Court is correct, in my view, to conclude that federal courts have jurisdiction to consider challenges to the legality of the detention of foreign nationals held at the Guantanamo Bay Naval Base in Cuba. While I reach the same conclusion, my analysis follows a different course. Justice Scalia exposes the weakness in the Court's conclusion that *Braden v. 30th Judicial Circuit Court of Ky., 410 U.S. 484* (1973), "overruled the statutory predicate to *Eisentrager*'s holding," *ante*, at 10—11. As he explains, the Court's approach is not a plausible reading of *Braden* or *Johnson v. Eisentrager, 339 U.S. 763* (1950). In my view, the correct course is to follow the framework of Eisentrager.

Eisentrager considered the scope of the right to petition for a writ of habeas corpus against the backdrop of the constitutional command of the separation of powers. The issue before the Court was whether the Judiciary could exercise jurisdiction over the claims of German prisoners held in the Landsberg prison in Germany following the cessation of hostilities in Europe. The Court concluded the petition could not be entertained. The petition was not within the proper realm of the judicial power. It concerned matters within the exclusive province of the Executive, or the Executive and Congress, to determine.

The Court began by noting the "ascending scale of rights" that courts have recognized for individuals depending on their connection to the United States. *Id.*, at 770. Citizenship provides a longstanding basis for jurisdiction, the Court noted, and among aliens physical presence within the United States also "gave the Judiciary power to act." *Id.*, at 769, 771. This contrasted with the "essential pattern for seasonable Executive constraint of enemy aliens." *Id.*, at 773. The place of the detention was also important to the jurisdictional question, the Court noted. Physical presence in the United States "implied protection," *id.*, at 777—778, whereas in *Eisentrager* "th[e] prisoners at no relevant time were within any territory over which the United States is sovereign," *id.*, at 778. The Court next noted that the prisoners in *Eisentrager* "were actual enemies" of the United States, proven to be so at trial, and thus could not justify "a limited opening of our courts" to distinguish the "many [aliens] of friendly personal disposition to whom the status of enemy" was unproven. *Id.*, at 778. Finally, the Court considered the extent to which jurisdiction would "hamper the war effort and bring aid and comfort to the enemy." *Id.*, at 779. Because the prisoners in *Eisentrager* were proven enemy aliens found and detained outside the United States, and because the existence of jurisdiction would have had a clear harmful effect on the Nation's military affairs, the matter was appropriately left to the Executive Branch and there was no jurisdiction for the courts to hear the prisoner's claims.

The decision in *Eisentrager* indicates that there is a realm of political authority over military affairs where the judicial power may not enter. The existence of this realm acknowledges the power of the President as Commander in Chief, and the joint role of the President and the Congress, in the conduct of military affairs. A faithful application of *Eisentrager*, then, requires an initial inquiry into the general circumstances of the detention to determine whether the Court has the authority to entertain the petition and to grant relief after considering all of the facts presented. A necessary corollary of *Eisentrager* is that there are circumstances in which the courts maintain the power and the responsibility to protect persons from unlawful detention even where military affairs are implicated. See also *Ex parte Milligan*, 4 Wall. 2 (1866).

The facts here are distinguishable from those in *Eisentrager* in two critical ways, leading to the conclusion that a federal court may entertain the petitions. First, Guantanamo Bay is in every practical respect a United States territory, and it is one far removed from any hostilities. The opinion of the Court well explains the history of its possession by the United States. In a formal sense, the United States leases the Bay; the 1903 lease agreement states that Cuba retains "ultimate sovereignty" over it. Lease of Lands for Coaling and Naval Stations, Feb. 23, 1903, U.S.-Cuba, Art. III, T. S. No. 418. At the same time, this lease is no ordinary lease. Its term is indefinite and at the discretion of the United States. What matters is the unchallenged and indefinite control that the United States has long exercised over Guantanamo Bay. From a practical perspective, the indefinite lease of Guantanamo Bay has produced a place that belongs to the United States, extending the "implied protection" of the United States to it. *Eisentrager, supra,* at 777–778.

The second critical set of facts is that the detainees at Guantanamo Bay are being held indefinitely, and without benefit of any legal proceeding to determine their status. In *Eisentrager*, the prisoners were tried and convicted by a military commission of violating the laws of war and were sentenced to prison terms. Having already been subject to procedures establishing their status, they could not justify "a limited opening of our courts" to show that they were "of friendly personal disposition" and not enemy aliens. 339 U.S., at 778. Indefinite detention without trial or other proceeding presents altogether different considerations. It allows friends and foes alike to remain in detention. It suggests a weaker case of military necessity and much greater alignment with the traditional function of habeas corpus. Perhaps, where detainees are taken from a zone of hostilities, detention without proceedings or trial would be justified by military necessity for a matter of weeks; but as the period of detention stretches from months to years, the case for continued detention to meet military exigencies becomes weaker.

In light of the status of Guantanamo Bay and the indefinite pretrial detention of the detainees, I would hold that federal-court jurisdiction is permitted in these cases. This approach would avoid creating automatic statutory authority to adjudicate the claims of persons located outside the United States, and remains true to the reasoning of *Eisentrager*. For these reasons, I concur in the judgment of the Court.

Source: Rasul v. Bush, 542 U.S. 466 (2004).

ANALYSIS

Justice Kennedy provided a succinct explanation for the Supreme Court's decision to allow detainees held at Guantanamo Bay to challenge their internment.

Essentially, the Supreme Court found that even though the presidency has some exclusive powers regarding the conduct of warfare, those powers do not include the ability to hold enemy captives indefinitely. This legal opinion focused upon the notion that the Bush administration had already decreed that the captives held at Guantanamo Bay would not be considered prisoners of war who could claim the protections of the Geneva Convention, a determination that placed the detainees into a legal limbo which had no guarantee that it would ever end. Because the detainees had not been charged with any crimes, they could not be classified as criminal prisoners, but if they were also not legally considered prisoners of war, there were few guidelines to explain the limits of their incarceration. The *Rasul v. Bush* case did not directly free any of the detainees, but it did force the government to justify why a given individual remained in captivity.

- **Document 59: Justice Sandra Day O'Connor Opinion, *Hamdi v. Rumsfeld***
- **When:** June 28, 2004
- **Where:** Washington, D.C.
- **Significance:** This case was brought on behalf of an American citizen, Yaser Esam Hamdi, who was captured fighting on behalf of the Taliban in Afghanistan. Hamdi argued that as a citizen of the United States, he had the constitutional right to challenge his detention at Guantanamo Bay. The government's response was that Hamdi, as a wartime captive, had no legal right to challenge his detention, which would be terminated at the conclusion of hostilities.

DOCUMENT

Opinion of O'Connor, J.
SUPREME COURT OF THE UNITED STATES
No. 03—6696
YASER ESAM HAMDI and ESAM FOUAD HAMDI, as next friend of YASER ESAM HAMDI, PETITIONERS *v.* DONALD H. RUMSFELD, SECRETARY OF DEFENSE, et al.
ON WRIT OF CERTIORARI TO THE UNITED STATES COURT OF APPEALS FOR THE FOURTH CIRCUIT
Justice O'Connor announced the judgment of the Court and delivered an opinion, in which The Chief Justice, Justice Kennedy, and Justice Breyer join.

At this difficult time in our Nation's history, we are called upon to consider the legality of the Government's detention of a United States citizen on United States soil as an "enemy combatant" and to address the process that is constitutionally owed to one who seeks to challenge his classification as such. The United States Court of Appeals for the Fourth Circuit held that petitioner's detention was legally authorized and that he was entitled to no further opportunity to challenge his enemy-combatant label. We now vacate and remand. We hold that although Congress authorized the detention of combatants in the narrow circumstances alleged here, due process demands that a citizen held in the United States as an enemy combatant be given a meaningful opportunity to contest the factual basis for that detention before a neutral decisionmaker.

I

This case arises out of the detention of a man whom the Government alleges took up arms with the Taliban during this conflict. His name is Yaser Esam Hamdi. Born an American citizen in Louisiana in 1980, Hamdi moved with his family to Saudi Arabia as a child. By 2001, the parties agree, he resided in Afghanistan. At some point that year, he was seized by members of the Northern Alliance, a coalition of military groups opposed to the Taliban government, and eventually was turned over to the United States military. The Government asserts that it initially detained and interrogated Hamdi in Afghanistan before transferring him to the United States Naval Base in Guantanamo Bay in January 2002. In April 2002, upon learning that Hamdi is an American citizen, authorities transferred him to a naval brig in Norfolk, Virginia, where he remained until a recent transfer to a brig in Charleston, South Carolina. The Government contends that Hamdi is an "enemy combatant," and that this status justifies holding him in the United States indefinitely—without formal charges or proceedings—unless and until it makes the determination that access to counsel or further process is warranted.

In June 2002, Hamdi's father, Esam Fouad Hamdi, filed the present petition for a writ of habeas corpus under 28 U.S.C. § 2241 in the Eastern District of Virginia, naming as petitioners his son and himself as next friend. The elder Hamdi alleges in the petition that he has had no contact with his son since the Government took custody of him in 2001, and that the Government has held his son "without access to legal counsel or notice of any charges pending against him." The petition contends that Hamdi's detention was not legally authorized. It argues that, "[a]s an American citizen, . . . Hamdi enjoys the full protections of the Constitution," and that Hamdi's detention in the United States without charges, access to an impartial tribunal, or assistance of counsel "violated and continue[s] to violate the Fifth and Fourteenth Amendments to the United States Constitution." The habeas petition asks that the court, among other things, (1) appoint counsel for Hamdi; (2) order respondents to cease interrogating him; (3) declare that he is being held in violation of the Fifth and Fourteenth Amendments; (4) "[t]o the extent Respondents contest any material factual allegations in this Petition, schedule an evidentiary hearing, at which Petitioners may adduce proof in support of their allegations"; and (5) order that Hamdi be released from his "unlawful custody." Although his habeas petition provides no details with regard to the factual circumstances surrounding his son's capture and detention, Hamdi's father has asserted in documents found elsewhere in the record that his son went to Afghanistan to do "relief work," and that he had been in that country less than two months before September 11, 2001, and could not have received military training. The 20-year-old was traveling on his own for the first time, his father says, and "[b]ecause of his lack of experience, he was trapped in Afghanistan once that military campaign began."

The District Court found that Hamdi's father was a proper next friend, appointed the federal public defender as counsel for the petitioners, and ordered that counsel be given access to Hamdi. The United States Court of Appeals for the Fourth Circuit reversed that order, holding that the District Court had failed to extend appropriate deference to the Government's security and intelligence interests. It directed the District Court to consider "the most cautious procedures first," and to conduct a deferential inquiry into Hamdi's status. It opined that "if Hamdi is indeed an 'enemy combatant' who was captured during hostilities in Afghanistan, the government's present detention of him is a lawful one."

On remand, the Government filed a response and a motion to dismiss the petition. It attached to its response a declaration from one Michael Mobbs (hereinafter "Mobbs Declaration"), who identified himself as Special Advisor to the Under Secretary of Defense for Policy. Mobbs indicated that in this position, he has been "substantially involved with matters related to the detention of enemy combatants in the current war against the al Qaeda terrorists and those who support and harbor them (including the Taliban)." He expressed his "familiar[ity]" with Department of Defense and United States military policies and procedures applicable to the detention, control, and transfer of al Qaeda and Taliban personnel, and declared that "[b]ased upon my review of relevant records and reports, I am also familiar with the facts and circumstances related to the capture of . . . Hamdi and his detention by U.S. military forces."

On the more global question of whether legal authorization exists for the detention of citizen enemy combatants at all, the Fourth Circuit rejected Hamdi's arguments that 18 U.S.C. § 4001(a) and Article 5 of the Geneva Convention rendered any such detentions unlawful. The court expressed doubt as to Hamdi's argument that §4001(a), which provides that "[n]o citizen shall be imprisoned or otherwise detained by the United States except pursuant to an Act of Congress," required express congressional authorization of detentions of this sort. But it held that, in any event, such authorization was found in the post-September 11 Authorization for Use of Military Force. Because "capturing and detaining enemy combatants is an inherent part of warfare," the court held, "the 'necessary and appropriate force' referenced in the congressional resolution necessarily includes the capture and detention of any and all hostile forces arrayed against our troops." The court likewise rejected Hamdi's Geneva Convention claim, concluding that the convention is not self-executing and that, even if it were, it would not preclude the Executive from detaining Hamdi until the cessation of hostilities.

Finally, the Fourth Circuit rejected Hamdi's contention that its legal analyses with regard to the authorization for the detention scheme and the process to which he was constitutionally entitled should be altered by the fact that he is an American citizen detained on American soil. Relying on *Ex parte Quirin*, 317 U.S. 1 (1942), the court emphasized that "[o]ne who takes up arms against the United States in a foreign theater of war, regardless of his citizenship, may properly be designated an enemy combatant and treated as such." "The privilege of citizenship," the court held, "entitles Hamdi to a limited judicial inquiry into his detention, but only to determine its legality under the war powers of the political branches. At least where it is undisputed that he was present in a zone of active combat operations, we are satisfied that the Constitution does not entitle him to a searching review of the factual determinations underlying his seizure there."

II

The threshold question before us is whether the Executive has the authority to detain citizens who qualify as "enemy combatants." There is some debate as to the proper scope of this term, and the Government has never provided any court with the full criteria that it uses in classifying individuals as such. It has made clear, however, that, for purposes of this case, the "enemy combatant" that it is seeking to detain is an individual who, it alleges, was "part of or supporting forces hostile to the United States or coalition partners" in Afghanistan and who "engaged in an armed conflict against the United States" there. We therefore answer only the narrow question before us: whether the detention of citizens falling within that definition is authorized.

The Government maintains that no explicit congressional authorization is required, because the Executive possesses plenary authority to detain pursuant to Article II of the Constitution. We do not reach the question whether Article II provides such authority, however, because we agree with the Government's alternative position, that Congress has in fact authorized Hamdi's detention, through the AUMF.

The AUMF authorizes the President to use "all necessary and appropriate force" against "nations, organizations, or persons" associated with the September 11, 2001, terrorist attacks. There can be no doubt that individuals who fought against the United States in Afghanistan as part of the Taliban, an organization known to have supported the al Qaeda terrorist network responsible for those attacks, are individuals Congress sought to target in passing the AUMF. We conclude that detention of individuals falling into the limited category we are considering, for the duration of the particular conflict in which they were captured, is so fundamental and accepted an incident to war as to be an exercise of the "necessary and appropriate force" Congress has authorized the President to use.

In light of these principles, it is of no moment that the AUMF does not use specific language of detention. Because detention to prevent a combatant's return to the battlefield is a fundamental incident of waging war, in permitting the use of "necessary and appropriate force," Congress has clearly and unmistakably authorized detention in the narrow circumstances considered here.

Hamdi objects, nevertheless, that Congress has not authorized the *indefinite* detention to which he is now subject. The Government responds that "the detention of enemy combatants during World War II was just as 'indefinite' while that war was being fought." We take Hamdi's objection to be not to the lack of certainty regarding the date on which the conflict will end, but to the substantial prospect of perpetual detention. We recognize that the national security underpinnings of the "war on terror," although crucially important, are broad and malleable. As the Government concedes, "given its unconventional nature, the current conflict is unlikely to end with a formal cease-fire agreement." The prospect Hamdi raises is therefore not far-fetched. If the Government does not consider this unconventional war won for two generations, and if it maintains during that time that Hamdi might, if released, rejoin forces fighting against the United States, then the position it has taken throughout the litigation of this case suggests that Hamdi's detention could last for the rest of his life.

III

Even in cases in which the detention of enemy combatants is legally authorized, there remains the question of what process is constitutionally due to a citizen who disputes his enemy-combatant status. Hamdi argues that he is owed a meaningful and timely hearing and that "extra-judicial detention [that] begins and ends with the submission of an affidavit based on third-hand hearsay" does not comport with the Fifth and Fourteenth Amendments. The Government counters that any more process than was provided below would be both unworkable and "constitutionally intolerable." Our resolution of this dispute requires a careful examination both of the writ of habeas corpus, which Hamdi now seeks to employ as a mechanism of judicial review, and of the Due Process Clause, which informs the procedural contours of that mechanism in this instance.

3

Striking the proper constitutional balance here is of great importance to the Nation during this period of ongoing combat. But it is equally vital that our calculus not give short shrift to the values that this country holds dear or to the privilege that is American citizenship. It is during our most challenging and uncertain moments that our Nation's commitment to due process is most severely tested; and it is in those times that we must preserve our commitment at home to the principles for which we fight abroad.

With due recognition of these competing concerns, we believe that neither the process proposed by the Government nor the process apparently envisioned by the District Court below strikes the proper constitutional balance when a United States citizen is detained in the United States as an enemy combatant. That is, "the risk of erroneous deprivation" of a detainee's liberty interest is unacceptably high under the Government's proposed rule, while some of the "additional or substitute procedural safeguards" suggested by the District Court are unwarranted in light of their limited "probable value" and the burdens they may impose on the military in such cases.

We therefore hold that a citizen-detainee seeking to challenge his classification as an enemy combatant must receive notice of the factual basis for his classification, and a fair opportunity to rebut the Government's factual assertions before a neutral decision-maker.

At the same time, the exigencies of the circumstances may demand that, aside from these core elements, enemy combatant proceedings may be tailored to alleviate their uncommon potential to burden the Executive at a time of ongoing military conflict. Hearsay, for example, may need to be accepted as the most reliable available evidence from the Government in such a proceeding. Likewise, the Constitution would not be offended by a presumption in favor of the Government's evidence, so long as that presumption remained a rebuttable one and fair opportunity for rebuttal were provided. Thus, once the Government puts forth credible evidence that the habeas petitioner meets the enemy-combatant criteria, the onus could shift to the petitioner to rebut that evidence with more persuasive evidence that he falls outside the criteria. A burden-shifting scheme of this sort would meet the goal of ensuring that the errant tourist, embedded journalist, or local aid worker has a chance to prove military error while giving due regard to the Executive once it has put forth meaningful support for its conclusion that the detainee is in fact an enemy combatant.

We think it unlikely that this basic process will have the dire impact on the central functions of war-making that the Government forecasts. The parties agree that initial captures on the battlefield need not receive the process we have discussed here; that process is due only when the determination is made to *continue* to hold those who have been seized. The Government has made clear in its briefing that documentation regarding battlefield detainees already is kept in the ordinary course of military affairs. Any fact-finding imposition created by requiring a knowledgeable affiant to summarize these records to an independent tribunal is a minimal one. Likewise, arguments that military officers ought not have to wage war under the threat of litigation lose much of their steam when factual disputes at enemy-combatant hearings are limited to the alleged combatant's acts. This focus meddles little, if at all, in the strategy or conduct of war, inquiring only into the appropriateness of continuing to detain an individual claimed to have taken up arms against the United States. While we accord the greatest respect and consideration to the judgments of military authorities in matters relating to the actual prosecution of a war, and recognize that the scope of that discretion necessarily is wide, it does not infringe on the core role of the military for the courts to exercise their own time-honored and constitutionally mandated roles of reviewing and resolving claims like those presented here.

In sum, while the full protections that accompany challenges to detentions in other settings may prove unworkable and inappropriate in the enemy-combatant setting, the threats to military operations posed by a basic system of independent review are not so weighty as to trump a citizen's core rights to challenge meaningfully the Government's case and to be heard by an impartial adjudicator.

IV

Hamdi asks us to hold that the Fourth Circuit also erred by denying him immediate access to counsel upon his detention and by disposing of the case without permitting him to meet with an attorney. Since our grant of certiorari in this case, Hamdi has been appointed counsel, with whom he has met for consultation purposes on several occasions, and with whom he is now being granted unmonitored meetings. He unquestionably has the right to access to counsel in connection with the proceedings on remand. No further consideration of this issue is necessary at this stage of the case.

Source: Hamdi v. Rumsfeld, 542 U.S. 507 (2004).

ANALYSIS

The U.S. Supreme Court found that Hamdi had the legal right to challenge his detention, and that the burden of proof for the allegations that led to his detention rested with the U.S. government. However, once the government supplied evidence that Hamdi should be held as an enemy combatant, the burden of proof would then shift back to Hamdi to demonstrate that the government was in error. O'Connor's opinion illustrated many of the legal pitfalls created by the detention program at Guantanamo Bay. In theory, prisoners of war are held until the end of hostilities. However, the international treaties that govern the treatment of prisoners of war were written with state conflicts in mind. The War on Terror, which is as much a fight against an ideology as a conventional conflict between warring powers, might very well last for several generations—and if so, any captives held by the United States would be essentially subject to life imprisonment without the benefit of a trial. *Hamdi v. Rumsfeld* did not trigger the release of any of the detainees at Guantanamo Bay, but it did open the possibility that they could challenge their detention, and possibly force the creation and implementation of military tribunals to determine which prisoners could be held indefinitely and which should be released at an earlier date.

- **Document 60: Abu Musab al Zarqawi's Letter to Al Qaeda Leadership**
- **When:** 2004
- **Where:** Iraq
- **Significance:** Al Zarqawi quickly became the most feared man in Iraq due to his leadership of the Al Qaeda offshoot operating in the aftermath of the American-led invasion. At his direction, Al Qaeda attacks were launched against coalition forces and Iraqi citizens, particularly members of the Shi'a majority. Even Osama bin Laden expressed some reservations at the ferocity of al Zarqawi's attacks, particularly those targeting Muslim civilians, but he was incapable of corralling al Zarqawi's activities.

DOCUMENT

Even if our bodies are far apart, the distance between our hearts is close.

Our solace is in the saying of the Imam Malik. I hope that both of us are well. I ask God the Most High, the Generous, [to have] this letter reach you clothed in the garments of health and savoring the winds of victory and triumph. Amen.

I send you an account that is appropriate to [your] position and that removes the veil and lifts the curtain from the good and bad [that are] hidden in the arena of Iraq.

As you know, God favored the [Islamic] nation with jihad on His behalf in the land of Mesopotamia. It is known to you that the arena here is not like the rest. It has positive elements not found in others, and it also has negative elements not found in others. Among the greatest positive elements of this arena is that it is jihad in the Arab heartland. It is a stone's throw from the lands of the two Holy Precincts and the al-Aqsa [Mosque]. We know from God's religion that the true, decisive

DID YOU KNOW?

Abu Musab al-Zarqawi

In 1999, Jordanian-born jihadist Abu Musab al-Zarqawi formed Jama'at al-Tawhid wal-Jihad (Organization of Monotheism and Jihad). In 2004, the group renamed itself Al Qaeda in Iraq and began operations against coalition forces in Iraq. It quickly established a reputation for extremely bloody and sensational attacks, particularly against Iraqi Shi'a civilian populations. These activities contradicted the priorities established by Osama bin Laden, who wished to have the group concentrate on American and coalition troops. One of the most notorious acts by the group was the beheading of U.S. military contractors, broadcast live on jihadi websites. Zarqawi quickly became the most-wanted terrorist in Iraq, and was killed in an airstrike in 2006. His death significantly hampered the group for a period of years, and many of its members became more interested in the formation of a new Islamic state under the group's new leader, Abu Bakr al-Baghdadi.

battle between infidelity and Islam is in this land, i.e., in [Greater] Syria and its surroundings. Therefore, we must spare no effort and strive urgently to establish a foothold in this land. Perhaps God may cause something to happen thereafter. The current situation, o courageous shaykhs, makes it necessary for us to examine this matter deeply, starting from our true Law and the reality in which we live.

Here is the current situation as I, with my limited vision, see it. I ask God to forgive my prattle and lapses. I say, having sought help from God, that the Americans, as you know well, entered Iraq on a contractual basis and to create the State of Greater Israel from the Nile to the Euphrates and that this Zionized American Administration believes that accelerating the creation of the State of [Greater] Israel will accelerate the emergence of the Messiah. It came to Iraq with all its people, pride, and haughtiness toward God and his Prophet. It thought that the matter would be somewhat easy. Even if there were to be difficulties, it would be easy. But it collided with a completely different reality. The operations of the brother mujahidin began from the first moment, which mixed things up somewhat. Then, the pace of operations quickened. This was in the Sunni Triangle, if this is the right name for it. This forced the Americans to conclude a deal with the Shi'a, the most evil of mankind. The deal was concluded on [the basis that] the Shi'a would get two-thirds of the booty for having stood in the ranks of the Crusaders against the mujahidin.

First: The Makeup [of Iraq]

In general, Iraq is a political mosaic, an ethnic mixture, and scattered confessional and sectarian disparities that only a strong central authority and a overpowering ruler have been able to lead, beginning with Ziyad Ibn Abihi (tr. note: 7th century A.D.) and ending with Saddam. The future faces difficult choices. It is a land of great hardships and difficulties for everyone, whether he is serious or not.

As for the details:

1. The Kurds

In their two Barazani and Talabani halves, these have given the bargain of their hands and the fruit of their hearts to the Americans. They have opened their land to the Jews and become their rear base and a Trojan horse for their plans. They (the Jews) infiltrate through their lands, drape themselves in their banners, and take them as a bridge over which to cross for financial control and economic hegemony, as well as for the espionage base for which they have built a large structure the length and breadth of that land. In general, Islam's voice has died out among them—the Kurds—and the glimmer of religion has weakened in their homes. The Iraqi Da'wa has intoxicated them, and the good people among them, few as they are, are oppressed and fear that birds will carry them away.

3 [*sic*]. The Shi'a

[They are] the insurmountable obstacle, the lurking snake, the crafty and malicious scorpion, the spying enemy, and the penetrating venom. We here are entering a battle on two levels. One, evident and open, is with an attacking enemy and patent infidelity. [Another is] a difficult, fierce battle with a crafty enemy who wears the garb of a friend, manifests agreement, and calls for comradeship, but harbors ill will and twists up peaks and crests.

Their greatest [act of] worship is to curse the Muslim friends of God from first to last. These are the people most anxious to divide the Muslims. Among their greatest principles are leveling charges of infidelity and damning and cursing the elite of those who have ruled matters, like the orthodox caliphs and the "ulama" of the Muslims, because of their belief that anyone who does not believe in the infallible imam, who is not present, does not believe in God and his Prophet, may God bless him and grant him salvation.

Second: The Current Situation and the Future

There is no doubt that the Americans' losses are very heavy because they are deployed across a wide area and among the people and because it is easy to procure weapons, all of which makes them easy and mouth-watering targets for the believers. But America did not come to leave, and it will not leave no matter how numerous its wounds become and how much of its blood is spilled. It is looking to the near future, when it hopes to disappear into its bases secure and at ease and put the battlefields of Iraq into the hands of the foundling government with an army and police that will bring the behavior of Saddam and his myrmidons back to the people. There is no doubt that the space in which we can move has begun to shrink and that the grip around the throats of the mujahidin has begun to tighten. With the deployment of soldiers and police, the future has become frightening.

Third: So Where are We?

Despite the paucity of supporters, the desertion of friends, and the toughness of the times, God the Exalted has honored us with good harm to the enemy. Praise be to God, in terms of surveillance, preparation, and planning, we have been the keys to all of the martyrdom operations that have taken place except those in the north. Praise be to God, I have completed 25 [operations] up to now, including among the Shi'a and their symbolic figures, the Americans and their soldiers, the police and soldiers, and the coalition forces. God willing, more are to come. What has prevented us from going public is that we have been waiting until we have weight on the ground and finish preparing integrated structures capable of bearing the consequences of going public so that we appear in strength and do not suffer a reversal. We seek refuge in God. Praise be to God, we have made good strides and completed important stages. As the decisive moment approaches, we feel that [our] body has begun to spread in the security vacuum, gaining locations on the ground that will be the nucleus from which to launch and move out in a serious way, God willing.

Fourth: The Work Plan

After study and examination, we can narrow our enemy down to four groups.

1. The Americans

These, as you know, are the most cowardly of God's creatures. They are an easy quarry, praise be to God. We ask God to enable us to kill and capture them to sow panic among those behind them and to trade them for our detained shaykhs and brothers.

2. The Kurds

These are a lump [in the throat] and a thorn whose time to be clipped has yet to come. They are last on the list, even though we are making efforts to harm some of their symbolic figures, God willing.

3. Soldiers, Police, and Agents

These are the eyes, ears, and hands of the occupier, through which he sees, hears, and delivers violent blows. God willing, we are determined to target them strongly in the coming period before the situation is consolidated and they control arrest[s].

4. The Shi'a

These in our opinion are the key to change. I mean that targeting and hitting them in [their] religious, political, and military depth will provoke them to show the Sunnis their rabies and bare the teeth of the hidden rancor working in their breasts.

5. The Work Mechanism

Our current situation, as I have previously told you, obliges us to deal with the matter with courage and clarity and to move quickly to do so because we consider that [unless we do so] there will be no result in which religion will appear. The solution that we see, and God the Exalted knows better, is for us to drag the Shi'a into the battle because this is the only way to prolong the fighting between us and the infidels. We say that we must drag them into battle for several reasons, which are:

1. They, i.e., the Shi'a, have declared a secret war against the people of Islam. They are the proximate, dangerous enemy of the Sunnis, even if the Americans are also an archenemy. The danger from the Shi'a, however, is greater and their damage is worse and more destructive to the [Islamic] nation than the Americans, on whom you find a quasi-consensus about killing them as an assailing enemy.

2. They have befriended and supported the Americans and stood in their ranks against the mujahidin. They have spared and are still sparing no effort to put an end to the jihad and the mujahidin.

3. Our fighting against the Shi'a is the way to drag the [Islamic] nation into the battle. We speak here in some detail. We have said before that the Shi'a have put on the uniforms of the Iraqi army, police, and security [forces] and have raised the banner of preserving the homeland and the citizen. Under this banner, they have begun to liquidate the Sunnis under the pretext that they are saboteurs, remnants of the Ba'th, and terrorists spreading evil in the land. With strong media guidance from the Governing Council and the Americans, they have been able to come between the Sunni masses and the mujahidin. I give an example that brings the matter close to home in the area called the Sunni Triangle—if this is the right name for it. The army and police have begun to deploy in those areas and are growing stronger day by day. They have put chiefs [drawn] from among Sunni agents and the people of the land in charge. In other words, this army and police may be linked to the inhabitants of this area by kinship, blood, and honor. In truth, this area is the base from which we set out and to which we return. When the Americans disappear from these areas—and they have begun to do so—and these agents, who are linked by destiny to the people of the land, take their place, what will our situation be?

5 [*sic*] – The Timing for Implementation

It is our hope to accelerate the pace of work and that companies and battalions with expertise, experience, and endurance will be formed to await the zero hour when we will begin to appear in the open, gain control the land at night, and extend it into daylight, the One and Conquering God willing. We hope that this matter, I mean the zero hour, will [come] four months or so before the promised government is formed. As you can see, we are racing against time. If we are able, as we hope, to turn the tables on them and thwart their plan, this will be good. If the other [scenario] [happens]—and we seek refuge in God—and the government extends its control over the country, we will have to pack our bags and break camp for another land in which we can resume carrying the banner or in which God will choose us as martyrs for his sake.

6. What About You?

You, gracious brothers, are the leaders, guides, and symbolic figures of jihad and battle. We do not see ourselves as fit to challenge you, and we have never striven to achieve glory for ourselves. All that we hope is that we will be the spearhead, the enabling vanguard, and the bridge on which the [Islamic] nation crosses over to the victory that is promised and the tomorrow to which we aspire. This is our vision, and we have explained it. This is our path, and we have made it clear. If you agree with us on it, if you adopt it as a program and road, and if you are convinced of the idea of fighting the sects of apostasy, we will be your readied soldiers, working under your banner, complying with your orders, and indeed swearing fealty to you publicly and in the news media, vexing the infidels and gladdening those who preach the oneness of God. On that day, the believers will rejoice in God's victory. If things appear otherwise to you, we are brothers, and the disagreement will not spoil [our] friendship. [This is] a cause [in which] we are cooperating for the good and supporting jihad. Awaiting your response, may God preserve you as keys to good and reserves for Islam and its people. Amen, amen.

Peace and the mercy and blessings of God be upon you.

Source: U.S. State Department, translation by the Coalition Provisional Authority, February 2004. Available online at http://2001-2009.state.gov/p/nea/rls/31694.htm.

ANALYSIS

Al Zarqawi's letter makes it extremely clear that he perceived the Shi'a of Iraq to be the foremost enemy to be confronted, with the American-led coalition occupying Iraq as the secondary enemy. In this communication, he gives lip service to following the dictates of bin Laden and the high command of Al Qaeda, but also makes it clear that he intended to continue his extremely bloody attacks upon soft targets. Zarqawi's ultimate goal was to provoke an Islamic civil war of extermination, in the expectation that superior Sunni numbers and resources would allow the annihilation of the Shi'a, whom he considered the most evil of humans due to their heresy. Had Zarqawi's plan been carried to fruition, the insurgency in Iraq would likely have devolved even further into sectarian violence, and might very well have grown to engulf the entire Middle East in conflict.

- **Document 61: Osama bin Laden's Letter to the American People**
- **When:** November 1, 2004
- **Where:** Afghanistan
- **Significance:** With this letter, bin Laden attempted to reach the American people directly with his claims regarding the September 11 attacks and the U.S. responses. He made the case that the attacks were the direct result of American policies, and would be repeated in the future if the United States did not cease meddling in the internal affairs of Middle Eastern nations.

DOCUMENT

Praise be to Allah who created the creation for his worship and commanded them to be just and permitted the wronged one to retaliate against the oppressor in kind. To proceed:

Peace be upon he who follows the guidance: People of America this talk of mine is for you and concerns the ideal way to prevent another Manhattan, and deals with the war and its causes and results.

Before I begin, I say to you that security is an indispensable pillar of human life and that free men do not forfeit their security, contrary to Bush's claim that we hate freedom.

If so, then let him explain to us why we don't strike for example—Sweden?

And we know that freedom-haters don't possess defiant spirits like those of the 19—may Allah have mercy on them.

No, we fight because we are free men who don't sleep under oppression. We want to restore freedom to our nation, just as you lay waste to our nation. So shall we lay waste to yours.

No one except a dumb thief plays with the security of others and then makes himself believe he will be secure. Whereas thinking people, when disaster strikes, make it their priority to look for its causes, in order to prevent it happening again.

But I am amazed at you. Even though we are in the fourth year after the events of September 11th, Bush is still engaged in distortion, deception and hiding from you the real causes. And thus, the reasons are still there for a repeat of what occurred.

DID YOU KNOW?

Caliphate

A caliphate is an Islamic government led by a political and religious successor to the Prophet Mohammed. Many Islamic empires have claimed to be the true caliphate, including the last pan-Islamic state, the Ottoman Empire. In the aftermath of World War I, the Ottoman Empire was dismantled, leading to the modern political organization of the Middle East. Many prominent Islamist terror organizations have called for the reestablishment of a caliphate that can unite all Muslims under a single banner. If such a caliphate came into being, it would potentially encompass an enormous geographic region stretching from North Africa to the Pacific Ocean, and including more than 1.6 billion Muslims. By any definition, such a caliphate would be regarded as a superpower with economic and political strength to rival any of the most powerful nations on earth.

So I shall talk to you about the story behind those events and shall tell you truthfully about the moments in which the decision was taken, for you to consider.

I say to you, Allah knows that it had never occurred to us to strike the towers. But after it became unbearable and we witnessed the oppression and tyranny of the American/Israeli coalition against our people in Palestine and Lebanon, it came to my mind.

The events that affected my soul in a direct way started in 1982 when America permitted the Israelis to invade Lebanon and the American Sixth Fleet helped them in that. This bombardment began and many were killed and injured and others were terrorized and displaced.

I couldn't forget those moving scenes, blood and severed limbs, women and children sprawled everywhere. Houses destroyed along with their occupants and high rises demolished over their residents, rockets raining down on our home without mercy.

The situation was like a crocodile meeting a helpless child, powerless except for his screams. Does the crocodile understand a conversation that doesn't include a weapon? And the whole world saw and heard but it didn't respond.

In those difficult moments many hard-to-describe ideas bubbled in my soul, but in the end they produced an intense feeling of rejection of tyranny, and gave birth to a strong resolve to punish the oppressors.

And as I looked at those demolished towers in Lebanon, it entered my mind that we should punish the oppressor in kind and that we should destroy towers in America in order that they taste some of what we tasted and so that they be deterred from killing our women and children.

And that day, it was confirmed to me that oppression and the intentional killing of innocent women and children is a deliberate American policy. Destruction is freedom and democracy, while resistance is terrorism and intolerance.

This means the oppressing and embargoing to death of millions as Bush Sr. did in Iraq in the greatest mass slaughter of children mankind has ever known, and it means the throwing of millions of pounds of bombs and explosives at millions of children—also in Iraq—as Bush Jr did, in order to remove an old agent and replace him with a new puppet to assist in the pilfering of Iraq's oil and other outrages.

So with these images and their like as their background, the events of September 11th came as a reply to those great wrongs, should a man be blamed for defending his sanctuary?

Is defending oneself and punishing the aggressor in kind, objectionable terrorism? If it is such, then it is unavoidable for us.

This is the message which I sought to communicate to you in word and deed, repeatedly, for years before September 11th.

And you can read this, if you wish, in my interview with Scott in Time Magazine in 1996, or with Peter Arnett on CNN in 1997, or my meeting with John Weiner in 1998.

You can observe it practically, if you wish, in Kenya and Tanzania and in Aden. And you can read it in my interview with Abdul Bari Atwan, as well as my interviews with Robert Fisk.

The latter is one of your compatriots and co-religionists and I consider him to be neutral. So are the pretenders of freedom at the White House and the channels controlled by them able to run an interview with him? So that he may relay to the

American people what he has understood from us to be the reasons for our fight against you?

If you were to avoid these reasons, you will have taken the correct path that will lead America to the security that it was in before September 11th. This concerned the causes of the war.

As for its results, they have been, by the grace of Allah, positive and enormous, and have, by all standards, exceeded all expectations. This is due to many factors, chief among them, that we have found it difficult to deal with the Bush administration in light of the resemblance it bears to the regimes in our countries, half of which are ruled by the military and the other half which are ruled by the sons of kings and presidents.

Our experience with them is lengthy, and both types are replete with those who are characterized by pride, arrogance, greed and misappropriation of wealth. This resemblance began after the visits of Bush Sr. to the region.

At a time when some of our compatriots were dazzled by America and hoping that these visits would have an effect on our countries, all of a sudden he was affected by those monarchies and military regimes, and became envious of their remaining decades in their positions, to embezzle the public wealth of the nation without supervision or accounting.

So he took dictatorship and suppression of freedoms to his son and they named it the Patriot Act, under the pretense of fighting terrorism. In addition, Bush sanctioned the installing of sons as state governors, and didn't forget to import expertise in election fraud from the region's presidents to Florida to be made use of in moments of difficulty.

All that we have mentioned has made it easy for us to provoke and bait this administration. All that we have to do is to send two mujahidin to the furthest point east to raise a piece of cloth on which is written al-Qaida, in order to make the generals race there to cause America to suffer human, economic, and political losses without their achieving for it anything of note other than some benefits for their private companies.

This is in addition to our having experience in using guerrilla warfare and the war of attrition to fight tyrannical superpowers, as we, alongside the mujahidin, bled Russia for 10 years, until it went bankrupt and was forced to withdraw in defeat.

All Praise is due to Allah.

So we are continuing this policy in bleeding America to the point of bankruptcy. Allah willing, and nothing is too great for Allah.

That being said, those who say that al-Qaida has won against the administration in the White House or that the administration has lost in this war have not been precise, because when one scrutinizes the results, one cannot say that al-Qaida is the sole factor in achieving those spectacular gains.

Rather, the policy of the White House that demands the opening of war fronts to keep busy their various corporations—whether they be working in the field of arms or oil or reconstruction—has helped al-Qaida to achieve these enormous results.

And so it has appeared to some analysts and diplomats that the White House and us are playing as one team towards the economic goals of the United States, even if the intentions differ.

And it was to these sorts of notions and their like that the British diplomat and others were referring in their lectures at the Royal Institute of International Affairs. [When they pointed out that] for example, al-Qaida spent $500,000 on the event, while America, in the incident and its aftermath, lost—according to the lowest estimate—more than $500 billion.

Meaning that every dollar of al-Qaida defeated a million dollars by the permission of Allah, besides the loss of a huge number of jobs.

As for the size of the economic deficit, it has reached record astronomical numbers estimated to total more than a trillion dollars.

And even more dangerous and bitter for America is that the mujahidin recently forced Bush to resort to emergency funds to continue the fight in Afghanistan and Iraq, which is evidence of the success of the bleed-until-bankruptcy plan—with Allah's permission.

It is true that this shows that al-Qaida has gained, but on the other hand, it shows that the Bush administration has also gained, something of which anyone who looks at the size of the contracts acquired by the shady Bush administration-linked mega-corporations, like Halliburton and its kind, will be convinced. And it all shows that the real loser is . . . you.

It is the American people and their economy. And for the record, we had agreed with the Commander-General Muhammad Ataa, Allah have mercy on him, that all the operations should be carried out within 20 minutes, before Bush and his administration noticed.

It never occurred to us that the commander-in-chief of the American armed forces would abandon 50,000 of his citizens in the twin towers to face those great horrors alone, the time when they most needed him.

But because it seemed to him that occupying himself by talking to the little girl about the goat and its butting was more important than occupying himself with the planes and their butting of the skyscrapers, we were given three times the period required to execute the operations—all praise is due to Allah.

And it's no secret to you that the thinkers and perceptive ones from among the Americans warned Bush before the war and told him: "All that you want for securing America and removing the weapons of mass destruction—assuming they exist—is available to you, and the nations of the world are with you in the inspections, and it is in the interest of America that it not be thrust into an unjustified war with an unknown outcome."

But the darkness of the black gold blurred his vision and insight, and he gave priority to private interests over the public interests of America.

So the war went ahead, the death toll rose, the American economy bled, and Bush became embroiled in the swamps of Iraq that threaten his future. He fits the saying "like the naughty she-goat who used her hoof to dig up a knife from under the earth."

So I say to you, over 15,000 of our people have been killed and tens of thousands injured, while more than a thousand of you have been killed and more than 10,000 injured. And Bush's hands are stained with the blood of all those killed from both sides, all for the sake of oil and keeping their private companies in business.

Be aware that it is the nation who punishes the weak man when he causes the killing of one of its citizens for money, while letting the powerful one get off, when he causes the killing of more than 1000 of its sons, also for money.

And the same goes for your allies in Palestine. They terrorize the women and children, and kill and capture the men as they lie sleeping with their families on the mattresses, that you may recall that for every action, there is a reaction.

Finally, it behooves you to reflect on the last wills and testaments of the thousands who left you on the 11th as they gestured in despair. They are important testaments, which should be studied and researched.

Among the most important of what I read in them was some prose in their gestures before the collapse, where they say: "How mistaken we were to have allowed the White House to implement its aggressive foreign policies against the weak without supervision."

It is as if they were telling you, the people of America: "Hold to account those who have caused us to be killed, and happy is he who learns from others' mistakes."

And among that which I read in their gestures is a verse of poetry. "Injustice chases its people, and how unhealthy the bed of tyranny."

As has been said: "An ounce of prevention is better than a pound of cure."

And know that: "It is better to return to the truth than persist in error." And that the wise man doesn't squander his security, wealth and children for the sake of the liar in the White House.

In conclusion, I tell you in truth, that your security is not in the hands of Kerry, nor Bush, nor al-Qaida. No.

Your security is in your own hands. And every state that doesn't play with our security has automatically guaranteed its own security.

And Allah is our Guardian and Helper, while you have no Guardian or Helper. All peace be upon he who follows the Guidance.

Source: English translation of a speech delivered by videotape on Al Jazeera Television, available at http://www.aljazeera.com/archive/2004/11/200849163336457223.html.

ANALYSIS

Although there are elements of ideology and religion contained within this letter, bin Laden definitely changed his approach to communications with the American public, particularly when compared to his earlier messages to the West, referenced in his statement. Rather than attempting to convince Americans to renounce their religions and embrace Islam, he instead chose to appeal on the grounds of economics and justice. He accused the Bush administration of placing private financial interests ahead of the lives of American citizens. At the same time, he threatened that terror attacks against American interests would continue as long as the American public did not repudiate the government's activities. Placing them in the context of historical attacks upon Muslim citizens, and drawing the connection between Israel and the United States, bin Laden sought to provoke a public outcry for isolationism as a means of saving the lives of military personnel and avoiding further budgetary deficits.

- **Document 62: Schmidt-Furlow Investigation into FBI Allegations of Detainee Abuse at Guantanamo Bay, Cuba Detention Facility**
- **When:** April 1, 2005
- **Where:** Davis-Monthan Air Force Base, Tucson, AZ
- **Significance:** Lieutenant General Randall Schmidt and Brigadier General John Furlow were tasked to conduct an investigation into allegations of detainee abuse at Guantanamo Bay. They found relatively minor violations of military policy, but determined that most of the allegations were unfounded.

DOCUMENT

EXECUTIVE SUMMARY

Detention and interrogation operations at Joint Task Force Guantanamo (JTF-GTMO) cover a three-year period and over 24,000 interrogations. This AR 15-6 investigation found only three interrogation acts in violation of interrogation techniques authorized by Army Field Manual 34-52 and DoD guidance. The AR 15-6 also found that the Commander of JTF-GTMO failed to monitor the interrogation of one high value detainee in late 2002. The AR 15-6 found that the interrogation of this same high value detainee resulted in degrading and abusive treatment but did not rise to the level of being inhumane treatment. Finally, the AR 15-6 found that the communication of a threat to another high value detainee was in violation of SECDEF [Secretary of Defense] guidance and the UCMJ [Uniform Code of Military Justice]. The AR 15-6 found no evidence of torture or inhumane treatment at JTF-GTMO.

SUMMARY OF FINDINGS

The findings above fall into three categories: Techniques that were authorized throughout the interrogation periods; techniques that were never authorized and finally, techniques that were originally unauthorized, and then subsequently authorized. The summary below only outlines the latter two categories of techniques to address whether the findings violated the UCMJ, international law, U.S. Law, regulations or directives.

Techniques that were never authorized: AR 15-6 determined the following acts were NEVER authorized under any interrogation guidance:

a) On at least two occasions between February 2002 and February 2003, two detainees were "short shackled" to the eye-bolt on the floor in the interrogation room;

b) Sometime in October 2002 duct tape was used to "quiet" a detainee.

c) Military interrogators threatened the subject of the second special interrogation and his family;

Techniques that became authorized after the fact: AR 15-6 determined the following acts were initially not authorized under existing interrogation guidance but later authorized as an approved technique.

a) On several occasions during 2002 and 2003, interrogators would adjust the air conditioner to make the detainees, to include the subject of the first Special Interrogation Plan, uncomfortable. This technique is now permitted under the SECDEF 16 Apr 03 guidance.

b) On several occasions prior to 2 Dec 02 and between 15 Jan 03 and 16 Apr 03 interrogators had detainees moved from one cell to another every few hours to disrupt sleep patterns and lower the ability to resist interrogation. This technique is now permitted under the SECDEF 16 Apr 03 guidance.

c) In October 2002 a Military Working Dog was brought into the interrogation room during the course of interrogation of the subject of the first Special Interrogation Plan and directed to growl, bark, and show his teeth at the detainee. This technique is subsequently approved for the interrogation of the subject of the first Special Interrogation Plan by SECDEF on 12 Nov 02.

d) The subject of the first Special Interrogation Plan was separated from other detainees in an isolation facility away from the general population from 8 Aug 02 to 12 Nov 02. This technique was subsequently approved for the interrogation of the subject of the first Special Interrogation Plan by SECDEF on 12 Nov 02.

In each of the incidents above the violations can best be characterized as violations of policy. The SECDEF's subsequent approval of each of the techniques clearly establishes the ultimate legitimacy of that technique and thus additional corrective action is not necessary.

Additional Matters: In addition to findings outlined above it is important to document some additional findings:

a) The team found no evidence that any detainee at GTMO was improperly documented or unaccounted for at any time. Every agency interviewee clearly indicated that they never knew of any "ghost detainees" at GTMO;

b) Several past interrogators at GTMO declined to be interviewed. In the case of personnel who are currently in a civilian status we had extremely limited authority to compel the individuals to cooperate with this investigation; of particular note was former SGT Erik Saar who has written a book into "activities" at GTMO. Despite repeated requests he declined to be interviewed;

c) During the course of this investigation, JTF-GTMO CG investigated and took action for personal misconduct of senior DoD personnel on GTMO. These allegations were reviewed and it was determined that they were not relevant to this investigation, and did not rise to a level to suggest a leadership environment with any impact on interrogation or detainee operations.

ADDITIONAL RECOMMENDATIONS

This AR15-6 recommends consideration of the following:

a) *Recommendation #23* Recommend a policy-level review and determination of the status and treatment of all detainees, when not classified as EPWs. This review needs to particularly focus on the definitions of humane treatment, military necessity, and proper employment of interrogation techniques (e.g. boundaries or extremes);

b) *Recommendation #24* Recommend study of the DoD authorized interrogation techniques to establish a framework for evaluating their cumulative impact in relation to the obligation to treat detainees humanely;

c) *Recommendation #25* Recommend a reevaluation of the DoD and Inter-agency interrogation training consistent with the new realities of the requirements of the global war on terror;

d) *Recommendation #26* Recommend a policy-level determination on role of Military Police in "setting the conditions" for intelligence gathering and interrogation of detainees at both the tactical level and strategic level facilities;

e) *Recommendation #27* Recommend an Inter-Agency policy review to establish "standards" for interrogations when multiple agencies and interrogation objectives are involved. Particular emphasis should be placed on setting policy for who has priority as the lead agency, the specific boundaries for the authorized techniques in cases with multiple agencies involved, a central "data-base" for all intelligence gathered at a detention facility, and procedures for record keeping to include historical, litigation support, lessons learned, and successful/unsuccessful intelligence gathering techniques.

Source: Army Regulation 15-6: Final Report, Investigation into FBI Allegations of Detainee Abuse at Guantanamo Bay, Cuba Detention Facility. Available online at https://www.thetorturedatabase.org/files/foia_subsite/pdfs/schmidt_furlow_report.pdf.

ANALYSIS

The American Civil Liberties Union (ACLU) obtained more than 5,000 documents through a Freedom of Information Act request for evidence of detainee abuse while in U.S. custody. The Schmidt-Furlow report addresses nearly two dozen allegations made by FBI interrogators of mistreatment of detainees. The authors of the report found that most of the allegations were actually instances of interrogation techniques that were approved for use with the detainees under Department of Defense regulations, but which the FBI interrogators thought should not be used. In the case of two special prisoners, each of whom was the subject of a unique interrogation plan, the report found that interrogators had pushed the boundaries of acceptable conduct, but that there should be no punitive action against the interrogators due to the special circumstances of the confinement.

- **Document 63: Lieutenant General Randall Schmidt, Testimony**
- **When:** August 24, 2005
- **Where:** Davis-Monthan Air Force Base, Tucson, AZ
- **Significance:** U.S. Air Force General Randall Schmidt was ordered to look into allegations of detainee abuse at Guantanamo Bay. While his final report (see Document 62) contained a few instances of interrogation techniques that had not been approved, he did not believe that the detainee situation had crossed the line into torture, and believed incomplete or flawed guidance was responsible for the questionable conduct.

DOCUMENT

Testimony of Lieutenant General Randall M. Schmidt

Taken 24 August, 2005 at Davis Monthan Air Force Base, Arizona

Q. Sir, just to start out can you provide us a quick background on why the AR 15-6 investigation that we now call the Schmidt Furlow Report was initiated?

A. Well like everybody else I was reading the papers about the abuse allegations at Guantanamo and I passed the papers everyday thanking God that I was not involved in that. I could envision myself with combat operations and training and things like that. I got the phone call from my boss, General Craddock, now the Commander of US Southern Command and he said he had kind of run into a stop on an investigation that was currently undergoing. That General Furlow had been tasked to run it—he had essentially two months underway with a small team looking into these allegation. I was unaware of that.

He said that he had been informed by the investigator General Furlow that, he was in a position where he had to interview officers senior to him. Two, specifically, and that unless he received some sort of extraordinary permissions or whatever that he'd need some help.

So General Craddock called me and said that he needed me to take over the investigation and as he saw it, I didn't have to go back and reinvent the investigation. And—I'll explain what the investigation was as I got into it, but he needed me to essentially take over, take it to completion, get the football across the goal line essentially with these two other interviews.

If you read the Geneva Conventions and also [Field Manual] 34-52, it will tell you that they're entitled to congregate. They're entitled to elect a leader. They're entitled to have representation, visits—I mean all kinds of stuff. And the write up it's almost like they're entitled to have a band. You know, and present grievances. And it's pretty crazy. They weren't entitled to that. The President said that they're not entitled to that, but they will be treated humanely and they will be given shelter, food, water and medicinal attention. I mean it just laid it out there.

So that became kind of the baseline for what was considered humane treatment. And there is no definition of what is "humane treatment." And I have Senators sending me—you know, answer these questions. What's the difference between inhuman and inhumane? I mean I'm just a dumb fighter pilot that did this investigation. So I said, okay, here's the judgment. The President said this. If they're—and there are no other guidance, if they were Enemy Prisoners of War it would be this. Okay? So somewhere in between. So we have kind of a threshold which I would probably recognize as what's torture. And there is a Convention against torture. I know what that is. There is humane treatment and nobody knows what that is, but there is a general fuzzy line.

And then it's up to me to recognize what abusive or degrading kind of treatment is. That's the protocol we used. The Secretary of Defense, when we started this, took responsibility for providing guidance through US Southern Command down to the JTFs [Joint Task Forces]. The JTFs 160 and 170 were set up as independent, parallel, almost non-cooperative sort of entities.

And the line between the two was really vague. The 160 JTF was detention operations, Military Police. They pretty much knew what they were doing. They were trying to figure out how to deal with the kinds of people they had. Violent people that had written off their lives already. It was like having psychotic murders row times six hundred. And it remains somewhat like that today, although they did kind of reach a plateau where there was a lot of spitting and things like that and cursing and throwing excrement and things like that are still kind of going on.

On the interrogations side it was a little bit—and I don't want to say it is out of control, but it was California Avocado Freestyle kind of a thing. Let's figure out what to do and how to interrogate these individuals when they're not Enemy Prisoners of War. They don't have a—they don't have an organizational construct. They're free agents. Dedicated—they've already signed off their lives. There is nothing left to lose kinds of individuals. It's like you have mass murders and said, okay, you know, these are your rules. These are—and they're going we don't do rules. And we don't do your sort of thing.

And the more serious the more influential individuals in that crowd have been trained in what we call "The Manchester Document" the rules of how to resist. They had gone to school on our FM 34-52. They knew we weren't going to torture them. They knew that they had rights. They knew that eventually they'd have the habeas entry into the legal system. They knew all this sort of stuff. And I mean you can—I've read their manual a few times.

And they've been through resistance training and they had a lot of time to think about. And when they sign to go to these missions, they know that if they don't die then they will deal with this and they do pretty well.

The interrogators had to deal with that. Okay? And it was a little chaotic.

So that was the situation. The guidance part of this was the one that was hardest to deduce. The Secretary of Defense got a request from General Dunlavey, saying we now have reached almost a dead-end on exploiting and getting relevant intelligence from people who we know, detainees, who we know in this population that we can get from them. Standard FM 34-52 techniques are not going to work. This was still very close to 2001 and this was approaching 2002 and we didn't know if we were going to get whacked again.

Source: Testimony of LTG Randall Schmidt, August 24, 2005. U.S. Army, Inspector General. Available online through the National Security Archive, http://nsarchive.gwu.edu/torturingdemocracy/documents/20050825.pdf.

ANALYSIS

While Schmidt related a number of examples of specific activities that he considered in the gray area between acceptable behavior and inhumane treatment, he ultimately did not find that there had been a specific intent to mistreat detainees. He felt that guidance issued from the top levels of the Bush administration was at best unclear and, at times, contradictory. Because certain unauthorized techniques had been utilized in a desperate bid to obtain actionable intelligence from high-value targets, Schmidt found there was evidence of wrongdoing, although pinning down the exact dates and actions proved almost impossible. More than anything, Schmidt was disappointed to find that the commander of the detention facility seemed to have little grasp of the treatment being meted out to detainees under his control, and his lack of administrative oversight led to a formal reprimand, but no charges being filed.

- **Document 64: National Security Strategy for the United States**
- **When:** March 16, 2006
- **Where:** Washington, D.C.
- **Significance:** The 2006 iteration of the National Security Strategy came at the nadir of Operation Iraqi Freedom, a conflict initially only tangentially linked to the War on Terror in 2003, but at the center of the war by 2006. In this document, President George W. Bush laid out his vision to guide national security agencies for the following four years.

DOCUMENT

Strengthen Alliances to Defeat Global Terrorism and Work to Prevent Attacks Against Us and Our Friends

A. Summary of National Security Strategy 2002

Defeating terrorism requires a long-term strategy and a break with old patterns. We are fighting a new enemy with global reach. The United States can no longer simply rely on deterrence to keep the terrorists at bay or defensive measures to thwart them at the last moment. The fight must be taken to the enemy, to keep them on the run. To succeed in our own efforts, we need the support and concerted action of friends and allies. We must join with others to deny the terrorists what they need to survive: safe haven, financial support, and the support and protection that certain nation-states historically have given them.

B. Current Context: Successes and Challenges

The war against terror is not over. America is safer, but not yet safe. As the enemy adjusts to our successes, so too must we adjust. The successes are many:

- Al-Qaida has lost its safe haven in Afghanistan.
- A multinational coalition joined by the Iraqis is aggressively prosecuting the war against the terrorists in Iraq.
- The al-Qaida network has been significantly degraded. Most of those in the al-Qaida network responsible for the September 11 attacks, including the plot's mastermind Khalid Shaykh Muhammad, have been captured or killed.

- There is a broad and growing global consensus that the deliberate killing of innocents is never justified by any calling or cause.
- Many nations have rallied to fight terrorism, with unprecedented cooperation on law enforcement, intelligence, military, and diplomatic activity.
- Numerous countries that were part of the problem before September 11 are now increasingly becoming part of the solution—and this transformation has occurred without destabilizing friendly regimes in key regions.
- The Administration has worked with Congress to adopt and implement key reforms like the Patriot Act which promote our security while also protecting our fundamental liberties.

The enemy is determined, however, and we face some old and new challenges:

- Terrorist networks today are more dispersed and less centralized. They are more reliant on smaller cells inspired by a common ideology and less directed by a central command structure.
- While the United States Government and its allies have thwarted many attacks, we have not been able to stop them all. The terrorists have struck in many places, including Afghanistan, Egypt, Indonesia, Iraq, Israel, Jordan, Morocco, Pakistan, Russia, Saudi Arabia, Spain, and the United Kingdom. And they continue to seek WMD in order to inflict even more catastrophic attacks on us and our friends and allies.
- The ongoing fight in Iraq has been twisted by terrorist propaganda as a rallying cry.
- Some states, such as Syria and Iran, continue to harbor terrorists at home and sponsor terrorist activity abroad.

C. The Way Ahead

From the beginning, the War on Terror has been both a battle of arms and a battle of ideas—a fight against the terrorists and against their murderous ideology. In the short run, the fight involves using military force and other instruments of national power to kill or capture the terrorists, deny them safe haven or control of any nation; prevent them from gaining access to WMD; and cut off their sources of support. In the long run, winning the war on terror means winning the battle of ideas, for it is ideas that can turn the disenchanted into murderers willing to kill innocent victims.

While the War on Terror is a battle of ideas, it is not a battle of religions. The transnational terrorists confronting us today exploit the proud religion of Islam to serve a violent political vision: the establishment, by terrorism and subversion, of a totalitarian empire that denies all political and religious freedom. These terrorists distort the idea of jihad into a call for murder against those they regard as apostates or unbelievers—including Christians, Jews, Hindus, other religious traditions, and all Muslims who disagree with them. Indeed, most of the terrorist attacks since September 11 have occurred in Muslim countries—and most of the victims have been Muslims.

To wage this battle of ideas effectively, we must be clear-eyed about what does and does not give rise to terrorism:

- Terrorism is not the inevitable by-product of poverty. Many of the September 11 hijackers were from middle-class backgrounds, and many terrorist leaders, like bin Laden, are from privileged upbringings.
- Terrorism is not simply a result of hostility to U.S. policy in Iraq. The United States was attacked on September 11 and earlier, well before we toppled the Saddam Hussein regime. Moreover, countries that stayed out of the Iraq war have not been spared from terror attack.
- Terrorism is not simply a result of Israeli-Palestinian issues. Al-Qaida plotting for the September 11 attacks began in the 1990s, during an active period in the peace process.
- Terrorism is not simply a response to our efforts to prevent terror attacks. The al-Qaida network targeted the United States long before the United States targeted al-Qaida. Indeed, the terrorists are emboldened more by perceptions of weakness than by demonstrations of resolve. Terrorists lure recruits by telling them that we are decadent and easily intimidated and will retreat if attacked.

The terrorism we confront today springs from:

- Political alienation. Transnational terrorists are recruited from people who have no voice in their own government and see no legitimate way to promote change in their own country. Without a stake in the existing order, they are vulnerable to manipulation by those who advocate a perverse vision based on violence and destruction.
- Grievances that can be blamed on others. The failures the terrorists feel and see are blamed on others, and on perceived injustices from the recent or sometimes distant past. The terrorists' rhetoric keeps wounds associated with this past fresh and raw, a potent motivation for revenge and terror.
- Sub-cultures of conspiracy and misinformation. Terrorists recruit more effectively from populations whose information about the world is contaminated by falsehoods and corrupted by conspiracy theories. The distortions keep alive grievances and filter out facts that would challenge popular prejudices and self-serving propaganda.
- An ideology that justifies murder. Terrorism ultimately depends upon the appeal of an ideology that excuses or even glorifies the deliberate killing of innocents. A proud religion—the religion of Islam—has been twisted and made to serve an evil end, as in other times and places other religions have been similarly abused.

Defeating terrorism in the long run requires that each of these factors be addressed. The genius of democracy is that it provides a counter to each.

- In place of alienation, democracy offers an ownership stake in society, a chance to shape one's own future.
- In place of festering grievances, democracy offers the rule of law, the peaceful resolution of disputes, and the habits of advancing interests through compromise.

- In place of a culture of conspiracy and misinformation, democracy offers freedom of speech, independent media, and the marketplace of ideas, which can expose and discredit falsehoods, prejudices, and dishonest propaganda.
- In place of an ideology that justifies murder, democracy offers a respect for human dignity that abhors the deliberate targeting of innocent civilians.

Democracy is the opposite of terrorist tyranny, which is why the terrorists denounce it and are willing to kill the innocent to stop it. Democracy is based on empowerment, while the terrorists' ideology is based on enslavement. Democracies expand the freedom of their citizens, while the terrorists seek to impose a single set of narrow beliefs. Democracy sees individuals as equal in worth and dignity, having an inherent potential to create and to govern themselves. The terrorists see individuals as objects to be exploited, and then to be ruled and oppressed.

Democracies are not immune to terrorism. In some democracies, some ethnic or religious groups are unable or unwilling to grasp the benefits of freedom otherwise available in the society. Such groups can evidence the same alienation and despair that the transnational terrorists exploit in undemocratic states. This accounts for the emergence in democratic societies of homegrown terrorists such as were responsible for the bombings in London in July 2005 and for the violence in some other nations. Even in these cases, the long-term solution remains deepening the reach of democracy so that all citizens enjoy its benefits.

The strategy to counter the lies behind the terrorists' ideology is to empower the very people the terrorists most want to exploit: the faithful followers of Islam. We will continue to support political reforms that empower peaceful Muslims to practice and interpret their faith. The most vital work will be done within the Islamic world itself, and Jordan, Morocco, and Indonesia have begun to make important strides in this effort. Responsible Islamic leaders need to denounce an ideology that distorts and exploits Islam for destructive ends and defiles a proud religion.

Many of the Muslim faith are already making this commitment at great personal risk. They realize they are a target of this ideology of terror. Everywhere we have joined in the fight against terrorism, Muslim allies have stood beside us, becoming partners in this vital cause. Pakistan and Saudi Arabia have launched effective efforts to capture or kill the leadership of the al-Qaida network. Afghan troops are in combat against Taliban remnants. Iraqi soldiers are sacrificing to defeat al-Qaida in their own country. These brave citizens know the stakes—the survival of their own liberty, the future of their own region, the justice and humanity of their own traditions—and the United States is proud to stand beside them.

The advance of freedom and human dignity through democracy is the long-term solution to the transnational terrorism of today. To create the space and time for that long-term solution to take root, there are four steps we will take in the short term.

- **Prevent attacks by terrorist networks before they occur.** A government has no higher obligation than to protect the lives and livelihoods of its citizens. The hard core of the terrorists cannot be deterred or reformed; they must be tracked down, killed, or captured. They must be cut off from the network of individuals and institutions on which they depend for support. That network must in turn be deterred, disrupted, and disabled by using a broad range of tools.

- **Deny WMD to rogue states and to terrorist allies who would use them without hesitation.** Terrorists have a perverse moral code that glorifies deliberately targeting innocent civilians. Terrorists try to inflict as many casualties as possible and seek WMD to this end. Denying terrorists WMD will require new tools and new international approaches. We are working with partner nations to improve security at vulnerable nuclear sites worldwide and bolster the ability of states to detect, disrupt, and respond to terrorist activity involving WMD.

- **Deny terrorist groups the support and sanctuary of rogue states.** The United States and its allies in the War on Terror make no distinction between those who commit acts of terror and those who support and harbor them, because they are equally guilty of murder. Any government that chooses to be an ally of terror, such as Syria or Iran, has chosen to be an enemy of freedom, justice, and peace. The world must hold those regimes to account.

- **Deny the terrorists control of any nation that they would use as a base and launching pad for terror.** The terrorists' goal is to overthrow a rising democracy; claim a strategic country as a haven for terror; destabilize the Middle East; and strike America and other free nations with ever-increasing violence. This we can never allow. This is why success in Afghanistan and Iraq is vital, and why we must prevent terrorists from exploiting ungoverned areas.

America will lead in this fight, and we will continue to partner with allies and will recruit new friends to join the battle.

Source: National Security Strategy of the United States, 2006, 8–12. Available at www.state.gov/documents/organization/64884.pdf.

ANALYSIS

As with the 2002 iteration of the National Security Strategy, the 2006 version considered terrorist activity to be one threat among many confronting the nation, and while terrorism was the most visible threat, it was not necessarily the most dangerous in the long term. The 2006 document took great pains to clarify what the administration considered to be the root causes of terrorism, pointing out that it is not necessarily an economic or religious problem, so much as an ideological one. The strategy illustrated the need to remain engaged in the information war with Al Qaeda, to include dominating the narrative of the causes of the war, retaining the moral high ground regarding the conduct of military operations, and preventing the growth of geographic safe havens. The strategy included an extensive reminder for unaligned nations that, in the mind of President Bush and his administration, any nation that allied itself with Al Qaeda would be considered a legitimate target for U.S. military action. Even providing a safe haven for Al Qaeda operatives could be considered a provocative act, regardless of whether the government in question deliberately allowed an Al Qaeda presence on its soil. If the Iraq War was considered an outgrowth of the fight against Al Qaeda by the Bush administration, this document served warning that the United States would not stop at invasions of Afghanistan and Iraq in its pursuit of Al Qaeda leadership. The organization was targeted for destruction regardless of its location, and uninvolved nations would do well to remain out of the way of American forces.

- **Document 65:** *Hamdan v. Rumsfeld*
- **When:** June 29, 2006
- **Where:** Washington, D.C.
- **Significance:** Salim Ahmed Hamdan worked as a bodyguard and personal driver for Osama bin Laden. In late 2001, he was captured by militia forces in Afghanistan and turned over to the U.S. military, which in turn sent him to the detainee facility at Guantanamo Bay, Cuba. In 2004, he was tried for conspiracy to commit acts of terrorism in a newly organized military commission. His lawsuit contended that the military commissions were illegally constituted and could not be used to put him on trial.

DOCUMENT

SUPREME COURT OF THE UNITED STATES
HAMDAN *v.* RUMSFELD, SECRETARY OF DEFENSE, ET AL.
CERTIORARI TO THE UNITED STATES COURT OF APPEALS FOR THE DISTRICT OF COLUMBIA CIRCUIT
No. 05–184. Argued March 28, 2006—Decided June 29, 2006

VI

Whether or not the Government has charged Hamdan with an offense against the law of war cognizable by military commission, the commission lacks power to proceed. The UCMJ conditions the President's use of military commissions on compliance not only with the American common law of war, but also with the rest of the UCMJ itself, insofar as applicable, and with the "rules and precepts of the law of nations," *Quirin*, 317 U. S., at 28— including, *inter alia*, the four Geneva Conventions signed in 1949. See *Yamashita*, 327 U. S., at 20–21, 23–24. The procedures that the Government has decreed will govern Hamdan's trial by commission violate these laws.

A

The commission's procedures are set forth in Commission Order No. 1, which was amended most recently on August 31, 2005—after Hamdan's trial had already

DID YOU KNOW?

Releases from Guantanamo Bay

The detention of enemy captives at Guantanamo Bay has caused a host of challenges. One of the substantial problems is the question of disposition—traditionally, prisoners of war are repatriated at the end of a conflict. However, the War on Terror has no obvious termination point, and the enemy fighters captured in the war are not acting on behalf of a nation; they are fighting for a non-state organization that presumably will not exist when the war ends. Some of these captives have been released to their home countries, where they have faced prosecution for various criminal offenses. The Saudi government established a reeducation program for terrorism suspects not accused of holding leadership positions. That program has shown some promise, but the recidivism rate for released prisoners remains high, and some nations absolutely refuse to accept the transfer of prisoners, or threaten to summarily execute them if they are returned.

begun. Every commission established pursuant to Commission Order No. 1 must have a presiding officer and at least three other members, all of whom must be commissioned officers. §4(A)(1). The presiding officer's job is to rule on questions of law and other evidentiary and interlocutory issues; the other members make findings and, if applicable, sentencing decisions. §4(A)(5). The accused is entitled to appointed military counsel and may hire civilian counsel at his own expense so long as such counsel is a U. S. citizen with security clearance "at the level SECRET or higher." §§4(C)(2)–(3).

The accused also is entitled to a copy of the charge(s) against him, both in English and his own language (if different), to a presumption of innocence, and to certain other rights typically afforded criminal defendants in civilian courts and courts-martial. See §§5(A)–(P). These rights are subject, however, to one glaring condition: The accused and his civilian counsel may be excluded from, and precluded from ever learning what evidence was presented during, any part of the proceeding that either the Appointing Authority or the presiding officer decides to "close." Grounds for such closure "include the protection of information classified or classifiable . . .; information protected by law or rule from unauthorized disclosure; the physical safety of participants in Commission proceedings, including prospective witnesses; intelligence and law enforcement sources, methods, or activities; and other national security interests." §6(B)(3). Appointed military defense counsel must be privy to these closed sessions, but may, at the presiding officer's discretion, be forbidden to reveal to his or her client what took place therein. *Ibid.*

Another striking feature of the rules governing Hamdan's commission is that they permit the admission of *any* evidence that, in the opinion of the presiding officer, "would have probative value to a reasonable person." §6(D)(1). Under this test, not only is testimonial hearsay and evidence obtained through coercion fully admissible, but neither live testimony nor witnesses' written statements need be sworn. See §§6(D)(2)(b), (3). Moreover, the accused and his civilian counsel may be denied access to evidence in the form of "protected information" (which includes classified information as well as "information protected by law or rule from unauthorized disclosure" and "information concerning other national security interests," §§6(B)(3), 6(D)(5)(a)(v)), so long as the presiding officer concludes that the evidence is "probative" under §6(D)(1) and that its admission without the accused's knowledge would not "result in the denial of a full and fair trial." §6(D)(5)(b). Finally, a presiding officer's determination that evidence "would not have probative value to a reasonable person" may be overridden by a majority of the other commission members. §6(D)(1).

Once all the evidence is in, the commission members (not including the presiding officer) must vote on the accused's guilt. A two-thirds vote will suffice for both a verdict of guilty and for imposition of any sentence not including death (the imposition of which requires a unanimous vote). §6(F). Any appeal is taken to a three-member review panel composed of military officers and designated by the Secretary of Defense, only one member of which need have experience as a judge. §6(H)(4). The review panel is directed to "disregard any variance from procedures specified in this Order or elsewhere that would not materially have affected the outcome of the trial before the Commission." *Ibid.* Once the panel makes its recommendation to the Secretary of Defense, the Secretary can either remand for further proceedings or forward the record to the President with his recommendation as to final disposition. §6(H)(5). The President then, unless he has delegated the task to the Secretary, makes the "final decision." §6(H)(6). He may change the commission's findings or sentence only in a manner favorable to the accused. *Ibid.*

B

Hamdan raises both general and particular objections to the procedures set forth in Commission Order No. 1. His general objection is that the procedures' admitted deviation from those governing courts-martial itself renders the commission illegal. Chief among his particular objections are that he may, under the Commission Order, be convicted based on evidence he has not seen or heard, and that any evidence admitted against him need not comply with the admissibility or relevance rules typically applicable in criminal trials and court-martial proceedings.

The Government objects to our consideration of any procedural challenge at this stage on the grounds that (1) the abstention doctrine espoused in *Councilman*, 420 U.S. 738, precludes pre-enforcement review of procedural rules, (2) Hamdan will be able to raise any such challenge following a "final decision" under the DTA, and (3) "there is . . . no basis to presume, before the trial has even commenced, that the trial will not be conducted in good faith and according to law."

C

In part because the difference between military commissions and courts-martial originally was a difference of jurisdiction alone, and in part to protect against abuse and ensure evenhandedness under the pressures of war, the procedures governing trials by military commission historically have been the same as those governing courts-martial. See, *e.g.*, 1 The War of the Rebellion 248 (2d series 1894) (General Order 1 issued during the Civil War required military commissions to "be constituted in a similar manner and their proceedings be conducted according to the same general rules as courts-martial in order to prevent abuses which might otherwise arise"). Accounts of commentators from Winthrop through General Crowder—who drafted Article of War 15 and whose views have been deemed "authoritative" by this Court, *Madsen*, 343 U.S., at 353—confirm as much. As recently as the Korean and Vietnam wars, during which use of military commissions was contemplated but never made, the principle of procedural parity was espoused as a background assumption.

There is a glaring historical exception to this general rule. The procedures and evidentiary rules used to try General Yamashita near the end of World War II deviated in significant respects from those then governing courts-martial. See 327 U.S. 1. The force of that precedent, however, has been seriously undermined by post-World War II developments.

D

The procedures adopted to try Hamdan also violate the Geneva Conventions. The Court of Appeals dismissed Hamdan's Geneva Convention challenge on three independent grounds: (1) the Geneva Conventions are not judicially enforceable; (2) Hamdan in any event is not entitled to their protections; and (3) even if he is entitled to their protections, *Councilman* abstention is appropriate. Judge Williams, concurring, rejected the second ground but agreed with the majority respecting the first and the last. As we explained in Part III, *supra*, the abstention rule applied in *Councilman*, 420 U.S. 738, is not applicable here. And for the reasons that follow, we hold that neither of the other grounds the Court of Appeals gave for its decision is persuasive.

VII

We have assumed, as we must, that the allegations made in the Government's charge against Hamdan are true. We have assumed, moreover, the truth of the message implicit in that charge—viz., that Hamdan is a dangerous individual whose beliefs, if acted upon, would cause great harm and even death to innocent civilians, and who would act upon those beliefs if given the opportunity. It bears emphasizing that Hamdan does not challenge, and we do not today address, the Government's power to detain him for the duration of active hostilities in order to prevent such harm. But in undertaking to try Hamdan and subject him to criminal punishment, the Executive is bound to comply with the Rule of Law that prevails in this jurisdiction.

The judgment of the Court of Appeals is reversed, and the case is remanded for further proceedings.

It is so ordered.

Source: Hamdan v. Rumsfeld, 548 U.S. 557 (2006).

ANALYSIS

Hamdan v. Rumsfeld is important because it established the Supreme Court's position that the military tribunals' process as constituted under Military Commission Order Number 1 (2002) did not meet the necessary requirements under either the Uniform Code of Military Justice or the Geneva Conventions Relative to Prisoners of War of 1949. Further, the Court found that the president did not have the power to establish a new system of jurisprudence without the direct approval of Congress, and, even with legislative approval, could not create a system that violated the U.S. Constitution. The Supreme Court did not rule that tribunals were in and of themselves inherently illegal, but required that the tribunals followed established rules of procedure and included sufficient legal counsel for the defense to present a case. The acceptance of hearsay, coerced testimony, and unsworn statements, allowed under the initial tribunals system, all fell short of the expectations established by the Supreme Court. Under the revamped system created by the Military

Commissions Act of 2006, Hamdan was convicted of one count of conspiracy to commit terrorism and sentenced to 66 months in confinement, most of which had already been served. In 2008, Hamdan was transferred to Yemeni custody and, one month later, released from captivity. Later that year, the U.S. Court of Appeals for the District of Columbia overturned his conviction.

- **Document 66: National Strategy for Combating Terrorism**
- **When:** September 2006
- **Where:** Washington, D.C.
- **Significance:** The 2006 version of the National Strategy for Combating Terrorism demonstrated the Bush administration's tendency to focus upon current events as the springboard for a long-term planning concept. Compared to the 2003 version (see Document 52) it is far more focused upon the specific challenges presented by the regional franchise terror organization Al Qaeda in Iraq, which had proven extremely capable and challenging during the Iraq insurgency.

DOCUMENT

Overview of America's National Strategy for Combating Terrorism

America is at war with a transnational terrorist movement fueled by a radical ideology of hatred, oppression, and murder. Our National Strategy for Combating Terrorism, first published in February 2003, recognizes that we are at war and that protecting and defending the Homeland, the American people, and their livelihoods remains our first and most solemn obligation.

Our strategy also recognizes that the War on Terror is a different kind of war. From the beginning, it has been both a battle of arms and a battle of ideas. Not only do we fight our terrorist enemies on the battlefield, we promote freedom and human dignity as alternatives to the terrorists' perverse vision of oppression and totalitarian rule. The paradigm for combating terrorism now involves the application of all elements of our national power and influence. Not only do we employ military power, we use diplomatic, financial, intelligence, and law enforcement activities to protect the Homeland and extend our defenses, disrupt terrorist operations, and deprive our enemies of what they need to operate and survive. We have broken old orthodoxies that once confined our counterterrorism efforts primarily to the criminal justice domain.

This updated strategy sets the course for winning the War on Terror. It builds directly from the National Security Strategy issued in March 2006 as well as the February 2003 National Strategy for Combating Terrorism, and incorporates our increased understanding of the enemy. From the beginning, we understood that the War on Terror involved more than simply finding and bringing to justice those who had planned and executed the terrorist attacks on September 11, 2001. Our strategy involved destroying the larger al-Qaida network and also confronting the radical ideology that inspired others to join or support the terrorist movement. Since 9/11, we have made substantial progress in degrading the al-Qaida network, killing or capturing key lieutenants, eliminating safehavens, and disrupting existing lines of support. Through the freedom agenda, we also have promoted the best long-term answer to al-Qaida's agenda: the freedom and dignity that comes when human liberty is protected by effective democratic institutions.

In response to our efforts, the terrorists have adjusted, and so we must continue to refine our strategy to meet the evolving threat. Today, we face a global terrorist movement and must confront the radical ideology that justifies the use of violence against innocents in the name of religion. As laid out in this strategy, to win the War on Terror, we will:

- Advance effective democracies as the long-term antidote to the ideology of terrorism;
- Prevent attacks by terrorist networks;
- Deny terrorists the support and sanctuary of rogue states;
- Deny terrorists control of any nation they would use as a base and launching pad for terror; and
- Lay the foundations and build the institutions and structures we need to carry the fight forward against terror and help ensure our ultimate success.

Today's Realities in the War on Terror

The terrorist attacks of September 11, 2001, were acts of war against the United States, peaceful people throughout the world, and the very principles of liberty and human dignity. The United States, together with our Coalition partners, has fought back and will win this war. We will hold the perpetrators accountable and work to prevent the recurrence of similar atrocities on any scale—whether at home or abroad. The War on Terror extends beyond the current armed conflict that arose out of the attacks of September 11, 2001, and embraces all facets of continuing U.S. efforts to bring an end to the scourge of terrorism. Ultimately, we will win the long war to defeat the terrorists and their murderous ideology.

Successes

- We have deprived al-Qaida of safe haven in Afghanistan and helped a democratic government to rise in its place. Once a terrorist sanctuary ruled by the repressive Taliban regime, Afghanistan is now a full partner in the War on Terror.
- A multinational coalition joined by the Iraqis is aggressively prosecuting the war against the terrorists in Iraq. Together, we are working to secure a united, stable, and democratic Iraq, now a new War on Terror ally in the heart of the Middle East.

- We have significantly degraded the al-Qaida network. Most of those in the al-Qaida network responsible for the September 11 attacks, including the plot's mastermind Khalid Shaykh Muhammad, have been captured or killed. We also have killed other key al-Qaida members, such as Abu Musab al-Zarqawi, the group's operational commander in Iraq who led a campaign of terror that took the lives of countless American forces and innocent Iraqis.
- We have led an unprecedented international campaign to combat terrorist financing that has made it harder, costlier, and riskier for al-Qaida and related terrorist groups to raise and move money.
- There is a broad and growing global consensus that the deliberate targeting of innocents is never justified by any calling or cause.
- Many nations have rallied to fight terrorism, with unprecedented cooperation on law enforcement, intelligence, military, and diplomatic activity.
- We have strengthened our ability to disrupt and help prevent future attacks in the Homeland by enhancing our counterterrorism architecture through the creation of the Department of Homeland Security, the Office of Director of National Intelligence, and the National Counterterrorism Center. Overall, the United States and our partners have disrupted several serious plots since September 11, including al-Qaida plots to attack inside the United States.
- Numerous countries that were part of the problem before September 11 are now increasingly becoming part of the solution—and this transformation has occurred without destabilizing friendly regimes in key regions.
- The Administration has worked with Congress to adopt, implement, and renew key reforms like the USA PATRIOT Act that promote our security while also protecting our fundamental liberties.

Yet while America is safer, we are not yet safe. The enemy remains determined, and we face serious challenges at home and abroad.

Challenges

- Terrorist networks today are more dispersed and less centralized. They are more reliant on smaller cells inspired by a common ideology and less directed by a central command structure.
- While the United States Government and its partners have thwarted many attacks, we have not been able to prevent them all. Terrorists have struck in many places throughout the world, from Bali to Beslan to Baghdad.
- While we have substantially improved our air, land, sea, and border security, our Homeland is not immune from attack.
- Terrorists have declared their intention to acquire and use weapons of mass destruction (WMD) to inflict even more catastrophic attacks against the United States, our allies, partners, and other interests around the world.
- Some states, such as Syria and Iran, continue to harbor terrorists at home and sponsor terrorist activity abroad.
- The ongoing fight for freedom in Iraq has been twisted by terrorist propaganda as a rallying cry.

- Increasingly sophisticated use of the Internet and media has enabled our terrorist enemies to communicate, recruit, train, rally support, proselytize, and spread their propaganda without risking personal contact.

Strategic Vision for the War on Terror

From the beginning, the War on Terror has been both a battle of arms and a battle of ideas—a fight against the terrorists and their murderous ideology. In the short run, the fight involves the application of all instruments of national power and influence to kill or capture the terrorists; deny them safe haven and control of any nation; prevent them from gaining access to WMD; render potential terrorist targets less attractive by strengthening security; and cut off their sources of funding and other resources they need to operate and survive. In the long run, winning the War on Terror means winning the battle of ideas. Ideas can transform the embittered and disillusioned either into murderers willing to kill innocents, or into free peoples living harmoniously in a diverse society.

The battle of ideas helps to define the strategic intent of our National Strategy for Combating Terrorism. The United States will continue to lead an expansive international effort in pursuit of a two-pronged vision:

- The defeat of violent extremism as a threat to our way of life as a free and open society; and
- The creation of a global environment inhospitable to violent extremists and all who support them.

Strategy for Winning the War on Terror

Long-term approach: Advancing effective democracy

The long-term solution for winning the War on Terror is the advancement of freedom and human dignity through effective democracy. Elections are the most visible sign of a free society and can play a critical role in advancing effective democracy. But elections alone are not enough. Effective democracies honor and uphold basic human rights, including freedom of religion, conscience, speech, assembly, association, and press. They are responsive to their citizens, submitting to the will of the people. Effective democracies exercise effective sovereignty and maintain order within their own borders, address causes of conflict peacefully, protect independent and impartial systems of justice, punish crime, embrace the rule of law, and resist corruption. Effective democracies also limit the reach of government, protecting the institutions of civil society. In effective democracies, freedom is indivisible. They are the long-term antidote to the ideology of terrorism today. This is the battle of ideas.

To wage the battle of ideas effectively, we must recognize what does and does not give rise to terrorism:

- Terrorism is not the inevitable by-product of poverty. Many of the September 11 hijackers were from middle-class backgrounds, and many terrorist leaders, like bin Laden, are from privileged upbringings.

- Terrorism is not simply a result of hostility to U.S. policy in Iraq. The United States was attacked on September 11 and many years earlier, well before we toppled the Saddam Hussein regime. Moreover, countries that did not participate in Coalition efforts in Iraq have not been spared from terror attacks.
- Terrorism is not simply a result of Israeli-Palestinian issues. Al-Qaida plotting for the September 11 attacks began in the 1990s, during an active period in the peace process.
- Terrorism is not simply a response to our efforts to prevent terror attacks. The al-Qaida network targeted the United States long before the United States targeted al-Qaida. Indeed, the terrorists are emboldened more by perceptions of weakness than by demonstrations of resolve. Terrorists lure recruits by telling them that we are decadent, easily intimidated, and will retreat if attacked.

The terrorism we confront today springs from:

- *Political alienation*. Transnational terrorists are recruited from populations with no voice in their own government and see no legitimate way to promote change in their own country. Without a stake in the existing order, they are vulnerable to manipulation by those who advocate a perverse political vision based on violence and destruction.
- *Grievances that can be blamed on others*. The failures the terrorists feel and see are blamed both on others and on perceived injustices from the recent or sometimes distant past. The terrorists' rhetoric keeps wounds associated with this past fresh and raw, a potent motivation for revenge and terror.
- *Subcultures of conspiracy and misinformation*. Terrorists recruit more effectively from populations whose information about the world is contaminated by falsehoods and corrupted by conspiracy theories. The distortions keep alive grievances and filter out facts that would challenge popular prejudices and self-serving propaganda.
- *An ideology that justifies murder*. Terrorism ultimately depends upon the appeal of an ideology that excuses or even glorifies the deliberate killing of innocents. Islam has been twisted and made to serve an evil end, as in other times and places other religions have been similarly abused.

Defeating terrorism in the long run requires that each of these factors be addressed. Effective democracy provides a counter to each, diminishing the underlying conditions terrorists seek to exploit.

- In place of alienation, democracy offers an ownership stake in society, a chance to shape one's own future.
- In place of festering grievances, democracy offers the rule of law, the peaceful resolution of disputes, and the habits of advancing interests through compromise.
- In place of a culture of conspiracy and misinformation, democracy offers freedom of speech, independent media, and the marketplace of ideas, which can expose and discredit falsehoods, prejudices, and dishonest propaganda.
- In place of an ideology that justifies murder, democracy offers a respect for human dignity that abhors the deliberate targeting of innocent civilians.

Democracy is the antithesis of terrorist tyranny, which is why the terrorists denounce it and are willing to kill the innocent to stop it. Democracy is based on empowerment, while the terrorists' ideology is based on enslavement. Democracies expand the freedom of their citizens, while the terrorists seek to impose a single set of narrow beliefs. Democracy sees individuals as equal in worth and dignity, having an inherent potential to create, govern themselves, and exercise basic freedoms of speech and conscience. The terrorists see individuals as objects to be exploited, and then to be ruled and oppressed.

Democracies are not immune to terrorism. In some democracies, some ethnic or religious groups are unable or unwilling to grasp the benefits of freedom otherwise available in the society. Such groups can evidence the same alienation and despair that the transnational terrorists exploit in undemocratic states. This accounts for the emergence in democratic societies of homegrown terrorists—even among second- and third-generation citizens. Even in these cases, the long-term solution remains deepening the reach of democracy so that all citizens enjoy its benefits. We will continue to guard against the emergence of homegrown terrorists within our own Homeland as well.

The strategy to counter the lies behind the terrorists' ideology and deny them future recruits must empower the very people the terrorists most want to exploit: the faithful followers of Islam. We will continue to support political reforms that empower peaceful Muslims to practice and interpret their faith. We will work to undermine the ideological underpinnings of violent Islamic extremism and gain the support of non-violent Muslims around the world. The most vital work will be done within the Islamic world itself, and Jordan, Morocco, and Indonesia, among others, have begun to make important strides in this effort. Responsible Islamic leaders need to denounce an ideology that distorts and exploits Islam to justify the murder of innocent people and defiles a proud religion.

Many of the Muslim faith are already making this commitment at great personal risk. They realize they are a target of this ideology of terror. Everywhere we have joined in the fight against terrorism, Muslim allies have stood beside us, becoming partners in this vital cause. They know the stakes—the survival of their own liberty, the future of their own region, the justice and humanity of their own traditions—and the United States is proud to stand beside them. Not only will we continue to support the efforts of our Muslim partners overseas to reject violent extremism, we will continue to engage with and strengthen the efforts of Muslims within the United States as well. Through outreach programs and public diplomacy we will reveal the terrorists' violent extremist ideology for what it is—a form of totalitarianism following in the path of fascism and Nazism.

Source: National Strategy for Combating Terrorism, March 2006, available at http://2001-2009.state.gov/s/ct/rls/wh/71803.htm.

ANALYSIS

The document notes that the War on Terror, like any international conflict, is both a struggle of violence and a struggle of ideas. In many ways, it constitutes a contest of learning and adaptation, and thus issuing a new strategy does not constitute abandoning the old one so much as refining the government's understanding of the nature of the conflict. The 2006 counterterrorism strategy has an interesting section denoting the successes of the previous five years, yet strangely, it makes only one mention of Osama bin Laden, to note his wealthy background. Trumpeting the successes of capturing or killing Al Qaeda leaders carried little weight so long as its inspirational leader and commander was still able to conduct his personal war upon the West. Another surprising characteristic of the document is the notion that the best long-term strategy for combating terrorism is to promote effective democracies, a position that ignores most of the terror-related history of the 20th century, when the most noteworthy attacks were almost exclusively carried out within democratic nations. Totalitarian regimes, in comparison, have had far more success at quashing terror organizations, in large part due to their ability to more effectively control economies, transportations systems, and the mass media. Ironically, this excerpt closes on the argument that terror organizations seek to impose a totalitarian vision upon the world akin to fascism or Nazism.

- **Document 67: Testimony of Khalid Sheikh Mohammed**
- **When:** March 10, 2007
- **Where:** Guantanamo Bay, Cuba
- **Significance:** Khalid Sheikh Mohammed has long been considered the operational planner for the September 11 attacks. In a military courtroom, he offered a prepared statement that many consider a confession of his involvement with Al Qaeda. However, Mohammed was subjected to waterboarding on several occasions, leading to accusations that the confession was coerced and would not stand up in a civil court.

DOCUMENT

Transcript of Combatant Status Review Tribunal Hearing for ISN 10024

I hereby admit and affirm without duress to the following:

1. I swore Bay'aat (i.e., allegiance) to Sheikh Usama Bin Laden to conduct Jihad of self and money, and also Hijrah (i.e., expatriation to any location in the world where Jihad is required).
2. I was a member of the Al Qaida Council.
3. I was the Media Operations Director for Al-Sahab, or The Clouds, under Dr. Ayman Al Zawahiri. Al-Sahab is the media outlet that provided Al-Qaida-sponsored information to Al Jazeera.

4. I was the Operational Director for Sheikh Usama Bin Laden for the organizing, planning, follow-up, and execution of the 9/11 Operation under the Military Commander, Sheikh Abu Hafs Al-Masri Subhi Abu Sittah.

5. I was the Military Operational Commander for all foreign operations around the world under the direction of Sheikh Usama Bin Laden and Dr. Ayman Al-Zawahiri.

6. I was directly in charge, after the death of Sheikh Abu Hafs Al-Masri Subhi Abu Sittah, of managing and following up on the Cell for the Production of Biological Weapons, such as anthrax and others, and following up on Dirty Bomb Operations on American soil.

7. I was Emir (i.e., commander) of Beit Al Shuhada (i.e., the Martyrs' House) in the state of Kandahar, Afghanistan, which housed the 9/11 hijackers. There I was responsible for their training and readiness for the execution of the 9/11 Operation. Also, I hereby admit and affirm without duress that I was a responsible participant, principal planner, trainer, financier (via the Military Council Treasury), executor, and/or a personal participant in the following;

    1. I was responsible for the 1993 World Trade Center Operation.

    2. I was responsible for the 9/11 Operation, from A to Z.

    3. I decapitated with my blessed right hand the head of the American Jew, Daniel Pearl, in the city of Karachi, Pakistan. For those who would like to confirm, there are pictures of me on the internet holding his head.

    4. I was responsible for the Shoe Bomber Operation to down two American airplanes.

    5. I was responsible for the Filka Island Operation in Kuwait that killed two American soldiers.

    6. I was responsible for the bombing of a nightclub in Bali, Indonesia, which was frequented by British and Australian nationals.

    7. I was responsible for planning, training, surveying, and financing the New (or Second) Wave attacks against the following skyscrapers after 9/11:

        1. Library Tower, California.

        2. Sears Tower, Chicago.

        3. Plaza Bank, Washington state.

        4. The Empire State Building, New York City.

8. I was responsible for planning, financing, & follow-up of Operations to destroy American military vessels and oil tankers in the Strait of Hormuz, the Strait of Gibraltar, and the Port of Singapore.

9. I was responsible for planning, training, surveying, and financing for the Operation to bomb and destroy the Panama Canal.

10. I was responsible for surveying and financing for the assassination of several former American Presidents, including President Carter.

11. I was responsible for surveying, planning, and financing for the bombing of suspension bridges in New York.

12. I was responsible for planning to destroy the Sears Tower by burning a few fuel or oil tanker trucks beneath it or around it.

13. I was responsible for planning, surveying, and financing for the operation to destroy Heathrow Airport, the Canary Wharf Building, and Big Ben on British soil.

14. I was responsible for planning, surveying, and financing for the destruction of many night clubs frequented by American and British citizens on Thailand soil.

15. I was responsible for surveying and financing for the destruction of the New York Stock Exchange and other financial targets after 9/11.

16. I was responsible for planning, financing, and surveying for the destruction of buildings in the Israeli city of Elat by using airplanes leaving from Saudi Arabia.

17. I was responsible for planning, surveying, and financing for the destruction of American embassies in Indonesia, Australia, and Japan.

18. I was responsible for surveying and financing for the destruction of the Israeli embassy in India, Azerbaijan, the Philippines, and Australia.

19. I was responsible for surveying and financing for the destruction of an Israeli El-Al Airlines flight on Thailand soil departing from Bangkok Airport.

20. I was responsible for sending several Mujahadeen into Israel to conduct surveillance to hit several strategic targets deep in Israel.

21. I was responsible for the bombing of the hotel in Mombasa that is frequented by Jewish travelers via El-Al airlines.

22. I was responsible for launching a Russian-made SA-7 surface-to-air missile on El-Al or other Jewish airliner departing from Mombasa.

23. I was responsible for planning and surveying to hit American targets in South Korea, such as American military bases and a few night clubs frequented by American soldiers.

24. I was responsible for financial, excuse me, I was responsible for providing financial support to hit American, Jewish, and British targets in Turkey.

25. I was responsible for surveillance needed to hit nuclear power plants that generate electricity in several U.S. states.

26. I was responsible for planning, surveying, and financing to hit NATO Headquarters in Europe.

27. I was responsible for the planning and surveying needed to execute the Bojinka Operation, which was designed to down twelve American airplanes full of passengers. I personally monitored a round-trip, Manila-to-Seoul, Pan Am flight.

28. I was responsible for the assassination attempt against President Clinton during his visit to the Philippines in 1994 or 1995.

29. I shared responsibility for the assassination attempt against Pope John Paul the second while he was visiting the Philippines.

30. I was responsible for the training and financing for the assassination of Pakistan's President Musharaf.

DID YOU KNOW?

Khalid Sheikh Mohammed

Khalid Sheikh Mohammed is the operational leader most closely associated with the September 11 attacks. He was born in Kuwait in 1965 to Pakistani parents. He joined the Muslim Brotherhood in 1981, and became increasingly radicalized while he pursued a mechanical engineering degree from North Carolina A&T University. After his graduation in 1986, Mohammed traveled to Afghanistan, where he joined the mujahideen and met prominent Islamist leaders, including Osama bin Laden. After the Soviet withdrawal in 1989, Mohammed remained allied with radical groups while considering plans to attack the United States. In the mid-1990s, he hit upon the idea of simultaneously hijacking multiple aircraft and deliberately flying them into targets on the ground. He developed a plan to take over 10 aircraft and turn them into suicide missiles, but eventually curtailed the plan to 4 airplanes in the final version. Mohammed was captured in Rawalpindi, Pakistan, in 2003, and has remained in U.S. military custody since that time. He underwent major interrogation while in American hands, including episodes of waterboarding that have undercut the likelihood of trial in a criminal court.

31. I was responsible for the attempt to destroy an American oil company owned by the Jewish former Secretary of State, Henry Kissinger, on the Island of Sumatra, Indonesia.

Personal Representative: Sir, that concludes the written portion of the Detainee's final statement and as he has alluded to earlier he has some additional comments he would like to make.

President: Alright. Before you proceed, Khalid Sheikh Muhammad, the statement that was just read by the Personal Representative, were those your words?

Detainee: Yes. And I want to add some of this one just for some verification. It like some operations before I join al Qaida. Before I remember al Qaida which is related to Bojinka Operation I went to destination involve to us in 94, 95. Some Operations which means out of al Qaida. It's like beheading Daniel Pearl. It's not related to al Qaida. It was shared in Pakistani, other group, Mujahadeen. The story of Daniel Pearl, because he stated for the Pakistani group that he was working with the both. His mission was in Pakistan to track about Richard Reed trip to Israel. Richard Reed, do you have trip? You send it Israel to make set for targets in Israel. His mission in Pakistan from Israeli intelligence, Mosad, to make interview to ask about when he was there. Also, he mention to them he was both. He have relation with CIA people and were the Mosad. But he was not related to al Qaida at all or UBL. It is related to the Pakistan Mujahadeen group. Other operations mostly are some word I'm not accurate in saying. I'm responsible but if you read the heading history. The line there.

Personal Representative: Also hereby admit and affirm without duress that I was a responsible participant, principal planner, trainer, financier.

Detainee: For this is not necessary as I responsible, responsible. But within these things responsible participant in finances.

In the name of God the most compassionate, the most merciful, and if any fail to retaliation by way of charity and. I apologize. I will start again. And if any fail to judge by the light of Allah has revealed, they are no better than wrong doers, unbelievers, and the unjust.

For this verse, I not take the oath. Take an oath is a part of your Tribunal and I'll not accept it. To be or accept the Tribunal as to be, I'll accept it. That I'm accepting American constitution, American law or whatever you are doing here. This is why religiously I cannot accept anything you do. Just to explain for this one, does not mean I'm not saying that I'm lying. When I not take oath does not mean I'm lying. You know very well peoples take oath and they will lie. You know the President he did this before he just makes his oath and he lied. So sometimes when I'm not making oath does not mean I'm lying.

Allah forbids you not with regards to those who fight you not for not for your faith nor drive you out of your homes from dealing kindly and justly with them. For Allah love those who are just. There is one more sentence. Allah only forbids you with regards to those who fight you for your faith and drive you out of your homes and support others in driving you out from turning to them for friendship and protection. It is as such to turn to them in these circumstances that do wrong.

So we are driving from whatever deed we do we ask about Koran or Hadith. We are not making up for us laws. When we need Fatwa from the religious we have to go back to see what they said scholar. To see what they said yes or not. Killing is prohibited in all what you call the people of the book, Jews, Judaism, Christianity, and Islam. You know the Ten Commandments very well. The Ten Commandments are shared between all of us. We all are serving one God. Then now kill you know it very well. But war language also we have language for the war. You have to kill. But you have to care if unintentionally or intentionally target if I have if I'm not at the Pentagon. I consider it is okay. If I target now when we target in USA we choose them military target, economical, and political. So, war central victims mostly means economical target. So if now American they know UBL. He is in this house they don't care about his kids and his. They will just bombard it. They will kill all of them and they did it. They kill wife of Dr. Ayman Zawahiri and his two daughters and his son in one bombardment. They receive a report that is his house be. He had not been there. They killed them. They arrested my kids intentionally. They are kids. They been arrested for four months they had been abused. So, for me I have patience. I know I'm not talk about what's come to me. The American have human right. So, enemy combatant itself, it flexible word. So I think God knows that many who been arrested, they been unjustly arrested. Otherwise, military throughout history know very well. They don't war will never stop. War start from Adam when Cain he killed Abel until now. It's never gonna stop killing of people. This is the way of the language. American start the Revolutionary War then they starts the Mexican then Spanish War then World War One, World War Two. You read the history. You know never stopping war. This is life. But if who is enemy combatant and who is not? Finally, I finish statement. I'm asking you to be fair with other people.

Source: Department of Defense, Verbatim Transcript of Combatant Status Review Tribunal Hearing for ISN 10024. Available online at http:// archive.defense.gov/news/transcript_ISN10024.pdf.

ANALYSIS

Khalid Sheikh Mohammed is the highest-ranking member of Al Qaeda who has been captured alive to date. He was captured on March 1, 2003, by agents of the Pakistani Intelligence Service and turned over to American custody. While in U.S. custody, he was subjected to the controversial practice of waterboarding, and he has alleged that he was tortured by foreign agents at the behest of the CIA. In this testimony, written in Arabic and delivered by a translator at the tribunal, Mohammed seeks to both justify his activities and take credit for every major Al Qaeda activity of the preceding two decades. This might indicate that Mohammed held a key position within Al Qaeda and that his capture had a massive effect upon the organization's ability to carry out large-scale attacks. It might also indicate that Mohammed sought to take the blame for as many actions as possible, shifting American attention away from other operatives who then might have a free hand in future attacks. He closes his statement with the suggestion that all of the members of Judaism, Christianity, and Islam serve the same God, and hence are bound by the same religious laws, but that members of all faiths have created new justifications to make war upon one another. In this fashion, Mohammed seeks to absolve Al Qaeda from any suggestion that its attacks were somehow worse or less acceptable than the types of killings perpetrated in the largest wars of the past.

4

DOCUMENTS FROM
THE PRESIDENCY
OF BARACK OBAMA, 2009–2016

- Document 68: Harold Koh, Speech to American Society on International Law
- **When:** March 25, 2010
- **Where:** Washington, D.C.
- **Significance:** Koh, serving as a special adviser to the State Department, offered his legal opinions regarding several of the most controversial aspects of the War on Terror. This excerpt includes discussions of the detainee situation at Guantanamo, the use of drones for targeted killings, and the distinctions between the laws of the battlefield and domestic law.

DOCUMENT

III. Current Legal Challenges
B. The Law of 9/11

We live in a time, when, as you know, the United States finds itself engaged in several armed conflicts. As the President has noted, one conflict, in Iraq, is winding down. He also reminded us that the conflict in Afghanistan is a "conflict that America did not seek, one in which we are joined by forty-three other countries ... in an effort to defend ourselves and all nations from further attacks." In the conflict occurring in Afghanistan and elsewhere, we continue to fight the perpetrators of 9/11: a non-state actor, al-Qaeda (as well as the Taliban forces that harbored al-Qaeda).

With this background, let me address a question on many of your minds: how has this Administration determined to conduct these armed conflicts and to defend our national security, consistent with its abiding commitment to international law? *Let there be no doubt: the Obama Administration is firmly committed to complying with all applicable law, including the laws of war, in all aspects of these ongoing armed conflicts.* As the President reaffirmed in his Nobel Prize Lecture, "Where force is necessary, we have a moral and strategic interest in binding ourselves to certain rules of conduct ... [E]ven as we confront a vicious adversary that abides by no rules ... the United States of America must remain a standard bearer in the conduct of war. That is what makes us different from those whom we fight. That is the source of our strength." We in the Obama Administration have worked hard since we entered office to ensure that

---

DID YOU KNOW?

Bowe Bergdahl

To date, only one U.S. service member has been captured and held as a prisoner by enemy forces in Afghanistan. On June 30, 2009, U.S. Sergeant Bowe Bergdahl walked away from his unit, stationed in Paktika Province. He left his equipment carefully stacked, and his disappearance triggered a massive search-and-rescue operation in the surrounding provinces, which failed to locate any trace of his whereabouts. In July 2009, representatives of the Taliban claimed to be holding Bergdahl, and soon released photos, videos, and other evidence of his capture. After months of negotiations conducted through the Qatari government, the United States agreed to release five prisoners from Guantanamo Bay in exchange for Bergdahl's safe return. He was released to U.S. custody on May 31, 2014. Critics of the exchange warned that it would embolden terror groups to kidnap American personnel in pursuit of future lopsided exchanges, but to date, no such actions against American service personnel have occurred. In late 2015, the army announced it would prosecute Bergdahl for desertion in the face of the enemy.

we conduct all aspects of these armed conflicts—in particular, detention operations, targeting, and prosecution of terrorist suspects—in a manner consistent not just with the applicable laws of war, but also with the Constitution and laws of the United States.

Let me say a word about each: detention, targeting, and prosecution.

1. Detention

With respect to detention, as you know, the last Administration's detention practices were widely criticized around the world, and as a private citizen, I was among the vocal critics of those practices. This Administration and I personally have spent much of the last year seeking to revise those practices to ensure their full compliance with domestic and international law, first, by unequivocally guaranteeing *humane treatment* for all individuals in U.S. custody as a result of armed conflict and second, by *ensuring that all detained individuals are being held pursuant to lawful authorities.*

a. Treatment

To ensure humane treatment, on his second full day in office, the President unequivocally banned the use of torture as an instrument of U.S. policy, a commitment that he has repeatedly reaffirmed in the months since. He directed that executive officials could no longer rely upon the Justice Department OLC opinions that had permitted practices that I consider to be torture and cruel treatment—many of which he later disclosed publicly—and he instructed that henceforth, all interrogations of detainees must be conducted in accordance with Common Article 3 of the Geneva Conventions and with the revised Army Field Manual. An interagency review of U.S. interrogation practices later advised—and the President agreed—that no techniques beyond those in the Army Field Manual (and traditional noncoercive FBI techniques) are necessary to conduct effective interrogations. That Interrogation and Transfer Task Force also issued a set of recommendations to help ensure that the United States will not transfer individuals to face torture. The President also revoked Executive Order 13440, which had interpreted particular provisions of Common Article 3, and restored the meaning of those provisions to the way they have traditionally been understood in international law. The President ordered CIA "black sites" closed and directed the Secretary of Defense to conduct an immediate review—with two follow-up visits by a blue ribbon task force of former government officials—to ensure that the conditions of detention at Guantanamo fully comply with Common Article 3 of the Geneva Conventions. Last December, I visited Guantanamo, a place I had visited several times over the last two decades, and I believe that the conditions I observed are humane and meet Geneva Conventions standards.

As you all know, also on his second full day in office, the President ordered Guantanamo closed, and his commitment to doing so has not wavered, even as closing Guantanamo has proven to be an arduous and painstaking process. Since the beginning of the Administration, through the work of my colleague Ambassador Dan Fried, we have transferred approximately 57 detainees to 22 different countries, of whom 33 were resettled in countries that are not the detainees' countries of origin. Our efforts continue on a daily basis. Just this week, five more detainees were transferred out of Guantanamo for resettlement. We are very grateful to those countries who have contributed to our efforts to close Guantanamo by resettling detainees;

that list continues to grow as more and more countries see the positive changes we are making and wish to offer their support.

B. Use of Force

In the same way, in all of our operations involving the *use of force*, including those in the armed conflict with al-Qaeda, the Taliban and associated forces, the Obama Administration is committed by word and deed to conducting ourselves in accordance with all applicable law. With respect to the subject of targeting, which has been much commented upon in the media and international legal circles, there are obviously limits to what I can say publicly. What I can say *is that it is the considered view of this Administration—and it has certainly been my experience during my time as Legal Adviser—that U.S. targeting practices, including lethal operations conducted with the use of unmanned aerial vehicles, comply with all applicable law, including the laws of war.*

The United States agrees that it must conform its actions to all applicable law. As I have explained, as a matter of international law, the United States is in an armed conflict with al-Qaeda, as well as the Taliban and associated forces, in response to the horrific 9/11 attacks, and may use force consistent with its inherent right to self-defense under international law. As a matter of domestic law, Congress authorized the use of all necessary and appropriate force through the 2001 Authorization for Use of Military Force (AUMF). These domestic and international legal authorities continue to this day.

As recent events have shown, al-Qaeda has not abandoned its intent to attack the United States, and indeed continues to attack us. Thus, in this ongoing armed conflict, the United States has the authority under international law, and the responsibility to its citizens, to use force, including lethal force, to defend itself, including by targeting persons such as high-level al-Qaeda leaders who are planning attacks. As you know, this is a conflict with an organized terrorist enemy that does not have conventional forces, but that plans and executes its attacks against us and our allies while hiding among civilian populations. That behavior simultaneously makes the application of international law more difficult and more critical for the protection of innocent civilians. Of course, whether a particular individual will be targeted in a particular location will depend upon considerations specific to each case, including those related to the imminence of the threat, the sovereignty of the other states involved, and the willingness and ability of those states to suppress the threat the target poses. In particular, this Administration has carefully reviewed the rules governing targeting operations to ensure that these operations are conducted consistently with law of war principles, including:

First, the principle of *distinction*, which requires that attacks be limited to military objectives and that civilians or civilian objects shall not be the object of the attack; and

Second, the principle of *proportionality*, which prohibits attacks that may be expected to cause incidental loss of civilian life, injury to civilians, damage to civilian objects, or a combination thereof, that would be excessive in relation to the concrete and direct military advantage anticipated.

In U.S. operations against al-Qaeda and its associated forces—including lethal operations conducted with the use of unmanned aerial vehicles—great care is taken to adhere to these principles in both planning and execution, to ensure that only legitimate objectives are targeted and that collateral damage is kept to a minimum.

Recently, a number of legal objections have been raised against U.S. targeting practices. While today is obviously not the occasion for a detailed legal opinion responding to each of these objections, let me briefly address four:

First, some have suggested that the *very act of targeting* a particular leader of an enemy force in an armed conflict must violate the laws of war. But individuals who are part of such an armed group are belligerents and, therefore, lawful targets under international law. During World War II, for example, American aviators tracked and shot down the airplane carrying the architect of the Japanese attack on Pearl Harbor, who was also the leader of enemy forces in the Battle of Midway. This was a lawful operation then, and would be if conducted today. Indeed, targeting particular individuals serves to narrow the focus when force is employed and to avoid broader harm to civilians and civilian objects.

Second, some have challenged *the very use of advanced weapons systems*, such as unmanned aerial vehicles, for lethal operations. But the rules that govern targeting do not turn on the type of weapon system used, and there is no prohibition under the laws of war on the use of technologically advanced weapons systems in armed conflict—such as pilotless aircraft or so-called smart bombs—so long as they are employed in conformity with applicable laws of war. Indeed, using such advanced technologies can ensure both that the best intelligence is available for planning operations, and that civilian casualties are minimized in carrying out such operations.

Third, some have argued that the use of lethal force against specific individuals fails to provide adequate process and thus constitutes *unlawful extrajudicial killing*. But a state that is engaged in an armed conflict or in legitimate self-defense is not required to provide targets with legal process before the state may use lethal force. Our procedures and practices for identifying lawful targets are extremely robust, and advanced technologies have helped to make our targeting even more precise. In my experience, the principles of distinction and proportionality that the United States applies are not just recited at meetings. They are implemented rigorously throughout the planning and execution of lethal operations to ensure that such operations are conducted in accordance with all applicable law.

Fourth and finally, some have argued that our targeting practices violate *domestic law*, in particular, the long-standing *domestic ban on assassinations*. But under domestic law, the use of lawful weapons systems—consistent with the applicable laws of war—for precision targeting of specific high-level belligerent leaders when acting in self-defense or during an armed conflict is not unlawful, and hence does not constitute "assassination."

In sum, let me repeat: as in the area of detention operations, this Administration is committed to ensuring that the targeting practices that I have described are lawful.

Source: Koh, Harold, "The Obama Administration and International Law," Speech to the Annual Meeting of the American Society of International Law,

Washington, D.C., March 25, 2010. Department of State. Available online at http://www.state.gov/s/l/releases/remarks/139119.htm.

ANALYSIS

Koh's remarks demonstrate many of the most challenging aspects of counterterrorism efforts. The government tasked with combating a terror organization is expected to follow all of the laws of armed conflict, even though its adversary will not pretend to obey the same limitations. President Obama quickly discovered the special challenges presented by engaging in such a conflict, but as Koh noted, he also took immediate steps to distance himself from some of the policies of his predecessor. In particular, the president's vow to close the Guantanamo Bay detention facility, and to prohibit the use of any form of torture, stood in stark contrast to the policies of the Bush administration.

- **Document 69: Anthony D. Romero Letter to Barack Obama**
- **When:** April 28, 2010
- **Where:** New York, NY
- **Significance:** Romero, the executive director of the American Civil Liberties Union, released this letter to express concerns to the president that many of the activities of the federal government conducted in the War on Terror should be considered illegal and unconstitutional, and must be stopped. In addition, he illustrated the longer-term ramifications of continuing the policy of extrajudicial killing, arguing that it should be stopped for practical as well as legal and moral reasons.

DOCUMENT

Dear Mr. President:

On behalf of the ACLU and its 500,000 members, I am writing to express our profound concern about recent reports indicating that you have authorized a program that contemplates the killing of suspected terrorists—including U.S. citizens—located far away from zones of actual armed conflict. If accurately described, this program violates international law and, at least insofar as it affects U.S. citizens, it is also unconstitutional.

The U.S. is engaged in non-international armed conflict in Afghanistan and Iraq and the lawfulness of its actions must be judged in that context. The program that you have reportedly authorized appears to envision the use of lethal force not just on the battlefield in Iraq, Afghanistan, or even the Pakistani border regions, but anywhere in the world, including against individuals who may not constitute lawful targets. The entire world is not a war zone, and war-time tactics that may be permitted on the battlefields in Afghanistan and Iraq cannot be deployed anywhere in the world where a terrorism suspect happens to be located. Your administration has eschewed the rhetoric of the "Global War on Terror." You should now disavow the sweeping legal theory that underlies that slogan.

Even in an armed conflict zone, individuals may be targeted only if they take a direct part in hostilities, for such time as they do so, or if they have taken up a continuous combat function. Propagandists, financiers, and other non-combat "supporters" of hostile groups cannot lawfully be targeted with lethal force. Applicable international humanitarian law also prohibits targeted killing except in order to prevent an individual's future participation in hostilities; fighters cannot be targeted solely as retribution for past actions. Furthermore, basic law-of-armed-conflict principles require that in such operations, civilians who are not taking direct part in hostilities must not be targeted, precautions must always be taken to spare the civilian population, anticipated civilian casualties must never be disproportionate to the expected concrete military advantage, and strikes must only occur when required by military necessity.

Outside armed conflict zones, the use of lethal force by the United States is strictly limited by international law and, at least in some circumstances, the Constitution. These laws permit lethal force to be used only as a last resort, and only to prevent imminent attacks that are likely to cause death or serious physical injury. According to news reports, the program you have authorized is based on "kill lists" to which names are added, sometimes for months at a time, after a secret internal process. Such a program of long-premeditated and bureaucratized killing is plainly not limited to targeting genuinely imminent threats. Any such program is far more sweeping than the law allows and raises grave constitutional and human rights concerns.

In a series of cases involving prisoners currently held by the U.S. at Guantanamo Bay, your administration has taken the position that the 2001 Authorization for Use of Military Force permits the detention of individuals captured anywhere in the world, even individuals who have no connection to the battlefield. For example, your administration has advanced that argument in the case of one of our clients—Mohammedou Salahi—who was detained in Mauritania. We do not think the AUMF can be read so broadly. In *Hamdi v. Rumsfeld*, the Supreme Court interpreted the AUMF consistently with international law, permitting the detention of a U.S. citizen captured in Afghanistan only because the detention of *battlefield* combatants was "so fundamental and accepted an incident to war as to be an exercise of the 'necessary and appropriate force' Congress has authorized the President

DID YOU KNOW?

Barack Obama

Barack Obama, the 44th president of the United States, was born in Honolulu, Hawaii, and attended Columbia University and Harvard Law School. He succeeded George W. Bush in office, and inherited the ongoing War on Terror from his predecessor. Obama changed some of the strategy pursued by the United States, but did not abandon the search for Osama bin Laden and his chief lieutenants. Obama placed a high priority upon withdrawing forces from Iraq and later Afghanistan, and placing more of the emphasis in the war upon the use of airpower and intelligence agencies. In particular, the Obama administration has relied heavily upon the use of remotely piloted aircraft, often called drones, which are armed with missiles and small bombs. These aircraft have been used for search-and-attack campaigns against key leaders, and have launched hundreds of lethal attacks against Al Qaeda operatives during the Obama presidency.

to use." 542 U.S. 507, 518 (2004). But even if the AUMF could be read to authorize the *detention* of suspected terrorists apprehended far from any zone of actual combat, it is a far more radical thing to propose that the AUMF authorizes the extrajudicial *execution* of those people. Outside of armed conflict zones, human rights law and the Constitution prescribe strict limits on the use of lethal force, limits that are narrower than those applicable in armed conflicts, and narrower than the standards governing detention. Targeted killing of suspects away from the battlefield is not a "fundamental and accepted . . . incident to war." Based on the available information, neither does your targeted killing program appear to be an exercise of "necessary and appropriate force" used only as a last resort to prevent imminent threats. The AUMF may be broad, but the authority it granted was not limitless, and it cannot now be construed to have silently overridden the limits prescribed by international law.

The program you have reportedly endorsed is not simply illegal but also unwise, because how our country responds to the threat of terrorism will in large measure determine the rules that govern *every* nation's conduct in similar contexts. If the United States claims the authority to use lethal force against suspected enemies of the U.S. anywhere in the world—using unmanned drones or other means—then other countries will regard that conduct as justified. The prospect of foreign governments hunting and killing their enemies within our borders or those of our allies is abhorrent.

The program you have endorsed also risks the deaths of innocent people. Over the last eight years, we have seen the government over and over again detain men as "terrorists," only to discover later that the evidence was weak, wrong, or non-existent. Of the many hundreds of individuals previously detained at Guantánamo, the vast majority have been released or are awaiting release. Furthermore, the government has failed to prove the lawfulness of imprisoning individual Guantánamo detainees in 34 of the 48 cases that have been reviewed by the federal courts thus far, even though the government had years to gather and analyze evidence for those cases and had itself determined that those prisoners were detainable. This experience should lead you to reject out of hand a program that would invest the CIA or the U.S. military with the unchecked authority to impose an extrajudicial death sentence on U.S. citizens and others found far from any actual battlefield.

Sincerely,

Anthony D. Romero

Executive Director

Source: Letter to President Obama Regarding Targeted Killings, April 28, 2010. Copyright (c) 2010, American Civil Liberties Union. Originally posted by the ACLU at https://www.aclu.org/letter/letter-president-obama-regarding-targeted -killings. Used by permission.

ANALYSIS

Romero expressed his concerns at a time when the United States was increasing the number of extrajudicial targeted killings as a part of the War on Terror. In 2008, Romero advised President-elect Obama to close the detention facility at

Guantanamo Bay on the first day of his presidency. Although the president issued orders to begin the process of closing the facility, it proved far more difficult than he envisioned as a candidate.

Romero's complaints about the extrajudicial killings program did little to curtail its expansion, to include the stalking and killing of American citizens. Although he raised the very real fear that the United States was creating a new era of conflict in which nations might feel entitled to attack their enemies anywhere, anytime, under the guise of combating terrorism, the United States expanded its remotely piloted airstrikes program, eventually launching these types of missions throughout East Africa, the Middle East, and Southwestern Asia.

- **Document 70: National Security Strategy of 2010**
- **When:** May 2010
- **Where:** Washington, D.C.
- **Significance:** The 2010 iteration of the National Security Strategy was the first version issued during the administration of President Barack Obama. As such, it was his first opportunity to unveil the direction of U.S. security activities in the broadest sense. Like previous versions, this document dealt with a wide variety of security threats, including the continuing conflict with Al Qaeda.

DOCUMENT

The United States is waging a global campaign against al-Qa'ida and its terrorist affiliates. To disrupt, dismantle and defeat al-Qa'ida and its affiliates, we are pursuing a strategy that protects our homeland, secures the world's most dangerous weapons and material, denies al-Qa'ida safe haven, and builds positive partnerships with Muslim communities around the world. Success requires a broad, sustained, and integrated campaign that judiciously applies every tool of American power—both military and civilian—as well as the concerted efforts of like-minded states and multilateral institutions.

We will always seek to delegitimize the use of terrorism and to isolate those who carry it out. Yet this is not a global war against a tactic—terrorism or a religion—Islam. We are at war with a specific network, al-Qa'ida, and its terrorist affiliates who support efforts to attack the United States, our allies, and partners.

Prevent Attacks on and in the Homeland: To prevent acts of terrorism on American soil, we must enlist all of our intelligence, law enforcement, and homeland security capabilities. We will continue to integrate and leverage state and major urban area fusion centers that have the capability to share classified information; establish a nationwide framework for reporting suspicious activity; and implement an integrated approach to our counterterrorism information systems to ensure that the

DID YOU KNOW?

Improvised Explosive Devices

Improvised explosive devices (IEDs) are homemade bombs, often made from stolen military ordnance, particularly artillery shells. They are often remote-detonated by a variety of means, including radio and cellular signals and hidden wires, or by a mechanical or magnetic trigger set off by the target in the same fashion as land mines. IEDs have proven devastatingly effective against coalition ground forces in Afghanistan and Iraq, causing the majority of casualties among coalition troops. IEDs have gradually become more sophisticated, including some designs created to penetrate armored vehicles through the use of shaped charges. The presence of IEDs in urban locales has forced radical changes in the method of conflict pursued by the coalition forces, and has proven a significant asymmetrical advantage for enemy units.

analysts, agents, and officers who protect us have access to all relevant intelligence throughout the government. We are improving information sharing and cooperation by linking networks to facilitate Federal, state, and local capabilities to seamlessly exchange messages and information, conduct searches, and collaborate. We are coordinating better with foreign partners to identify, track, limit access to funding, and prevent terrorist travel. Recognizing the inextricable link between domestic and transnational security, we will collaborate bilaterally, regionally, and through international institutions to promote global efforts to prevent terrorist attacks.

Strengthen Aviation Security: We know that the aviation system has been a particular target of al-Qa'ida and its affiliates. We must continue to bolster aviation security worldwide through a focus on increased information collection and sharing, stronger passenger vetting and screening measures, the development of advanced screening technologies, and cooperation with the international community to strengthen aviation security standards and efforts around the world.

Deny Terrorists Weapons of Mass Destruction: To prevent acts of terrorism with the world's most dangerous weapons, we are dramatically accelerating and intensifying efforts to secure all vulnerable nuclear materials by the end of 2013, and to prevent the spread of nuclear weapons. We will also take actions to safeguard knowledge and capabilities in the life and chemical sciences that could be vulnerable to misuse.

Deny Al-Qa'ida the Ability to Threaten the American People, Our Allies, Our Partners and Our Interests Overseas: Al-Qa'ida and its allies must not be permitted to gain or retain any capacity to plan and launch international terrorist attacks, especially against the U.S. homeland. Al Qa'ida's core in Pakistan remains the most dangerous component of the larger network, but we also face a growing threat from the group's allies worldwide. We must deny these groups the ability to conduct operational plotting from any locale, or to recruit, train, and position operatives, including those from Europe and North America.

Afghanistan and Pakistan: This is the epicenter of the violent extremism practiced by al-Qa'ida. The danger from this region will only grow if its security slides backward, the Taliban controls large swaths of Afghanistan, and al-Qa'ida is allowed to operate with impunity. To prevent future attacks on the United States, our allies, and partners, we must work with others to keep the pressure on al-Qa'ida and increase the security and capacity of our partners in this region.

In Afghanistan, we must deny al-Qa'ida a safe haven, deny the Taliban the ability to overthrow the government, and strengthen the capacity of Afghanistan's security forces and government so that they can take lead responsibility for Afghanistan's future. Within Pakistan, we are working with the government to address the local, regional, and global threat from violent extremists.

We will achieve these objectives with a strategy comprised of three components.

- First, our military and International Security Assistance Force (ISAF) partners within Afghanistan are targeting the insurgency, working to secure key population centers, and increasing efforts to train Afghan security forces. These military resources will allow us to create the conditions to transition to Afghan responsibility. In July 2011, we will begin reducing our troops responsibly, taking into account conditions on the ground. We will continue to advise and assist Afghanistan's Security Forces so that they can succeed over the long term.

- Second, we will continue to work with our partners, the United Nations, and the Afghan Government to improve accountable and effective governance. As we work to advance our strategic partnership with the Afghan Government, we are focusing assistance on supporting the President of Afghanistan and those ministries, governors, and local leaders who combat corruption and deliver for the people. Our efforts will be based upon performance, and we will measure progress. We will also target our assistance to areas that can make an immediate and enduring impact in the lives of the Afghan people, such as agriculture, while supporting the human rights of all of Afghanistan's people—women and men. This will support our long-term commitment to a relationship between our two countries that supports a strong, stable, and prosperous Afghanistan.

- Third, we will foster a relationship with Pakistan founded upon mutual interests and mutual respect. To defeat violent extremists who threaten both of our countries, we will strengthen Pakistan's capacity to target violent extremists within its borders, and continue to provide security assistance to support those efforts. To strengthen Pakistan's democracy and development, we will provide substantial assistance responsive to the needs of the Pakistani people, and sustain a long-term partnership committed to Pakistan's future. The strategic partnership that we are developing with Pakistan includes deepening cooperation in a broad range of areas, addressing both security and civilian challenges, and we will continue to expand those ties through our engagement with Pakistan in the years to come.

Deny Safe Havens and Strengthen At-Risk States: Wherever al-Qa'ida or its terrorist affiliates attempt to establish a safe haven—as they have in Yemen, Somalia, the Maghreb, and the Sahel—we will meet them with growing pressure. We also will strengthen our own network of partners to disable al-Qa'ida's financial, human, and planning networks; disrupt terrorist operations before they mature; and address potential safe-havens before al-Qa'ida and its terrorist affiliates can take root. These efforts will focus on information-sharing, law enforcement cooperation, and establishing new practices to counter evolving adversaries. We will also help states avoid becoming terrorist safe havens by helping them build their capacity for responsible governance and security through development and security sector assistance.

Deliver Swift and Sure Justice: To effectively detain, interrogate, and prosecute terrorists, we need durable legal approaches consistent with our security and our values. We adhere to several principles: we will leverage all available information and intelligence to disrupt attacks and dismantle al-Qa'ida and affiliated terrorist organizations; we will bring terrorists to justice; we will act in line with the rule of law and due process; we will submit decisions to checks and balances and accountability; and we will insist that matters of detention and secrecy are addressed in a manner consistent with our Constitution and laws. To deny violent extremists one of their most potent recruitment tools, we will close the prison at Guantanamo Bay.

Resist Fear and Overreaction: The goal of those who perpetrate terrorist attacks is in part to sow fear. If we respond with fear, we allow violent extremists to succeed far beyond the initial impact of their attacks, or attempted attacks—altering our society and enlarging the standing of al-Qa'ida and its terrorist affiliates far beyond its actual reach. Similarly, overreacting in a way that creates fissures between America and certain regions or religions will undercut our leadership and make us less safe.

Contrast Al-Qa'ida's Intent to Destroy with Our Constructive Vision: While violent extremists seek to destroy, we will make clear our intent to build. We are striving to build bridges among people of different faiths and regions. We will continue to work to resolve the Arab-Israeli conflict, which has long been a source of tension. We will continue to stand up for the universal rights of all people, even for those with whom we disagree. We are developing new partnerships in Muslim communities around the world on behalf of health, education, science, employment, and innovation. And through our broader emphasis on Muslim engagement, we will communicate our commitment to support the aspirations of all people for security and opportunity. Finally, we reject the notion that al-Qa'ida represents any religious authority. They are not religious leaders, they are killers; and neither Islam nor any other religion condones the slaughter of innocents.

Source: White House, www.whitehouse.gov/sites/default/files/rss_viewer/national_security_strategy.pdf.

ANALYSIS

When compared to the 2002 and 2006 National Security Strategies (see Documents 47 and 64), the 2010 strategy is much more defensive in nature. The Obama administration placed a greater emphasis upon hardening and protecting potential targets rather than engaging in costly interventions. The president was elected on a promise to end the wars in Iraq and Afghanistan, and believed that the best mechanism to guarantee the safety and security of American citizens was first and foremost to stop provoking new attacks. However, it was impossible for the U.S. military to immediately walk away from the ongoing conflicts, and hence a more managed drawdown and gradual withdrawal of forces proved to be the key operating concept during the first Obama administration.

- **Document 71: Brian Michael Jenkins, Testimony before the House Committee on Homeland Security**
- **When:** May 26, 2010
- **Where:** Washington, D.C.
- **Significance:** Jenkins is a RAND analyst who studies the danger presented by homegrown terrorists within the United States. In this testimony, he offered a broad overview of the threat from radicalized U.S. citizens.

DOCUMENT

A Determined, Resilient, Opportunistic and Adaptable Foe

Nearly nine years after 9/11, the principal terrorist threat still comes from a galaxy of jihadist groups that subscribe to or have been influenced by al Qaeda's ideology of a global armed struggle against the West. The complexity of the movement defies easy assessment. The ability of al Qaeda's central leadership to directly project its power through centrally planned and managed terrorist attacks has been reduced. Terrorist organizations now confront a more hostile operating environment: Al Qaeda has not been able to carry out a major terrorist attack in the West since the London bombings of 2005. For the time being, it has concentrated its resources and efforts on the conflicts in Afghanistan and Pakistan.

This should not imply that we are at a tipping point in the struggle against terrorism. Al Qaeda, its affiliates, and its allies, remain determined to continue to attack, and they have proved to be resilient, opportunistic, and adaptable, capable of morphing to meet new circumstances. Complacency on our part would be dangerous.

A More Decentralized Terrorist Campaign

To carry on its international terrorist campaign, al Qaeda now relies on its affiliates, principally in North Africa, Iraq, and the Arabian Peninsula, and on its continuous exhortation to followers to do whatever they can, wherever they are. Other terrorist groups, while concentrating on local contests, have adopted al Qaeda's vision of a global struggle and may launch their own attacks or assist volunteers seeking support.

Emphasis on Do-It-Yourself Terrorism

The United States remains al Qaeda's primary target. Some analysts believe that al Qaeda is under

---

DID YOU KNOW?

David Petraeus

General David Petraeus is the most well-known and successful U.S. military commander to emerge during the War on Terror. A graduate of West Point, he also holds a PhD from Princeton University. During his career in uniform, he commanded the Multinational Forces—Iraq; the International Stabilization Force in Afghanistan; and the U.S. Central Command, which has regional responsibility for both zones of conflict. He personally oversaw the writing of a joint army/marines counterinsurgency manual, *FM 3-24: Counterinsurgency*, which has received much credit for improving the military situation in both locations. In 2011, Petraeus retired from active duty and was named by President Barack Obama to serve as the director of the Central Intelligence Agency. In 2012, barely a year into his tenure at the head of the CIA, he was forced to resign after an extramarital affair with Paula Broadwell, his biographer, emerged into the public eye. Petraeus has continued as a consultant regarding the conflict with Al Qaeda and the Islamic State.

growing pressure to prove that it can carry out another attack on U.S. soil in order to retain its credentials as the vanguard of the jihadist movement. Such an attack could take the form of an operation planned from abroad, like the Christmas Day airline bombing attempt, or it could be do-it-yourself attempts by homegrown terrorists responding to al Qaeda's call to action. Inevitably, one or more of these attacks may succeed.

Terrorist attempts are not evidence of our failure to protect the nation from terrorism, nor should they be cause for feigned outrage and divisive finger-pointing. They provide opportunities to learn lessons and improve defenses. The attempts reflect that we are at war—although the term has been largely discarded—and as in any war, the other side attacks.

America's Homegrown Terrorists

According to a recent RAND paper, there were 46 reported cases of radicalization and recruitment to jihadist terrorism in the United States between 9/11 and the end of 2009. This number does not include attacks from abroad. In all, 125 persons were involved in the 46 cases. Two more cases and several more arrests in 2010 bring the total to 131 persons. Half of the cases involve single individuals; the remainder are tiny conspiracies. The number of cases and the number of persons involved both increased sharply in 2009. Whether this presages a trend we cannot yet say. But these cases tell us that radicalization and recruitment to jihadist terrorism do happen here. They are clear indications of terrorist intent. The threat is real.

No Deep Reservoirs of Potential Recruits

Fortunately, the number of homegrown terrorists, most of whom are Muslims, is a tiny turnout in a Muslim American community of perhaps 3 million. (By contrast, several thousand Muslim Americans serve in the U.S. armed forces.) Al Qaeda's exhortations to violence are not resonating among the vast majority of Muslim Americans. There are veins of extremism, handfuls of hotheads, but no deep reservoirs from which al Qaeda can recruit. America's would-be jihadists are not Mao's fish swimming in a friendly sea.

The cases do not indicate an immigration or border-control problem. Almost all of those arrested for terrorist-related crimes are native-born or naturalized U.S. citizens or legal permanent residents. Most of them have lived in the United States for many years. There is no evidence that they were radicalized before coming to the United States. No armies of "sleepers" have infiltrated the country.

The Criminal Justice System Works

The cases also tell us that the U.S. criminal justice system works. With the exception of Jose Padilla, who was initially held as an enemy combatant, the individuals arrested in these cases (except for those who left to join jihad fronts abroad) were brought before U.S. courts and convicted or now await trial.

About a quarter of those identified have links with jihadist groups—al Qaeda, Lashkar-e-Taiba, or the Taliban—but there is no underground network of foreign terrorist operatives, and there are no terrorist gangs in the United States like those active in the 1970s, when the level of terrorist violence was much higher than it is today.

Amateurs Are Still Dangerous

Twenty-five of the 131 terrorists identified in the United States since 9/11 received some kind of terrorist indoctrination or training. Judging by the results, it was not very good. Al Qaeda clearly has quality-control problems. The plots have been amateurish. Only two attempts succeeded in causing casualties—significantly, both were carried out by lone gunmen, a problem in the United States that transcends terrorism. But amateurs are still dangerous. There is no long mile between the terrorist wannabe and the lethal zealot.

America's jihadists may suffer from substandard zeal. Only one became a suicide bomber, although Major Nidal Hasan may not have expected to survive his murderous rampage at Fort Hood. The rest planned to escape.

Most American jihadists appear to have radicalized themselves rather than having been recruited in the traditional sense. However, itinerant proselytizing recruiters appear in some of the cases, and active recruiting does occur in prisons. Many homegrown terrorists begin their journey to violent jihad on the Internet.

Diverse Personal Motives

The process of radicalization and recruitment to jihadist terrorist violence is complex and reflects a combination of individual circumstances and ideological motivations. Personal crisis and political cause are often paired in the process.

What does the jihadist acolyte seek in terrorism? Although recruitment may involve the rhetoric of religious belief, turning to violent jihad does not seem to result from profound religious discernment. Few jihadists appear to have more than a superficial knowledge of Islam. On the other hand, radicalization and recruitment do appear to be opportunities for an ostentatious display of piety, conviction, and commitment to their beliefs, ultimately expressed in violence.

Jihadists often use the need to avenge perceived assaults on Islam—insults to the religion, atrocities inflicted upon its believers, aggression by infidels against its people and territory, anger at specific U.S. policies—to justify their actions. These certainly are jihadist recruiting themes, but volunteer terrorists also view jihad as an opportunity for adventure, a chance to gain status in a subculture that exalts violence, to overcome perceived personal humiliation and prove manliness, to demonstrate prowess, to be perceived as a warrior in an epic struggle.

For lonely hearts, joining jihad offers a camaraderie that can sweep the more malleable along to schemes they would otherwise not have contemplated. For those who feel powerless, violent action offers the secret pleasures of clandestinity and power that come with the decision to kill.

Al Qaeda's ideology also has become a vehicle for resolving personal discontents, an opportunity to start life over, to transcend personal travail and turmoil through bloody violence, to soothe a restless soul with the spiritual comfort of an absolute ideology that dismisses the *now* as a brief passage between a glorious mythical past and eternal paradise. The jihadist may see terrorism as a path to glory in every sense of that word.

The Message to Would-Be Terrorists: No Path to Glory

Dealing with domestic radicalization does not mean countering jihadist propaganda. It means applying the law. What one believes is a matter of conscience.

What one does to impose his or her beliefs on others concerns everyone. When a course of action involves the threat or use of violence, it becomes a matter of law. America's response to homegrown terrorism must, above all, be based upon the law.

The individualistic quality of radicalization and recruitment to jihadist terrorism in the United States suggests a counter-recruitment strategy that focuses on dissuading individuals from joining al Qaeda's version of jihad. This can be accomplished not through ideological or theological debate with al Qaeda's online communicators, but by deterrence through arrests, by treating terrorists and would-be terrorists as ordinary criminals, by stripping them of political pretensions.

The message to would-be terrorists should be that they can trust no one. They will fail. They will be detected and apprehended. They will be treated as ordinary criminals and will spend a long time in a prison cell. They will receive no applause. They will disgrace their families and their communities. They will be labeled fools. Their lives will be wasted. There will be no glory.

Authorities could go further and consider something like Italy's so-called "repentant program," in which convicted terrorists were offered reduced sentences in return for their cooperation. This kind of program differs from routine plea-bargaining and from efforts abroad to rehabilitate terrorists. A "repentant" program would reward those who not only provide authorities with operational intelligence, but also contribute to understanding the recruitment process itself, and who actively participate in efforts to discourage others from following the same destructive path. It would let the denunciations of al Qaeda motivator al-Awlaki come from his own acolytes.

Local Authorities Are Best Placed to Counter Recruiting

Preventing future terrorist attacks will require the active cooperation of the American Muslim community, which is the target of jihadist recruiting. It will require effective domestic intelligence collection. Both are best accomplished by local authorities.

The first line of defense against radicalization and recruitment to jihadist terrorism in the Muslim-American community *is* the Muslim-American community. America's invasion of Iraq, its support for Ethiopia's invasion of Somalia, and its current military efforts in Afghanistan and Pakistan have created some pockets of resentment, but polls indicate little support for al Qaeda's jihadist fantasies among American Muslims. Cooperation against terrorism means more than the public denunciations of al Qaeda that many non-Muslim Americans demand as proof of Muslims' patriotism, nor should tips to police be the sole metric.

Much of the defense against jihadist radicalization will be invisible—quiet discouragement, interventions by family members and friends, and when necessary, discreet assistance to the authorities. Reports indicate that this is already taking place.

Community policing can maintain the cooperation that is needed. This does not involve police in religious or political debates, which are matters for the community. It requires building and maintaining trust between the community and local authorities and understanding local communities and diasporas, their problems, and their concerns.

Community cooperation will not prevent all terrorist attempts. Respected community leaders may have limited influence over more radical elements or may have no clue about tiny conspiracies or individuals who are on an interior journey to terrorism.

Members of the community must realize that while they play an important role in discouraging terrorism, they cannot be intermediaries in criminal investigations or intelligence operations aimed at preventing terrorist attacks. American Muslims should not regard themselves or be perceived by others as targets because they are Muslims. But being Muslim brings no privileged or separate status.

Disruption of Terrorist Plots: An Undeniable Intelligence Success

Twenty-five of the reported cases of homegrown terrorism involved plots to carry out attacks in the United States. Only three—including the failed Times Square bombing attempt—got as far as implementation, an undeniable intelligence success. And no doubt, other terrorist plots have been disrupted without arrests, while the publicized success of authorities has had a deterrent effect on still other plotters.

Intelligence has improved since 9/11. Federal government agencies share more information with each other and with local police departments and fusion centers, although there are still some problems. But connecting dots is not enough, and the emphasis on information-sharing should not distract us from the difficult and delicate task of domestic intelligence collection.

Domestic Intelligence Collection Remains Haphazard

The diffuse nature of today's terrorist threat and the emphasis on do-it-yourself terrorism challenge the presumption that knowledge of terrorist plots will come first to federal authorities, who will then share this information with state and local authorities. It is just as likely—perhaps more likely—that local law enforcement could be the first to pick up the clues of future conspiracies.

Local police departments are best placed to collect domestic intelligence. Their ethnic composition reflects the local community. They know the territory. They don't rotate to a new city every three or four years. They report to local authorities. But they often lack an understanding of intelligence and require resources and training.

Despite the clear need for improved domestic intelligence, collection remains haphazard. The Joint Terrorism Task Forces are extremely effective, but they are case-oriented, and investigation differs from intelligence. The fusion centers are venues for sharing information and have diverse responsibilities, but few collect intelligence.

An Army of On-Line Jihadists but Few Terrorists

The Internet plays an important role in contemporary terrorism, as jihadists have effectively demonstrated. It allows global communications, critical to a movement determined to build an army of believers. It facilitates recruiting. It is accessible to seekers, reinforcing and channeling their anger. It creates online communities of like-minded extremists, engaging them in constant activity. It is a source of instruction. It facilitates clandestine communication.

The Internet, however, has not enabled al Qaeda, despite its high volume of sophisticated communications, to provoke a global intifada. Its websites and chat rooms outnumber its Western recruits. Its on-line exhortations to Americans have produced a very meager return—an army of on-line jihadists, but only a tiny cohort of terrorists in the real world. And while the Internet offers would-be terrorists a continuing tutorial on tactics and improvised weapons, again thus far, this has not yet significantly improved terrorist skills.

Moreover, the Internet provides insights into jihadist thinking and strategy and has proved to be a source of intelligence leading to arrests. This must be kept in perspective when considering countermeasures. These might include ways to address the issue of anonymity and facilitate investigations—and here, terrorist use of the Internet represents only one facet of a much larger problem of cyber-crime.

I have no doubt that jihadists will attempt further terrorist attacks. Some will succeed. That is war. But I also have no doubt that these attacks will not defeat this republic or destroy its values without our active complicity, as long as we do not yield to terror.

Source: "Internet Terror Recruiting and Tradecraft: How Can We Address an Evolving Tool While Protecting Free Speech," Hearing before the Subcommittee on Intelligence, Information Sharing, and Terrorism Risk Assessment, May 26, 2010. Serial No. 111-67. Washington, D.C.: Government Printing Office, 2010.

ANALYSIS

It is illustrative that Jenkins notes a significant rise in radicalization efforts and homegrown jihadism beginning in 2009. This shift was a deliberate effort on the part of Al Qaeda to conduct some form of attacks within the United States, and suggests that U.S. efforts at national security and counterterrorism had inhibited the chances of Al Qaeda operatives infiltrating and attacking. Instead, Al Qaeda recruiters began to focus upon the use of the Internet for communication with potential radicals within the United States, focusing upon the young and marginalized elements of Muslim communities in America. While this approach yielded some successes, the net effect has not been close to what Al Qaeda leadership hoped to achieve. Jenkins argues that the key to preventing homegrown terrorism is to control the narrative that surrounds such activities, and prevent the potential actors from being seen as anything but pathetic criminals bent upon destruction, far from the heroic image that many have been presented as the ideal.

- **Document 72:** *Al-Aulaqi v. Obama*
- **When:** December 7, 2010
- **Where:** Washington, D.C.
- **Significance:** The father of Anwar al-Awlaki filed a lawsuit to demand the removal of his son from the U.S. government's targeted killing list. He argued that the government did not have the right to kill American citizens without judicial review, but the suit was dismissed when the Court found that he did not have legal standing to demand such a review.

DOCUMENT

Anwar Al-Aulaqi's Access to the Courts

Plaintiff has failed to provide an adequate explanation for his son's inability to appear on his own behalf, which is fatal to plaintiff's attempt to establish "next friend" standing. In his complaint, plaintiff maintains that his son cannot bring suit on his own behalf because he is "in hiding under threat of death" and any attempt to access counsel or the courts would "expos[e] him to possible attack by Defendants." But while Anwar Al-Aulaqi may have chosen to "hide" from U.S. law enforcement authorities, there is nothing preventing him from peacefully presenting himself at the U.S. Embassy in Yemen and expressing a desire to vindicate his constitutional rights in U.S. courts. Defendants have made clear—and indeed, both international and domestic law would require—that if Anwar Al-Aulaqi were to present himself in that manner, the United States would be "prohibit[ed] [from] using lethal force or other violence against him in such circumstances."

Plaintiff argues that to accept defendants' position—that Anwar Al-Aulaqi can access the U.S. judicial system so long as he "surrenders"—"would require the Court to accept at the standing stage what is disputed on the merits," since the Court would then be acknowledging that Anwar Al-Aulaqi is, in fact, currently "a participant in an armed conflict against the United States." Not so. The Court's conclusion that Anwar Al-Aulaqi can access the U.S. judicial system by presenting himself in a peaceful manner implies no judgment as to Anwar Al-Aulaqi's status as a potential terrorist. *All* U.S. citizens may avail themselves of the U.S. judicial system if they present themselves peacefully, and *no* U.S. citizen may simultaneously avail himself of the U.S. judicial system and evade U.S. law enforcement authorities. Anwar Al-Aulaqi is thus faced with the same choice presented to all U.S. citizens.

It is certainly possible that Anwar Al-Aulaqi could be arrested—and imprisoned—if he were to come out of hiding to seek judicial relief in U.S. courts. Without expressing an opinion as to the likelihood of Anwar Al-Aulaqi's future arrest or imprisonment, it is significant to note that an individual's incarceration does not render him unable to access the courts within the meaning of *Whitmore*. Indeed, "prisoners can, and do, bring civil suits all the time." Given that an individual's actual incarceration is insufficient to show that he lacks access to the courts, the mere prospect of Anwar Al-Aulaqi's future incarceration fails to satisfy *Whitmore*'s "inaccessibility" requirement.

Plaintiff argues, however, that if his son were to seek judicial relief, he would not be detained as an ordinary federal prisoner, but instead would be subject to "indefinite detention without charge." It is true that courts have, in some instances, granted "next friend" standing to enemy combatants being held "incommunicado." For example, in *Padilla v. Rumsfeld*, 352 F.3d 695 (2d Cir. 2003), *rev'd and remanded on other grounds*, 542 U.S. 426 (2004), the Second Circuit granted an attorney "next friend" standing to file a habeas petition on behalf of an American citizen who was being detained as an enemy combatant at a U.S. naval base in South Carolina. The court in *Padilla* had little difficulty concluding that the real party in interest was unable to "access the courts" under *Whitmore*, as he had been denied "any contact with his counsel, his family or any other non-military personnel" for eighteen months. Similarly, in *Hamdi v.Rumsfeld*, 296 F.3d 278 (4th Cir. 2002), *vacated on other grounds*,

542 U.S. 507 (2004), the Fourth Circuit permitted the father of a military detainee to petition the court on his son's behalf, as the son was being "held incommunicado and subjected to an infinite detention … without access to a lawyer."

But unlike the detainees in *Padilla* and *Hamdi*, Anwar Al-Aulaqi is not in U.S. custody, nor is he being held incommunicado against his will. To the extent that Anwar Al-Aulaqi is currently incommunicado, that is the result of his own choice. Moreover, there is reason to doubt whether Anwar Al-Aulaqi is, in fact, incommunicado. Since his alleged period of hiding began in January 2010, Anwar Al-Aulaqi has communicated with the outside world on numerous occasions, participating in AQAP video interviews and publishing online articles in the AQAP magazine *Inspire*. Anwar Al-Aulaqi has continued to use his personal website to convey messages to readers worldwide, and a July 2010 online article written by Anwar Al-Aulaqi advises readers that they "may contact Shayk [Anwar] Al-Aulaqi through any of the emails listed on the contact page." Needless to say, Anwar Al-Aulaqi's access to e-mail renders the circumstances of his existing, self-made "confinement" far different than the confinement of the detainees in *Padilla* and *Hamdi*.

Even if Anwar Al-Aulaqi were to be captured and detained, the conditions of his confinement would still need to be akin to those in *Padilla* and *Hamdi* before his father could be accorded standing to proceed as Anwar Al-Aulaqi's "next friend." In cases brought by purported "next friends" on behalf of detainees at Guantanamo Bay, courts have not presumed that the detainees lack access to the U.S. judicial system, but have required the would-be "next friends" to make a *showing* of inaccessibility.

Because Anwar Al-Aulaqi has not yet been detained, it is impossible to determine whether the nature of any such hypothetical detention would be more similar to that in *Padilla* and *Hamdi*, or to the Guantanamo Bay cases in which detainees have been found capable of bringing suit on their own behalf. Regardless, the mere prospect of future detention is insufficient to warrant a finding that Anwar Al-Aulaqi currently lacks access to the courts.

Source: Al-Aulaqi v. Obama (2010). Civil Action No. 10-1469 (JDB). Available online at https://www.aclu.org/sites/default/files/field_document/2010-12-7-AulaqivObama-Decision.pdf.

ANALYSIS

This section of the Court's decision illustrates an interesting quandary for American citizens placed upon the targeted killing list. If they turn themselves over to U.S. custody, they will have access to the full court system to adjudicate their situation, but they will also be potentially placing themselves into indefinite confinement. As the Court notes, though, a target can hardly claim protection from the courts and flee from their jurisdiction at the same time. A separate section of the decision ruled that Nasser al-Awlaki, Anwar's father, could not claim "next friend" status, a legal position that would allow him to file a lawsuit on behalf of his son. Essentially, the only way that Anwar al-Awlaki could pursue judicial relief of a government intention to kill him would be to place himself under the control of that government.

- **Document 73: Statement by President Obama on the Death of Osama bin Laden**
- **When:** May 2, 2011
- **Where:** Washington, D.C.
- **Significance:** President Obama announced that U.S. Special Forces had raided a compound in Pakistan and killed Osama bin Laden in the process.

DOCUMENT

Good evening. Tonight, I can report to the American people and to the world that the United States has conducted an operation that killed Osama bin Laden, the leader of al Qaeda, and a terrorist who's responsible for the murder of thousands of innocent men, women, and children.

It was nearly 10 years ago that a bright September day was darkened by the worst attack on the American people in our history. The images of 9/11 are seared into our national memory—hijacked planes cutting through a cloudless September sky; the Twin Towers collapsing to the ground; black smoke billowing up from the Pentagon; the wreckage of Flight 93 in Shanksville, Pennsylvania, where the actions of heroic citizens saved even more heartbreak and destruction.

And yet we know that the worst images are those that were unseen to the world. The empty seat at the dinner table. Children who were forced to grow up without their mother or their father. Parents who would never know the feeling of their child's embrace. Nearly 3,000 citizens taken from us, leaving a gaping hole in our hearts.

On September 11, 2001, in our time of grief, the American people came together. We offered our neighbors a hand, and we offered the wounded our blood. We reaffirmed our ties to each other, and our love of community and country. On that day, no matter where we came from, what God we prayed to, or what race or ethnicity we were, we were united as one American family.

We were also united in our resolve to protect our nation and to bring those who committed this vicious attack to justice. We quickly learned that the 9/11 attacks were carried out by al Qaeda—an organization headed by Osama bin Laden, which had openly declared war on the United States and was committed to killing innocents in our country and around

---

DID YOU KNOW?

Zero Dark Thirty

On December 19, 2012, Sony Pictures released *Zero Dark Thirty*, a film directed by Kathryn Bigelow and distributed by Columbia Pictures. The film purported to tell the true story of the hunt for Osama bin Laden. It culminated with a recreation of the raid that killed the Al Qaeda leader, which occurred on May 2, 2011. The film depicted scenes of torturing Al Qaeda prisoners and suggested such interrogations were key to determining bin Laden's location. The movie received broad critical acclaim, five Academy Award nominations, and earned more than $130 million. In many ways, it drove the U.S. public's understanding of the hunt for and killing of bin Laden, even though the filmmakers made deliberate decisions to streamline the story and characters involved to fit the format. After the film's release, allegations surfaced that the director and her staff had been given access to classified materials to enhance the story's accuracy, although none of the filmmakers has been prosecuted for such an offense.

the globe. And so we went to war against al Qaeda to protect our citizens, our friends, and our allies.

Over the last 10 years, thanks to the tireless and heroic work of our military and our counterterrorism professionals, we've made great strides in that effort. We've disrupted terrorist attacks and strengthened our homeland defense. In Afghanistan, we removed the Taliban government, which had given bin Laden and al Qaeda safe haven and support. And around the globe, we worked with our friends and allies to capture or kill scores of al Qaeda terrorists, including several who were a part of the 9/11 plot.

Yet Osama bin Laden avoided capture and escaped across the Afghan border into Pakistan. Meanwhile, al Qaeda continued to operate from along that border and operate through its affiliates across the world.

And so shortly after taking office, I directed Leon Panetta, the director of the CIA, to make the killing or capture of bin Laden the top priority of our war against al Qaeda, even as we continued our broader efforts to disrupt, dismantle, and defeat his network.

Then, last August, after years of painstaking work by our intelligence community, I was briefed on a possible lead to bin Laden. It was far from certain, and it took many months to run this thread to ground. I met repeatedly with my national security team as we developed more information about the possibility that we had located bin Laden hiding within a compound deep inside of Pakistan. And finally, last week, I determined that we had enough intelligence to take action, and authorized an operation to get Osama bin Laden and bring him to justice.

Today, at my direction, the United States launched a targeted operation against that compound in Abbottabad, Pakistan. A small team of Americans carried out the operation with extraordinary courage and capability. No Americans were harmed. They took care to avoid civilian casualties. After a firefight, they killed Osama bin Laden and took custody of his body.

For over two decades, bin Laden has been al Qaeda's leader and symbol, and has continued to plot attacks against our country and our friends and allies. The death of bin Laden marks the most significant achievement to date in our nation's effort to defeat al Qaeda.

Yet his death does not mark the end of our effort. There's no doubt that al Qaeda will continue to pursue attacks against us. We must—and we will—remain vigilant at home and abroad.

As we do, we must also reaffirm that the United States is not—and never will be—at war with Islam. I've made clear, just as President Bush did shortly after 9/11, that our war is not against Islam. Bin Laden was not a Muslim leader; he was a mass murderer of Muslims. Indeed, al Qaeda has slaughtered scores of Muslims in many countries, including our own. So his demise should be welcomed by all who believe in peace and human dignity.

Over the years, I've repeatedly made clear that we would take action within Pakistan if we knew where bin Laden was. That is what we've done. But it's important to note that our counterterrorism cooperation with Pakistan helped lead us to bin Laden and the compound where he was hiding. Indeed, bin Laden had declared war against Pakistan as well, and ordered attacks against the Pakistani people.

Tonight, I called President Zardari, and my team has also spoken with their Pakistani counterparts. They agree that this is a good and historic day for both of our nations. And going forward, it is essential that Pakistan continue to join us in the fight against al Qaeda and its affiliates.

The American people did not choose this fight. It came to our shores, and started with the senseless slaughter of our citizens. After nearly 10 years of service, struggle, and sacrifice, we know well the costs of war. These efforts weigh on me every time I, as Commander-in-Chief, have to sign a letter to a family that has lost a loved one, or look into the eyes of a service member who's been gravely wounded.

So Americans understand the costs of war. Yet as a country, we will never tolerate our security being threatened, nor stand idly by when our people have been killed. We will be relentless in defense of our citizens and our friends and allies. We will be true to the values that make us who we are. And on nights like this one, we can say to those families who have lost loved ones to al Qaeda's terror: Justice has been done.

Tonight, we give thanks to the countless intelligence and counterterrorism professionals who've worked tirelessly to achieve this outcome. The American people do not see their work, nor know their names. But tonight, they feel the satisfaction of their work and the result of their pursuit of justice.

We give thanks for the men who carried out this operation, for they exemplify the professionalism, patriotism, and unparalleled courage of those who serve our country. And they are part of a generation that has borne the heaviest share of the burden since that September day.

Finally, let me say to the families who lost loved ones on 9/11 that we have never forgotten your loss, nor wavered in our commitment to see that we do whatever it takes to prevent another attack on our shores.

And tonight, let us think back to the sense of unity that prevailed on 9/11. I know that it has, at times, frayed. Yet today's achievement is a testament to the greatness of our country and the determination of the American people.

The cause of securing our country is not complete. But tonight, we are once again reminded that America can do whatever we set our mind to. That is the story of our history, whether it's the pursuit of prosperity for our people, or the struggle for equality for all our citizens; our commitment to stand up for our values abroad, and our sacrifices to make the world a safer place.

Let us remember that we can do these things not just because of wealth or power, but because of who we are: one nation, under God, indivisible, with liberty and justice for all.

Thank you. May God bless you. And may God bless the United States of America.

Source: Barack Obama, Remarks on the Death of Al Qaida Terrorist Organization Leader Usama bin Laden, May 1, 2011. *Public Papers of the Presidents of the United States: Barack Obama* (2011, Book 1). Washington, D.C.: Government Printing Office, 480–482.

ANALYSIS

President Obama felt the need to notify the American public on the death of Osama bin Laden as soon as it had been confirmed by the attackers, and thus made this press announcement at nearly midnight on the East Coast. While the death of Al Qaeda's leader was undoubtedly received with joy in many quarters, the fact that he was discovered hiding in Pakistan came as a surprise to many citizens. Pakistan had served as an ally in the fight against Al Qaeda, and the discovery that bin Laden had hidden in a compound in Abbottabad, less than a mile from the Pakistani National Military Academy, led many to believe that the Pakistani government was complicit in his ability to hide from coalition forces. The raid on bin Laden's compound was launched without notifying the Pakistani government, a fact that President Obama glossed over when describing the success of the raid and the reaction of both governments. In reality, the Pakistani government was furious at the incursion upon its sovereign territory, regardless of the outcome, and the implicit mistrust of the U.S. military community toward the Pakistani government. However, President Obama calculated that the risk of angering an ally in the War on Terror was outweighed by the possibility that someone in the Pakistani government might tip off bin Laden, leading him to escape once more.

* **Document 74: National Strategy for Countering Terrorism**
* **When:** July 2011
* **Where:** Washington, D.C.
* **Significance:** Although the 2010 National Security Strategy placed much less emphasis upon the threat of terrorism than previous editions, President Obama's administration released a stand-alone document to discuss the overarching strategy governing the U.S. counterterrorism efforts under his regime.

DOCUMENT

Overview of the National Strategy for Counterterrorism

This National Strategy for Counterterrorism articulates our government's approach to countering terrorism and identifies the range of tools critical to this Strategy's success. This Strategy builds on groundwork laid by previous strategies and many aspects of the United States Government's enduring approach to countering terrorism. At the same time, it outlines an approach that is more focused and specific than were previous strategies.

The United States deliberately uses the word "war" to describe our relentless campaign against al-Qa'ida. However, this Administration has made it clear that we are not at war with the tactic of terrorism or the religion of Islam. We are at war with a specific organization—al-Qa'ida.

U.S. efforts require a multidepartmental and multinational effort that goes beyond traditional intelligence, military, and law enforcement functions. We are engaged in a broad, sustained, and integrated campaign that harnesses every tool of American power—military, civilian, and the power of our values—together with the concerted efforts of allies, partners, and multilateral institutions. These efforts must also be complemented by broader capabilities, such as diplomacy, development, strategic communications, and the power of the private sector. In addition, there will continue to be many opportunities for the Executive Branch to work with Congress, consistent with our laws and our values, to further empower our counterterrorism professionals with the tools and resources necessary to maximize the effectiveness of our efforts.

> **DID YOU KNOW?**
>
> **Ayman al-Zawahiri**
>
> Ayman al-Zawahiri spent two decades as Osama bin Laden's chief deputy within Al Qaeda. He was born in 1951 in Egypt, where he became a radical opponent of the regime, joining the Muslim Brotherhood as a teenager. He helped found Islamic Jihad in 1973 while completing his medical degree, and he assumed control of the terror organization in 1984. He met bin Laden in Saudi Arabia in 1986, and helped found Al Qaeda two years later. After 20 years as one of the leading intellectuals within the group, Zawahiri assumed command after bin Laden's death in 2011.

Structure of the Strategy. This Strategy sets out our overarching goals and the steps necessary to achieve them. It also includes specific areas of focus tailored to the regions, domains, and groups that are most important to achieving the President's goal of disrupting, dismantling, and defeating al-Qa'ida and its affiliates and adherents while protecting the American people.

The *Overarching Goals* articulate the desired end states that we aim to create, understanding that success requires integrated, enduring, and adaptive efforts. Success also requires strategic patience: Although some of these end states may not be realized for many years, they will remain the focus of what the United States aims to achieve.

The *Areas of Focus* are the specific regions and al-Qa'ida-affiliated groups that the Strategy prioritizes.

The Threat We Face

The preeminent security threat to the United States continues to be from *al-Qa'ida and its affiliates and adherents.*

A decade after the September 11, 2001 terrorist attacks, the United States remains at war with al-Qa'ida. Although the United States did not seek this conflict, we remain committed, in conjunction with our partners worldwide, to disrupt, dismantle, and eventually defeat al-Qa'ida and its affiliates and adherents to ensure the security of our citizens and interests.

The death of Usama bin Laden marked the most important strategic milestone in our effort to defeat al-Qa'ida. It removed al-Qa'ida's founder and leader and most influential advocate for attacking the United States and its interests abroad. But, as the President has made clear, Usama bin Laden's demise does not mark the end of our effort. Nor does it mark the end of al-Qa'ida, which will remain focused on striking the United States and our interests abroad.

Since 2001 the United States has worked with its partners around the globe to put relentless pressure on al-Qa'ida—disrupting terrorist plots, measurably reducing the financial support available to the group, and inflicting significant leadership losses. Despite our many successes, al-Qa'ida continues to pose a direct and significant threat to the United States.

In addition to plotting and carrying out specific attacks, al-Qa'ida seeks to inspire a broader conflict against the United States and many of our allies and partners. To rally individuals and groups to its cause, al-Qa'ida preys on local grievances and propagates a self-serving historical and political account. It draws on a distorted interpretation of Islam to justify the murder of Muslim and non-Muslim innocents. Countering this ideology—which has been rejected repeatedly and unequivocally by people of all faiths around the world—is an essential element of our strategy.

Although its brutal tactics and mass murder of Muslims have undermined its appeal, al-Qa'ida has had some success in rallying individuals and other militant groups to its cause. Where its ideology does resonate, the United States faces an evolving threat from groups and individuals that accept al-Qa'ida's agenda, whether through formal alliance, loose affiliation, or mere inspiration. Affiliated movements have taken root far beyond al-Qa'ida's core leadership in Afghanistan and Pakistan, including in the Middle East, East Africa, the Maghreb and Sahel regions of northwest Africa, Central Asia, and Southeast Asia. Although each group is unique, all aspire to advance al-Qa'ida's regional and global agenda—by destabilizing the countries in which they train and operate, attacking U.S. and other Western interests in the region, and in some cases plotting to strike the U.S. Homeland.

Adherence to al-Qa'ida's ideology may not require allegiance to al-Qa'ida, the organization. Individuals who sympathize with or actively support al-Qa'ida may be inspired to violence and can pose an ongoing threat, even if they have little or no formal contact with al-Qa'ida. Global communications and connectivity place al-Qa'ida's calls for violence and instructions for carrying it out within easy reach of millions. Precisely because its leadership is under such pressure in Afghanistan and Pakistan, al-Qa'ida has increasingly sought to inspire others to commit attacks in its name. Those who in the past have attempted attacks in the United States have come from a wide range of backgrounds and origins, including U.S. citizens and individuals with varying degrees of overseas connections and affinities.

Beyond al-Qa'ida, other foreign terrorist organizations threaten U.S. national security interests. These groups seek to undermine the security and stability of allied and partner governments, foment regional conflicts, traffic in narcotics, or otherwise pursue agendas that are inimical to U.S. interests. Whether these are groups that operate globally, as Hizballah or Hamas do, or are terrorist organizations located and focused domestically, we are committed to working vigorously and aggressively to counter their efforts and activities even as we avoid conflating them and al-Qa'ida into a single enemy.

Principles That Guide Our Counterterrorism Efforts
Although the terrorist organizations that threaten us are far from monolithic, our CT efforts are guided by core principles: Adhering to U.S. Core Values; Building

Security Partnerships; Applying CT Tools and Capabilities Appropriately; and Building a Culture of Resilience

We are committed to upholding our most cherished values as a nation not just because doing so is right but also because doing so enhances our security. Adherence to those core values—respecting human rights, fostering good governance, respecting privacy and civil liberties, committing to security and transparency, and upholding the rule of law—enables us to build broad international coalitions to act against the common threat posed by our adversaries while further delegitimizing, isolating, and weakening their efforts.

The United States is dedicated to upholding the rule of law by maintaining an effective, durable legal framework for CT operations and bringing terrorists to justice. U.S. efforts with partners are central to achieving our CT goals, and we are committed to building security partnerships even as we recognize and work to improve shortfalls in our cooperation with partner nations.

Our CT efforts must also address both near and long-term considerations—taking timely action to protect the American people while ensuring that our efforts are in the long-term security interests of our country. Our approach to political change in the Middle East and North Africa illustrates that promoting representative and accountable governance is a core tenet of U.S. foreign policy and directly contributes to our CT goals.

At the same time, we recognize that no nation, no matter how powerful, can prevent every threat from coming to fruition. That is why we are focused on building a culture of resilience able to prevent, respond to, or recover fully from any potential act of terror directed at the United States.

Adhering to U.S. Core Values

The United States was founded upon a belief in a core set of values that is written into our founding documents and woven into the very fabric of our society. Where terrorists offer injustice, disorder, and destruction the United States must stand for freedom, fairness, equality, dignity, hope, and opportunity. The power and appeal of our values enables the United States to build a broad coalition to act collectively against the common threat posed by terrorists, further delegitimizing, isolating, and weakening our adversaries.

- Respect for Human Rights. Our respect for universal rights stands in stark contrast with the actions of al-Qa'ida, its affiliates and adherents, and other terrorist organizations. Contrasting a positive U.S. agenda that supports the rights of free speech, assembly, and democracy with the death and destruction offered by our terrorist adversaries helps undermine and undercut their appeal, isolating them from the very population they rely on for support. Our respect for universal rights must include living them through our own actions. Cruel and inhumane interrogation methods are not only inconsistent with U.S. values, they undermine the rule of law and are ineffective means of gaining the intelligence required to counter the threats we face. We will maximize our ability to collect intelligence from individuals in detention by relying on our most effective tool—the skill, expertise, and professionalism of our personnel.

- Encouraging Responsive Governance. Promoting representative, responsive governance is a core tenet of U.S. foreign policy and directly contributes to our CT goals. Governments that place the will of their people first and encourage peaceful change directly contradict the al-Qa'ida ideology. Governments that are responsive to the needs of their citizens diminish the discontent of their people and the associated drivers and grievances that al-Qa'ida actively attempts to exploit. Effective governance reduces the traction and space for al-Qa'ida, reducing its resonance and contributing to what it fears most—irrelevance.
- Respect for Privacy Rights, Civil Liberties, and Civil Rights. Respect for privacy rights, civil liberties, and civil rights is a critical component of our Strategy. Indeed, preservation of those rights and liberties is essential to maintain the support of the American people for our CT efforts. By ensuring that CT policies and tools are narrowly tailored and applied to achieve specific, concrete security gains, the United States will optimize its security and protect the liberties of its citizens.
- Balancing Security and Transparency. Democratic institutions function best in an environment of transparency and open discussion of national issues. Wherever and whenever possible, the United States will make information available to the American people about the threats we face and the steps being taken to mitigate those threats. A well-informed American public is a source of our strength. Information enables the public to make informed judgments about its own security, act responsibly and with resilience in the face of adversity or attack, and contribute its vigilance to the country's collective security. Yet at times, some information must be protected from disclosure—to protect personnel and our sources and methods of gathering information and to preserve our ability to counter the attack plans of terrorists.

Upholding the Rule of Law. Our commitment to the rule of law is fundamental to supporting the development of an international, regional, and local order that is capable of identifying and disrupting terrorist attacks, bringing terrorists to justice for their acts, and creating an environment in every country around the world that is inhospitable to terrorists and terrorist organizations.

Maintaining an Effective, Durable Legal Framework for CT Operations. In the immediate aftermath of the September 11, 2001 attacks, the United States Government was confronted with countering the terrorist threat in an environment of legal uncertainty in which long-established legal rules were applied to circumstances not seen before in this country. Since then we have refined and applied a legal framework that ensures all CT activities and operations are placed on a solid legal footing. Moving forward, we must ensure that this legal framework remains both effective and durable. To remain effective, this framework must provide the necessary tools to defeat U.S. adversaries and maintain the safety of the American people. To remain durable this framework must withstand legal challenge, survive scrutiny, and earn the support of Congress and the American people as well as our partners and allies. It must also maintain sufficient flexibility to adjust to the changing threat and environment.

Bringing Terrorists to Justice. The successful prosecution of terrorists will continue to play a critical role in U.S. CT efforts, enabling the United States to disrupt and deter terrorist activity; gather intelligence from those lawfully held in U.S. custody; dismantle organizations by incarcerating key members and operatives; and gain a measure of justice by prosecuting those who have plotted or participated in attacks. We will work with our foreign partners to build their willingness and capacity to bring to justice suspected terrorists who operate within their borders. When other countries are unwilling or unable to take action against terrorists within their borders who threaten the United States, they should be taken into U.S. custody and tried in U.S. civilian courts or by military commission.

Building Security Partnerships

The United States alone cannot eliminate every terrorist or terrorist organization that threatens our safety, security, or interests. Therefore, we must join with key partners and allies to share the burdens of common security.

- *Accepting Varying Degrees of Partnership.* The United States and its partners are engaged in the full range of cooperative CT activities—from intelligence sharing to joint training and operations and from countering radicalization to pursuing community resilience programs. The United States partners best with nations that share our common values, have similar democratic institutions, and bring a long history of collaboration in pursuit of our shared security. With these partners the habits of cooperation established in other security-related settings have transferred themselves relatively smoothly and efficiently to CT.

  In some cases partnerships are in place with countries with whom the United States has very little in common except for the desire to defeat al-Qa'ida and its affiliates and adherents. These partners may not share U.S. values or even our broader vision of regional and global security. Yet it is in our interest to build habits and patterns of CT cooperation with such partners, working to push them in a direction that advances CT objectives while demonstrating through our example the value of upholding human rights and responsible governance. Furthermore, these partners will ultimately be more stable and successful if they move toward these principles.

- *Leveraging Multilateral Institutions.* To counter violent extremists who work in scores of countries around the globe, the United States is drawing on the resources and strengthening the activities of multilateral institutions at the international, regional, and subregional levels. Working with and through these institutions can have multiple benefits: It increases the engagement of our partners, reduces the financial burden on the United States, and enhances the legitimacy of our CT efforts by advancing our objectives without a unilateral, U.S. label. The United States is committed to strengthening the global CT architecture in a manner that complements and reinforces the CT work of existing multilateral bodies. In doing so, we seek to avoid duplicating and diluting our own or our partners' efforts, recognizing that many of our partners have capacity limitations and cannot participate adequately across too broad a range of multilateral fora.

Source: White House, www.whitehouse.gov/sites/default/files/counterterrorism
_strategy.pdf.

ANALYSIS

As a public document, the National Strategy for Countering Terrorism obviously cannot reveal the tactical plans for the United States regarding military, law enforcement, and intelligence agency activities regarding terrorist organizations. Rather, the document is intended to explain the broad foundations of the U.S. approach to winning the War on Terror. In particular, the refusal to forego fundamental rights guaranteed by the Constitution, even in the face of a terrorist threat, is key to understanding the federal approach to counterterrorism. Furthermore, the United States offers a competing vision for the means by which different cultures and nations should interact with one another, on the grounds of mutual respect and acceptance of diversity. It is important to note the strong international partnership approach preferred by the Obama administration, which is in stark contrast to the Bush administration's position that in the War on Terror, there can be no neutral ground, and thus nations were either with or against the United States. The hard line adopted by Bush alienated many world leaders, while the Obama administration attempted to bring as many nations into the coalition against terrorism as possible.

- **Document 75: Remarks by President Obama on the Death of Anwar al-Awlaki**
- **When:** September 30, 2011
- **Where:** White House, Washington, D.C.
- **Significance:** Anwar al-Awlaki, an American citizen, had risen to be one of the key leaders of Al Qaeda in the Arabian Peninsula, the deadliest regional franchise of Al Qaeda. In this address, President Obama discussed the decision to target and kill an American citizen in the fight against Al Qaeda.

DOCUMENT

Before I begin, I want to say a few words about some important news. Earlier this morning, Anwar al-Awlaki—a leader of al Qaeda in the Arabian Peninsula—was killed in Yemen. The death of Awlaki is a major blow to al Qaeda's most active operational affiliate. Awlaki was the leader of external operations for al Qaeda in the Arabian Peninsula. In that role, he took the lead in planning and directing efforts to murder innocent Americans. He directed the failed attempt to blow up an airplane on Christmas Day in 2009. He directed the failed attempt to blow up U.S. cargo planes in 2010.

And he repeatedly called on individuals in the United States and around the globe to kill innocent men, women and children to advance a murderous agenda.

The death of al-Awlaki marks another significant milestone in the broader effort to defeat al Qaeda and its affiliates. Furthermore, this success is a tribute to our intelligence community, and to the efforts of Yemen and its security forces, who have worked closely with the United States over the course of several years.

Awlaki and his organization have been directly responsible for the deaths of many Yemeni citizens. His hateful ideology—and targeting of innocent civilians—has been rejected by the vast majority of Muslims, and people of all faiths. And he has met his demise because the government and the people of Yemen have joined the international community in a common effort against Al Qaeda.

Al Qaeda in the Arabian Peninsula remains a dangerous—though weakened—terrorist organization. And going forward, we will remain vigilant against any threats to the United States, or our allies and partners. But make no mistake: This is further proof that al Qaeda and its affiliates will find no safe haven anywhere in the world.

DID YOU KNOW?

Anwar al-Awlaki

Anwar al-Awlaki was an American-born Islamic imam and lecturer who fled the United States and joined Al Qaeda in the Arabian Peninsula. He became its spiritual leader and one of the chief spokespeople of Al Qaeda while hiding from U.S. intelligence and law enforcement agencies. He is credited with inspiring dozens of terror attacks against the United States and its allies in the War on Terror, largely through his sermons on the Internet. He was also linked to at least three of the September 11 hijackers through a mosque they frequented in Falls Church, Virginia. On September 30, 2011, an American remotely piloted aircraft fired a missile at a vehicle carrying al-Awlaki and another American, Samir Khan, killing both. Al-Awlaki's death dealt a major blow to Al Qaeda's online recruitment efforts, but it came at a cost. Many civil liberties organizations in the United States decried the strike on the grounds that the U.S. government had effectively hunted down and killed two American citizens without a trial or any form of judicial oversight.

Working with Yemen and our other allies and partners, we will be determined, we will be deliberate, we will be relentless, we will be resolute in our commitment to destroy terrorist networks that aim to kill Americans, and to build a world in which people everywhere can live in greater peace, prosperity and security.

Leon, Marty, Ash, Sandy, men and women of this department, both uniformed and civilian—we still have much to do: From bringing the rest of our troops home from Iraq this year, to transitioning to Afghan lead for their own security, from defeating al Qaeda, to our most solemn of obligations—taking care of our forces and their families, when they go to war and when they come home.

None of this will be easy, especially as our nation makes hard fiscal choices. But as Commander-in-Chief, let me say it as clearly as I can. As we go forward we will be guided by the mission we ask of our troops and the capabilities they need to succeed. We will maintain our military superiority. We will never waver in defense of our country, our citizens or our national security interests. And the United States of America—and our Armed Forces—will remain the greatest force for freedom and security that the world has ever known.

Source: White House Office of the Press Secretary, Remarks by the President at the "Change of Office" Chairman of the Joint Chiefs of Staff Ceremony, September 30, 2011. Available online at https://www.whitehouse.gov/the-press -office/2011/09/30/remarks-president-change-office-chairman-joint-chiefs-staff -ceremony.

ANALYSIS

This discussion of the death of al-Awlaki was inserted into a speech marking the promotion of Admiral Mike Mullen to Chairman of the Joint Chiefs of Staff, making Mullen the highest-ranking military officer in the nation. Coming less than five months after the raid that killed Osama bin Laden, the news that Anwar al-Awlaki had been killed was hailed as another major victory in the War on Terror. However, only two weeks later, Awlaki's teenaged son, also an American citizen by birth, was killed by an airstrike in Yemen, an attack that provoked an enormous amount of criticism of the administration for its seeming desire to kill terror suspects on any pretext. While the attack upon Anwar al-Awlaki eliminated a key enemy leader who had inspired dozens of attacks upon U.S. citizens, the lack of judicial oversight regarding his killing and, even more so, the killing of his son gave pause to many observers.

- **Document 76: Jeh Johnson, Department of Defense General Counsel, Speech to Yale Law School**
- **When:** February 22, 2012
- **Where:** New Haven, CT
- **Significance:** Jeh Johnston's speech to the Yale Law School offered remarks upon the lawful use of force, including assassinations and targeted killings, in the War on Terror.

DOCUMENT

Just before becoming President, Barack Obama told his transition team that the rule of law should be one of the cornerstones of national security in his Administration. In retrospect, I believe that President Obama made a conscious decision three years ago to bring in to his Administration a group of strong lawyers who would reflect differing points of view. And, though it has made us all work a lot harder, I believe that over the last three years the President has benefited from healthy and robust debate among the lawyers on his national security team, which has resulted in carefully delineated, pragmatic, credible and sustainable judgments on some very difficult legal issues in the counterterrorism realm—judgments that, for the most part, are being accepted within the mainstream legal community and the courts.

Tonight I want to summarize for you, in this one speech, some of the basic legal principles that form the basis for the U.S. military's counterterrorism efforts against Al Qaeda and its associated forces. These are principles with which the top national security lawyers in our Administration broadly agree. My comments are general in nature about the U.S. military's legal authority, and I do not comment on any operation in particular.

First: in the conflict against an *unconventional* enemy such as al Qaeda, we must consistently apply *conventional* legal principles. We must apply, and we have applied, the law of armed conflict, including applicable provisions of the Geneva Conventions and customary international law, core principles of distinction and proportionality, historic precedent, and traditional principles of statutory construction. Put another way, we must not make it up to suit the moment.

Against an unconventional enemy that observes no borders and does not play by the rules, we must guard against aggressive interpretations of our authorities that will discredit our efforts, provoke controversy and invite challenge. As I told the Heritage Foundation last October, over-reaching with military power can result in national security setbacks, not gains. Particularly when we attempt to extend the reach of the military on to U.S. soil, the courts resist, consistent with our core values and our American heritage—reflected, no less, in places such as the Declaration of Independence, the Federalist Papers, the Third Amendment, and in the 1878 federal criminal statute, still on the books today, which prohibits willfully using the military as a posse comitatus unless expressly authorized by Congress or the Constitution.

Second: in the conflict against al Qaeda and associated forces, the bedrock of the military's domestic legal authority continues to be the Authorization for the Use of Military Force passed by the Congress one week after 9/11. "The AUMF," as it is often called, is Congress' authorization to the President to:

use all necessary and appropriate force against those nations, organizations, or persons he determines planned, authorized, committed, or aided the terrorist attacks that occurred on September 11, 2001, or harbored such organizations or persons, in order to prevent any future acts of international terrorism against the United States by such nations, organizations or persons.

Ten years later, the AUMF remains on the books, and it is still a viable authorization today.

In the detention context, we in the Obama Administration have interpreted this authority to include: those persons who were part of, or substantially supported, Taliban or al-Qaeda forces or associated forces that are engaged in hostilities against the United States or its coalition partners.

This interpretation of our statutory authority has been adopted by the courts in the habeas cases brought by Guantanamo detainees, and in 2011 Congress joined

---

DID YOU KNOW?

The Islamic State as the JV Team?

On January 27, 2014, reporter David Remnick published "Going the Distance: On and Off the Road with Barack Obama" in *The New Yorker*. The article was based upon a series of interviews with the president, including one conducted three days earlier in the White House. In that interview, Remnick recorded the following response to an inquiry about the resurgence of terrorist organizations in Iraq and Syria:

> "The analogy we use around here sometimes, and I think is accurate, is if a jayvee team puts on Lakers uniforms that doesn't make them Kobe Bryant," Obama said, resorting to an uncharacteristically flip analogy. "I think there is a distinction between the capacity and reach of a bin Laden and a network that is actively planning major terrorist plots against the homeland versus jihadists who are engaged in various local power struggles and disputes, often sectarian."

The suggestion that the Islamic State might be considered the "junior varsity" team when compared to Al Qaeda angered many terrorism experts, who felt that the president was not taking seriously the threat presented by the emergent group. Although the White House later suggested that the remarks were taken out of context and not explicitly referring to the Islamic State, so much as generally referring to violent radical factions within Iraq, political opponents repeatedly used the remark to argue that the president did not understand the security situation in Iraq.

the Executive and Judicial branches of government in embracing this interpretation when it codified it almost word-for-word in Section 1021 of this year's National Defense Authorization Act, 10 years after enactment of the original AUMF. (A point worth noting here: contrary to some reports, neither Section 1021 nor any other detainee-related provision in this year's Defense Authorization Act creates or expands upon the authority for the military to detain a U.S. citizen.)

But, the AUMF, the statutory authorization from 2001, is not open-ended. It does not authorize military force against anyone the Executive labels a "terrorist." Rather, it encompasses only those groups or people with a link to the terrorist attacks on 9/11, or associated forces.

Nor is the concept of an "associated force" an open-ended one, as some suggest. This concept, too, has been upheld by the courts in the detention context, and it is based on the well-established concept of co-belligerency in the law of war. The concept has become more relevant over time, as al Qaeda has, over the last 10 years, become more de-centralized, and relies more on associates to carry out its terrorist aims.

An "associated force," as we interpret the phrase, has two characteristics to it: (1) an organized, armed group that has entered the fight alongside al Qaeda, and (2) is a co-belligerent with al Qaeda in hostilities against the United States or its coalition partners. In other words, the group must not only be aligned with al Qaeda. It must have also entered the fight against the United States or its coalition partners. Thus, an "associated force" is not any terrorist group in the world that merely embraces the al Qaeda ideology. More is required before we draw the legal conclusion that the group fits within the statutory authorization for the use of military force passed by the Congress in 2001.

Third: there is nothing in the wording of the 2001 AUMF or its legislative history that restricts this statutory authority to the "hot" battlefields of Afghanistan. Afghanistan was plainly the focus when the authorization was enacted in September 2001, but the AUMF authorized the use of necessary and appropriate force against the organizations and persons connected to the September 11th attacks—al Qaeda and the Taliban—without a geographic limitation.

The legal point is important because, in fact, over the last 10 years al Qaeda has not only become more decentralized, it has also, for the most part, migrated away from Afghanistan to other places where it can find safe haven.

However, this legal conclusion too has its limits. It should not be interpreted to mean that we believe we are in any "Global War on Terror," or that we can use military force whenever we want, wherever we want. International legal principles, including respect for a state's sovereignty and the laws of war, impose important limits on our ability to act unilaterally, and on the way in which we can use force in foreign territories.

Fourth: I want to spend a moment on what some people refer to as "targeted killing." Here I will largely repeat Harold's much-quoted address to the American Society of International Law in March 2010. In an armed conflict, lethal force against known, individual members of the enemy is a long-standing and long-legal practice. What is new is that, with advances in technology, we are able to target military objectives with much more precision, to the point where we can identify, target and strike a single military objective from great distances.

Should the legal assessment of targeting a single identifiable military objective be any different in 2012 than it was in 1943, when the U.S. Navy targeted and shot down over the Pacific the aircraft flying Admiral Yamamoto, the commander of the Japanese navy during World War Two, with the specific intent of killing him? Should we take a dimmer view of the legality of lethal force directed against individual members of the enemy, because modern technology makes our weapons more precise? As Harold stated two years ago, the rules that govern targeting do not turn on the type of weapon system used, and there is no prohibition under the law of war on the use of technologically advanced weapons systems in armed conflict, so long as they are employed in conformity with the law of war. Advanced technology can ensure both that the best intelligence is available for planning operations, and that civilian casualties are minimized in carrying out such operations.

On occasion, I read or hear a commentator loosely refer to lethal force against a valid military objective with the pejorative term "assassination." Like any American shaped by national events in 1963 and 1968, the term is to me one of the most repugnant in our vocabulary, and it should be rejected in this context. Under well-settled legal principles, lethal force against a valid *military* objective, in an armed conflict, is consistent with the law of war and does not, by definition, constitute an "assassination."

Fifth: as I stated at the public meeting of the ABA Standing Committee on Law and National Security, belligerents who also happen to be U.S. citizens do not enjoy immunity where non-citizen belligerents are valid military objectives. Reiterating principles from *Ex Parte Quirin* in 1942, the Supreme Court in 2004, in *Hamdi* v. *Rumsfeld*, stated that "[a] citizen, no less than an alien, can be 'part of or supporting forces hostile to the United States or coalition partners' and 'engaged in an armed conflict against the United States.'"

Sixth: contrary to the view of some, targeting decisions are not appropriate for submission to a court. In my view, they are core functions of the Executive Branch, and often require real-time decisions based on an evolving intelligence picture that only the Executive Branch may timely possess. I agree with Judge Bates of the federal district court in Washington, who ruled in 2010 that the judicial branch of government is simply not equipped to become involved in targeting decisions.

As I stated earlier in this address, within the Executive Branch the views and opinions of the lawyers on the President's national security team are debated and heavily scrutinized, and a legal review of the application of lethal force is the weightiest judgment a lawyer can make. (And, when these judgments start to become easy, it is time for me to return to private law practice.)

My legal colleagues and I who serve in government today will not surrender to the national security pressures of the moment. History shows that, under the banner of "national security," much damage can be done—to human beings, to our laws, to our credibility, and to our values. As I have said before, we must adopt legal positions that comport with common sense, and fit well within the mainstream of legal thinking in the area, consistent with who we are as Americans.

I have talked today about legally sustainable and credible ways to wage war, not to win peace. All of us recognize this should not be the normal way of things, and that the world is a better place when the United States does indeed lead by the power of an example, and not by the example of its power.

In addition to my uncle, one of my personal heroes is my former law partner Ted Sorensen, who died a little over a year ago. Ted was John F. Kennedy's speechwriter, one of his closest advisors, and himself one of the most eloquent communicators of our time.

In May 2004 Ted Sorensen gave one of the best speeches I've ever heard. It was right after the Abu Ghraib scandal broke. He said this, which I will never forget:

Last week a family friend of an accused American guard in Iraq recited the atrocities inflicted by our enemies on Americans and asked: Must we be held to a different standard? My answer is YES. Not only because others expect it. We must hold ourselves to a different standard. Not only because God demands it, but because it serves our security. Our greatest strength has long been not merely our military might but our moral authority. Our surest protection against assault from abroad has been not all our guards, gates and guns or even our two oceans, but our essential goodness as a people.

My goal here tonight was to inform and to educate. My other reason for being here is to appeal directly to the students, to ask that you think about public service in your career. Law students become trained in the law for many different reasons, with many different traits and interests. Some are naturally suited for transactions, to help structure deals. Others want to be in the courtroom, and love advocacy. There are so many facets of the law—and people who want to pursue them—that help make our profession great.

Thank you for listening.

Source: Jeh Charles Johnson, General Counsel of the Department of Defense, Dean's Lecture at Yale Law School: "National Security Law, Lawyers, and Lawyering in the Obama Administration," February 22, 2012. Full text at http://www.cfr.org/defense-and-security/jeh-johnsons-speech-national-security-law-lawyers-lawyering-obama-administration/p27448.

ANALYSIS

Johnson's speech laid out the legal challenges presented by the War on Terror. He sought to reassure the audience that the Obama administration has maintained a firm commitment to prosecuting the war against Al Qaeda in a legal fashion, while also pointing out that the authorization to use military force against the terror organization did not set geographic or technological boundaries. In addition to parsing out the differences between assassinations and the legitimate use of military force by a variety of means, Johnson also suggested some of the key limitations upon the use of military operations to combat Al Qaeda. Perhaps most tellingly, he noted that the United States was not in a "Global War on Terror," a distinction that the administration made on a number of previous occasions. However, less than four years later, the United States commenced airstrikes against the Islamic State in Iraq and the Levant, without a renewed or amended military authorization, a decision that suggested that the administration was willing to stretch the limits of the conflict with Al Qaeda to their limits.

- **Document 77: National Security Strategy 2015**
- **When:** February 2015
- **Where:** Washington, D.C.
- **Significance:** After six years in office, the security priorities of President Obama had substantially changed from the positions adopted prior to assuming the office. The 2015 National Security Strategy reflected a shift in the attitude toward international interventions. It was the first version of the strategy released after the death of Osama bin Laden, and the importance of terrorism as a national security priority was greatly reduced from the previous iteration.

DOCUMENT

The threat of catastrophic attacks against our homeland by terrorists has diminished but still persists. An array of terrorist threats has gained traction in areas of instability, limited opportunity, and broken governance. Our adversaries are not confined to a distinct country or region. Instead, they range from South Asia through the Middle East and into Africa. They include globally oriented groups like al-Qa'ida and its affiliates, as well as a growing number of regionally focused and globally connected groups—many with an al-Qa'ida pedigree like ISIL, which could pose a threat to the homeland.

We have drawn from the experience of the last decade and put in place substantial changes to our efforts to combat terrorism, while preserving and strengthening important tools that have been developed since 9/11. Specifically, we shifted away from a model of fighting costly, large-scale ground wars in Iraq and Afghanistan in which the United States—particularly our military—bore an enormous burden. Instead, we are now pursuing a more sustainable approach that prioritizes targeted counterterrorism operations, collective action with responsible partners, and increased efforts to prevent the growth of violent extremism and radicalization that drives increased threats. Our leadership will remain essential to disrupting the unprecedented flow of foreign terrorist fighters to and from conflict zones. We will work to address the underlying conditions that can help foster violent extremism such as poverty, inequality, and repression. This means supporting alternatives to extremist messaging and greater economic opportunities for women and disaffected

DID YOU KNOW?

FBI Most Wanted Terrorists

The FBI began maintaining a list of its "Most Wanted Fugitives" in 1950. In the 21st century, the FBI maintains separate lists of most wanted terrorists, criminals wanted for crimes against children, cyber criminals, and domestic terrorists. In 2016, the most wanted terrorists were:

Jehad Serwan Mostafa
Ibrahim Salih Mohammed Al-Yacoub
Mohammed Ali Hamadei
Joanne Deborah Chesimard
Abdul Rahman Yasin
Daniel Andreas San Diego
Isnilon Totoni Hapilon
Ali Saed Bin Ali El-Hoorie
Husayn Muhammad Al-Umari
Jaber A. Elbaneh
Ali Atwa
Abd Al Aziz Awda
Jamel Ahmed Mohammed Ali Al-Badawi
Raddulan Sahiron
Ayman Al-Zawahiri
Ramadan Abdullah Mohammad Shallah
Hasan Izz-Al-Din
Abdullah Ahmed Abdullah
Muhammad Ahmed Al-Munawar
Muhammad Abdullah Khalil Hussain Ar-Rahayyal
Wadoud Muhammad Hafiz Al-Turki
Liban Haji Mohamed
Ahmad Ibrahim Al-Mughassil
Ahmad Abousamra
Adnan G. El Shukrijumah
Jamal Saeed Abdul Rahim
Saif Al-Adel

Of these 27, 25 are known or suspected members of radical Islamist organizations. All are wanted in conjunction with attacks against U.S. citizens. Most of the fugitives are accompanied by a monetary reward for aid rendered in the capture or conviction of the subject. The size of the monetary awards ranges from $50,000 for Abousamra to $25 million for Zawahiri.

youth. We will help build the capacity of the most vulnerable states and communities to defeat terrorists locally. Working with the Congress, we will train and equip local partners and provide operational support to gain ground against terrorist groups. This will include efforts to better fuse and share information and technology as well as to support more inclusive and accountable governance.

In all our efforts, we aim to draw a stark contrast between what we stand for and the heinous deeds of terrorists. We reject the lie that America and its allies are at war with Islam. We will continue to act lawfully. Outside of areas of active hostilities, we endeavor to detain, interrogate, and prosecute terrorists through law enforcement. However, when there is a continuing, imminent threat, and when capture or other actions to disrupt the threat are not feasible, we will not hesitate to take decisive action. We will always do so legally, discriminately, proportionally, and bound by strict accountability and strong oversight. The United States—not our adversaries—will define the nature and scope of this struggle, lest it define us.

Our counterterrorism approach is at work with several states, including Somalia, Afghanistan and Iraq. In Afghanistan, we have ended our combat mission and transitioned to a dramatically smaller force focused on the goal of a sovereign and stable partner in Afghanistan that is not a safe haven for international terrorists. This has been made possible by the extraordinary sacrifices of our U.S. military, civilians throughout the interagency, and our international partners. They delivered justice to Osama bin Laden and significantly degraded al-Qa'ida's core leadership. They helped increase life expectancy, access to education, and opportunities for women and girls. Going forward, we will work with partners to carry out a limited counterterrorism mission against the remnants of core al-Qa'ida and maintain our support to the Afghan National Security Forces (ANSF). We are working with NATO and our other partners to train, advise, and assist the ANSF as a new government takes responsibility for the security and well-being of Afghanistan's citizens. We will continue to help improve governance that expands opportunity for all Afghans, including women and girls. We will also work with the countries of the region, including Pakistan, to mitigate the threat from terrorism and to support a viable peace and reconciliation process to end the violence in Afghanistan and improve regional stability.

We have undertaken a comprehensive effort to degrade and ultimately defeat ISIL. We will continue to support Iraq as it seeks to free itself from sectarian conflict and the scourge of extremists. Our support is tied to the government's willingness to govern effectively and inclusively and to ensure ISIL cannot sustain a safe haven on Iraqi territory. This requires professional and accountable Iraqi Security Forces that can overcome sectarian divides and protect all Iraqi citizens. It also requires international support, which is why we are leading an unprecedented international coalition to work with the Iraqi government and strengthen its military to regain sovereignty. Joined by our allies and partners, including multiple countries in the region, we employed our unique military capabilities to arrest ISIL's advance and to degrade their capabilities in both Iraq and Syria. At the same time, we are working with our partners to train and equip a moderate Syrian opposition to provide a counterweight to the terrorists and the brutality of the Assad regime. Yet, the only lasting solution to Syria's civil war remains political—an inclusive political transition that responds to the legitimate aspirations of all Syrian citizens.

Source: White House, www.whitehouse.gov/sites/default/files/docs/2015_national_security_strategy.pdf.

ANALYSIS

The 2015 National Security Strategy is concerned with far more than just expounding upon the security challenges facing the United States. It actually offers a broad vision of foreign policy and the international advantages possessed by the United States. It also noted that U.S. interests in the Middle East face a greater threat from a newly emergent group, the Islamic State in Iraq and the Levant (ISIL). Perhaps most importantly, the policy relegates terrorism to a relatively remote threat—while it notes that terrorism continues to be a thorny issue, it devotes far less space to discussing efforts to combat terrorism than it does to offering a shift in foreign policy focus from the Middle East to the Pacific Region. This shift has its roots in both economic and political factors beyond the scope of this work, but it promises to be a major adjustment in American foreign relations and military priorities.

- **Document 78: Secretary of Defense Ash Carter's Remarks to the House Armed Services Committee**
- **When:** December 1, 2015
- **Where:** Washington, D.C.
- **Significance:** Secretary of Defense Ash Carter was asked to speak to the House Armed Services Committee about the national strategy to combat the Islamic State. He offered an overview of current

activities designed to curtail the expansion of the group, and to
bring about its eventual downfall. His remarks demonstrated the
progress of the military campaign against the Islamic State, but
devoted little space to the homeland security challenge presented
by the group. The next day, two individuals who pledged allegiance
to the Islamic State attacked a community center in San Bernardino, California, in the sixth deadliest terror attack on U.S. soil.

DOCUMENT

The United States' strategy requires leveraging all the components of our nation's
might to destroy ISIL. Every instrument of national power—diplomatic, military,
law enforcement, homeland security, economic, informational—is engaged and
every national security agency is contributing to one of the strategy's nine lines of
effort. We're defending the homeland, acting to defeat ISIL in its core in Syria
and Iraq, and taking appropriate action wherever else in the world this evil organization metastasizes.

The Defense Department contributes to nearly all the lines of effort, but protecting the homeland is among our highest priorities. We're adapting to meet ISIL's
threat, including assuring the security of Defense Department installations and personnel. And, just last week, I hosted some of the top national security and law
enforcement leaders at the Pentagon to discuss efforts to cut off the flow of foreign
fighters.

We at the Defense Department, of course, are also centrally responsible for the
military campaign, which will be the focus of my statement to this Committee.
Through our own action and those of our coalition partners, the military campaign
will destroy ISIL's leadership and forces, and deprive it of resources, safe haven,
and mobility—all while we seek to identify and then enable capable, motivated
local forces on the ground to expel ISIL from its territory, hold and govern it, and
ensure that victory sticks.

That's the right strategic approach for two principal reasons. First, it emphasizes
the necessity of capable, motived local forces—as the only force that can assure a
lasting victory. Such forces are hard to find, but they do exist. And we can enable
them—and we are constantly looking for effective ways to expand doing so—but
we cannot substitute for them.

And, second, this strategic approach sets the conditions for a political solution to
the civil war in Syria and to crippling sectarianism in Iraq, which are the only
durable ways to prevent a future ISIL-like organization from re-emerging. And that's
why the diplomatic work, led by Secretary Kerry and the State Department, is the
first and most critical line of effort in our strategy.

We are gathering momentum on the battlefield in Syria and Iraq. And today,
I will describe how the U.S. is continuing to accelerate the military campaign
against ISIL, and what more we're asking of our global partners. While I cannot
describe everything in this unclassified setting, I do want to take a few extra minutes

this morning to give as much detail as possible about the new things we are doing to accelerate ISIL's defeat.

We're at war. We are using the might of the finest fighting force the world has ever known. Tens of thousands of U.S. personnel are operating in the broader Middle East region, and more are on the way. We have some of our most advanced air and naval forces attacking ISIL. U.S. troops are advising and assisting ground operations in Syria and Iraq. I will describe briefly some of these efforts and how we can accelerate them.

In northern Syria, local forces, with our support, are fighting along the Ma'ra line, engaging ISIL in the last remaining pocket of access into Turkey. Meanwhile, a coalition of Syrian Arabs that we helped equip in Northeastern Syria—with statutory authorizations and funds provided by Congress—are fighting alongside Kurdish forces and have recaptured important terrain, most recently pushing ISIL out of the town of Al Hawl and at least 900 square kilometers of surrounding territory. They are now focused on moving south to isolate ISIL's nominal capital of Raqqa, with the ultimate objective of collapsing its control over the city.

This momentum on the ground in northern Syria has been enabled by increased coalition airstrikes. In early November, we deployed additional strike aircraft to Incirlik Air Base in Turkey. Those and other

> ## DID YOU KNOW?
>
> ### The Formation of the Islamic State
>
> The leadership of the Islamic State is largely composed of former members of Al Qaeda in Iraq. In particular, it has many Baathist former members of the Iraqi Army who served under Saddam Hussein. The group has deliberately striven to provoke a civil war between Iraqi Sunnis, Iraqi Shi'a, and Kurds, a goal Al Qaeda leaders believed should be postponed until Western influence had been driven from the Middle East. When the rivalry between the two groups became intolerable, the Islamic State formally renounced its ties to Al Qaeda and proclaimed the existence of a new caliphate encompassing territory in Iraq and Syria. In 2013, the group's leader, Abu Bakr al-Baghdadi, rebranded the group ad-Dawlah al-Islamiyah fi 'l-'Iraq wa-sh-Sham (Islamic State of Iraq and the Levant). In 2014, the group formally separated from Al Qaeda and declared a new Islamic caliphate, rapidly capturing territory in Iraq and Syria. Despite attacks by a U.S.-led coalition, the group expanded its geographic control in 2015, and began to establish branches in Afghanistan, Algeria, Egypt, India, Indonesia, Libya, Mali, Nigeria, Pakistan, Saudi Arabia, Turkey, and Yemen. By 2016, the Islamic State had become the largest, best funded, and most active terror organization in the world.

aircraft in the region combined with improved intelligence allowed us, in November, to significantly increase our airstrikes against ISIL, to the highest level since the start of our operations in August 2014.

To build on that momentum, we're sending—on President Obama's orders and the Chairman's and my advice—Special Operations forces personnel to Syria to support the fight against ISIL. American special operators bring a unique suite of capabilities that make them force multipliers: they will help us garner valuable ground intelligence, further enhance our air campaign, and enable local forces that can regain and then hold territory occupied by ISIL. Where we find further opportunity to leverage such capability, we will be prepared to expand it.

Next, in the south of Syria, we are also taking advantage of opportunities to open a southern front on ISIL, by enabling fighters, trained and equipped by us and other Coalition partners, to conduct strikes inside Syria. We are also enhancing the border control and defenses of a key ally, Jordan, with additional military assets and planning assistance.

In northern Iraq, Pershmerga units, with the help of U.S. air power and advisers, have retaken the town of Sinjar, cutting the main line of communication between Raqqa and Mosul, the two largest cities under ISIL's control. To move people and supplies, ISIL now must rely on backroads, where we will locate and destroy them.

Elsewhere in Iraq, we have about 3,500 troops at six locations in Iraq in support of Iraqi Security Forces, or ISF. There, we've been providing increased lethal fire and augmenting the existing training, advising, and assisting program. And we're prepared to do more as Iraq shows capability and motivation in the counter-ISIL fight and in resolving its political divisions.

The progress in the Sunni portions of Iraq—as the campaign to recapture Ramadi shows—has been slow, much to our and Prime Minister Abadi's frustration. Despite his efforts, sectarian politics and Iranian influence have made building a multi-sectarian ISF difficult, with some notable exceptions, such as the effective U.S.-trained counter-terrorism forces. We continue to offer additional U.S. support of all kinds and urge Baghdad to enroll, train, arm, and pay Sunni Arab fighters, as well as local Sunni Arab police forces, to hold territory recaptured from ISIL.

All these efforts—from northern Syria through Iraq—have shrunk the ISIL-controlled territory in both. Importantly, we now have an opportunity to divide ISIL's presence in Iraq from that in Syria. This could be important because, while both countries are plagued by ISIL, each, as I said earlier, has different political pathologies that provide the opportunity for extremism, and they ultimately require different kinds of political progress to assure lasting victory.

Next, in full coordination with the Government of Iraq, we're deploying a specialized expeditionary targeting force to assist Iraqi and Kurdish Peshmerga forces and to put even more pressure on ISIL. These special operators will over time be able to conduct raids, free hostages, gather intelligence, and capture ISIL leaders. That creates a virtuous cycle of better intelligence, which generates more targets, more raids, and more momentum. The raids in Iraq will be done at the invitation of the Iraqi government and focused on defending its borders and building the ISF's own capacity. This force will also be in a position to conduct unilateral operations into Syria.

Next, we are also significantly expanding U.S. attacks on ISIL's infrastructure and sources of revenue, particularly its oil revenue. Over the past several weeks, because of improved intelligence and understanding of ISIL's operations, we've intensified the air campaign against ISIL's war-sustaining oil enterprise, a critical pillar of ISIL's financial infrastructure. In addition to destroying fixed facilities like wells and processing facilities, we've destroyed nearly 400 of ISIL's oil tanker trucks, reducing a major source of its daily revenues. There's more to come too.

And we're improving our capability to eliminate ISIL's leadership, by conducting raids using the expeditionary targeting force I discussed a moment ago and targeted airstrikes. Since I last appeared before this committee in June, we have removed some key ISIL figures from the battlefield—Hajji Mutaz, ISIL's second in command; Junaid Hussein, a key external operative actively plotting against our servicemembers; Mohammed Emwazi, a.k.a "Jihadi John," an ISIL executioner; and Abu Nabil, ISIL's leader in Libya. Like previous actions, these strikes serve notice to ISIL that no target is beyond our reach.

Finally, even as we work to defeat ISIL in Syria and Iraq, where its parent tumor has grown, we also recognize ISIL has metastasized elsewhere. The threat posed by ISIL, and groups like it, can span regions and our own combatant commands. That's why the Defense Department is organizing a new way to leverage infrastructure we've already established in Afghanistan, the Levant, East Africa, and Southern Europe into a unified capability to counter transnational and transregional threats like ISIL.

An example of this network in action was our recent strike on Abu Nabil, where assets from several locations converged to successfully kill this ISIL leader in Libya.

As that strike shows, there's a lot of potential here, but to do more, we need to be creative, and consider changes to how the Defense Department works and is structured. This could be an important focus of any new Goldwater-Nichols-type reforms, which I know this committee, and particularly Chairman Thornberry, is exploring. I welcome this timely review and look forward to working with you on it, as we complete our own ongoing reform initiatives in the Department.

Source: House Armed Services Committee, available at http://docs.house.gov/ meetings/AS/AS00/20151201/104236/HHRG-114-AS00-Wstate-Carter A-20151201.pdf.

ANALYSIS

Carter's overview provided a clear explanation of current military activities led by the United States in Iraq and Syria, targeting the Islamic State. Although Carter acknowledged the importance of other instruments of military power in combating the organization, as the secretary of defense, it is only natural that his focus would remain upon military operations. Critics of the military response to the Islamic State came from both ends of the political spectrum. Some argued that the United States was not taking the threat of the Islamic State seriously, and that airstrikes and a small contingent of ground forces would not be enough to check the progress of the nascent caliphate. Others claimed that Congress had not authorized military action against the Islamic State, and that the president was attempting to use the authorization for the use of military force against Al Qaeda as justification to attack any radical group in the Middle East. Although the Islamic State had very publicly executed American hostages, for most U.S. citizens, the group did not represent a threat in the same fashion as Al Qaeda. While the group had perpetrated horrific attacks in other countries, it had achieved little success on American soil. However, the day after Carter's testimony, two Islamic State adherents conducted a mass shooting in San Bernardino, California, an action that drove home the very real threat presented by the Islamic State, even within the United States.

- **Document 79: President Obama's Address to the Nation on U.S. Counterterrorism Strategy**
- **When:** December 6, 2015
- **Where:** Washington, D.C.

- **Significance:** Four days before these remarks, two radicalized individuals entered a community center in San Bernardino, California, and opened fire upon a meeting with semi-automatic weapons. They killed 14 civilians and wounded more than a dozen. Hours later, the suspects were killed in a firefight with local law enforcement. As the investigation unfolded, the president chose to offer remarks on the incident in a national address.

DOCUMENT

Good evening. On Wednesday, 14 Americans were killed as they came together to celebrate the holidays. They were taken from family and friends who loved them deeply. They were White and Black, Latino and Asian, immigrants and American-born, moms and dads, daughters and sons. Each of them served their fellow citizens, and all of them were part of our American family.

Tonight I want to talk with you about this tragedy, the broader threat of terrorism, and how we can keep our country safe.

The FBI is still gathering the facts about what happened in San Bernardino, but here is what we know. The victims were brutally murdered and injured by one of their coworkers and his wife. So far, we have no evidence that the killers were directed by a terrorist organization overseas or that they were part of a broader conspiracy here at home. But it is clear that the two of them have—had gone down the dark path of radicalization, embracing a perverted interpretation of Islam that calls for war against America and the West. They had stockpiled assault weapons, ammunition, and pipe bombs. So this was an act of terrorism, designed to kill innocent people.

Our Nation has been at war with terrorists since Al Qaida killed nearly 3,000 Americans on 9/11. In the process, we've hardened our defenses, from airports to financial centers to other critical infrastructure. Intelligence and law enforcement agencies have disrupted countless plots here and overseas and worked around the clock to keep us safe. Our military and counterterrorism professionals have relentlessly pursued terrorist networks overseas, disrupting safe havens in several different countries, killing Usama bin Laden, and decimating Al Qaida's leadership.

Over the last few years, however, the terrorist threat has evolved into a new phase. As we've become better at preventing complex, multifaceted attacks like 9/11, terrorists turned to less complicated acts of violence like the mass shootings that are all too common in our society. It is this type of attack that we saw at Fort Hood in 2009, in Chattanooga earlier this year, and now in San Bernardino. And as groups like ISIL grew stronger amidst the chaos of war in Iraq and then Syria, and as the Internet erases the distance between countries, we see growing efforts by terrorists to poison the minds of people like the Boston Marathon bombers and the San Bernardino killers.

For 7 years, I have confronted this evolving threat each morning in my intelligence briefing. And since the day I took this office, I've authorized U.S. forces to take out terrorists abroad precisely because I know how real the danger is. As Commander in Chief, I have no greater responsibility than the security of the American people. As a father to two young daughters who are the most precious part of my life, I know that we see ourselves with friends and coworkers at a holiday party like the one in San Bernardino. I know we see our kids in the faces of the young people killed in Paris. And I know that after so much war, many Americans are asking whether we are confronted by a cancer that has no immediate cure.

Well, here's what I want you to know: The threat from terrorism is real, but we will overcome it. We will destroy ISIL and any other organization that tries to harm us. Our success won't depend on tough talk or abandoning our values or giving into fear. That's what groups like ISIL are hoping for. Instead, we will prevail by being strong and smart, resilient and relentless, and by drawing upon every aspect of American power.

Here's how. First, our military will continue to hunt down terrorist plotters in any country where it is necessary. In Iraq and Syria, airstrikes are taking out ISIL leaders, heavy weapons, oil tankers, infrastructure. And since the attacks in Paris, our closest allies—including France, Germany, and the United Kingdom—have ramped up their contributions to our military campaign, which will help us accelerate our effort to destroy ISIL.

Second, we will continue to provide training and equipment to tens of thousands of Iraqi and Syrian forces fighting ISIL on the ground so that we take away their safe havens. In both countries, we're deploying special operations forces who can accelerate that offensive. We've stepped up this effort since the attacks in Paris, and we'll continue to invest more in approaches that are working on the ground.

Third, we're working with friends and allies to stop ISIL's operations: to disrupt plots, cut off their financing, and prevent them from recruiting more fighters. Since the attacks in Paris, we've surged intelligence sharing with our European allies. We're working with Turkey to seal its border with Syria. And we are cooperating with Muslim-majority countries—and with our Muslim communities here at home—to counter the vicious ideology that ISIL promotes online.

Fourth, with American leadership, the international community has begin—begun to establish a process—and timeline—to pursue ceasefires and a political resolution to the Syrian war. Doing so will allow the Syrian people and every country, including our allies, but also countries like Russia, to focus on the common goal of destroying ISIL, a group that threatens us all.

This is our strategy to destroy ISIL. It is designed and supported by our military commanders and counterterrorism experts, together with 65 countries that have joined an American-led coalition. And we constantly examine our strategy to determine when additional steps are needed to get the job done. That's why I've ordered the Departments of State and Homeland Security to review the visa waiver program [visa program; White House correction] under which the female terrorist in San Bernardino originally came to this country. And that's why I will urge high-tech and law enforcement leaders to make it harder for terrorists to use technology to escape from justice.

Finally, if Congress believes, as I do, that we are at war with ISIL, it should go ahead and vote to authorize the continued use of military force against these terrorists. For over a year, I have ordered our military to take thousands of airstrikes against ISIL targets. I think it's time for Congress to vote to demonstrate that the American people are united and committed to this fight.

My fellow Americans, these are the steps that we can take together to defeat the terrorist threat. Let me now say a word about what we should not do. We should not be drawn once more into a long and costly ground war in Iraq or Syria. That's what groups like ISIL want. They know they can't defeat us on the battlefield. ISIL fighters were part of the insurgency that we faced in Iraq. But they also know that if we occupy foreign lands, they can maintain insurgencies for years, killing thousands of our troops, draining our resources, and using our presence to draw new recruits.

The strategy that we are using now—airstrikes, special forces, and working with local forces who are fighting to regain control of their own country—that is how we'll achieve a more sustainable victory. And it won't require us sending a new generation of Americans overseas to fight and die for another decade on foreign soil.

Here's what else we cannot do. We cannot turn against one another by letting this fight be defined as a war between America and Islam. That too is what groups like ISIL want. ISIL does not speak for Islam. They are thugs and killers, part of a cult of death, and they account for a tiny fraction of more than a billion Muslims around the world, including millions of patriotic Muslim Americans who reject their hateful ideology. Moreover, the vast majority of terrorist victims around the world are Muslim. If we're to succeed in defeating terrorism, we must enlist Muslim communities as some of our strongest allies, rather than push them away through suspicion and hate.

That does not mean denying the fact that an extremist ideology has spread within some Muslim communities. This is a real problem that Muslims must confront, without excuse. Muslim leaders here and around the globe have to continue working with us: to decisively and unequivocally reject the hateful ideology that groups like ISIL and Al Qaida promote; to speak out against not just acts of violence, but also those interpretations of Islam that are incompatible with the values of religious tolerance, mutual respect, and human dignity.

But just as it is the responsibility of Muslims around the world to root out misguided ideas that lead to radicalization, it is the responsibility of all Americans, of every faith, to reject discrimination. It is our responsibility to reject religious tests on who we admit into this country. It's our responsibility to reject proposals that Muslim Americans should somehow be treated differently. Because when we travel down that road, we lose. That kind of divisiveness, that betrayal of our values, plays into the hands of groups like ISIL. Muslim Americans are our friends and our neighbors, our coworkers, our sports heroes. And yes, they are our men and women in uniform who are willing to die in defense of our country. We have to remember that.

My fellow Americans, I am confident we will succeed in this mission because we are on the right side of history. We were founded upon a belief in human dignity, that no matter who you are or where you come from or what you look like or what religion you practice, you are equal in the eyes of God and equal in the eyes of the law. Even in this political season, even as we properly debate what steps I and future Presidents must take to keep our country safe, let's make sure we never forget what makes us exceptional. Let's not forget that freedom is more powerful than fear; that we have always met challenges—whether war or depression, natural disasters or terrorist attacks—by coming together around our common ideals as one Nation and one people. So long as we stay true to that tradition, I have no doubt America will prevail.

Thank you. God bless you, and may God bless the United States of America.

Source: Weekly Compilation of Presidential Documents, 2015, no. 0874. Available at https://www.gpo.gov/fdsys/browse/collection.action?collectionCode=CPD.

ANALYSIS

The San Bernardino attacks resulted in one of the deadliest terror attacks in U.S. history. The perpetrators, Syed Rizwan Farook and Tashfeen Malik, were soon proven to be radical Islamists who had pledged their support to the Islamic State. Malik, who had entered the United States on a fiancé visa, appeared to be the first of the pair to be radicalized, marking one of the rare known occurrences of a wife radicalizing her husband. The couple left behind a two-year old child, an action that also does not fit the normal profile of lone-wolf attackers.

President Obama took pains to remind the nation that the vast majority of Muslims do not agree with the aims of the Islamic State, but in a nod to the political realities, he did acknowledge the dangers associated with radicalization efforts being conducted by violent extremists. Building off of the ramifications of a single attack, the president called for Congress to renew and expand the authorization to use military force to explicitly allow military attacks against the Islamic State.

- **Document 80: President Obama, State of the Union Address**
- **When:** January 12, 2016
- **Where:** Washington, D.C.
- **Significance:** This was President Obama's last opportunity to deliver a State of the Union address, and many expected him to make a significant attempt to cement his legacy with his remarks. With only a year remaining in his presidency, and a very contentious primary election season under way, the president outlined a series of very broad proposals that might be commenced during his administration, but which would require many years to reach fruition. While much of the speech was dedicated to domestic affairs, a segment of his remarks discussed his vision for the ongoing struggle with violent extremism.

DOCUMENT

Let me tell you something: The United States of America is the most powerful nation on Earth. Period. Period. It's not even close. It's not even close. It's not even close. We spend more on our military than the next eight nations combined. Our troops are the finest fighting force in the history of the world. All right. No nation attacks us directly, or our allies, because they know that's the path to ruin. Surveys show our standing around the world is higher than when I was elected to this office, and when it comes to every important international issue, people of the world do not look to Beijing or Moscow to lead. They call us. So I think it's useful to level set here, because when we don't, we don't make good decisions.

Now, as someone who begins every day with an intelligence briefing, I know this is a dangerous time. But that's not primarily because of some looming superpower out there, and it's certainly not because of diminished American strength. In today's world, we're threatened less by evil empires and more by failing states.

The Middle East is going through a transformation that will play out for a generation, rooted in conflicts that date back millennia. Economic headwinds are blowing in from a Chinese economy that is in significant transition. Even as their economy severely contracts, Russia is pouring resources in to prop up Ukraine and Syria, client states that they saw slipping away from their orbit. And the international system we built after World War II is now struggling to keep pace with this new reality. It's up to us, the United States of America, to help remake that system. And to do that well, it means that we've got to set priorities. Priority number one is protecting the American people and going after terrorist networks. Both Al Qaida and now ISIL pose a direct threat to our people, because in today's world, even a handful of terrorists who place no value on human life, including their own, can do a lot of damage. They use the Internet to poison the minds of individuals inside our country. Their actions undermine and destabilize our allies. We have to take them out.

DID YOU KNOW?

Operation Inherent Resolve

On June 15, 2014, a U.S.-led coalition commenced Operation Inherent Resolve, a military campaign against the Islamic State in Iraq and the Levant (ISIL). Consisting primarily of airstrikes by Western air forces coupled with ground advances by regional armies, the campaign seeks to roll back ISIL conquests in Iraq and Syria, and ultimately to destroy the conventional fighting capabilities of the terror organization. In the first 18 months of operations, the United States and its coalition partners launched over 10,000 airstrikes against the terror group.

But as we focus on destroying ISIL, over-the-top claims that this is world war III just play into their hands. Masses of fighters on the back of pickup trucks, twisted souls plotting in apartments or garages, they pose an enormous danger to civilians; they have to be stopped. But they do not threaten our national existence. That is the story ISIL wants to tell. That's the kind of propaganda they use to recruit. We don't need to build them up to show that we're serious, and we sure don't need to push away vital allies in this fight by echoing the lie that ISIL is somehow representative of one of the world's largest religions. We just need to call them what they are: killers and fanatics who have to be rooted out, hunted down, and destroyed.

And that's exactly what we're doing. For more than a year, America has led a coalition of more than 60 countries to cut off ISIL's financing, disrupt their plots, stop the flow of terrorist fighters, and stamp out their vicious ideology. With nearly 10,000 airstrikes, we're taking out their leadership, their oil, their training camps, their weapons. We're training, arming, and supporting forces who are steadily reclaiming territory in Iraq and Syria.

If this Congress is serious about winning this war and wants to send a message to our troops and the world, authorize the use of military force against ISIL. Take a vote. Take a vote. But the American people should know that with or without congressional action, ISIL will learn the same lessons as terrorists before them. If you doubt America's commitment—or mine—to see that justice is done, just ask Usama bin Laden. Ask the leader of Al Qaida in Yemen, who was taken out last year, or the perpetrator of the Benghazi attacks, who sits in a prison cell. When you come after Americans, we go after you. And it may take time, but we have long memories, and our reach has no limits.

Our foreign policy has to be focused on the threat from ISIL and Al Qaida, but it can't stop there. For even without ISIL, even without Al Qaida, instability will continue for decades in many parts of the world: in the Middle East, in Afghanistan and parts of Pakistan, in parts of Central America, in Africa and Asia. Some of these places may become safe havens for new terrorist networks. Others will just fall victim to ethnic conflict or famine, feeding the next wave of refugees. The world will look to us to help solve these problems, and our answer needs to be more than tough talk or calls to carpet-bomb civilians. That may work as a TV sound bite, but it doesn't pass muster on the world stage.

We also can't try to take over and rebuild every country that falls into crisis, even if it's done with the best of intentions. That's not leadership; that's a recipe for quagmire, spilling American blood and treasure that ultimately will weaken us. It's the lesson of Vietnam; it's the lesson of Iraq. And we should have learned it by now.

Now, fortunately there is a smarter approach: a patient and disciplined strategy that uses every element of our national power. It says America will always act, alone if necessary, to protect our people and our allies, but on issues of global concern, we will mobilize the world to work with us and make sure other countries pull their own weight. That's our approach to conflicts like Syria, where we're partnering with local forces and leading international efforts to help that broken society pursue a lasting peace. That's why we built a global coalition, with sanctions and principled diplomacy, to prevent a nuclear-armed Iran. And as we speak, Iran has rolled back its nuclear program, shipped out its uranium stockpile, and the world has avoided another war.

The point is, American leadership in the 21st century is not a choice between ignoring the rest of the world—except when we kill terrorists—or occupying and rebuilding whatever society is unraveling. Leadership means a wise application of military power and rallying the world behind causes that are right. It means seeing our foreign assistance as a part of our national security, not something separate, not charity.

Source: *Weekly Compilation of Presidential Documents*, 2016, no. 0012. Available at https://www.gpo.gov/fdsys/browse/collection.action?collectionCode=CPD.

ANALYSIS

With this speech, the president worked not only to define his own legacy, but also to shape the national strategy and public perceptions regarding the Islamic State. The strategy walks a fine line, in that the president wants to destroy the Islamic State, but do so at minimal risk to American service personnel. Thus, the focus remains upon airstrikes in support of local forces, and a refusal to commit large numbers of ground troops to the fight. Given that the Islamic State possesses no significant air defenses, this strategy minimizes the likelihood of U.S. casualties. However, it also makes it difficult to ascertain the level of progress against the enemy, and minimizes the ability to influence the civilian population within the area dominated by the Islamic State. While the president's call not to attempt to fix every failed state pleased many isolationists, the policy of engaging in the use of military force against terror organizations that are not allied with Al Qaeda, and hence not necessarily a part of the 2001 authorization to use military force, suggests that the president has run out of other mechanisms to influence the turmoil in the Middle East.

CHRONOLOGY OF MODERN TERRORISM AND U.S. RESPONSE

May 1, 1961	Antuilo Ramierez Ortiz hijacks a National Airlines plane and demands transportation to Cuba. It is the first U.S. aircraft hijacking.
October 25, 1978	President Jimmy Carter signs the Foreign Intelligence Surveillance Act, designed to facilitate investigations of foreign citizens suspected of espionage or terrorism.
December 26, 1979	Soviet forces enter Afghanistan in support of a puppet regime, triggering a decade-long war against the mujahideen.
October 23, 1983	Hezbollah operatives detonate truck bombs at American and French compounds in Beirut, killing 242 U.S. troops and 58 French troops.
August 11, 1988	Osama bin Laden and Abdullah Azzam found Al Qaeda.
December 21, 1988	Pan Am Flight 103 is destroyed over Lockerbie, Scotland, when a bomb detonates aboard the airplane. A total of 270 people are killed, including 11 hit by falling wreckage. Libyan intelligence agents are later blamed for the attack.
February 15, 1989	Soviet forces complete their withdrawal from Afghanistan.
August 2, 1990	Iraqi forces invade Kuwait and threaten attacks upon Saudi Arabia.
February 26, 1993	A truck bomb detonates in the World Trade Center, killing 6 and wounding more than 1,000. Ramzi Ahmed Yousef is later proven to be the organizer of the attack.
March 20, 1995	Aum Shinrikyo members release Sarin nerve gas on the Tokyo subway system during rush hour. Twelve commuters are killed, and more than 5,000 are incapacitated.
April 19, 1995	Timothy McVeigh detonates a truck bomb outside the Alfred P. Murrah Building in Oklahoma City, killing 169.

June 25, 1996	A truck bomb detonates outside of Khobar Towers, a U.S. military housing facility in Dharan, Saudi Arabia, killing 19 U.S. personnel and wounding more than 500.
August 23, 1996	Osama bin Laden formally declares war upon the United States and demands the evacuation of all Western troops from Saudi Arabia.
August 7, 1998	Bombs explode outside the U.S. embassies in Nairobi, Kenya, and Dar es Salaam, Tanzania. Twelve U.S. citizens and nearly 300 foreign citizens are killed, and more than 5,000 are wounded.
August 20, 1998	In retaliation for the bombings of U.S. embassies in Kenya and Tanzania, Tomahawk cruise missiles strike Al Qaeda camps in Afghanistan and Sudan.
June 7, 1999	The Federal Bureau of Investigation places Al Qaeda leader Osama bin Laden on the "Ten Most Wanted" list.
October 12, 2000	The USS Cole is attacked by an explosives-laden boat, killing 17 sailors and injuring 39.
January 25, 2001	President William Clinton's outbound counterterrorism adviser, Richard Clarke, warns incoming National Security Advisor Condoleezza Rice about the dangers presented by Al Qaeda.
May 30, 2001	Federal Aviation Administration security manager Michael Canavan implores airlines to pay greater attention to security measures.
August 6, 2001	Central Intelligence Agency analysts deliver a briefing to President George W. Bush, warning of an imminent Al Qaeda attack upon the United States.
September 11, 2001	Nineteen Al Qaeda operatives simultaneously hijack four aircraft. Two are deliberately flown into the World Trade Center in New York City, one is flown into the Pentagon in Washington, D.C., and one crashes in a field in Pennsylvania. A total of 2,996 are killed in the attacks; thousands more are wounded.
September 18, 2001	The U.S. Congress formally passes the Authorization for the Use of Military Force, allowing President Bush to use the military and intelligence assets of the nation to hunt down the perpetrators of the September 11 attacks.
September 20, 2001	President George W. Bush addresses a joint session of Congress and vows revenge upon al Qaeda for the September 11 attacks.
September 28, 2001	Hezbollah commander Sayyed Hassan Nasrallah blames the September 11 attacks upon a joint U.S.–Israeli plot to justify an invasion of the Middle East.

September 28, 2001	The UN General Assembly passes a resolution calling upon all member states to freeze the assets of Al Qaeda and affiliated groups.
September–October 2001	An unknown perpetrator mails envelopes laced with anthrax spores to five media outlets and two U.S. senators, prompting several building closures and causing five deaths.
October 7, 2001	The United States commences airstrikes against Taliban and Al Qaeda targets in Afghanistan.
October 26, 2001	President George W. Bush signs the USA PATRIOT Act into law.
November 10, 2001	President George W. Bush addresses the UN General Assembly and calls upon member nations for support in the war against Al Qaeda.
December 22, 2001	Richard Reid attempts to detonate explosives hidden in his shoes while aboard American Airlines Flight 63.
January 9, 2002	John Yoo provides the Bush administration rationale for detaining captured enemies at Guantanamo Bay but not providing them with prisoner-of-war status under the Geneva Convention.
March 21, 2002	Secretary of Defense Donald Rumsfeld institutes a military tribunal system to put Al Qaeda members on trial for terrorism activities.
October 12, 2002	Suicide bombers outside a nightclub in Bali, Indonesia, kill more than 200, including 7 Americans.
November 15, 2002	The National Commission on Terrorist Attacks upon the United States, also called the 9/11 Commission, is chartered and tasked with investigating the 9/11 attacks.
November 2002	Osama bin Laden releases a letter to the American people explaining Al Qaeda's grievances and explaining how to end terror attacks against the U.S. homeland.
March 20, 2003	A U.S.-led coalition commences an invasion of Iraq, ostensibly to disarm the Iraqi government of weapons of mass destruction and eliminate its support of terror organizations.
April 16, 2003	Secretary of Defense Donald Rumsfeld authorizes specific "enhanced interrogation techniques" for use at Guantanamo Bay.
March 11, 2004	Ten bombs detonate aboard Madrid commuter trains, killing nearly 200. The attacks occur 30 months after 9/11.
March 24, 2004	Former presidential counterterrorism adviser Richard Clarke testifies before the 9/11 Commission and apologizes to the nation for failing to detect and prevent the September 11 attacks.

June 28, 2004	The U.S. Supreme Court issues decisions in *Rasul v. Bush* and *Hamdan v. Rumsfeld*.
July 22, 2004	The 9/11 Commission releases its final report.
July 7, 2005	Four suicide bombers attack subway trains in London, killing more than 50.
June 7, 2006	An airstrike kills Abu Musab al-Zarqawi, commander of Al Qaeda in Iraq.
February 10, 2007	General David Petraeus is named commander of Multi-National Force—Iraq, and begins implementing a major troop surge in the hope of providing stability.
March 10, 2007	Khalid Sheikh Mohammed formally confesses to planning the 9/11 attacks, in addition to a host of other Al Qaeda operations, during a Combatant Status Review tribunal hearing at Guantanamo Bay, Cuba.
November 5, 2009	Major Nidal Malik Hasan, an army psychiatrist, opens fire at a military facility in Fort Hood, Texas, killing 13 and wounding 30.
December 25, 2009	Umar Farouk Abdulmutallab attempts to detonate a bomb about an international flight. He had smuggled the explosives onto the airplane by concealing them in his underwear.
April 28, 2010	Anthony Romero, president of the American Civil Liberties Union, writes an open letter to President Barack Obama calling for an end to extrajudicial targeted killings.
May 1, 2010	Faisal Shahzad attempts to detonate a car bomb in Times Square.
September 23, 2010	Iranian president Mahmoud Ahmadinejad delivers a speech before the UN General Assembly in which he blames the 9/11 attacks upon a U.S. government plot. A general walkout ensues.
May 2, 2011	U.S. Navy SEALs attack a compound in Abbottabad, Pakistan, and kill Osama bin Laden.
June 16, 2011	Al Qaeda's website formally announces the succession of Ayman al-Zawahiri to command the organization.
September 30, 2011	American-born Al Qaeda spokesperson Anwar al-Awlaki is killed by a missile fired by an unmanned aircraft in Yemen.
February 9, 2012	Somalian terror organization al Shabaab formally announces its allegiance to Al Qaeda.
September 11, 2012	Militants attack the U.S. consulate in Benghazi, Tripoli, and assassinate Ambassador J. Christopher Stevens.
April 15, 2013	Two bombs explode near the finish line of the Boston Marathon. Chechen brothers Dzhokhar and Tamerlan Tsarnaev are later found to have placed the bombs.

June 13, 2014	The United States commences airstrikes targeting the Islamic State in Iraq and the Levant.
December 28, 2014	The North Atlantic Treaty Organization formally ends combat operations in Afghanistan.
January 3–7, 2015	Boko Haram militants attack several northern Nigerian villages, killing more than 2,000 civilians.
January 7, 2015	Gunmen linked to Al Qaeda in the Arabian Peninsula attack the offices of *Charlie Hebdo*, a satire magazine based in Paris, France, killing 12 and wounding 10.
March 18, 2015	Three Islamic State gunmen attack the Bardo Museum in Tunis, killing 22 victims including 20 foreign tourists. One of the attackers remains at large.
March 26–27, 2015	Al-Shabaab operatives attack the Makka al-Mukarama hotel in Mogadishu, Somalia, killing 24 and wounding 28.
June 26, 2015	Seifiddine Rezgui Yacoubi, an Islamic State operative, opens fire at a tourist resort near Sousse, Tunisia, killing 38 tourists and wounding 39 more.
October 10, 2015	Members of the Islamic State detonate two suicide bombs in Ankara, Turkey, killing 102 and wounding 508.
October 31, 2015	Metrojet Flight 9268 is destroyed after a bomb exploded during the flight, killing 224 mostly Russian passengers and crew. The Islamic State took credit for the attack, and claimed it was retaliation for Russian airstrikes in Syria.
November 12, 2015	Two suicide bombers attack a Beirut suburb, killing 43 mostly Shi'a victims. The Islamic State later claims responsibility.
November 13, 2015	Eight attackers launch three coordinated attacks at six locations in Paris, France, killing 130 and wounding nearly 400. The attackers are members of the Islamic State.
December 2, 2015	Syed Rizwan Farook and Tashfeen Malik attack a community center in San Bernardino, California, killing 14 and wounding 21. They are later shown to have pledged allegiance to the Islamic State.
January 15–16, 2016	Al Qaeda in the Islamic Maghreb operatives attack a restaurant and hotel in Ouagadougou, Burkina Fason, killing 30 and wounding 60.
January 20, 2016	Tehrik-i-Taliban Pakistan gunmen attack Bacha Khan University in Charsadda, Pakistan, killing 20 and wounding 60.
June 12, 2016	Omar Mateen opens fire in an Orlando nightclub, killing 49 and wounding 53. He pledges allegiance to the Islamic State in a telephone call to 911 during the attack.
July 14, 2016	Mohamed Lahouaiej-Bouhlel drives a cargo truck into crowds celebrating Bastille Day in Nice, France, killing 85 and wounding 307. Two days later the Islamic State claimed responsibility for the attack.

BIBLIOGRAPHY

Aboul-Enein, Youssef H. *Militant Islamist Ideology: Understanding the Global Threat*. Annapolis, MD: Naval Institute Press, 2010.

Atwan, Abdel Bari. *The Secret History of Al Qaeda*. Berkeley, CA: University of California Press, 2006.

Aust, Stefan, et al. *Inside 9/11: What Really Happened*. New York: St. Martin's Press, 2001.

Ball, Howard. *The USA PATRIOT Act of 2001: Balancing Civil Liberties and National Security*. Santa Barbara, CA: ABC-CLIO, 2004.

Benjamin, Daniel, and Steven Simon. *The Age of Sacred Terror*. New York: Random House, 2002.

Bergen, Peter L. *The Osama bin Laden I Know: An Oral History of Al Qaeda's Leader*. New York: Free Press, 2006.

Bloom, Mia. *Dying to Kill: The Allure of Suicide Terror*. New York: Columbia University Press, 2005.

Bowden, Mark. *Finish: The Killing of Osama bin Laden*. New York: Atlantic Monthly Press, 2012.

Burgat, François. *Islamism in the Shadow of Al-Qaeda*. Trans. Patrick Hutchinson. Austin, TX: University of Texas Press, 2008.

Burleigh, Michael. *Blood & Rage: A Cultural History of Terrorism*. New York: HarperCollins, 2009.

Campbell, Kurt M., and Michèle A. Flournoy. *To Prevail: An American Strategy for the Campaign Against Terrorism*. Washington, DC: Center for Strategic and International Studies Press, 2001.

Chaliand, Gérard, and Arnaud Blin, eds. *The History of Terrorism: From Antiquity to Al Qaeda*. Berkeley, CA: University of California Press, 2007.

Clarke, Richard A. *Against All Enemies: Inside America's War on Terror*. New York: Free Press, 2004.

Clinton, Bill. *My Life*. New York: Vintage, 2005.

Clinton, Hillary Rodham. *Hard Choices*. New York: Simon & Schuster, 2014.

Coburn, Davin. *Civilian Warriors: The Inside Story of Blackwater and the Unsung Heroes of the War on Terror*. New York: Penguin, 2013.

Coll, Steve. *Ghost Wars: The Secret History of the CIA, Afghanistan, and Bin Laden, from the Soviet Invasion to September 10, 2001*. New York: Penguin, 2010.

Dunbar, David, and Brad Reagan. *Debunking 9/11 Myths: Why Conspiracy Theories Can't Stand Up to the Facts*. New York: Hearst Books, 2006.

Dunnigan, James F. *The Next War Zone: Confronting the Global Threat of Cyberterrorism*. New York: Citadel Press, 2002.

Ensalaco, Mark. *Middle Eastern Terrorism: From Black September to September 11*. Philadelphia, PA: University of Pennsylvania Press, 2007.

Forst, Brian. *Terrorism, Crime, and Public Policy*. New York: Cambridge University Press, 2008.

Fouda, Yosri, and Nick Fielding. *Masterminds of Terror: The Truth Behind the Most Devastating Terrorist Attack the World Has Ever Seen*. New York: Arcade Publishing, 2003.

Freeh, Louis J., and Howard Means. *My FBI: Bringing Down the Mafia, Investigating Bill Clinton, and Fighting the War on Terror*. New York: St. Martin's Press, 2005.

Gates, Robert M. *Duty: Memoirs of a Secretary at War*. New York: Knopf, 2014.

Gerges, Fawaz A. *The Far Enemy: Why Jihad Went Global*. New York: Cambridge University Press, 2005.

Greenberg, Karen J. *The Least Worst Place: Guantanamo's First 100 Days*. New York: Oxford University Press, 2009.

Greenberg, Karen J., and Joshua L. Dratel, eds. *The Enemy Combatant Papers: American Justice, the Courts, and the War on Terror*. New York: Cambridge University Press, 2008.

Griffin, David Ray. *Debunking 9/11*, revised ed. Northampton, MA: Olive Branch Press, 2007.

Gunaratna, Rohan. *Inside Al Qaeda: Global Network of Terror*. New York: Columbia University Press, 2002.

Gurr, Nadine, and Benjamin Cole. *The New Face of Terrorism: Threats from Weapons of Mass Destruction*. New York: I.B. Tauris, 2005.

Habeck, Mary R. *Knowing the Enemy: Jihadist Ideology and the War on Terror*. New Haven, CT: Yale University Press, 2006.

Hardy, Colleen E. *The Unlawful Detention of Enemy Combatants during the War on Terror*. El Paso, TX: LFB Scholarly Publishing, 2009.

Hashmi, Taj ul-Islam. *Global Jihad and America: The Hundred-Year War Beyond Iraq and Afghanistan*. Thousand Oaks, CA: SAGE Publications, 2014.

Hersh, Seymour M. *Chain of Command: The Road from 9/11 to Abu Ghraib*. New York: HarperCollins, 2004.

Hoffman, Bruce. *Inside Terrorism*. New York: Columbia University Press, 2006.

Holloway, David. *9/11 and the War on Terror*. Edinburgh: Edinburgh University Press, 2008.

Ibrahim, Raymond, ed. and trans. *The Al Qaeda Reader*. New York: Broadway Books, 2007.

Jacquard, Roland. *In the Name of Osama bin Laden: Global Terrorism and the Bin Laden Brotherhood*. Durham, NC: Duke University Press, 2002.

Jaffer, Jameel, and Amrit Singh. *Administration of Torture: A Documentary Record from Washington to Abu Ghraib and Beyond*. New York: Columbia University Press, 2007.

Kaplan, Fred. *The Insurgents: David Petraeus and the Plot to Change the American Way of War*. New York: Simon & Schuster, 2013.

Kean, Thomas H., Lee H. Hamilton, and Benjamin Rhodes. *Without Precedent: The Inside Story of the 9/11 Commission*. New York: Knopf, 2006.

Kepel, Gilles, and Jean-Pierre Milelli, eds. *Al Qaeda in Its Own Words*. Cambridge, MA: Belknap Press, 2008.

Klaidman, Daniel. *Kill or Capture: The War on Terror and the Soul of the Obama Presidency*. Boston, MA: Houghton Mifflin Harcourt, 2013.

Lang, Anthony F., Jr., and Amanda Russell Beattie, eds. *War, Torture and Terrorism*. New York: Routledge, 2009.

Lawrence, Bruce, ed. *Messages to the World: The Statements of Osama bin Laden*. New York: Verso, 2005.

Levi, Michael. *On Nuclear Terrorism*. Cambridge, MA: Harvard University Press, 2007.

Lewis, Jeffrey William. *The Business of Martyrdom: A History of Suicide Bombing*. Annapolis, MD: Naval Institute Press, 2012.

Lewis, Michael W. *The War on Terror and the Laws of War: A Military Perspective*. New York: Oxford University Press, 2009.

McChrystal, Stanley. *My Share of the Task*. New York: Penguin, 2013.

McDermott, Terry. *Perfect Soldiers: The Hijackers: Who They Were, Why They Did It*. New York: HarperCollins, 2005.

Mockaitis, Thomas R. *The "New" Terrorism: Myths and Reality*. Westport, CT: Praeger, 2007.

Mohamedou, Mohammad-Mahmoud Ould. *Understanding Al Qaeda: The Transformation of War*. London: Pluto, 2007.

Morrell, Michael J. *The Great War of Our Time: The CIA's Fight against Terrorism from al Qa'ida to ISIS*. New York: Twelve, 2015.

Mudd, Philip. *Takedown: Inside the Hunt for Al Qaeda*. Philadelphia, PA: University of Pennsylvania Press, 2013.

Murawiec, Laurent. *The Mind of Jihad*. New York: Cambridge University Press, 2008.

Murphy, Dean E. *September 11: An Oral History*. New York: Doubleday, 2002.

Nacos, Brigitte L. *Mass-Mediated Terrorism: The Central Role of the Media in Terrorism and Counterterrorism*, 2nd ed. Lanham, MD: Rowman & Littlefield, 2007.

Naftali, Timothy. *Blind Spot: The Secret History of American Counterterrorism*. New York: Basic Books, 2005.

Naylor, Sean. *Not a Good Day to Die: The Untold Story of Operation Anaconda*. New York: Berkley Books, 2005.

The 9/11 Commission Report: Final Report of the National Commission on Terrorist Attacks Upon the United States. New York: W.W. Norton, 2004.

Owen, Mark. *No Easy Day: The Autobiography of a Navy SEAL*. New York: Dutton, 2012.

Panetta, Leon. *Worthy Fights: A Memoir of Leadership in War and Peace*. New York: Penguin, 2014.

Pape, Robert A. *Dying to Win: The Strategic Logic of Suicide Terrorism*. New York: Random House, 2005.

Polk, William R. *Violent Politics: A History of Insurgency, Terrorism, & Guerrilla War from the American Revolution to Iraq*. New York: HarperCollins, 2007.

Posner, Gerald. *Why America Slept: The Failure to Prevent 9/11*. New York: Ballantine, 2003.

Randal, Jonathan. *Osama: The Making of a Terrorist*. New York: Knopf, 2004.

Redfield, Marc. *The Rhetoric of Terror: Reflections on 9/11 and the War on Terror*. New York: Fordham University Press, 2009.

Riedel, Bruce. *Deadly Embrace: Pakistan, America, and the Future of the Global Jihad*. Washington, DC: Brookings Institution Press, 2011.

Risen, James. *State of War: The Secret History of the CIA and the Bush Administration*. New York: Free Press, 2006.

Robinson, Adam. *Bin Laden: Behind the Mask of the Terrorist*. New York: Arcade Publishing, 2001.

Robinson, Linda. *Masters of Chaos: The Secret History of the Special Forces*. New York: Public Affairs, 2004.

Rogers, A. P. V. *Law on the Battlefield,* 3rd ed. New York: Manchester University Press, 2012.

Rubin, Barry, and Judith Colp Rubin, eds. *Anti-American Terrorism and the Middle East.* New York: Oxford University Press, 2002.

Rumsfeld, Donald. *Known and Unknown.* New York: Sentinel, 2011.

Saar, Erik, and Viveca Novak. *Inside the Wire.* New York: Penguin Press, 2005.

Sageman, Marc. *Understanding Terror Networks.* Philadelphia, PA: University of Pennsylvania Press, 2004.

Scheuer, Michael. *Through Our Enemies' Eyes: Osama bin Laden, Radical Islam, and the Future of America.* Washington, DC: Potomac Books, 2006.

Schmitt, Eric. *Counterstrike: The Untold Story of America's Secret Campaign against Al Qaeda.* New York: St. Martin's, 2012.

Shemella, Paul, ed. *Fighting Back: What Governments Can Do about Terrorism.* San Francisco, CA: Stanford Security Studies, 2011.

Stanton, Doug. *Horse Soldiers: The Extraordinary Story of a Band of U.S. Soldiers Who Rode to Victory in Afghanistan.* New York: Scribner, 2009.

Strawser, Bradley Jay, ed. *Killing by Remote Control: The Ethics of an Unmanned Military.* New York: Oxford University Press, 2013.

Talbott, Strobe, and Nayan Chanda, eds. *The Age of Terror: America and the World after September 11.* New York: Basic Books, 2001.

Tenet, George, and Bill Harlow. *At the Center of the Storm: My Years at the CIA.* New York: HarperCollins, 2007.

Terry, James P. *The War on Terror: The Legal Dimension.* Lanham, MD: Rowman & Littlefield, 2013.

Thomas, Andrew R. *Aviation Insecurity: The New Challenges of Air Travel.* Amherst, NY: Prometheus Books, 2003.

Warrick, Joby. *Black Flags: The Rise of ISIS.* New York: Doubleday, 2015.

Woodward, Bob. *Bush at War.* New York: Simon & Schuster, 2002.

Wright, Lawrence. *The Looming Tower: Al Qaeda and the Road to 9/11.* New York: Knopf, 2006.

INDEX

ABOUT THE AUTHOR

PAUL J. SPRINGER is a full professor of comparative military studies and the chair of the Department of Research at the Air Command and Staff College, Maxwell Air Force Base, Alabama. His published work includes *America's Captives: Treatment of POWs from the Revolutionary War to the War on Terror*; Praeger's *Outsourcing War to Machines: The Military Robotics Revolution*; ABC-CLIO's *Military Robots and Drones: A Reference Handbook* and *Cyber Warfare: A Reference Handbook*; and Routledge's *Transforming Civil War Prisons: Lincoln, Lieber, and the Laws of War*. Springer holds a doctorate in military history from Texas A&M University and is a senior fellow of the Foreign Policy Research Institute in Philadelphia.